OREGON BREWERIES

BRIAN YAEGER

STACKPOLE BOOKS

For I. P. Yae

Published by
STACKPOLE BOOKS
5067 Ritter Road
Mechanicsburg, PA 17055
www.stackpolebooks.com

The authors and the publisher encourage readers to visit the breweries and sample their beers, and recommend that those who consume alcoholic bever-ages travel with a designated nondrinking driver.

Printed in the United States of America

10 9 8 7 6 5 4 3 2 1

FIRST EDITION

Cover design by Tessa J. Sweigert
Author photo by Max Gerber
Labels and logos used with the permission of the breweries

Library of Congress Cataloging-in-Publication Data

Yaeger, Brian.
    Oregon breweries / Brian Yaeger. — First edition.
      pages   cm
    Includes index.
    ISBN 978-0-8117-1211-8
    1. Breweries—Oregon—Guidebooks. 2. Oregon—Guidebooks. I. Title.
TP573.U6Y34 2014
663'.309795—dc23

                                             2014029495

Contents

Acknowledgments

I may have written this book single-handedly (well, I used one hand when it came to trying the hundreds of beers it took to "research" all of Oregon's breweries, but both hands to type), but I didn't do it alone. Such an undertaking relied on the huge assistance and encouragement of many, chiefly my very supportive wife, Kimberley, a.k.a. Half Pint. The fact that she gave me her blessing to go off on journeys around the Great State of Oregon with a brand new baby at home would've been gracious enough. That she spent so much time helping to edit and guide the manuscript makes her deserving of some kind of wifely medal, which in this case is a bottle of The Abyss.

Speaking of editing, thanks to John Holl, my new editor at *All About Beer* magazine, for throwing my name into Stackpole's hat to pen the Oregon volume in the fantastic series of brewery guidebooks by state. Likewise, a huge vow of appreciation to Brittany Stoner (and Kyle Weaver) at Stackpole. Holl is the co-author of two such titles—*Indiana Breweries* and *Massachusetts Breweries*—so I'd just like to say: Hey, you can fit two Indianas and three Massachusettses into Oregon! I guess that means I then owe him five beers. Speaking of *All About Beer*, although I'd just published *Red, White, and Brew: An American Beer Odyssey*, that was the first beer magazine to publish me and set me on the path to being a freelance beer writer. I'm grateful to publisher Daniel Bradford and contributing editor Julie Anne Johnson for the continued support. I look forward to some pints of that delicious North Carolina beer with you soon.

I can't thank enough my friends and colleagues in the Oregon beer writing and blogging community. The list starts with the Dean of American Beer Writers, Fred Eckhardt, who penned *A Treatise on Lager Beers* before the esteemed Michael Jackson and Charlie Papazian published their first books. Deep into his eighties, he remains active in the beer scene and his charitable birthday party, FredFest at Hair of the Dog, is not to be missed.

The Brew Site (TheBrewSite.com) is believed to be the longest-running beer blog in the country since 2004. Blogger and author Jon Abernathy has always been one of my top resources for Oregon beer news as well as drinking companion when visiting the brewery boomtown of Bend. Lisa Morrison, better known as The Beer Goddess (Beer Goddess.com) hosts the radio program "Beer O'Clock" and writes for a host of national and local publications. There's no finer treat than enjoying a glass of an amazing new Oregon brew with her at Belmont Station. John Foyston has kept the *Oregonian* (OregonLive.com/Beer) readers informed about beer goings-on for some twenty years. By my count, twenty-seven of the nearly two hundred breweries in the state were operating when he started; I hope someone writes about me one day that I've been doing this since back when Oregon only had two hundred breweries (there were merely 140 when I started this project).

There are so many folks who champion our breweries, and I'm sure I'm forgetting some, but I always enjoy getting to share a round with Jeff Alworth, the renowned author of Beervana.blogspot.com who had a beer column in Portland's *Willamette Week* eight years before I did. On that note, thanks to arts and culture editor Martin Cizmar for kicking up the beer coverage. Ezra Johnson-Greenough is a great festival organizer, blogs at NewSchoolBeer.com, and is always happy to drink my rare and expensive bottles. Abram Goldman-Armstrong isn't just the editor of *Northwest Brewing News*, he's also on the frontlines of that other craft beverage renaissance, having just launched Cider Riot. Angelo De Ieso and Daruss "DJ" Paul keep the highly-respected Brewpublic.com going, which De Ieso—who's blessed with insane optimism and positivity—has kept up since 2008. Lucy Birmingham (LucyBurningham.com) champions beer and bikes. Christian DeBenedetti, Adrienne So, and Jason Notte are more Portland-based beer writers found in a potpourri of periodicals. Emily Engdahl maintains OregonBeerCountry.org, blogs for *1859* magazine, and is the executive director for the Pink Boots Society for women in the beer industry. Pete Dunlop covers the professional beer biz via BeervanaBuzz.com while Sanjay Reddy takes the opposite approach with his Not So Professional Beer Blog. Somewhere in between is Bill Night from It's Pub Night and the "Piss & Vinegar" column at The New School. Kris Thered writes beer reviews and more at BitteredUnits.blogspot.com while Eric Steen (EricMSteen.com) puts his arts background to work devising artistic and progressive beer events and programs such as Beers Made by Walking. And Mike Besser, a.k.a. the BrewDad (dot-com), is an honorary Oregonian in this fellow brewdad's mind.

From Brewvana tour operator Ashley Rose Salvitti to online broadcasters Eric Buist and his team behind Hopstories, Damian DeBuiser of The Brew Happy Show, and Charlie Herrin of Beer Traveler TV, not to mention Ritch "SNOB Ritch" Marvin, whose amazing photographs capture the beers, people, and places, there's an unending list of people who make Oregon the great place it is for beer lovers.

To my own parents, who believe you're not really an author until you've written two books, thank you for having pushed me to be a real author since that infamous letter to the news stations. Writing about beer is my way of covering the good in this world. Mom, keep exploring IPAs. Dad, I've got a cold hefeweizen with your name on it.

And I shan't forget the actual brewery owners, brewers, and publicans who make drinking one's way across the PNW so dang delicious and adventurous. So let's get to them, the stars of the show, who all graciously gave of their time and wisdom, poured of their beer, and befriended with their charm.

Foreword

Oregon breweries are so Oregon. They are a celebration of where we live and who we are. Hops have been grown in the Willamette Valley of Oregon for over one hundred years. It's the hops that impart those fabulous flavors, aromas, and that pretty blond head to beer. It seems to be no coincidence that these two industries, craft brewing and hop growing, are both thriving. The craft-brew industry has brought a change to hop farming like no other in variety and taste. And there have been changes in hop production over those hundred years that continue to improve efficiencies and hop quality. Today, the focus of change is on new hop varieties coming to the market at a crazy pace to satisfy the innovative brewers and curious consumers. It's a melding of businesses and passions.

Change happens, but hop farming is hop farming, and how my grandparents farmed to produce the annual harvest and how I manage my crops are very similar: boots on the ground, working with Mother Nature. I thought for a time that I could manipulate or manage the big Mother N, but no, she rules. One late spring day, after I had returned from college for the summer work season, we had a freak hailstorm flatten a twenty-acre field of hops. My father was leaving that next day on a business trip. As we stood at the edge of the field discussing our options to save the crop, we reached the conclusion that nothing much could be done. I was instructed to simply wait for the plants to regrow new shoots and then retrain those shoots up the network of strings. If lucky, we would have a third of our expected production to harvest. My dad could see my frustration, and so it was time for a lesson in hop history. The story was simply put, as farming stories of our family tend to be. And it was very familiar, only this time it was my grandfather standing in a hopyard flattened by hail with my father at his side. And what was the solution then? My grandfather threw his hands casually in the air and announced, "Well, all we can do is wait. Your mother and I are going to the beach." That portion of hop growing has not changed; you do your best to guide a crop through the growing season by walking the fields and anticipating crop needs, but have patience—it can all change in an instant. I think of that story often as I walk our hop fields today. I think of the luxury I have in walking in the steps of both my father and grandfather. I think of their lessons in patience. And I think of how delighted they would be to see the changes in how hops are perceived and truly honored in today's brewing world.

It's not just the number of hop varieties available to a brewer but how, when, and why an artisan brewer will choose to use them. It's exciting and flavorful. The variety and uses of hops places a signature on every brewery, brewer, and brew. It's a grand reason to discover what's brewing in all the corners of Oregon. It's a great homegrown story of hop growing and craft beer.

Gayle Goschie
Goschie Farms, Inc.
Celebrating 110 years of hop growing

Introduction

Oregonians enjoy beer from Oregon's 192 breweries (and counting). They really like breweries in their own neighborhood. Breweries belong to a neighborhood, but not the other way around, and the locals rejoice when a new brewpub opens. The issue of saturation frequently arises —"Do we really need another brewery?" but it's not about need. We need shelter. We need power, gas, and water. Those are utilities. Craft beer isn't something we use; we savor it. Last I checked there are no artisanal gas companies, no hand-cranked electric companies. If beer were simply a utility, we'd only need two or three gargantuan, industrial beer factories to service everyone (ahem). Perhaps you're saying, "No, I *need* craft beer," but I'd counter that you *want* craft beer because flavor matters, provenance matters, and supporting the people responsible for providing you with it is important.

Why Beer? Why Oregon?

How to put this even-handedly? All across the United States, from coast to coast, the Mexican border to the Canadian border, there are phenomenal brewing cultures to soak up and calling out one as the best above all others is not just difficult, it's impossible and foolhardy. Having said that, Oregon can claim to be the best spot on the map for such a beer scene and boasts more than enough world-class breweries to support such a bold assertion. How many other states are nicknamed "Beervana?" Well, that's just me gushing. Oregon's brewers themselves don't need to brag and boast; they just make a whole lot of great beers across the entire spectrum of styles (and beyond) and welcome locals and visitors alike with open arms and honest pints.

I should add that while you'll discover crisp pilsners, robust imperial stouts, and funky wild ales, IPAs reign supreme. We're blessed by proximity to America's two primary hop-growing regions. Washington's Yakima Valley excels in bittering hops and Oregon's Willamette Valley produces bushels of aroma hops that make sitting in a local beer garden a fragrant, divine experience. (No, it doesn't rain all year long, so such outdoor patios are plentiful.) Situated between the Cascade and Coast mountains, the Willamette Valley straddles the North

45th Parallel, where the rainy, cool climate constitutes excellent growing conditions similar to Bavaria's Hallertau region.

But beer isn't just hops. It's the barley that you'll begin to find growing out in the eastern plains. It's the water sourced from stellar watersheds and aquifers, thanks to pristine rainfall and snowmelt that enables brewers statewide to benefit from some of the softest, low-mineral water one could hope for. It's the yeast that more often than not comes from Wyeast Labs, founded in Hood River in 1986, a company that has directly fostered the craft beer revolution. But let's not forget the growing number of brave brewers who rely on spontaneous fermentation, so clearly the atmosphere supports an exciting direction in the next wave of brewing. Last but not least, it's the people.

Can it be any surprise that F. H. Steinbart, America's oldest homebrew supply shop, established in 1918, is in the same city—Portland—that has the record number of breweries? The Oregon Brew Crew is one of the largest and oldest homebrewing clubs in the country, and many alumni have founded breweries. And credit must be paid to the group of pioneers including Brian and Mike McMenamin (McMenamin Brothers Brewing), Kurt and Rob Widmer (Widmer Bros. Brewing), Dick Ponzi (BridgePort), and Fred Bowman and Art Larrance (Portland Brewing), who wrote a bill that led to legalizing brewpubs in Oregon in 1985. Beyond these folks, it is common for brewers employed at one company to move to another or eventually launch their own. Brewmaster Larry Sidor began his brewing career at Olympia in Tumwater, Washington, but thanks to Pabst, who bought both "Oly" and Blitz-Weinhard, he has some Henry's to his credit, too, and later became the brewmaster at Deschutes in Bend before cofounding Crux. Brewmaster John Harris brewed from square one at McMenamins in Portland, then headed to Deschutes (before Sidor's time) and later returned to Portland for Full Sail before starting his own Ecliptic. Stories like these play out over the years and throughout each region. I don't call it turnover; I call it pollination. Craft brewers are fraternal and independent, and everyone adds his or her own style, ideas, and panache.

Take the Scenic Route(s)

The trickiest part about planning a "beercation" to Oregon is probably whether or not to focus on Portland. After all, Portland is home to more breweries than any other city on the planet (over fifty and counting). If that seems crazy—how could a city of approximately 600,000 people support so many breweries and brewpubs?—that's just indicative of the way locally crafted suds are engrained in the culture. If there's a bar or restaurant without at least a couple of Oregon-brewed options on tap or in bottles or cans, I've never found myself there. Tap-rooms offering twenty or more Northwest ales and lagers are the norm. Portlanders habitually explore new brews, making it fun for both the brewers and imbibers to experiment.

But Oregon is a huge state, and it's preposterous to think Portland is the only place hopping. Most of the breweries are not within the larger Portland Metro. Furthermore, Oregon is one of the most picturesque states. A beer trip will bring you to verdant mountain villages, breath-taking coastal hamlets, outdoor playgrounds in the high desert, lush river valleys, college towns, and historic townships along the Oregon Trail. It's my firm belief that Lewis and Clark secretly left St. Louis because they wanted to explore somewhere better for brewing.

Captain William Clark wrote of this area in 1805: "Welcome to the theater of majestic beauty—the Great Northwest." Forty-seven years later, Henry Saxer established the Liberty Brewery in Portland when the city itself was only eight years old. Henry Weinhard contributed greatly to the local brewing evolution, launching his brewery here in 1856. (Oregon gained statehood in 1859.) By the end of the nineteenth century, he'd become such a successful beer magnate that he offered to pump in beer to flow from the Skidmore Fountain, today known as the area where the infamous Voodoo Donuts is located. While a few of the larger industrial breweries had outposts here, such as Blitz-Weinhard Brewery (that bounced around in ownership among the conglomerates like Stroh, Pabst, and Miller and is now the multi-use Brewery Blocks in downtown Portland's Pearl District), it would take over a century for the Pacific Northwest to earn its place in the pantheon of epic brewing regions, thanks to the efforts of pioneers whom we'll meet in this book.

Perhaps most telling about the depth and breadth of Oregon's brewing history, as well as its present and future, is how many of the first wave of craft breweries originated here and the fact that they not only survived but are among the largest producers in the country. It's not like Pennsylvania or Wisconsin, which have sixth-generation-run brewing companies. What the state lacks in historical tradition it makes up for in entrepreneurship and innovation. In Portland there's BridgePort (1984), Widmer Bros. (1984), and Portland Brewing (1986), plus the brewpub that started it all, McMenamin Brothers' Hillsdale Brewery (1984). Then there's Full Sail in Hood River (1987), Deschutes in Bend (1988), and Rogue in Newport (1988). As for the present, more than thirty breweries opened in 2013, as small as single-barrel nanobreweries in the most remote corners of the state and as large as 30-barrel production breweries in places like Bend, where it feels like new breweries will have to start opening on top of existing ones just to find room.

So where does it all end? It doesn't! The story of Oregon brewing is never-ending. It's like one of those choose-your-own-adventure books but without any dead ends. It's ridiculously exciting and terribly thirst-inducing. Whether you're exploring Oregon for its breweries and taking in the scenery as a result or setting out to hike, bike, paddle, surf, kitesurf, ski, or roll on through, fortunately there's a cold one waiting for you at the end of each day's adventure, no matter where your expedition takes you. We can all drink to that.

Frothy Statistics

Oregonians enjoy 32 percent more craft beer than the next leading state's denizens in terms of pints per capita. Like 71 percent of stats, I made that up on the spot. But in all seriousness, we drank over 33 percent of the 1.4 million barrels produced in-state in 2013 and, conversely, 53 percent of the beer consumed in-state was brewed in-state. That's according to the Oregon Brewers Guild. A barrel equals two standard 15.5-gallon kegs or 248 sixteen-ounce pints.

Not going off of figures presented by the Guild but based on my own visits, research, and the Oregon Liquor Control Commission (OLCC)'s reports, as of July 2014 there are 192 brewing facilities—all but thirteen make beer at a single-site brewery—operated by 165 brewing companies. In other words, the McMenamins Brewing Co. runs seventeen different breweries around the state. And they cannot make beer fast enough. No matter how many barrels of beer they produce a year and no matter how many new companies arrive on the scene, others still need to expand to keep up with demand. That might be the nutshell story of the state of Oregon beer.

More impressive facts gleaned from the Guild are that Oregon's brewing companies employ more than six thousand people and add hundreds more to this work force each year. Better still, there are some thirty thousand jobs directly connected to the industry, ranging from hop farmers to distributors to beertenders and probably to the guys making branded koozies for some breweries. All told, beer has a $3 billion impact on the state.

After this, the frothy stats turn into fuzzy ones. The Guild reports that of the 2.8 million barrels of beer consumed in Oregon in 2013, just over a half million barrels were brewed here, meaning 18 percent never crossed a state line. But that ignores overall craft beer consumption, data that the Brewers Association (BA), a national advocacy group, collects and reports. (The BA complicates matters by excluding Oregon's largest brewery, Widmer Bros., because of AB InBev's minority stake in Craft Brew Alliance, Widmer's parent company.) Regardless, the brewed-in-state stat neglects the market research group IRI's figures that Portland, for example, consumes some 40 percent craft beer overall (more than any other city). Using the BA's report that 7.8 percent by volume of the United States' $100 billion beer industry is comprised of craft beer, Portlanders drink five times the national average of the good stuff.

One more super fun stat, and then we'll move on to what all this means in terms of visiting Oregon breweries on the whole. According to a breakdown of beer styles consumed in Beervana, 25.2 percent of sales to consumers in 2012 was India Pale Ale. And that reflected a 24 percent growth. People here want hops, and they want them now. Put another way, over a quarter of all beer sold and enjoyed in the Beaver State isn't just craft beer, it's against-the-grain, hyper-aromatic, bitterness galore IPA. If you're wondering why practically every Oregon brewery makes at least one IPA, that's why: demand. You won't hear any of the multigenerational family hop farms—for example, Goschie Farms or Crosby Hop Farms, both near Salem—complaining.

The Scenic Route's Nonroutine Scenery

Each of the breweries in this book has its own unique story and distinct characters, not to mention distinguishing beers. I've singled out one beer from each brewery as The Pick, the beer not to miss when visiting. (For the few entries that don't feature a Pick, it's because I did not get the chance to sample a commercially available beer, not because I didn't deem any worthy of spotlighting.) The question I dislike most is, "What's your favorite brewery?" (Or the equally impossible, "What's your favorite beer?") I always enjoy visiting a brewery and drinking the freshest possible representation of their art.

There are some areas that are more concentrated that others, naturally, directly connected to population. Portland is the largest city in Oregon and has one brewery for every twelve thousand residents or so. The Guild reports that 12 percent of the people who come for work or pleasure hit a brewery. Bend, in Central Oregon, boasts twenty breweries among its roughly eighty thousand residents, meaning every four thousand Bendites get their own brewery. *Visit Bend* states that as of 2013 a full 40 percent of tourists visited at least one of those. Lane County doesn't have nearly as high a brewery-per-capita rate, but when you consider that five of its thirteen are reached along a single-mile walk, it's clear why Eugene's Whiteaker is called the Brewery District. And one of the most naturally gorgeous chunks of Earth, Hood

BREWERY LOCATIONS

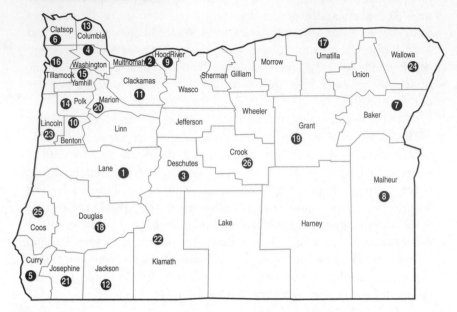

❶ Agrarian Ales

❷ Alameda Brewing Co.

❸ The Ale Apothecary

❹ Ambacht Brewing

❺ Arch Rock Brewing Co.

❻ Astoria Brewing Co. / Wet Dog Café

❷ Awesome Ales

❷ Baerlic Brewing Co.

❼ Barley Brown's Brew Pub / Baker City
   Brewing Co.

❷ Base Camp Brewing Co.

❽ Beer Valley Brewing Co.

❸ Below Grade Brewing

❸ Bend Brewing Co.

❾ Big Horse Brewing / Horsefeathers
   Restaurant

❻ Bill's Tavern and Brewhouse

❿ Block 15 Restaurant & Brewery

❸ Boneyard Beer

⓫ Boring Brewing Co.

❷ Breakside Restaurant & Pub Brewery

⓫ Breakside Taproom & Brewery

❶ Brewers Union Local 180

⓬ BricktownE Brewing Co.

❸ Bridge 99 Brewery

❷ BridgePort Brewing Co.

❷ Buckman Botanical Brewery (Rogue Ale's
   Green Dragon Pub)

❼ Bull Ridge Brew Pub

⓫ Bunsenbrewer Fermentation Laboratory
   and Public House

❻ Buoy Beer Co.

❷ Burnside Brewing Co.

❿ Calapooia Brewing Co.

⓬ Caldera Brewing Co.

⓭ Captured by Porches Brewing Co.

❷ Cascade Brewing Barrel House

❹ Cascade Brewing & Raccoon Lodge

❸ Cascade Lakes Brewing Co.

⓮ Chatoe Rogue Farmstead Nanobrewery

⓯ Chehalem Valley Brewing Co.

❺ Chetco Brewing Co.

❶ Claim 52 Brewing

❷ Coalition Brewing Co.

⓭ Columbia County Brewing

❷ Columbia River Brewing Co.

2 The Commons Brewery
21 Conner Fields Brewing
3 Crux Fermentation Project

16 De Garde Brewing
10 Deluxe Brewing Co.
3 Deschutes Brewery
2 Deschutes Brewery Portland Public House
9 Double Mountain Brewery & Taproom
17 Dragon's Gate Brewery
18 Draper Brewing

2 Ecliptic Brewing
19 1188 Brewing Co.
1 The Elk Horn Brewery
1 Eugene City Brewery (Rogue Ales Public House)
2 Ex Novo Brewing Co.

1 Falling Sky Brewing
2 Fat Head's Portland
11 Fearless Brewing Co.
11 Feckin Irish Brewing Co.
12 Fire Cirkl
16 Fire Mountain Brewery / Outlaw Brew House
2 Fire on the Mountain Brewing Co.
10 Flat Tail Brewery
6 Fort George Brewery + Public House
9 Full Sail Brewing Co.

2 Gigantic Brewing Co.
20 Gilgamesh Brewing
15 Golden Valley Brewery
3 GoodLife Brewing Co.
15 Grain Station Brew Works
21 Griess Family Brews
2 Ground Breaker Brewing

2 Hair of the Dog Brewing Co.
15 Heater Allen Brewing
17 Hermiston Brewing Co.
6 Hondo's Brew & Cork
2 Hopworks Urban Brewery

1 Hop Valley Brewing Co.
2 Humble Brewing

21 JD's Sports Bar & Brewery
3 Juniper Brewing Co.

2 Kells Brewpub
22 Klamath Basin Brewing Co. / The Creamery Brewpub & Grill
2 Krauski's Brewskis / The Hoppy Brewer

17 Laht Neppur Brewing Co.
2 Laurelwood Public House & Brewery
9 Logsdon Farmhouse Ales
2 Lompoc Brewing
15 Long Brewing Co.
2 Lucky Labrador Hawthorne Brew Pub
2 Lucky Labrador Quimby Beer Hall

2 The Mash Tun Brewpub
4 Max's Fanno Creek Brewpub
10 Mazama Brewing
2 McMenamins
2 McMenamins Concordia Brewery at Kennedy School
4 McMenamins Cornelius Pass Roadhouse Brewery
2 McMenamins Crystal Ballroom Brewery
2 McMenamins Edgefield Brewery
2 McMenamins Fulton Pub & Brewery
1 McMenamins High Street Brewery
2 McMenamins Hillsdale Brewery & Public House
23 McMenamins Lighthouse Brewery
10 McMenamins on Monroe
11 McMenamins Old Church & Pub
3 McMenamins Old St. Francis School Brewery
18 McMenamins Roseburg Station Pub & Brewery
20 McMenamins Thompson Brewery
22 Mia & Pia's Pizzeria & Brewhouse
2 Migration Brewing Co.
11 Mt. Hood Brewing Co. (Ice Axe Grill)
24 Mutiny Brewing

(2) Natian Brewery
(23) Newport Brewing Co. / Bier One
(1) Ninkasi Brewing Co.

(1) Oakshire Brewing
(3) Oblivion Brewing Co.
(2) Occidental Brewing Co.
(4) The Old Market Pub & Brewery
(3) Old Mill Brew Wërks
(18) Old 99 Brewing Co.
(2) Old Town Brewing Co.
(12) Opposition Brewing Co.
(10) Oregon Trail Brewery

(16) Pelican Brewing Co.
(9) Pfriem Family Brewers
(2) Pints Brewing Co.
(1) Plank Town Brewing Co.
(3) Platypus Pub / The Brew Shop
(12) Portal Brewing Co.
(2) Portland Brewing Co.
(2) Portland U-Brew & Pub
(17) The Prodigal Son Brewery and Pub
(2) Pyramid Brewing Co.

(20) RAM Restaurant & Brewery (Big Horn Brewing)
(3) Rat Hole Brewing
(4) Red Ox Brewing
(3) Riverbend Brewing and Sports Pub
(2) Rock Bottom Restaurant & Brewery
(23) Rogue Ales
(23) Rusty Truck Brewing

(20) Salem Ale Works
(1) Sam Bond's Brewing Co.
(20) Santiam Brewing
(2) Sasquatch Brewing Co.
(6) Seaside Brewing Co.
(20) Seven Brides Brewing
(25) 7 Devils Brewing Co.
(11) Short Snout Brewing

(3) Silver Moon Brewing
(10) Sky High Brewing
(3) Smith Rock Brewing
(9) Solera Brewery
(26) Solstice Brewing Co.
(12) Southern Oregon Brewing Co.
(12) Standing Stone Brewing Co.
(1) Steelhead / McKenzieBrewing Co.
(11) Stickmen Brewery & Skewery
(2) StormBreaker Brewing
(3) Sunriver Brewing Co.
(12) Swing Tree Brewing Co.

(8) Tandem Brewing
(3) 10 Barrel Brewing Co.
(24) Terminal Gravity Brewing
(2) 13 Virtues Brewing Co. / Philadelphia's Steaks & Hoagies
(3) Three Creeks Brewing Co.
(4) Three Mugs Brewing Co.
(9) Thunder Island Brewing Co.
(5) Tight Lines Brewery
(2) Tugboat Brewing Co.
(23) Twisted Snout Brewery and Public House / Pig Feathers BBQ
(4) Two Kilts Brewing Co.
(18) Two-Shy Brewing

(2) Upright Brewing
(4) Uptown Market Brewery

(20) Vagabond Brewing
(4) Vertigo Brewing
(1) Viking Braggot Co.

(12) Walkabout Brewing Co.
(2) Widmer Brothers Brewing
(3) Wild Ride Brewing Co.
(21) Wild River Brewing & Pizza Co.
(23) Wolf Tree Brewery
(3) Worthy Brewing Co.

(23) Yachats Brewery, Market, and Farmstore

River, only boasts a population of some seven thousand but supports five breweries.

On the flipside, there's something rewarding about exploring off the beaten trail to discover some of the most rural breweries, such as 1188 Brewing in the elk hunter's paradise of John Day in Eastern Oregon, or the all-cask ale Brewers Union Local 180 in the tranquil town of Oakridge that mountain bikers who crave the surrounding single-track trails in the Cascade Mountains like to keep for themselves.

I thought I was done spouting statistics, but this last set is a goodie. Among thirty-six counties, twenty-eight have breweries found in nearly seventy cities, so no matter where you go there's absolutely a brewery nearby. Overall, Oregon claimed the title of most breweries per capita with 6.3 for every 100,000 residents over the age of twenty-one. Eat it, Vermont, with only 6.2 among the same metric.

Please, please, please, if you're coming to Oregon for the beer, don't miss the opportunity to immerse yourself in the scenic Northwest a step beyond the pint. Circumnavigate the farmlands in the Willamette Valley (where the beauty of hop vines growing up trestles over ten feet high is superseded by the pungency of all that fresh *Humulus lupulus*). Cruise the coast, but spend plenty of time with your bare feet in the water (anything more than that may require a thick wetsuit; the ocean's freezing) looking for orange and purple starfish among the tide pools. Burn off the previous night's round by lacing up your boots and hiking the Ten Falls Canyon Trail in Silver Falls State Park, where even kids can easily reach (you guessed it) ten waterfalls, including several where the trail goes behind the cascading current. A more challenging hike is Yocum Ridge, a sixteen-mile loop with a 3,600-foot elevation gain on Mt. Hood, providing assured solitude along Sandy River. Of course, in Southern Oregon the deep blue waters of Crater Lake, Oregon's only National Park, are a destination all their own.

I conducted hundreds of interviews and spent countless hours chatting with the amicable, inspiring, and talented brewers of this fine state, but one of my favorite quotes instead came from an interview I read on The New School blog, courtesy of Pfriem Family Brewers' Josh Pfriem. He said: "If you look at where some of the greatest breweries in the world are located, they fall in cities saturated with breweries. In Germany you have Munich, Dusseldorf, Köln, Bamberg. In Belgium there is Watou (which my son is named after), Brussels, etc. Places such as Burton-on-Trent in England, Portland, San Diego, and Fort Collins also come to mind. The beauty of these places is that they are all known for beer. They have become 'beer destinations' on the map, with communities of brewers inspiring each other to keep making better and more interesting beer. Located in Hood River, we are nestled into one of the most beautiful places in the world, with a plethora of hops and grain being grown all around us. The water is from the aquifers of Mt. Hood, and most folks live a lifestyle based around drinking beer."

To this I'd like to add that when you visit a place like Munich, you're obligated to quaff liters of Weisse beer. In Köln, good luck finding anything but their indigenous Kolsch. Bamberg is beautiful and I personally love their smoky rauchbiers, but all that liquid bonfire could create palate fatigue. So soak up that pilsner in Plzeň (or Prague), but when it comes to Oregon, while it behooves you to try Northwest IPAs, after that, it's wide open.

Pace yourself. Hydrate. And don't race around trying to hit every single brewery during your beercation. Because you can't. It took me ages to visit all of the breweries in the following pages in a reasonable and responsible manner. I hope for your benefit that your first pilgrimage to Beervana won't be your last. Savor every drop, every vista, and every accommodating beertender and person sitting beside you at the bar or outside playing cornhole.

Portland

The hops growing in my backyard don't get much direct sunlight, and that's not a joke about how cloudy it is in Portland all the time. I simply set up a makeshift trestle using a second-story eave and voilà, usable Nugget hops within a few seasons. (I chose that varietal for the corny reason of brewing a Little Nugget IPA once my kid is old enough to help Daddy homebrew.) The point is, if usable hops grow in even less-than-ideal conditions, it's no surprise that the better and more horticultural homebrewers around town have pretty nifty little hopyards going, and it's not uncommon to find wild hops growing along telephone poles. Fortunately, there are perfect hopyards an hour south of Portland in the Willamette Valley so every brewery can (and does) make fresh hop beers during harvest season. Plan a trip in September. The truth is, hops need plenty of sun and it's that dearth of sunshine that prevents some people from moving to Portland, but we've got to have some type of population control.

The city of Portland, incorporated in 1851, is divided into four quadrants. The Willamette River divides the west and east halves of the city, while Burnside Street slices north from south so everything is clearly in, say, the southeast or northwest quadrants. There's also North Portland, "the fifth quadrant," which lies farther west than parts of even Northwest or Southwest, but that's how Portland rolls and the river flows. The city's home to some 600,000 people, but that goes way up when looking at all of Portland Metro among three counties. Most of Portland is in Multnomah County, but some land spills into Clackamas and Washington Counties. Among those three counties, there are currently seventy-five breweries.

Still, Portland's not exactly a major market, but that doesn't stop Portlanders from thinking it's the center of the universe. Luckily there are enough ice packs in the media to keep the city's collective head from swelling. Portland never took top honors in Charlie Papazian's Beer City USA national poll; Ashland, North Carolina, always eked out a win, even though Portland is famously known as Beervana and supports more breweries and brewpubs than any other city on Earth. The java fiends at *Travel + Leisure* deemed our neighbors to the north, Seattle, as the better coffee city despite PDX's boasting nearly as many coffee bean roasting companies—fifty-plus—as brewing companies (for a complete list, see pages 395–396). And *Bicycling* magazine placed Minneapolis as the better bike-friendly city over Portland, despite hosting the largest Naked Bike Ride, during which many of the eight thousand riders wear only a helmet and a smile. The sketch comedy show *Portlandia* lampoons every aspect of the culture.

But Portland does take a lot seriously. Denizens are happier with the Major League Soccer **Timbers**—every home game is played in front of a capacity crowd—than nabbing an NFL franchise. #RCTID. (And win or lose, this will always be Rip City when it comes to the Blazers.) People in Stumptown are serious about their trees; **Forest Park**, the largest urban park in America, offers over seventy miles of hikeable trails. Rose City is home to one seriously large rose garden; the **International Rose Test Garden**, in bloom from April through October, offers some seven thousand rose bushes in more pinks and other warm colors than you knew existed.

Of particular note are the six hundred-plus food carts that operate in city limits, where you can find everything from khao man gai (killer Thai chicken) to grilled PB&Js (with or without Sriracha sauce or capicola) to those late night troughfulls of poutine that make Cartopia great. Speaking of cured meats, it's a bit over the top how many ways there are to enjoy greasy bacon in these parts. Personal favorites include atop a Liège-style waffle with brie and basil, infused in vodka for bloody Marys (then garnished with a slice), and candied bits sprinkled over maple ice cream melting over pan-fried cornbread.

And the last impressive number that gets bandied about a lot, though I've yet to see the formal survey to support it, is that Portland wears the crown in most strip clubs per capita. There are vegan strip clubs, punk strip clubs, and one with Stripperoke (the girls strip while you perform karaoke on stage). What many are legitimately surprised about is that no one has opened a Strip Club Brewpub. Just think of the slogans!

Seeing how this is a guidebook, shopping at **Powell's Books** is as compulsory as quaffing a pint at a brewery or taproom. Folks think they're only going to "pop in" to check out this city block large indie bookseller (there's a reason it's called Powell's City of Books), only to find themselves absconding from the new releases in the green room to the mysteries in the gold room before being entranced by the rare books room (anything with a hundred dollar price tag is on the cheap side). It's worth noting that in the orange room's vast cooking section, tomes on beer alone account for four shelves (good luck finding four beer books at other large retailers).

Throughout the city, its residents, and the playful culinary, fashion, and art scenes, beer doesn't make cameos. It's completely woven into the culture. That bearded buy riding down the street is way more likely to be a brewer than a lumberjack. (But beards aren't a telltale sign.) There isn't some secret society of beer geeks; they're called Portlanders. It's why PDX drinks the highest percentage of craft beer— around 50 percent—in the country. If you visited a brewery a week in Portland, it'd take you over a year to check out every brewery's pub or tasting room, so the idea of hitting them all in one visit is ridiculous. Instead, explore the neighborhoods, ignore the drizzle, and discover that you're never more than a few blocks from another tasty glass.

BridgePort Brewing Co.

1318 Northwest Marshall Street,
Portland, OR 97209
(503) 241-7179 • BridgeportBrew.com
Twitter @BridgePortBrew

BridgePort, née Columbia River Brewery in 1984, is Oregon's oldest surviving craft brewery. Founders Dick and Nancy Ponzi—the owners of Ponzi Vineyards—were instrumental in getting the laws changed in Oregon to allow brewpubs and tasting rooms (theirs opened in 1986). And BridgePort deserves the lion's share of credit for popularizing India Pale Ale in America. More than thirty years later, they still make time to brew beers like Long Ball, a golden ale designed for the Hillsboro Hops Short Season-A baseball team.

Dick stated in an interview with Pete Dunlop, author of the historical book *Portland Beer*, "An advantage we had coming from wine was we knew about stainless steel . . . We weren't afraid to fabricate our own stuff." Eleven years later, fabricating their own stuff had taken its toll. "It became too much of a job and we started to think about getting out. With Pinot Noir, we had to educate some distributors, but it wasn't bad. With beer, we had to do it over and over. We got tired of the grind."

Enter the Gambrinus Co., which bought Bridge-Port in 1996. Based in San Antonio, it's the tenth largest brewing company in America, with holdings including the Spoetzl Brewery (famous for Shiner Bock) in Shiner, Texas, and the Trumer

Beers brewed: Year-round: IPA, Kingpin Double Red Ale. Seasonals: Old Knucklehead Barleywine, Bear Hug Cherry Chocolate Stout, Stumptown Tart Belgian Berry Ale, Hop Harvest Fresh-Hopped Pilsner. Limited releases: Hop Czar IPA Series, Long Ball Golden Ale, Mettle & Mash Hibiscus Ginger Saison.

The Pick: India Pale Ale. It smacks of pineapple rind and pinecones mixed with some orange pith and lawn clippings, but mostly it tastes important. Today, a 5.5 percent alcohol, 50 IBUs IPA would be deemed a session IPA (or a pale ale), but this led many beer lovers and brewers to their *a-ha* moments with hoppy potential. And it's still great among the current landscape.

Brauerei in Berkeley, California. Gambrinus continued to brew Bridge-Port's lineup developed by original brewmaster Karl Ockert, a graduate in fermentation sciences from University of California, Davis. That included its early flagship, Blue Heron, debuted in 1987 for the Audubon Society but retired in 2013. Earlier, they'd retired Pintail, a copper ESB. British bitters were a gateway style for me into more intriguing beer, which might explain why they're considered part of the old guard of beer styles. But in 1996, BridgePort unleashed the vanguard BridgePort India Pale Ale, a beer the term "game changer" was created for.

One of the first things Gambrinus president Carlos Alvarez did was bring in Australian brewmaster Phil Sexton. "In the mid-nineties, there was talk about hoppier and more bitter beers, but this seemed to be disconnected from the basics: balance, harmony, and drinkability," Sexton said, explaining the creation of his IPA. "Alongside the hop fields of Yakima [Washington], I put it to [then head brewer] Bill Lundeen that without copying the already well-established American pale ale, we should take it to the next level, using local hops and bottle fermentation for natural preserving.

"We were looking for fruit esters rather than the more nutty dry style of the English versions; Cascades and Chinooks loaned themselves very well to this, and the introduction of a hop back allowed us to extract high levels of aromatic oil without driving up the IBU [International Bitterness Units]."

IPA wasn't new; its history dates back to the eighteenth century. In America, Ballantine brewed one from 1939 until the 1990s. Anchor Liberty premiered in 1975 and was hopped like, but not called, an IPA. Grant's Brewpub opened in Yakima in 1982 and made the first craft IPA. But BridgePort IPA was the first to be bottled, marketed, and distributed to a wider market, and hence it was many people's first experience with this bold, bitter beer, everything being relative. "Originally it was 60 IBUs, but we found that to be a little high," Sexton continued. "It's fair to say there were some raised eyebrows about our [expensive] hop bill at the time."

Discussing this landmark beer with Ockert, who had left the company in 1990 but returned by 1996, he understated, "It got popular." More specifically, he mentioned, "We won gold medals at GABF . . . It owned the category because no one was making anything like it . . . And it helped jumpstart the hops industry in Oregon. We have great hops here."

Those medals came in 1997 and 1999 when IPA was still a niche style. Ironically, when they entered it into the GABF American-style IPA category—the most crowded of three separate IPA categories—in 2009, Ockert recalled, "The judges' notes came back saying, 'Not true to style.'" By his retirement from BridgePort in 2010, he was still receiving hate email from people who said it couldn't possibly be called an IPA because it didn't approach 100 IBUs.

I love that story. And like most people who appreciate a well-balanced beer that's designed to be enjoyed, not conquered, I love BridgePort IPA. A mind-blowing stat that most people outside of the Northwest can't even fathom is that IPA constitutes over 25 percent of every beer bought and consumed in Oregon. Not just craft beer—all beer. That's entirely thanks to BridgePort. And it's the third best-selling brand within the category to this day.

As for the brewery, it is always evolving and keeping up with the times. Jeff Edgerton, who began his brewing industry career in 1989 as a lab tech at the first brewery that put Portland on the map—Blitz-Weinhard—came aboard in 1998. He ascended to brewmaster when Ockert retired. One beer he oversaw was Hop Czar, a bodacious entry in the imperial IPA category that BridgePort introduced in 2008. It proved so popular that, in an interesting move, the company spun the brand into a "constant exploration" series of progressive IPAs, starting with Citra Dry-Hopped IPA, nicknamed Citra Czar, in early 2014. Next came Topaz Copper IPA, featuring Topaz hops that newly reached our shores from Australia.

"Brewing craft beer is an art form in and of itself," said Alvarez, "but you still have to follow Marketing 101 principles for packaging and branding if you are to compete beyond your own brewpub." As for said brewpub, it's located in the Pearl District and is naturally the best place in town to drink their beer. The handsome, two-story space attached to the brewery occupying a former rope factory features dark, brick walls and high, timber ceilings. It doubles as an art gallery. The in-house bakery makes their own breads and pretzels, and all sorts of deliciousness comes out of the smoker, including pulled pork and wild salmon. The Sellwood Pizza is topped with chicken, bacon, and mozzarella (all smoked) and an IPA barbecue sauce. It screams for a pint of Kingpin Double Red for hoppy and sweet flavors to complement the various toppings.

Reflecting on BridgePort entering its fourth decade, Edgerton commented, "It's great to be turning thirty, but it's even more exciting to see how far the craft-brewing industry has come."

BridgePort Brewing Co.

Opened: 1984.

Owner: Gambrinus Co.

Brewers: Jeff Edgerton (brewmaster), Eric Munger (head brewer), and Jeff Thompson (production manager).

System: 80-barrel.

Annual production: 60,000 barrels.

Distribution: Oregon and seventeen other states.

Hours: Sunday and Monday, 11:30 a.m. to 10 p.m.; Tuesday through Thursday, 11:30 a.m. to 11 p.m.; Friday and Saturday, 11:30 a.m. to midnight.

Tours: Saturdays at 1 p.m., 3 p.m., and 5 p.m. Must be ages ten and up; no open-toed shoes. First come, first served. Groups should contact Molly Ishkanian (molly@r-west.com).

Takeout beer: Bottles, growlers, and dock sales.

Gift shop: Shirts, hoodies, hats, and beerware.

Food: Starters, sandwiches and burgers, salads, and pizzas. Try the grilled smoked bratwurst with bacon-braised red cabbage.

Deschutes Brewery Portland Public House

210 Northwest 11th Avenue, Portland, OR 97209
(503) 296-4906 • DeschutesBrewery.com/locations/portland
Twitter @DeschutesPDXPub

To save residents and Beervana pilgrims the 162-mile drive to Bend, as part of Deschutes's twentieth anniversary in 2008 the company opened a brewpub in the heart of Portland's Pearl District. Through the ornately framed windows behind the bar (not to mention a giant one in the reception entrance), visitors catch glimpses of the brewery where Ben Kehs and Jason Barbe brew some core brands (Mirror Pond, Inversion IPA, and seasonals such as Jubelale) and experimental beers. So in a way, they run a part-time pilot brewery.

Running this brewhouse is something all of Deschutes's assistant brewmasters try to do in rotation. So although Kehs—who began working at Deschutes in 2004—still owns a home in Bend, he loves living and brewing in Portland and doesn't have an end time in mind. Part of the pub's value, Kehs said, is that it "exposes a lot more people to who we are as a brewery. You'll be able to find more IPAs on tap here. People weren't as crazy for IPAs on tap [in Bend] as they are here." Indeed, it's rare to find fewer than five IPA (or IPA-like) taps.

And that's not counting Armory XPA, dubbed an Experimental Pale Ale for its groundbreaking inclusion of Citra hops back before the varietal became an industry darling. Now a brand in Deschutes's core portfolio, Armory was actually the very first beer brewed here. As such, it's considered the flagship of the PDX pub. Those same Citras were critical to the development of Chainbreaker White IPA, the harbinger of the new, hybridized style and also formulated here.

To complete the trinity of R&D beers conceived of in Portland and now brewed year-round, Kehs told me that Fresh Squeezed IPA—one of my very favorites among Deschutes beers and IPAs

Beers brewed: Year-round: Armory XPA, Deschutes River Ale, Mirror Pond Pale Ale, Chainbreaker White IPA, Inversion IPA, Black Butte Porter, Obsidian Stout (nitro). Seasonals: Jubelale, Deschutes River Ale, and more.

The Pick: King Cone IPA. I prefer to try beers unique to this pub and fresh hop ales are always a distinctive treat. As many as five are brewed here each harvest. King Cone's aroma exudes towering citrus and pine from the Cascades but the big finish is actually a sweeter fruit flavor like cantaloupe-strawberry juice, all thanks to conditioning hops from nearby Goschie Farms.

across the board—originated 162 miles outside of Bend. "We get experimental hop varieties," he said, adding that when they first got a hold of what is now called Citra, it was just known by its experimental number. "Last year, we got Mosaics when they were still 369s." I'm developing a love affair with Mosaic hops and the tropical fruit flavors they impart. When Kehs offered me a sample of his latest batch of Fresh Squeezed at the start of fresh hop season, the suggestion of POG juice—the ubiquitous blend of passion fruit, orange, and guava found all over Hawaii—was instantaneous.

This pub is not just some marketing angle to install a presence in Portland—it is part and parcel of the Deschutes Brewery. Kehs told me that the company's cobrewmaster Cam O'Connor visits weekly and retrieves samples of every project to sample around back at HQ. President and founder Gary Fish partakes in the tasting panels. That's not to say they don't mind having a satellite pub where they get to sell more of the company Frisbees. But inside, with a fireplace to unwind in front of, walls covered in homey framed photos and sketches, and the large space with the aesthetic of a masculine lodge, Deschutes Portland Public House most certainly is its own destination. If I had to guess, despite the fact that the restaurant is on the Westside and the population is on the Eastside, I'd say it's the most visited brewpub in Portland.

Deschutes Brewery Portland Public House

Opened: 2008.

Owner: Gary Fish (see page 311).

Brewers: Ben Kehs (assistant brewmaster) and Jason Barbe (assistant brewer).

System: 25-hectoliter (about 21 barrels).

Annual production: 1,800 barrels.

Distribution: Portland.

Hours: Sunday through Tuesday, 11 a.m. to 10 p.m.; Wednesday and Thursday, 11 a.m. to 11 p.m.; Friday and Saturday, 11 a.m. to midnight.

Tours: Daily, noon to 4 p.m. on the hour.

Takeout beer: Growlers and bottles.

Gift shop: The host area doubles as a large gift shop with all manner of apparel and souvenirs, including a rainbow of branded Frisbee golf discs.

Food: Solid pub staples and some creative offerings including Obsidian Stout Mac and Cheese that's an entrée not a side and a burger with Mirror Pond aioli (plus an elk and a bison burger). The S'mores Butterscotch Stout Cake is otherworldly.

Events: Street Fare annual festival of beer, food, and music. The Abyss release party the second Thursday of November. Anniversary party on June 27.

Fat Head's Portland

131 Northwest 13th Avenue, Portland, OR 97209
FatHeadsPortland.com • Twitter @FatHeadsPDX

Inspired by the news that Ohio's Fat Head's—already represented in Cleveland and Pittsburgh—is leapfrogging the Midwest and Mountain states to open a taphouse in Beervana, I'm now in favor of a brewery from every state sending a brewpub representative to turn Stumptown into a quasi United Nation of Beer.

Owner-brewer Matt Cole said he "spent quite a bit of time in Oregon and Washington working with hop growers and fell in love with the area." Opening a Fat Head's in Portland "gets us closer to the growers. And the beer scene, in general, is vibrant. It just made sense."

Cole is keenly aware that fresher hops make fresher beers. He said the Ohio plant uses 42,000 pounds, equaling a half-million bucks a year of the fragrant flowers. He's enthusiastic about using experimental hops from each harvest for fresh-hop beers among the fifteen taps at the Pearl District brewery, located around the corner from the Deschutes, Rogue, and 10 Barrel pubs. "You're only as good as what you put into your beer," he said. He's also excited to brew with Oregon staples like hazelnuts and coffee in beers ranging from Bavarian lagers to Belgian ales. "I fell in love with Portland because it's such a foodie town," he said.

Fat Head's Portland

Opening: 2014.
Owner: Matt Cole.
Brewers: Mike Hunsaker and Owen Lamb.
System: 10-barrel.
Annual production: 3,000 barrels (planned).
Distribution: Northern Oregon.
Hours: TBD.
Tours: By request.
Takeout beer: Growlers.
Gift shop: "Headgear" including hats, apparel, cycling jerseys, and swag.
Food: "Headwich" sandwiches ("relatively close to the size of your head," including the Pot Head with pot roast and Head Banger with British bangers) and more pub grub featuring some Oregon goods.

Beers brewed: Year-round: Head Hunter IPA, Hop JuJu Imperial IPA, Sunshine Daydream Session IPA. Seasonals: Trail Head Pale Ale, Güdenhoppy Pils, Oompa Loompa Chocolate Cream Stout, Bean Me Up Imperial Coffee Stout, and barrel-aged beers.

Kells Brewpub

210 Northwest 21st Avenue, Portland, OR 97210
(503) 719-7175 • KellsBrewpub.com
Twitter @KellsBrewPub

I think almost everyone—beer drinker, globetrotter, or armchair adventurer—yearns to drink in the romance and the stout that epitomizes Irish beer. If not fresh at the Guinness brewery, we fancy the notion of enjoying a few pints with our mates at a cozy local pub. That's why Irish bars are so popular across America and the world, and why the McAleese family opened Kells Irish Restaurant and Pub in Seattle in 1983.

Established by Ethna McAleese and her eldest son Gerard, that pub is now operated by Gerard's brother Patrick. Gerard and his wife own the Kells in downtown Portland, opened in 1991. A third pub owned by a third brother, Paul, opened in San Francisco in 1996. Mary McAleese, former president of Ireland and the brothers' fourth cousin, isn't planning on opening a pub on the Emerald Isle.

There *is* a fourth pub however, in Portland's Alphabet District just over a mile from the original in Old Town, and it amalgamates Irish tradition with Oregon sensibilities by operating as a veritable brewpub. It's also smaller and hosts traditional Irish folk music, compared to the larger pub's rock music vibe. This newest Kells pub began with Gerard's son Garrett, who started out working at the Old Town location as a kid, bussing and hosting, then moved up to server and bartender once he was of age. He later found himself studying and homebrewing in Argentina of all places, where he befriended a pair who had launched an artisanal brewery. Eventually he returned home to Portland to work in an Irish pub. See? Everyone likes the idea.

Beers brewed: Year-round: Irish Lager, IPA (Irish Pale Ale), Irish Red Ale, seasonals.

For ages, Kells pubs served a proprietary Irish Lager brewed by Rogue Ales. But Garrett continued homebrewing and convinced his dad they'd have full control over the beer if he brewed it himself (and a few other styles, too, while he's at it). Garrett equates his lager to Harp. At 4.5 percent alcohol, it's a light, crisp beer with a creamy finish. The Irish red ale, also 4.5 percent, is the one that wins over Irish guests and also converts

The Pick: Irish Pale Ale is a great combo of floral and piney flavors. Irish imbibers may find it too bitter for their palates, but locals like me appreciate balanced IPAs at comparatively low 6.2 percent ABV.

many of their remaining patrons who order(ed) Bud Light. Since it's Portland brewed, it's a touch hoppier than Smithwick's, but Garrett and the brewing team of consultants Dave Fleming (a veteran brewer with long stints at Lompoc and Lucky Lab) and Ray Farrell—both half Irish—use all English hops. The IPA (in this case, Irish Pale Ale) is an English-style IPA rather than the more prevalent Northwest style and is made with English malts and a blend of English and Northwest hops.

Incidentally, Kells isn't confined to brewing Irish-style beers. When they were invited to the Holiday Ale Fest, Garrett made a beer based off his homebrewed oatmeal porter and warmed it up as a Mexican Mocha Porter, adding 6 gallons of coffee, 10 pounds of chocolate, and 4 different peppers including habaneros for a 10-barrel batch. It was one of my favorite beers at the 2012 winter fest. This rich beer would pair nicely with their shepherd's pie made with ground beef simmered in Guinness, complementing it with Mexican mole notes. If by some freak chance you're not in a beer mood, they also have a hundred-plus whiskeys. Naturally, Jameson graces the Whiskey Wings housemade barbecue sauce.

As for that Guinness, I had one last question for Garrett during my visit to the pub. I sat with him in a hand-built wooden booth across from the fireplace, facing a large, backlit work of stained glass. It was salvaged from Upstate New York's St. Patrick's Chapel, which was built in 1892 and burned down some 170 years later, and depicts the church's patron saint. I asked Garrett if he'd do a dry Irish stout. "You always want to try," he responded, "but out of respect . . ." he tapered off, pantomiming a tip o' the hat to Ireland's legendary brew.

Kells Brewpub

Opened: 2012.

Owners: Gerard and Lucille McAleese.

Brewers: Garrett McAleese, Dave Fleming, and Ray Farrell.

System: 20-barrel.

Annual production: 1,200 barrels.

Distribution: Kells pubs in Portland and Seattle.

Hours: Monday through Friday, 11:30 a.m. to close; Saturday and Sunday, 9 a.m. to close.

Tours: Just ask.

Takeout beer: Growlers.

Gift shop: T-shirts, caps, and more.

Food: Irish and American fare, including shepherd's pie and fish and chips.

Events: St. Patrick's Day Irish Festival.

Other location: Kells Irish Restaurant and Pub (112 SW 2nd Ave., Portland; 503-227-4057; KellsIrish.com/portland).

Lucky Labrador Quimby Beer Hall

1945 Northwest Quimby Street, Portland, OR 97209
(503) 517-4352 • LuckyLab.com
Twitter @LuckyLabPDX

Most people think of the duo in Grant Wood's iconic painting *American Gothic* as husband and wife, but in actuality they're father and daughter. You know the one. They're standing stoically on their farm, the man firmly holding a pitchfork while the woman is empty-handed. But not at Lucky Labrador's Quimby Beer Hall. The mural painted in dual panels along the back patio wall portrays the spinster more like a brewster, pint in hand. (The other panel depicts it as a hop farm—not that Iowa has abundant hop crops along its 42nd Parallel, but they do exist.) As for the pint in her hand, brewer Ben Flerchinger wouldn't say exactly what beer it is, but considering she's smiling a bit as compared to Wood's portrait, I'm going to say it's Super Dog IPA, Lucky Lab's best-selling beer that boasts a pound of dry hops per barrel.

This outpost of the Lucky Labrador Brewing opened in 2006 as the third location (following the original brewpub on Southeast Hawthorne Boulevard, page 60, and the public house in Southeast's Multnomah Village), housed in the former Freightliner Trucks factory dating back to the 1940s. Flerchinger has been the brewer here since day one, having begun his professional brewing career at the Hawthorne location where he climbed the ladder from bartender to keg washer to brewer thanks to his budding interest as a homebrewer at the time.

If there's one thing that sets this Northwest location apart from its Southeast forbearer, it's that this brewpub offers eighteen taps to the other's twelve, so Flerchinger relishes the leeway to brew more experimentally. Sure, many of the 30-barrel batches are devoted to Super Dog IPA since it's the bestseller here and those kegs need to satisfy Lucky Lab's two brewery-less pubs (and limited bottling), but Flerchinger still gets to play around. He said he's always tinkering with his ginger beer—upping the ginger spice or perhaps adding a pronounced hop spice—and conceiving

Beers brewed: Year-round: Blue Dog Pale Ale, Top Dog Extra Special Pale Ale, Super Dog IPA, SlabTown Wheat Stout. Seasonals: Scottish Holiday, Solar Flare Ale, Crystal Weizen, Hawthorne's Best Bitter, Ginger Beer, Irish Stout, and more.

The Pick: Super Dog IPA is a big, fluffy IPA with a wet nose and offers lots to love, especially for fans of grapefruity hops and ample malt body.

various ways to build an IPA. He usually has three or four on tap at a time. Out of the lineup of beers in the Got Hops? Series of experimental IPAs, he says those hopped with dank Summit hops are the most popular. And then there are the ones he ages in spent barrels. Though I've seen others around town, he lays claim to doing the first IPA aged in Old Tom Gin barrels (even more rare considering gin isn't typically aged in oak barrels) wherein the floral hops and gin botanicals intermarry amiably and deliciously. His Black Sheep CDA aged in bourbon barrels yielded chocolate and berry flavors I never would've expected.

But don't lose sight of the fact that, above all, this is a great space for hanging out with two- and four-legged friends. Labradors and dogs of all breeds are welcome on the patio, but unless your pooch is an art critic keep him from standing too close to the mural, please. Inside, though your eyes are drawn to the Andy Warholian dog paintings, there's an event space that has hosted weddings, bar mitzvahs, and corporate parties. The outside is ideal for quaffing some pints while your pooch lounges at your feet. Granted this is the Westside and surrounded by apartments and condos so there are fewer dog owners, it's not the Lucky Lab unless there are labs and puppies galore enjoying their masters' quaffing a few pints.

Lucky Labrador Quimby Beer Hall

Opened: 2006.
Owners: Alex Stiles and Gary Geist (see page 60).
Brewer: Ben Flerchinger.
System: 30-barrel.
Annual production: 2,500 barrels.
Distribution: Oregon.
Hours: Monday through Wednesday, 11 a.m. to 11 p.m.; Thursday through Saturday, 11 a.m. to midnight; Sunday, noon to 10 p.m.
Tours: By appointment.
Takeout beer: Bombers, growlers, and keg dock sales.
Gift shop: The back wall displays T-shirts, bike jerseys, hoodies, and caps.
Food: Pizzas, sandwiches, and salads. Vegetarian friendly.
Extras: The Tour de Lab is a bike ride visiting the Lucky Lab pubs in September and benefits the DoveLewis animal hospital across the street from the Quimby pub (as do roughly 90 percent of the company's charitable givings). Dogs always allowed; minors until 9 p.m.
Other locations: Multnomah Village Public House (7675 SW Capitol Highway, Portland; 503-244-2537). North Tap Room (1700 N. Killingsworth St., Portland; 503-505-9511).

Pints Brewing Co.

412 Northwest 5th Avenue, Portland, OR 97209
(503) 564-BREW (2739) • PintsBrewing.com
Twitter @PintsBrewing

Coffeehouse by day. Brewpub and "urban taproom" by night. American domination by tomorrow.

Owner Chad Rennaker is like Rich "Uncle" Penny-bags (generally known as "the Monopoly guy"), only without the top hat. Rennaker is a real-life real estate developer, but instead of putting little green houses or red condos on his properties he's building brewpubs. It began with Pints in Old Town Portland, and then came Ponderosa Brewing Co. in Albuquerque.

In 2012, Rennaker and his wife, Dana, opened a spot downstairs from their offices for all things brewed. From 7 a.m. to 11:30 a.m. during the week, it's Pints Everyday Coffee. Within half an hour, the coffee-house sign comes down, revealing the taps hidden in the morning. The skylights cast a heavenly spotlight on the 3.5-barrel brewhouse (with 7-barrel fermenters) helmed by brewmaster Alan Taylor. His pre-Pints stints included Widmer Brothers, and before that Germany, where he studied, hence his amazing pronunciation of—and penchant for—German beer styles. Incidentally, when his AmeriKaner in Berliner Weisse is available on draft (soured with *Lactobacillus*), imported, traditional woodruff syrup replaces the cafe's Torani bottles.

I love the Berliner Weisse, but the most popular beer here is Seismic IPA. (The sporadically available imperial version is Seismic Upgrade.) Among the ten taps, there are four standards, including a light blond, a hoppy red, and a mocha-like stout; two seasonals; and two "randoms." Given Taylor's proclivity for German varieties (although he certainly has established an eclectic program with many Belgian- and American-tinged recipes), those randoms could include an eisbock or a weizendoppelbock, both quite malty sweet yet with enough spicy balance. But more often Mini Whammy and Tripel Whammy are found; the

Beers brewed: Year-round: Brick House Blonde, Seismic IPA, Rip Saw Red, Steel Bridge Stout. Seasonals: Green Line Organic IPA, Seismic Upgrade Imperial IPA, Norbert Vienna Lager, Mini Whammy Grisette, Tripel Whammy, AmeriKaner in Berliner Weisse, Konvention Kolsch, Barleywine.

The Pick: Seismic IPA. There are no faults in Seismic IPA, a very regional flavor packed with Columbus hops for bitterness (75 IBUs). Cascades flesh out the hop bouquet and Simcoe and Amarillos are used in earth-shattering dry-hopping.

former is a session Grisette farmhouse ale and the latter (named for fans of the eighties game show *Press Your Luck*) is a warming Belgian tripel redolent of Juicy Fruit gum.

Taylor, who has been brewing professionally since 1997, said Pints is the first brewery he has worked where he has 100 percent creative control. The brewery has veered slightly from the path established by inaugural brewer Zach Beckwith (now at Three Creeks in Sisters), who preached fundamentals as if he were a college basketball coach. Upon Pints' opening, I recall Beckwith saying, "Other menus look more like a soup list than a beer list." I mention that mostly to segue into the fact that they've since added a food menu that is short, focuses on fundamentals (burgers and deli sandwiches), and does offer a daily house-made soup. But overall, in Taylor's words, the self-proclaimed urban taproom is a "really comfortable place to have some nice beers."

Comfy, yes, yet fairly industrial, too. Sitting at outdoor tables when the weather permits is ideal, but inside the walls are all brick, the floor plan is open with high ceilings, and the brew system is flush against the back wall. Taylor said it reminds him of Northern Europe and since his wife's from Hamburg, he'd know. Another aspect he enjoys about the layout is that since there are tables by the brewery, patrons feel comfortable talking to him, which occurs daily. At least it did. We'll see what his office looks like as he transitions to "Corporate Brewmaster" for the line of brewpubs under Rennaker's umbrella. Beyond Oregon and New Mexico, properties planned to get their own brewpub include ones in Hawaii and Arizona. They're all warmer, but here in Portland, there are hops growing along trellises outside the Rennakers' offices, visible above the pub as you enter, and Albuquerque and Phoenix aren't exactly renowned for their hops.

Pints Brewing Co.

Opened: 2012.
Owner: Chad Rennaker.
Brewers: Alan Taylor (brewmaster) and Matt Kollaja (head brewer).
System: 3.5-barrel.
Annual production: 350 barrels.
Distribution: Portland and a bit beyond.
Hours: Monday through Saturday, 11:30 a.m. to 11 p.m.; Sunday, noon to 9 p.m.
Tours: Just walk in the back and if Alan's brewing, he's happy to talk.
Takeout beer: Growlers (two-for-one fills on Saturdays).
Gift shop: Threads and glass.
Food: Sandwiches and salads. The BLT's roasted garlic mayo literally seals the deal.

Portland and Pyramid Brewing

2730 Northwest 31st Avenue, Portland, OR 97210
(503) 228-5269 • PortlandBrewing.com • PyramidBrew.com
Twitter @PortlandBrewing • @PyramidBrew

Portland Brewing has been halfway around the world, all without leaving its namesake hometown. Founded by Art Larrance and Fred Bowman in 1986, the brewery was later owned by an initial investor, a Scot named Robert "Mac" MacTarnahan, until 2004 when Seattle-based Pyramid Brewing (founded in 1984 as Hart Brewing) took over. In 2008, Vermont's Magic Hat Brewing acquired Pyramid and renamed Portland Brewing as MacTarnahan's. Collectively, the company was called Independent Brewers United (with the clever acronym IBU, which also denotes beer's international bitterness units).

From there, North American Breweries folded IBU into its other properties—such as Labatt USA, spun off from the Canadian brewing concern—in 2010, with all of them run from offices at Genesee Brewing in Rochester, New York. Finally, in 2012 Florida Ice & Farm Co. shelled out for all of the above, adding them to their portfolio that also includes Costa Rica's largest beer brand, Imperial, plus bottled beverages ranging from Heineken to Pepsi. Through it all, MacTarnahan's Amber and Pyramid Hefeweizen have remained classic beers in the canon of Northwest brewing. And if Cerveza Imperial seems out of place, it's not—Florida Ice & Farm Co. (FIFCo) is based not in the Sunshine State, but in Costa Rica.

The brewery and taproom greets visitors to the industrial sliver between Forest Park and the Willamette River with twelve taps of mostly Pyramid brands. Portland Brewing only has three available year-round: the IPA, Zigzag River Lager, and that famous amber that still bears the name of the brewery's mid-era owner. (Incidentally, Mac wasn't just Portland Brewing's financial savior; he was also a record-holding athlete in both track and wrestling.) It also continually formulates some intriguing, tasty seasonals. In the fall, Noble Scot—the toasty, malt-leaning Scottish ale that pairs excellently with shepherd's pie—is steadfast. It's followed by their newest creation, Royal Anne Cherry Stout, obviously cherry-driven. Brewed with chocolate malts and puréed Oregon-grown Royal Anne cherries (most often found in maraschinos), this winter warmer that clocks in at nearly 8 percent alcohol is like drinking a chocolate-covered cherry or those cherry liqueurs encased in chocolate and wrapped in gold foil. (I'm not the only one who loves those things, am I?)

There are ongoing matters of branding, but in early 2013, having nothing to do with developing new brand identities or beer styles, MacTarnahan's reverted back to Portland Brewing, the name it had for its first eighteen years.

Original founders Larrance and Bowman were high school buddies and have remained friends all these years later. Larrance founded Cascade Brewing in 1995; its Raccoon Lodge in Hillsboro is a seminal public house, whereas its Cascade Barrel Room in Southeast Portland has developed a global reputation as the "House of Sour" (as in beers soured by wild yeasts). He quickly recalled the "leverage situation" that nudged him out the door once he no longer held a majority interest in Portland Brewing and asserted that "the company was controlled by non-brewing people." Unarguably, there have been some curious actions taken, but only three other Portland breweries have been around longer, and long is the list of ones that came after but didn't last. Some Portland neighborhoods have become crowded with brewpubs—not saturated, mind you, just crowded. But FIFCo's Portland/Pyramid Brewery and Taproom has found its niche in a fitting setting that is industrial yet flanked by evergreen trees and a deep blue river that adroitly reflects the name Portland.

Portland beers: Year-round: MacTarnahan's Amber Ale, IPA, ZigZag River Lager. Seasonals: Rose Hip Gold and Oyster Stout (spring); Full Bloom, India Pale Lager, and Oregon Honey Beer (summer); Noble Scot (fall); Blackwatch Cream Porter and Royal Anne Cherry Stout (winter).

Pyramid beers: Year-round: Hefeweizen, Apricot Wheat Ale, Thunderhead IPA, Outburst Imperial IPA, IPL, Wheaten IPA, Weiss Cream. Seasonals: Strawberry Blonde Saison, Curve Ball Blonde Ale, Oktoberfest, Snow Cap Winter Warmer.

The Pick: MacTarnahan's Amber. Once the flagship style of microbrewing, this sweet amber ale with a tickle of Cascade hops remains their best-selling brand, indicating the hoppy arms race that ensued after its release in 1992 left plenty of drinkers battle fatigued.

Portland and Pyramid Brewing

Opened: 1984 (Pyramid); 1986 (Portland).

Owner: Florida Ice & Farm Co.

Brewer: Ryan Pappe.

System: 125-barrel.

Annual production: Unknown, but 29,000 barrels shipped throughout Oregon.

Distribution: Portland distributes to Oregon and sixteen other states. Pyramid distributes to an additional nineteen states, for a combined total of thirty-six.

Hours: Monday, 11 a.m. to 9 p.m.; Tuesday through Thursday, 11 a.m. to 10 p.m.; Friday, 11 a.m. to 11 p.m.; Saturday, noon to 11 p.m.; Sunday, noon to 9 p.m.

Tours: Saturday, noon to 3 p.m.

Takeout beer: Growlers, bottles, and dock sales.

Gift shop: Extensive merchandise.

Food: Classic "brewhouse cuisine" ranging from poutine to "porkwich."

Festival: The annual release of Noble Scot includes a bagpiper piping, traditional Scottish fare, and more.

McMenamins Crystal Ballroom Brewery

1332 West Burnside Street, Portland, OR 97209
(503) 225-0047
Mcmenamins.com/CrystalBallroom
Twitter @CaptainNeon

Long before it was resurrected as the Crystal Brewery, the Cotillion Hall opened in 1914 thanks to Michael "Montrose" Ringler, who piously abstained from alcohol yet not from dancing, even though, as McMenamins historian Tim Hills wrote, "Portland residents could be arrested for dancing." In the 1930s, after the Great Depression when Jazz and dancing were illicit—Ringler had been incarcerated on such charges—the hall became the Crystal Ballroom and the "floating dance floor" started hosting line dancing. The floor was built on springs to absorb the brunt of fancy footwork and was directly inspired by the "elastic floor" that my vaudevillian great-grandparents danced on in San Francisco. It's believed the Crystal's is the last one in existence in the country.

Over the years the timbre changed: James Brown, Wilson Pickett, Janis Joplin, The Grateful Dead, Portland's late, great Elliot Smith, and currently great The Decemberists. In between the Grateful Dead and Elliot Smith was the psychedelic heyday when bands such as The Electric Prunes (note to anyone born after 1970 like myself: that's not a fictitious group) were deemed a bad influence (by those born before 1940) on the area's misguided youth, so the Crystal Ballroom was shut down in 1968. McMenamins reopened it in 1997.

Beers brewed: Year-round: Hammerhead Pale Ale, Terminator Stout, Ruby, IPA. Seasonals: Black Widow, Thundercone Fresh Hop, Orzel Bialy Baltic Porter, Mad Hatter IIPA, and more.

The Pick: Mad Hatter Imperial IPA. If you see this one on, order it while it's hot. Actually, the huge amount of hops was hot—they're literally steeped in hot water to create a floral, zesty, herbal tea that is then added to the wort's long boil. It has the maltiness and alcohol strength (9 percent) of an imperial IPA, but the way the hops are introduced keeps the bitterness well below the radar, creating a fragrant, flavorful beer devoid of "imperial" intimidation.

The ground-level Ringlers Pub is a large room with a long bar in the middle, lots of dark wood, and a canopy with a mosaic spreading over the bar and clear up through the ceiling into the second-floor brewhouse. The walls, bedecked with vintage signs and pictures, still showcase the original Cotillion Hall sign. There are several billiard tables behind the bar (pool is free until 6 p.m.). Upstairs, Lola's Room—named for the first female police chief and Montrose Ringler's chief nemesis, Lola Baldwin—hosts DJ nights and more intimate live shows compared to the ballroom directly overhead, which is easily one of my favorite venues for its size, acoustics, aesthetic, and last but not least, options for house brewed beer.

The Crystal complex includes the Crystal Hotel directly across Northwest 13th Avenue, still on Burnside. The original building, built in 1911, was converted into the Majestic Hotel in 1946. Its next permutation was a gay bathhouse that closed in 2007. The ground-floor restaurant is Zeus Café, named for former owner Nate Zusman. My favorite element is the surrounding stained glass denoting "Dark Star" by the Grateful Dead. Literally. Crystal panels depict the song note for note. It's a distinctly McMenamins touch, and the song is a favorite of the Deadhead brothers. It almost diverts one's eyes away from the Turkish chandeliers. The windows are all able to roll out or open wide, but if you're chilly, don't worry—heaters are built into every booth and guests can control the temperature themselves. Talk about climate control and comfort.

Downstairs, Al's Den is a cool grotto bar that hosts weeklong residencies (starting with REM's Peter Buck). Live music 365 nights a year provides a chic dinner option. And while moderation is key for drinking beer (or house wine, cider, and spirits), the hotel has fifty-one rooms. Staff artists styled them all after musical acts that have jammed at the Crystal, from James Brown to Flogging Molly. The Heart of Glass room, for example, portrays Deborah Harry paddling in a heart-shaped boat through a flood while the headboard is adorned with a giant painting of a glass heart and Blondie's lyrics scrawled across the top of the walls, ticker-tape style.

It would probably please Ringler that the Cotillion Hall is still in use a century later, but I'm not sure he'd love that it sees its fair share of spilt beer—brewed downstairs from his lavish dance floor—during concerts. Dancing and drinking are no longer outlawed, but it's tricky to do both simultaneously.

McMenamins Crystal Ballroom Brewery

Opened: 1997.

Owners: Brian and Mike McMenamin (see page 92).

Brewer: Dan Black.

System: 6-barrel.

Annual production: 1,818 barrels.

Distribution: Portland.

Pub Hours (Ringlers): Sunday through Wednesday, 11:30 a.m. to 1 a.m.; Thursday through Saturday, 11:30 a.m. to 2:30 a.m.

Tours: Walk-in tours when brewer is available.

Takeout beer: Growlers, limited bottles, and kegs.

Gift shop: Plenty of apparel, glassware, and souvenirs.

McMenamins Fulton Pub & Brewery

0618 Southwest Nebraska Street, Portland, OR 97239
(503) 246-9530 • Mcmenamins.com/Fulton
Twitter @CaptainNeon

Jake Reisch operated a diner called Reisch's Place that, supposedly, he also ran as a speakeasy, having built this Fulton neighborhood hole-in-the-wall in the grips of Prohibition. There are photos of him and his wife, whose family had one of Portland's first breweries (The United States Brewery), on what McMenamins Fulton manager Andy McFall calls "the history wall."

The McMenamins converted this space into their second brewery in 1988. Beyond the usual McMenamins-style art, check out the gallery of sorts above the bar, where a patron converted dozens of coasters into his small, circular canvases. The other in-house artist is Oregon native Ryan Mott, the twenty-first brewer here, though it's his twelfth brewpub within the empire where he has mashed in.

Mere blocks from Willamette Park and along the river, this cozy bar with a beer garden out back, replete with a firepit, maintains a hyper-local vibe. Mott's not a whacky brewer and proudly keeps Nebraska Bitter as the flagship since it originated at this pub, but visit circa Cinco de Mayo and feel the burn of liquid del fuego, Jalapa Ale, the golden jalapeño brew commemorating the pub's anniversary.

McMenamins Fulton Pub & Brewery

Opened: 1988.
Owner: Brian and Mike McMenamin (see page 92).
Brewer: Ryan Mott.
System: 6-barrel.
Annual production: 1,000 barrels.
Distribution: On-premises and at three nearby pubs.
Hours: Monday through Thursday, 11 a.m. to midnight;
Friday, 11 a.m. to 1 a.m.; Saturday, 11 a.m. to midnight;
Sunday, 11 a.m. to 11 p.m.
Tours: Walk-in tours when the brewer is available.
Takeout beer: Growlers and dock sales.
Gift shop: Mc-merch (shirts and other items).
Food: McMenamins pub grub.

Beers brewed: Year-round: Hammerhead Pale Ale, Terminator Stout, Ruby, IPA, Nebraska Bitter. Seasonals: Autumn Fest, Jalapa, Squirtie Pale Ale, and more.

The Pick: Nebraska Bitter. Garnering its name from the street it's brewed on, this accessible English-style bitter derives its blond roots from Crystal malt and a citric kick solely from Cascade hops.

McMenamins Hillsdale Brewery & Public House

1505 Southwest Sunset Boulevard, Portland, OR 97239
(503) 246-3938 • Mcmenamins.com/Hillsdale
Twitter @CaptainNeon

Fri., Oct. 25
8:32 Start fill—gas on
8:40 110 gal H2O
10:00 100 lbs extract . . .

Thus begins the handwritten brew sheet of the very first ever brewpub beer made on this spot in 1985, thanks to the efforts of some crazy folks like Brian and Mike McMenamin, who changed the law to allow breweries to actually sell beer on-site. The crumpled and yellowed sheet of paper is casually framed on the wall just inside the entrance, near a photo of said McMenamin brothers (looking a fair bit younger than they do today).

Yes, as the sheet documents, they were using malt extract initially. In 1985, there was no such thing as "craft beer" and few had heard the term "microbrew." They only put in a brewery here at the Hillsdale location because as tiny as the kitchen is—the brewery is right in the kitchen—it was at least roomier than the Barley Mill in Southeast Portland, the first McMenamins pub, opened in 1983. The then-3-barrel batch (it's now a company-norm 6-barrel system) called for a total of 5 pounds of hops, starting with Willamettes and finishing with Tettnangers that were added to the "overwhelming-outrageous" boil, noted with four stars for added exuberance. Of course there was excitement in the air. Oregon's first brewpub became a reality.

According to the Oregon Brewers Guild, in 1985 there were twenty-one non-corporate breweries in all of America. "The only rule is that there are no rules," Mike McMenamin said at the time. To get a sense of the early days, I met with McMenamins general manager Rob Vallance at the brewery—initially referred to as Captain Neon's

Beers brewed: Year-round: Hammerhead Pale Ale, Terminator Stout, Ruby, IPA. Seasonals: Jam Session IPA, Black Widow, Purple Haze, Thundercone, and more.

The Pick: Ruby. Stalwarts will kill me for not selecting Hammerhead, or possibly Terminator, but Ruby Ale defines a style that McMenamins originated: the fruited wheat ale. Despite the 42 pounds of Oregon-fresh and processed raspberries per batch, more than hinted at in each pour's pink hue, it's very much a bready, refreshing wheat beer that has a slight berry aroma and aftertaste rather than bombarding the palate like a Framboise. And at under 4.5 percent alcohol, it doesn't bombard the liver, either.

Fermentation Chamber—to chat. Vallance first brewed for the company at the Lighthouse Brewery (not a real lighthouse) in 1994, though he had begun working for them three years earlier. We sat beneath the neon yellow sun and blue moon, archetypal artwork from McMenamins' long-standing in-house artist Lyle Hehn. Vallance mentioned that Mike McMenamin, who's a huge Deadhead, went by the handle Captain Neon. More importantly, he explained that the "no rules" rule meant trying things that, up until such time, had been forbidden in brewing by the government. Like fruit. The inaugural brewer, Ron Wolf, whose brewing résumé included the vaunted original craft brewery Anchor in San Francisco, brewed a batch where he went out to the parking lot fence and picked wild blackberries to throw in. (Mars Bars are hardly fruit, but those also went into an early batch.) Wolf's longest lasting mark was his twelfth batch, a hearty stout created to satisfy the Irish brothers' love of Guinness, called Terminator.

Company-wide, there are only three mandatory beers that all brewers make (four counting a non-specific IPA). Besides Terminator, they are Ruby and Hammerhead. Both originated at Hillsdale in 1986, but not as Ruby or Hammerhead per se. "It was originally Ruby Tuesday," said Vallance, "but we had to change it because of the burger chain." The process and recipe have changed, naturally, but today it calls for 42 pounds of puréed Oregon raspberries and it "absolutely sells the most," even more than hoppy Hammerhead or the super hoppy IPAs.

As for Hammerhead Pale Ale, batch number 37 wasn't originally just called Hammerhead, and it wasn't a pale ale. It was Old Hammerhead Strong Ale and it stayed that way for about a year until a new brewer named John Harris was hired in 1986. He's now a legendary brewer in Oregon, having transitioned from Hillsdale to founding brewer at Deschutes before moving back to Portland as Full Sail's brewmaster, finally becoming creator of his own Ecliptic Brewing in 2013. Back then, he converted Hillsdale from extract brewing to all-grain, giving beers like Hammerhead the complexity that only caramelly Crystal malts can bring, while upping the hop bill with grapefruity Cascades to make it an early classic Northwest pale ale.

The rest is history. But the pub is still the hub of the neighborhood, fairly literally. It's on the spot where Hillsdale's founding father, John Slavin, built his home in 1850. It's where the Pierce Sanitorium operated from 1918–1924, fifty years before becoming a Skipper's Fish & Chips. It still looks like Skipper's, not a pioneer house or tuberculosis treatment facility in the vein of other McMenamins properties retaining the original building styles, but along with all of the Hehn artwork adorning the walls and ceiling, that's part of its charm. And it's still the best bet to get the Captain Neon Burger with blue cheese sauce and bacon.

McMenamins Hillsdale Brewery & Public House

Opened: 1985.

Owners: Mike and Brian McMenamin (see page 92).

Brewer: Tyler Newton.

System: 6-barrel.

Annual production: 650 barrels.

Hours: Monday through Thursday, 11 a.m. to midnight; Friday and Saturday, 11 a.m. to 1 a.m.; Sunday, noon to 11 p.m.

Tours: Walk-ins when the brewer is available.

Takeout beer: Growlers, limited bottles, and dock sales.

Gift shop: Apparel, glassware, and souvenirs.

Food: Wide-ranging menu of pub staples. The Captain Neon Burger with blue cheese sauce is the way to go.

Events: The third Saturday of February marks the annual Hillsdale Brewfest, their original of many such fests, where the winning beer from twenty McMenamin brewers gets to represent the company at the Oregon Brewers Festival.

The Old Market Pub & Brewery

6959 Southwest Multnomah Boulevard, Portland, OR 97223
(503) BIG-BEER (244-2337) • DrinkBeerHere.com
Twitter @OMPBrew

Owners Andy and Shelly Bigley were freshly into their thirties when, as McMenamins alumni, they decided to open their own neighborhood-centric, family-oriented brewpub. It seemed fitting to name the old produce market and cannery Old Market Pub since Dance Studio Pub—referencing the market's adjoining space that's also part of this 15,000-square-foot compound—doesn't have the same ring.

With the recent departure of brewer Tomas Sluiter, who left to launch his own Culmination Brewing, Bobby Stevens is in charge of the 15-barrel brewhouse. That means sating hopheads with fresh Bombay IPA. And chili heads, if such beer lovers truly exist, need to try Hot Tamale. But the liquid star here is Mr. Toad's Wild Red Ale. It's saved from being overly malty by dry-hopping.

Within this ginormous hall, families and sports fans can find ample tables, drinking games including pool and shuffleboard, and Oregon Lottery video poker (so try to keep your kiddoes from playing in that area). Because Old Market Pub is such a dining haven for Multnomah families, Andy lamented that he'll soon have to change the menu options or prices simply to keep above water. It was a point of pride that nothing on the menu, at least until recently, was over ten dollars, despite the generous portions. But the small increase isn't without its benefits. He's contemplating upgrading to Painted Hills organic beef for the burgers. They already use only organic malts for all the beers.

Can't be bothered to trek out to Multnomah? A fifteen-minute drive into Southeast Portland will take you to The Broadway Grill & Brewery, a second pub that isn't branded as Old Market Pub but still offers the same beers and menu. Notice it has "brewery" in the name, even though it doesn't actually have one. To that, Andy added the word "yet." The pub is interesting because it has an entire room for video poker and lottery games,

Beers brewed: Year-round: Mr. Toad's Wild Red Ale, British Bombay IPA, Ol' Granny Smith Apple Ale, Hot Tamale Chili Beer, Hop On!, Great White Wheat, and seasonals.

The Pick: Hop On! This beer is devoid of a classic style, but at 5 percent ABV yet 87 IBUs it fits the bill of a Northwest ale that's got great body and is opulently perfumed with hops. Even *Arrested Development* fans can't steer clear of this Hop On!

from which minors are banned, but also a diaper deck in the bathrooms. So stay tuned to see what else he's got up his sleeve, because it's increasingly rare to find a brewpub in Portland that has an entire mile radius all to itself.

The Old Market Pub & Brewery

Opened: 1994.

Owners: Andy and Shelly Bigley.

Brewer: Bobby Stevens.

System: 15-barrel.

Annual production: 800 barrels.

Distribution: Pubs only.

Hours: Monday through Thursday, 11 a.m. to midnight; Friday, 11 a.m. to 1 a.m.; Saturday, 9 a.m. to 1 a.m.; Sunday, 9 a.m. to 11 p.m.

Tours: By request.

Takeout beer: Growler fills.

Gift shop: A variety of gear, from T-shirts to sweat pants.

Food: Standard pub fare; perhaps the only place in Oregon that serves Cincinnati-style "three-way chili."

Other location: The Broadway Grill & Brewery (1700 NE Broadway, Portland; 503-284-4460).

Rock Bottom Restaurant & Brewery

206 Southwest Morrison Street,
Portland, OR 97204
503-796-BREW (2739)
RockBottom.com/portland
Twitter @RockBottomPdx

The most admirable aspect about Rock Bottom breweries is that each of the national chain's thirty-seven brewpubs has its own brewery on-site where the respective brewmasters have free reign to create their own beers—at least in part. After nearly two decades, Rock Bottom merged with Gordon Biersch and formed CraftWorks in 2010, becoming the largest operator of beer-focused casual dining restaurants, including Old Chicago and smaller regional chains. Brewmaster Charlie Hutchins, an Indiana native, is charged with brewing the company's four core beers (Cologne-style Kolsch, Belgian-style White Ale, Red Ale, and IPA), and even though the recipe looks the same on paper, what you get in the glass ends up being quite different, especially here in Portland.

Out of every Rock Bottom brewery, Portland's is the only one brewing with hop leaves instead of pelletized hops (and always has been). These fresher hops, including coveted Simcoes and Centennials, grant beers such as the IPA—and especially the Imperial IPA on tap during my last visit—that sticky, lip-smacking quality emblematic of Northwest ales. Not to mention, the Portland location is the only Rock Bottom that gets to use a hopback—a chamber filled with additional hops through which the wort passes before beginning fermentation, and which also acts as a de facto filter—in the brewhouse for added floral aroma.

Beers brewed: Year-round: Kolsch, White Ale, Red Ale, IPA, rotating dark ale. Seasonals: Three in rotation always on tap.

That brewhouse is located upstairs from the main dining area and features all-glass walls. Hutchins referred to it as a "brewquarium" and said most brewers at pubs with visible breweries come in super early to finish their brewing before customers arrive. But, he said, even when his work is on display, most patrons don't take notice.

The clientele is heavily business folks at lunch, given its enviable central downtown location, with a swelling happy hour crowd. Families on vacation make up another big chunk of the tabs. You're not

The Pick: Cascadian Dark Ale. Straight stouts are outstanding, but Hutchins Pacific-Northwestifies the requisite dark ale by augmenting it with a regional love of hops. It's what everyone else calls a Black IPA but in these parts is known as a Cascadian Dark Ale.

likely to find many locals since they tend to keep it hyper-local by supporting their neighborhood brewpubs or taprooms, which explains the proliferation of breweries east of the Willamette River.

But Rock Bottom most certainly is a Portland brewery. While all the breweries in the chain are required to have at least one dark beer on tap, Hutchins is a fan of making his a CDA. What everyone else calls a Black IPA is known here in Cascadia (Oregon, Washington, parts of Idaho, and British Columbia) as a Cascadian Dark Ale. So yes, it's just as black as a stout and features some of the same dark roasted malts, but it's hopped to the hilt like an India Pale Ale.

Hutchins acknowledged that there is a Rock Bottom culture and that it's common for brewers to hop around from one outpost to another. But as a veteran since 2008 of this location (truth be told, in ultra-rare Portland brewer fashion it's his first and only brewery experience), his focus is on the classics. The hoppy beers amp up the bitterness and aroma of the hops. The witbier isn't subtle with its coriander and orange peel, just as the winter seasonal coffee stout doesn't skimp on the java. But you won't find any head-scratchers here, or what Hutchins calls "pie beers" (e.g. the brewer tossed a whole pie into the mash).

Parent company CraftWorks' only direction for the other three taps (bringing the total to eight) is that whatever the house brewer puts on, it should sell. Given all these elements, Rock Bottom is one of the best-selling brewpubs for on-premises sales in town.

Rock Bottom Restaurant & Brewery

Opened: 1994.

Owner: CraftWorks Restaurants and Breweries, Inc.

Brewmaster: Charlie Hutchins.

System: 9-barrel.

Annual production: 1,500 barrels.

Distribution: On-premises only.

Hours: Sunday through Thursday, 11 a.m. to midnight; Friday and Saturday, 11 a.m. to 1:30 a.m.

Tours: By appointment only.

Takeout beer: Growler fills/refills.

Gift shop: T-shirts, hoodies, and glassware for sale at the entrance/exit.

Food: Casual dining heavy on the burgers and fries and continental crowd-pleasing fare.

Sasquatch Brewing Co.

6440 SW Capitol Highway, Portland, OR 97239
(503) 402-1999 • SasquatchBrewery.com
Twitter @SasquatchBrew

Homebrewer and Oregon native Tom Sims's goal in 2012 was to offer the families of Hillsdale their own "local." Ever since, locals have been bellying up to the bar at Sasquatch (although families, naturally, opt for tables). Upon entering, there's a welcoming front bar that fits a cozy four, maybe five, barstools. Head left for the larger space that's still rather comfy to enjoy a hearty and possibly even healthy sit-down meal. The food is fresh and locally sourced with plenty of veggie options to counter the burger and sandwich menu. Where that leaves items like deep-fried kimchi pickles, which appeal to both veggies and carnies, I'm not sure. If you want something to do with your fingers besides pop fried pickles, grab one of the Etch-A-Sketches in the game bin up front for the little ones. (Yeah, that's the ticket, for the little ones.) And when the weather abides, soak up some Vitamin D on the front patio with your pooch at your feet. This is how Sims achieved his goal.

Beer-wise, there's certainly something for everyone who isn't a minor or a canine. To dip your toes into the beer pool (sorry, it's a metaphor; there's no actual pool of beer), there's Oregon Session Ale, house-described as an "introduction to craft beer," which is easily a pub favorite. So is the Woodboy dry-hopped IPA that's bittered with Centennials but dry hopped with Cascades for a floral bouquet and citrus finish. Or, as long as we're dealing with mythical, wild, and unobtainable beasts like the brewery's namesake sasquatches, dive in with Moby Dick Imperial IPA, a monstrous beer that tips the scales at 10.2 percent ABV under a tsunami of 90 IBUs. On the dark side of the brew, there's Bertha Brown for fans of beers that emulate chocolate roastiness and Hairy Knuckle Stout, which, like Bertha, is often served on nitro. It leans more toward the warming side with oatmeal in the base and hints of coffee in the nose and on the tongue.

Beers brewed: Year-round: Oregon Session Ale, Belgian Blonde Ale, Healy Heights Pale Ale, Woodboy Dry-Hopped IPA, Moby Dick Imperial IPA, Bertha Brown Ale, Hairy Knuckles Stout. Seasonals: Celilo CDA, Vanilla Bourbon Cream Ale.

The Pick: Oregon Session Ale. Flaked maize in the grain bill means anyone can get down with this creamy, light-bodied ale (only 4.7 percent ABV). It has a pilsner malt base for a honeyed biscuit flavor that still features aromatic Willamette Valley hops.

Somewhat interestingly, there is a total of twenty-five taps in house, a full eight of which are devoted to cider. A few even have grapes flowing through them. But more interestingly, house manager Alex Beard told me that they're not just big fans of cider—they also have been federally approved to make their own. He cautioned not to expect all eight cider taps to go from guest brands to Sasquatch-made ciders, "but who knows?"

Nevertheless, they remain an "IPA-centric" brewpub since they abide by the mantra of brewing what they like to drink. Sims not only makes the beers but also hand-built the brewery, squeezed into the rear of the pub, and other fixtures, even down to the tap handles. As Beard noted, "He is generally our handyman and carpenter," proving that it's more important to have good hands than a real Bigfoot.

Sasquatch Brewing Co.

Opened: 2012.
Owner and brewer: Tom Sims.
System: 7-barrel.
Annual production: 800 barrels.
Distribution: Oregon.
Hours: Monday through Thursday, 3 p.m. to 11 p.m.; Friday and Saturday, noon to midnight; Sunday, noon to 9 p.m.
Tours: By request.
Takeout beer: Growlers and dock sales.
Gift shop: Shirts, hats, and glassware.
Food: Snacks such as deep-fried "kimchee" pickles and brown sugar-crusted ribs; small plates including beet fritters, sandwiches, and burgers (ask about the seasonal burger); and large plates ranging from hanger steak to quinoa hash.
Events: The occasional open-mic night, including adorable kids' open mics.

Tugboat Brewing Co.

711 Southwest Ankeny Street, Portland, OR 97205
(503) 226-2508 • www.d2m.com/Tugwebsite

The Tug: perhaps the most mysterious, misunderstood, and maligned brewery in Beervana.

It's mysterious because despite operating since 1993 almost no one knows about it. Seriously. And despite being centrally located downtown, just a block away from the intersection of Burnside and Broadway that everyone can pinpoint in their sleep, it's off the main road in what feels like an alley, meaning most foot traffic walks right by. (Perhaps that foot traffic is headed toward Mary's Club, Rose City's first topless—now nude—bar in a city that prides itself on having more strip clubs per capita than any other city. See? We're not just about the breweries here.)

It's misunderstood because when customers walk in and see that only a third of the eighteen taps are house beers they may not get that this is a brewery rather than a bar with a few private label beers. Having said that, expect as many as half of the house taps to be dry.

And it's maligned because beer geeks, or "the beer sniffers" as founder Megan McEnroe-Nelson calls them, huddle en masse inside Bailey's Taproom, which opened directly across the tiny alley-like street in 2007. While it's one of the most impressive taprooms in town, offering twenty well-curated drafts, evidently their clientele and Tugboat's don't mix. Once when I checked in at Tugboat via Twitter, a notorious Portland beer snob replied, "There must be some mistake—did someone at Tugboat get a hold of your phone?"

For all the beer drinkers intimidated by the atmosphere across the street where imbibers can generally engage in beer-speak with the best of them, Megan and her tiny staff happily welcome all guests, whether they know a pale ale from a pale lager or not. None of the beers on tap are that challenging. Then again, sip fresh Hop Gold and you'd swear they garnished the pint glass with grapefruit pith. And their 13 (sometimes 14) percent Chernobyl Double Russian Imperial Stout is an extreme beer. It goes down so smoothly that she made the

Beers brewed: Year-round: Hop Gold, Thunderbolt Pale Ale, Rye P.A., Chernobyl Double Russian Imperial Stout, seasonals.

The Pick: Chernobyl. True to its name, this is a double imperial and mutates between 13 and 14 percent ABV. No visit is complete without trying this viscous, leathery number fit for a Romanov.

responsible call to only sell it by the half pint. As such, it makes for the perfect nightcap. If you need two nightcaps and you're still sitting on (and not beside) your barstool, you can get another.

Her husband, Terry, is the brewer. They both worked on-site even before the brewery. She operated Café Omega and he specialized in watch restoration, previously running his business called Time For Fun from the adjoining space. They knocked down the wall and got a liquor license in 1991. Within two years they were brewing, despite Megan's only being nineteen years old. (Terry was already over twenty-one.) Running a microbrewery may seem like the most awesome, fun job for a nineteen-year-old (and it's unequivocally up there for anyone at any age) but she recalled "it was a lot of work [and] very tiring." Having said that, sporting a brunette bob and an omnipresent smile as she poured beers and offered samples, her girlish appearance remained.

Overall, Tugboat effortlessly exudes a comfortable and convivial atmosphere: stacks of old books, well-worn board games, cool jazz raining down from the speakers yet still enabling conversations to remain audible, and a thin trickle of patrons—out-of-towners, after-work crowds, and barflies alike—with whom you'd actually want to converse. Beer sniffers who dismiss Tugboat as for the dogs haven't met patron-turned-bartender Linsel Greene, the Goldendoodle of beer slingers. It all fits with the original concept for the brewery. The name has regional significance. Portland, compared to San Francisco and Seattle, is small and inland, so commercial vessels traveling via the Columbia River require tugboat assistance. Tugboats, like the brewery, aren't very fancy, Megan said. But "They're small, powerful, and hard-working. And a little bit salty."

Tugboat Brewing Co.

Opened: 1993.

Owners: Megan McEnroe-Nelson and Terry Nelson.

Brewer: Terry Nelson.

System: 4-barrel.

Annual production: 135 barrels.

Hours: Monday, 5 p.m. to 10 p.m.; Tuesday through Thursday, 4 p.m. to midnight; Friday, 4 p.m. to 1 a.m.; Saturday, 4 p.m. to 1 a.m.

Tours: No. It's a 4-barrel system in a tiny room, what's to see?

Takeout beer: They'll fill growlers or jars but don't sell growlers.

Gift shop: No, but they did just get some T-shirts in.

Food: Short and oddball menu of snacks and small plates such as mac and cheese, nachos, smoked salmon, and Chinese pork tenderloin, all $6–$7.

Baerlic Brewing Co.

2235 Southeast 11th Avenue, Portland, OR 97214
503-477-9418 • BaerlicBrewing.com
Twitter @BaerlicBrewing

Baerlic adds to the Hosford-Abernethy neighborhood's bustling brewing scene that includes The Commons and (formerly known as) Ground Breaker Breweries. It's a stone's throw from what beer writer/Beer Goddess Lisa Morrison dubbed the "Beermuda Triangle," which consists of Lucky Labrador, Green Dragon, and Cascade Barrel House. Let's add Hair of the Dog and Base Camp while we're at it, making it more of a Beermuda Pentagon. And we can't forget retail destinations Apex, Beer-Mongers, and Imperial.

Of the brewery and taproom with a patio, cofounder Rik Hall pitched it as "born out of an undying passion for the perfect pint of beer." They offer snacks and such but not a full menu, along with ten taps to wash everything down, all set in a warm, cozy bar sans TVs to affect the ambiance.

The name, Hall explained, translates to "of barley" in Old English and is pronounced "bear-lick." Like "a bear licking the foam off a frosty mug," he said. "But feel free to use it whenever you want to describe something that's both honest and delicious," he added, "as in, 'these waffles are baerlic.'" Indeed, waffles are "baerlic," but Hall and co-owner Ben Parsons are aware that the pub is moving into the former space of Portland's once-beloved bagel shop Kettleman's, so I like to think they're putting a twist on that old monk's milieu by saying they'll be making liquid bagels.

Beers brewed: Invincible IPA, Cavalier Cream Ale, Primeval Brown Ale, Noble Stout, Dry-hopped Barleywine, and an ever-evolving list of one-off, barrel-aged, and experimental beers.

Baerlic Brewing Co.

Opened: 2014.

Owners and brewers: Rik Keller Hall and Ben Parsons.

System: 10-barrel.

Annual production: TBD.

Distribution: Goal is on-premises only.

Hours: Tuesday through Thursday, 4 p.m. to 10 p.m.; Friday, 2 p.m. to 11 p.m.;
Saturday, noon to 11 p.m.; Sunday, noon to 10 p.m.

Tours: Upon request.

Takeout beer: Growlers, 22s, and dock sales.

Food: Cheese, charcuterie, and snacks.

Base Camp Brewing Co.

930 Southeast Oak Street, Portland, OR 97214
503-477-7479 • BaseCampBrewingCo.com
Twitter @BaseCampBrewing

It's funny. Base Camp's tasting room is outfitted with woodwork from six native trees, granite from a nearby quarry, and photographs depicting mountainous hikes, snowy slopes, and serene surf, all inviting you to the playgrounds of the great outdoors. (Kayakers immediately notice the canoe hanging from the rafters.) Yet all anyone wants to do in this urban base camp is sit inside at the bar or al fresco in the garden drinking beer. Owner-brewer Justin Fay's outdoorsiness manifests itself in all aspects of the design, from tasty beers with names like In-Tents and Intrepid to the garden's flora comprised of edible, native plants.

This high-concept brewery is a welcome addition to the Buckman neighborhood, which a handful of breweries already call home. One way Base Camp differentiated itself was by debuting not with an IPA, but with an IPL. The intensely flavored In-Tents India Pale Lager is a quixotic hybrid of fragrant, bitter IPA and Old World lager aged on house-toasted oak. Brewers have long been hybridizing IPAs, so In-Tents forewent ale yeast in favor of lager yeast. But this ain't no hoppy PBR, nor would it be described as dry or crisp. Fay, head brewer Paul Thurston, and lead brewer Austin Kneen age—or lager—In-Tents on house-toasted oak chips, enriching it with caramel notes.

"We're a lager brewery," Fay proclaimed as we sat in the high-ceilinged tasting room. "We're trying to help portray our ideas behind how we create beers with, as Thurston put it, 'great respect for [the] tradition in the thousands of years of history behind it.' But we're taking our artistic leeway to create something new." Thurston added, "There's a lot of confusion about what lager is. Many simply think American adjunct [beers]." Alas, that's what the big boys make. Thurston's past brewing experience came from Rogue Ales

Beers brewed: Year-round: In-Tents India Pale Lager, Northwest Fest, Ripstop Rye Pils, Lost Meridian Wit, Celestial CDL, S'more Stout. Seasonals: Intrepid IPA, Midnight in Wallonia, Carabiner Cream Ale, Cross Channel Mild, Rauch the Boat, Acclimator Doppelbock, and more.

The Pick: S'more Stout. There aren't any actual graham crackers, marshmallows, or chocolate bars in this stout, but biscuit malt imparts a grahaminess, roast malt conveys the chocolate character, and that sweet vanilla gooeyness comes in at the finish, while smoked malt lends an overall campfire quality. Each glass is garnished with a toasted marshmallow. Ingenious and delicious!

and BridgePort Brewing. Kneen worked at Pyramid and, like practically all other craft brewers, churned out ales. That means the beers ferment warm instead of cooler, bottom-fermenting lagers. Just as heat rises, ale yeast do their microbiological magic at the top of fermentation tanks while chillier lager yeasties work down low.

Base Camp's other lagers include Celestial Cascadian Dark Lager (one of the first commercial CDLs), Northwest Fest, Ripstop Rye Pils, Acclimator Doppelbock, and Rauch the Boat. That last one, a PacNorthwest take on a Bamberg rauchbier (*rauch* is German for "smoke"), features a hefty 20 percent Bamberger malt that's smoked instead of kilned or roasted. I love its bonfire flavor that, with the hint of caramel from the rest of the malt bill, tastes vaguely like candied bacon. Having said that, during wintry fire season, I look forward to S'more Stout, garnished with a mini-mallow roasted with a brûlée torch.

When it comes to retail, some call Base Camp's eye-catching, 22-ounce containers "aluma bottles" or "bottle cans." But the guys just call them bottles. The aluminum bottles feature striking colors; In-Tents is as green and beautiful as the great outdoors.

As for the actual greens surrounding the beer garden, Fay is prone to nibbling on them. He said he realizes they should be labeled since we're not all knowledgeable foragers. When I asked him about what they had growing, he pointed out miner's lettuce, highbush cranberries, trillium, and oxalis. Like I would know trillium from oxalis. Well, oxalis looks like radioactive-grown three-leaf clovers, and since Fay promised that everything's safe to eat, I now know it tastes like a super tart plum. It's nice, but stick with foraging for beer.

Base Camp Brewing Co.

Opened: 2012.

Owner: Justin Fay.

Brewers: Justin Fay, Paul Thurston (head brewer), and Austin Kneen (lead brewer).

System: 25-barrel.

Annual production: 1,750 barrels.

Distribution: Oregon, Washington, Northern California, and Vermont.

Hours: Sunday through Wednesday, noon to 9 p.m.; Thursday through Saturday, 11 a.m. to midnight.

Tours: Just ask.

Takeout beer: Bottles, growler-fills, and dock sales.

Gift shop: Apparel and glassware.

Food: The pizza and Mediterranean food carts parked on-site are semipermanent. S'mores kits ($2.50) available at the bar.

Buckman Botanical Brewery
(Rogue Ale's Green Dragon Pub)

928 Southeast Ninth Avenue, Portland, OR 97214
503-517-0660
BuckmanBrewery.com • PDXGreenDragon.com
Twitter @BuckmanBrewery, @PDXGreenDragon

The beloved Green Dragon Pub with its nineteen rotating taps closed for the second time on November 17, 2008. On November 18, it reopened under new ownership. That's president Brett Joyce's super abridged version of how the pub with the loyal following landed under the umbrella of Rogue Ales, whose Portland offices are catty-corner.

They've since more than doubled the tap list, including moving dartboards to make room for "the back thirty." And lest you think most of those handles would go to Rogue brands, with over sixty draft or cask beers, you can count the number from Rogue on one hand. Yeah, there was already a brewing system in place, but Joyce casually pointed out that it didn't work, so they eventually bought another.

The 15-barrel brewery, set in the Buckman neighborhood (that Beer Goddess Lisa Morrison dubbed the "Beermuda Triangle" for its eight breweries within a half-mile radius), uses teas, herbs, spices, and other botanicals. Certainly, hops are botanicals, but Buckman's is truly going rogue. "Our view is that Portland doesn't need [another] hoppy brewery," explained Joyce. In response to, or in defiance of, the hops race that has many local brewers making IPAs first and Imperial IPAs second, the Buckman Botanical Brewery focuses exclusively on "no-hop/low-hop [beers], never an IPA. We can do something more experimental, things that Rogue wouldn't do."

Brewer Danny Connors spent a couple of years brewing down at the main Rogue brewery in Newport under brewmaster John Maier (nicknamed "More Hops"). It's safe to say Maier won't take over the Buckman brewery anytime soon. Connors

Beers brewed: Year-round: Chamomellow Pale Ale, Ginger Pale Ale, Orange Peel Ale, Apple Beer. Seasonals: Pumpkin Kolsch, Red Nectar Ale, Parnold Almer Kolsch.

The Pick: Pumpkin Kolsch. People tend to love or hate pumpkin beers, and many who say they hate them really just detest the idea of a beer that tastes like pumpkin pie. By building on a light, dry Kolsch base, the squash's true, delicate flavor shines through (yes, enhanced by pie spice) and could be enjoyed even while not trick-or-treating. But for a real treat, try the version aged in Rogue's Hazelnut Spice Rum barrels. Scary good.

explained that the "no-hop/low-hop" is really more about the latter rather than about brewing true gruits (sans hops). A sparse amount of hops is used for bittering but never, ever for finishing.

It'd be difficult to call any of Buckman's beers a flagship since the brewery is perceived as creating weird beers, but Connors said the Ginger Pale Ale is the most popular by far. I'll never forget the first time I had it, though it wasn't at the pub. For a short while Buckman Botanical operated a cart at a food-truck "pod" near my house. I ordered the ginger ale to go with my lunch of Korean bulgogi beef, but I wasn't handed a housemade soft drink. Instead, I sipped a true ale, spiced with ginger—12 pounds, grated fresh, per 15-barrel batch, I'd later discover.

Orange Peel Ale tastes like it's dry hopped with orange peel, but Connors said that ingredient is added at the end of the boil. He made another beer based on their comparatively popular Chamomellow, wherein he added lemon peels to this already tea'ed up beer to emulate the beverage popularized by tee 'n tea fan Arnold Palmer.

What's funny about the house beers, made on the brewing system directly visible through floor-to-ceiling windows inside the Green Dragon, is that they get their own set of five taps drilled into the back wall, fairly removed from the main bar. They really are distinct from everything else. Having said that, there's a separate 1-barrel system reserved for the Oregon Brew Crew, a homebrew club that gets to tap a pro-am beer every Wednesday night, though its members are not inclined to forego big hops like Buckman Botanical.

Buckman Botanical Brewery (Rogue Ale's Green Dragon Pub)

Opened: 2010.

Owner: Brett Joyce (see Rogue Ales, page 172).

Brewer: Danny Connors.

System: 15-barrel.

Annual production: 1,200 barrels.

Distribution: A few accounts around town.

Hours: Sunday through Wednesday, 11 a.m. to 11 p.m.; Thursday through Saturday, 11 a.m. to 1 a.m.

Tours: Weekdays at 4 p.m.

Takeout beer: Growlers, kegs, and limited hand-bottling in bombers.

Gift shop: Apparel and growlers located in the back.

Food: Pub grub.

Events: Meet the Brewer events every Thursday, Firkin Fest in June, The Wedge cheese festival organized by the Oregon Cheese Guild, Pumpkin Fest in October, and a Nanofest supporting local nanobreweries.

Cascade Brewing Barrel House

939 Southeast Belmont Street, Portland, OR 97214
(503) 265-8603 • CascadeBrewingBarrelHouse.com
Twitter @CascadeBrewing

It's called a "sour shower" because honored guests, who often have no experience using a mallet to traditionally tap a cask, wind up not plugging the bung swiftly enough and having the contents—beer inoculated with wild microorganisms that don't throw dried fruit or spice flavors like regular ale yeast but funky, tart notes best described as sour—washing over the person or persons standing in front, or sometimes even patrons seated at the front bar. Remember Gallagher, the comedian who barraged fans in the front row of his performances with fruit he squashed with a sledgehammer? Think that, but without the pulp.

But that's just the once-a-week, six o'clock Tap It Tuesdays, when a new, masterfully blended creation typically soured with *Lactobacillus* and *Pediococcus* (they don't use *Brettanomyces* like most sour ale brewers) is served "live from the barrel." (They literally outfit a hole in the wall with an entire oak barrel and rely on gravity to liberate the contents rather than serve these concoctions draft-style from a keg.) At all other times, Cascade Barrel House is a "sour head's" Louvre (or at least a mid-sized city's MoMA). Even the 750-milliliter bottles lined up on the bar present a striking palette (and palate): the red-labeled Strawberry, orange Tangerine Dream, yellow Figaro, green The Vine, blue Blueberry, and violet-wrapped Elderberry. I've heard people describe visits as religious moments.

Not surprisingly, as if preaching from the Dais of Sour, brewmaster Ron Gansberg—who has been with Cascade since it opened in 1998, though his brewing career began at BridgePort in 1986—sermonized, "There's this enlightenment and expansion through experience of different beers.

Beers brewed: Year-round: Kriek, Apricot, Portland Ale, Cascade IPA, Razberry Wheat. Seasonal sour beers: Blueberry, Strawberry, The Vine, Sang Noir, Honey Ginger Lime, Vlad the Imp Aler, Bourbonic Plague, Noyaux, and more. Others: Stouts, saisons, goses, and more.

The Pick: Noyaux. Given the veritable farmers market of fruit beers that are puckeringly acidic in a complementary way (the cherry Kriek and Blueberry ales are not to be missed), Noyaux one-ups its Apricot cousin. It's a blend of blond ales oak-aged for over a year then aged on apricot "noyaux," the meat inside the pits denatured through roasting, so it lends both apricot and almond tones, plus a kiss of raspberries. The result, at around 10 percent ABV, is simply otherworldly.

We see a lot of people going through that IPA hop excursion, and when you come out to the top of that and are looking for something else, sour beers are a wonderful, new journey. It offers an intense sensory experience as the equal to any hoppy beer. But in some ways I think it's more refreshing with the combination of flavors, fruits, spices, strength, and sweetness that all combine together to create a rich and varied experience."

Amen, brother. Hallelujah.

A pilgrimage is the journey undertaken by the devout to a sacred space. For those who genuflect at the funk altar, Cascade Barrel House is a worthy mecca, but I must mention that the beers aren't actually brewed here. The brewery is situated in the ground floor of the Raccoon Lodge in the Southwest Portland suburb of Raleigh Hills next to Beaverton. Seven miles west, it offers an entirely different ambiance than Portland's Barrel House.

Art Larrance, a key figure in Oregon's brewpub legislation that kickstarted the industry in 1985, founded Cascade Brewing after his initial enterprise, Portland Brewing, cofounded with his childhood chum Fred Bowman, left a, uh, sour taste in his mouth thanks to the majority shareholders. But he and Bowman are still friends; there's a photo of them on the wall, along with Bert Grant, who opened America's first modern brewpub, taken during the first brew in January 1986. The following year Larrance and company created the Oregon Brewers Festival that now ushers in over eighty thousand thirsty revelers. Cascade Brewing opened in 1998 with Gansberg at the helm, whom Larrance hired away from Portland Brewing. Gansberg bears a resemblance to Dick Cheney but uses his powers for good. He makes non-intimidating beers such as Portland Ale, Cascade IPA, and Razberry Wheat, but his trademark "Northwest-style sour ales" are what made Cascade Brewing famous.

Speaking to Larrance about Cascade's new direction while at the tapping of a beer called Pumpkin Smash (made with 750 pounds of flame-roasted gourds), he summarized, "We'd been looking for our magic elixir before the roof was on the Raccoon Lodge . . . Out of default, we picked this style because there was nothing else left."

As Gansberg further explained, "I wanted something that'd tie in my background of making wine, ciders, fruit wines, and sodas all together. . . . At one point we were just another tree in a tall forest. It's difficult to distinguish oneself, to differentiate. [Sour beers] were so intriguing, going into it with a steep learning curve and perils." Sour beers are notoriously difficult to make because of the unpredictable nature of the wild bacteria used. "Each one of these batches is like laying the keel of a ship. Each one is intended for a certain voyage and destination. We'll make several beers side by side with slight variations. We'll see if they went where we thought they would. And whether or not how we equipped them as far as recipe, strength, etcetera holds up to the voyage."

This is where lead blender Preston Weesner factors in. He helps concoct those new blends destined for the live barrel tappings "to answer," as Gansberg put it, "the ever-present question, 'What's new?'" He lauded Weesner for his great sense of taste and mental catalog of the six-hundred-plus wine and spirit barrels each in various stages of aging different beers at all times.

Thanks to the analog team efforts, the *New York Times* rated Cascade Kriek—the first in their sour program since local Bing cherries felt like a natural ingredient to try—the #1 sour beer in America. That isn't blasphemy, but I think the newspaper of record simply wasn't around when Vlad the Imp Aler was on tap or when those rare bottles were released. Fans may vacillate on which is their favorite draw of alchemy, but Vlad's interplay of strong and spiced blond ales, matured in choice barrels for tart and tannic results, ought to be somewhere in the top two.

When Gansberg walked up to the stage during the 2009 Great American Beer Festival (GABF) to receive his silver medal in the Barrel-Aged Sour Beer category for Vlad the Imp Aler, in his excitement, he missed the announcement that his Bourbonic Plague won gold. Bourbonic is the bourbon-aged version of their spiced porter, Bain du Bruge, and I recall hearing that the judges argued over which beer should get top honors, not knowing both hailed from the same brewery.

Cascade Brewing Barrel House

Opened: 2010 (Cascade Brewing/Raccoon Lodge, 1998; see page 123)

Owner: Art Larrance.

Brewers: Ron Gansberg (brewmaster and "chief imaginer") and Preston Weesner (lead blender).

System: 10-barrel.

Annual production: 900 barrels.

Distribution: Oregon, California, New York, and more.

Hours: Sunday through Tuesday, noon to 10 p.m.; Wednesday and Thursday, noon to 11 p.m.; Friday and Saturday, noon to midnight.

Tours: By appointment.

Takeout beer: 750-milliliter bottles of select sour ales and growlers of any non-sour beer.

Gift shop: T-shirts, hoodies, and a bike jersey.

Food: Small plates such as cheese and charcuterie. Specials have included escargot or figs sautéed in Apricot Sour with smoked tomato pesto.

Coalition Brewing Co.

COALITION
BREWING CO.

2705 Southeast Ankeny Street, Portland, OR, 97214
(503) 894-8080 • CoalitionBrewing.com
Twitter @CoalitionBrewin

The Twenty-Eighth Avenue corridor gets paid short shrift around town. Maybe Twenty-Eighth's lack of goodly, hoodly identity explains the oversight when people list the city's top destinations. But in my opinion, the businesses—predominantly outstanding restaurants and cafés—that stretch from Northeast Glisan Street to Southeast Pine Street qualify it as Portland's best kept secret for a walking street. How excellent that it's bookended by Coalition Brewing on the south end and Migration Brewing on the north end.

Coalition launched as an alliance between Elan Walsky and Kiley Hoyt. Despite being homebrewers who'd received formal brewing education through the Siebel Institute in Chicago, their serendipitous encounter occurred at Steinbart, Portland's venerable homebrew supply shop. They not only struck up a conversation as Walsky, who worked there at the time, waited on her, but also discovered they both had an idea to open a small local brewery. Freakily, they both had the name Hobo Brewing in mind. Hoyt had migrated her way from the East Coast to the West and had gone so far as to start Hobo as an LLC. For Walsky's part, "The only things I can draw are a cartoon Godzilla and a cartoon hobo," he said, adding, "I just always liked that word." Alas, so did the lawyer who contacted them about a remote California brewery that makes a wheat beer by that name, one of the sixty beers I've found with the word "hobo."

The pair checked out potential spaces all over town, eventually settling on Southeast Ankeny. For years, Coalition operated in two addresses—a pub on the south side of the street and the brewing operation on the north. But when the lease expired in May 2014, they doubled down on being a production brewery. Gone are their inventive

Beers brewed: Year-round: King Kitty Red, Bump's Bitter ESB, Mr. Pigs Pale Ale, Two Dogs IPA, WU Cream Ale, Loving Cup Maple Porter. Seasonals: Sourpuss Berliner Weisse, Wheat the People, Space Fruit (citrus IPA), Simple ISA, Hanso VS Bulleit (bourbon-aged stout), Bourbon Loving Cup, Oud School Sour Belgian Brown.

The Pick: Loving Cup Maple Porter. This British-style porter is on the dry side, offering the desired chocolatiness but without being thick or sweet. It also features Grade A maple syrup from Hoyt's native Vermont, which is more pronounced in the aroma than in the swallow.

"meatloaf cupcakes" with mashed potato "frosting," but the pod behind the former pub includes some of Rose City's best food carts serving grilled cheese sandwiches, Tuscan cuisine, and the best falafel this side of Jerusalem because that's how Portland rolls. (Food trucks don't roll.) The new tasting room at the brewery remains kid and pet friendly.

Most of their straightforward beers began as homebrew recipes. Two Dogs IPA features grassy and lemony hops and is named for a former brewer's two dogs. King Kitty Red garners its name from a neighborhood cat who hung out in a tree near the brewery, while Mr. Pigs Pale isn't pork-inspired at all but got the name of Hoyt's cat. Green Pig is the name of their autumnal fresh-hop pale ale. Continuing the feline motif, they make a great seasonal, sour Berliner Weisse in collaboration with Wyeast Labs called Sourpuss. On a hot day, reach for Rooster's Cream, a light-bodied ale with flaked barley. Hoyt swears having so many animal themed brands "wasn't planned that way."

Besides those named for pets and livestock, a personal favorite of mine is Loving Cup, unique among Portland beers. Hoyt is a Vermont native, so it makes sense that Coalition offers a porter brewed with maple syrup sourced from the Green Mountain State. It's available year-round in draft, though it's wisely bottled each autumn when it becomes their best-selling seasonal brand. Grade A medium syrup gives the beer a sweet, sappy kick. Since it's lower in fermentable sugars than grade B, it's right in line with the porter's existing dryness, keeping it a sessionable 5.4 percent alcohol so it doesn't fill you up, be it at Thanksgiving or any homemade pancake breakfast. They also make a bourbon-aged Loving Cup with Burnside Bourbon barrels from nearby Eastside Distillery. Now if only they'd take my suggestion of brewing a beer called Two Hobos, or in keeping with the animal theme, perhaps Bonobo Hobo.

Coalition Brewing Co.

Opened: 2010.
Owners: Elan Walsky and Kiley Hoyt.
Brewers: Elan Walsky and Dave Fleming.
System: 10-barrel.
Annual production: 1,250 barrels.
Distribution: Oregon and Washington.
Hours: TBD.
Tours: By appointment only.
Takeout beer: Growler fills, limited bombers, and tallboy cans.
Gift shop: Shirts, hoodies, and growlers.

The Commons Brewery

THE COMMONS +BREWERY+

630 Southeast Belmont Street, Portland, OR 97214
(503) 343-5501 • CommonsBrewery.com
Twitter @CommonsBrewery

The first beer I had with Mike Wright was called Blue Foot, a Flanders Red-style ale, slightly sweet and sour with notes of cherries aged in a Pinot Noir barrel. He brewed it in his garage. But we weren't at his house; nor, in fact, were we drinking his homebrew. We were at Victory Bar, a few blocks away on what has since become a bustling strip of Southeast Division Street, and the woman behind the bar didn't even know he was the brewer. That's because Wright had launched his nanobrewery, then called Beetje Brewery, in the summer of 2010 and within months had racked up all of a half dozen accounts.

Early the next year, when Wright grew confident he'd produce 30 barrels by year's end, I asked him what he figured his eventual growth might look like. He said he'd consider a few hundred barrels to be "a wild success." Before the end of 2011, he grew the business almost 500 percent, but that's not saying much considering it debuted producing "just shy of 1.5-barrel [batches] . . . on a mish-mash of pieces, some new, some old."

Funnily enough, he initially turned his homebrewery into a commercial one really just to see if he could. Quite literally in the fall of 2009, the impetus for Wright's admittedly non-glamorous start occurred "just to challenge the system." Would the OLCC and TTB actually approve of a garage-based brewery? He was so skeptical about pulling off this stunt that once his ruse developed traction it took him around a year to even devise a business plan. He might have swept the whole thing under the rug were it not for the urging from local beer blogger Angelo De Ieso of Brewpublic.com to participate in

Beers brewed: Year-round: Urban Farmhouse Ale, Flemish Kiss, Pils, Blonde, Madrone, Walnut, Ambree, Avant. Seasonals: Winter: Little Brother (Belgian dark strong), Bourbon Little Brother, Oatmeal Stout. Spring: Myrtle, Biere Royale (black current lactic sour ale), Biere de Garde. Summer: Wit, Haver Bier (oatmeal saison), Berliner Weisse. Fall: Sticke, Fleur de Ferme. Beetje Series: Brotherly Love, Eleanor, Plum Bretta, Harold, Eidolon, and more.

The Pick: Urban Farmhouse Ale. This beautiful, delicate flagship continues to create a love affair with saisons. At a relatively mild 5.3 percent ABV, the fruity and peppery esters, embellished with rye in the grain bill, pleases beer geeks while the golden color, low bitterness, and lively carbonation keep it approachable for those who fear craft beer is out to ambush their palates.

a celebration of small, local breweries, dubbed Microhopic. So Wright made a beer now called Urban Farmhouse Ale.

The name Beetje (pronounced "bee-cha") is, appropriately, a Flemish word akin to "little bit." It referred to both the demure size of Wright's farmhouse-style, inner-city, garage-based brewery and also the easy-drinking beers themselves. No 10 percent double IPAs from this guy. Wright's beers use actual Belgian yeasts smuggled back from a trip that was part pilgrimage, part homecoming, given that his wife is Belgian-born.

The legal brewery launched as a whimsical challenge, but the Belgian-style beers were no lark. Beetje underwent a metamorphosis into the 7-barrel brewery, and The Commons is no longer a nanobrewery or based in the garage. Nor is Wright the sole brewer now. He hired Sean Burke, then a recent graduate from the Siebel Institute's Doemens Academy in Germany. It was sort of like graduating from Le Cordon Bleu and landing his first gig at a new bistro in Paris. In no time, the brewery started earning accolades analogous to Michelin stars.

In 2012 at Portland's Cheers to Belgian Beers, one of the most unique and specialized festivals, The Commons' entry, Eleanor—a wine barrel-aged golden farmhouse ale soured with a cocktail of *Brettanomyces* and other propogated cultures —won People's Choice and returns as part of the brewery's aptly-named Beetje Series. Months later, The Commons struck silver at the GABF with a brett'ed pale ale called Flemish Kiss, this time voted on by a panel of certified beer judges. A year later, they hauled home two more medals for lemony-tart Myrtle, fermented with *Lactobacillus*, and the flagship Urban Farmhouse, a beer so beloved around town that *Willamette Week* named it Beer of the Year. The Commons beers are appreciated on a local level and respected on a national level. At the 2014 World Beer Cup, an international panel of judges blind taste tested Flemish Kiss and awarded it another medal.

It isn't a surprise that The Commons launched as formidably as it did. On that fateful day, quaffing the Flanders Red, Wright confessed, "Yes, I'd like to do this full time some day." He believed that was years out on the horizon, because who leaves a stable career as an IT manager when he's got a family to provide for? But, he added, "I think every nanobrewer would like to do this full time."

So forgive me if I credit (or blame) The Commons' success, in part, for the proliferation of nanobreweries around Portland and parts beyond. The nanobrewery route is a popular method of breaking into the industry, just as food carts (nearly a thousand-strong around Portland) are trendy among those who really dream of opening a proper brick-and-mortar restaurant. But Wright made it look so easy (it's not) and many of the dozen teensy breweries subsequently launched in the greater metro solicited his expertise. He explained that when budding brewers and entrepreneurs approach him and say, "'Hey man, I'm gonna start a nano and have a bunch of questions,' I answer all of them, of course, but [they] need to understand that a nano is not a viable business model."

Hence, heeding his own advice, Wright committed to real growth for the simple reason of expanding his customer base, now well beyond that half dozen from the relative early days. The current brewery is in industrial Hosford-Abernethy (yet a few blocks from quaint Ladd's Addition) and is small but inviting. It provides a social atmosphere for guests to stand around the 7-barrel system after ordering a favorite beer on draft or happening upon a one-off that may be herbal, sour, smoky, or entirely unfamiliar in this nearly-anything-goes environment. The latter comes courtesy of the original (now pilot) cobbled-together system where the Beetje Series beers, sold in limited bottlings at the brewery, originate. The first was called Brotherly Love, a variation on Little Brother, a Belgian dark strong ale but matured in bourbon barrels with red tart cherries and roasted Peruvian cocoa nibs.

Then again, The Commons' success being what it is, they're already scouting new locations nearby, with plans to upgrade to a 15-barrel system. An expanded location will fit more thirsty patrons and events such as a beer and cheese fest during Portland Beer Week. That's decidedly no little bit, but there's no such issue as too much of a good thing.

The Commons Brewery

Opened: 2011.

Owner: Mike Wright.

Brewers: Sean Burke and Mike Wright.

System: 15-barrel and 7-barrel.

Annual production: 900 barrels.

Distribution: Oregon; Boise, Idaho; and Vancouver, British Columbia.

Hours: Tuesday through Sunday, noon to 10 p.m.

Takeout beer: Growlers (mostly year-round beers only) and bottles.

Tours: Available upon request.

Food: No food served but outside food is allowed. Light snacks are sometimes provided.

Extras: No minors permitted. Anniversary party in December turns into an epic beer geek bottle-sharing event.

Gigantic Brewing Co.

5224 Southeast 26th Street, Portland,
OR 97202
(503) 208-3416 • GiganticBrewing.com
Twitter @GiganticBrewing

Brewing veterans Ben Love (formerly of Hopworks) and Van Havig (ex-Rock Bottom) united to create a 15-barrel brewery with the stated goal of never selling more than 4,000 barrels a year, and they're already three-quarters of the way there. Gigantic can refer to a lot of things, but clearly they're not gunning for any list of biggest breweries.

Then again, in a short amount of time they've become a pretty big deal in Portland, as the packed picnic tables out front can attest to (when the weather complies). They did it with huge hops and a blatant disregard for cultivating any other fan-favorite beers. To paraphrase Gigantic's stated mission, they aim to "make the best damn IPA in Portland," while every other flavorful beer comes out just once to "create new interpretations of classic styles" and "ignore those same style guidelines completely." Is it *the* best? Impossible to say. *One* of the best? Sure.

The Gigantic rock stars include burly, bearded Ben Love, a native Oregonian though he, like many of his colleagues, got his start brewing in the Midwest. His C.V. includes Oregon breweries Pelican and Hopworks, from where he departed to found Gigantic with lanky, increasingly shiny-domed Van Havig. Havig isn't like a rock star just because he's a brewmaster. It's because he dropped out of the London School of Economics just like Mick Jagger did. Havig also decided to brew out West after his first brewery gig in the Midwest. That led him to Rock Bottom and a sixteen-year service culminating at the one in Portland before he split, citing irreconcilable differences, so to speak. He eventually brought brewer Scott Guckel with him, who affably helps pronounce his last name as "a cross between a giggle and a chuckle." The production brewery is located, fittingly, in an industrial section of Southeast Portland—both Love and Havig

Beers brewed: Year-round: Gigantic IPA. Seasonals: Massive! Barleywine. One-offs: Everything else.

The Pick: IPA. Gigantic prudently picked one core beer and is doing it well. This bombastic IPA, a first-off, should be an IOA since it's more of an orange-colored ale. What's more, the perfumed scent of Curaçao oranges serves notice that the motif will continue through the complementary bitter notes of orange zest and pith, along with the sweet flavor of orange blossom honey mixed in with the malt.

reside in the quadrant—near Reed College, which claims Havig as an alumnus.

Regarding their quintessential and bodacious Northwest IPA that accounts for over 60 percent of sales, Havig opined, "It's fun to make new beers. But brewing isn't really about creating new recipes. Brewing's about process. So if the majority of what this brewery does is IPA and we can continue to try and improve it, I think that's much more about craft than making something new all the time. I mean, how do you get good at anything? You repeat it! If you just make new shit all the time, you're just half-assing."

"Unless you make it really well," Love interrupted.

Remember, in addition to crafting the best IPA they can, every other release is fleeting, likely never to return and be honed. Fortuitously, there are only two chefs in this gigantic kitchen and they're both on the same page. The ephemeral, quarterly releases are conceived and created, as Havig explained, "when one of us wants to do a particular beer and then takes the lead. Ben does more of the recipes than I do. He comes up with whatever idea. Then we'll talk our way through each one."

Thus far, such concepts have included The City that Never Sleeps, which melded a vigorous, toasty imperial schwarzbier with funky, earthy saison; and Ume Umai, brewed with black rice and aged on plums, resulting in a beer that was neither black nor particularly plummy as one might expect but pleasurably dry, slightly tart, and tawny. Too Much Coffee Man was another black saison made with cold-brewed coffee courtesy of Coava Coffee, an excellent roaster three miles north but still in Southeast, which eschewed the more expected English porter base for something akin to a Belgian farmhouse ale. The beer took its name from the comic by local artist Shannon Wheeler who, naturally, also designed the label.

I won't say that the artwork that graces each label is as important as the fluid art inside each bottle, but it has become a notable characteristic of Gigantic releases. In an era chock-full of collaboration beers where two breweries partner up, Gigantic has its own art director in Rob Reger, who helps Love and Havig line up artists who, according to Love, "are really well known in the art world [even if] outside people don't know who they are." It reminds me of the way beer geeks rave about brewers who may be rock stars in the beer world but remain anonymous outside its hallowed bierhalls. "We don't give them any direction, just . . . the name of the beer," Havig said. "We pay them a decent amount." The collective results have ended up looking like a panoply of comic book covers. Best of all, they all get framed and hung on the otherwise dark gray walls inside the brewery's tasting room for a vibe that brings to mind the gallery of concert posters inside the Fillmore. A few customers have even bought some.

It helps that another art collaborator is the Hellion Gallery in Old Town, where you'll always find Gigantic beer on tap during the First Thursday art crawl. Gigantic even made a yeast-forward Belgian golden ale called Hellion, dry hopped with Sorachi Ace and Simcoe, but since each release sticks around on draft for just one season, don't expect to find it at the gallery. One caveat that the guys told me about is their plan to re-release Massive—a barleywine that underwent an eight-hour boil—each year. Local artist AJ Fosik created the label, reminiscent of the skull(s) of Cerberus the mythological three-headed dog, and I'm told he's down for doing a new one every year, just as the recipe itself will be different. I'll be looking forward to seeing how Massive 2.0 turns out, as well as what the second generation of the Massive label will look like hanging in the Gigantic Tap Room. Well, Tap Room and Champagne Lounge is the official name. The name isn't a joke, even if Love said it started out that way: "We're a beer bar. We didn't want to have red and white wine." They don't. They do have a small selection of the other carbonated, fermented beverage and a couple of guest drafts, but I think it's safe to say that they'll never tap the beer market as the Champagne of Beers.

Gigantic Brewing Co.

Opened: 2012.

Owners: Ben Love and Van Havig.

Brewers: Ben Love, Van Havig, and Scott Guckel.

System: 15-barrel.

Annual production: 3,000 barrels.

Distribution: Oregon, Washington, California, Alaska, Vermont, Chicago, British Columbia, and intermittent points beyond.

Hours: Seasonal; check before you visit.

Tours: By appointment.

Takeout beer: Growlers, 22s, and dock sales.

Gift shop: Gigantic apparel and glassware.

Food: Food trucks occasionally parked nearby.

Extras: No minors allowed, but dogs allowed in the patio.

Ground Breaker Brewing

715 Southeast Lincoln Street, Portland, OR 97214
(503) 974-4467 • GroundBreakerBrewing.com
Twitter @GroundBreakerBrewing

Ground Breaker Brewing, originally called Harvester, debuted in late 2011 as the nation's only dedicated gluten-free craft brewery. Ground Breaker's Northwest-style ales are crafted from not only sorghum, like most gluten-free options on the market, but also Willamette Valley chestnuts, certified gluten-free oats, pure cane sugar, and Willamette Valley hops. In other words, Ground Breaker's beers are made without barley, wheat, rye, corn, etc. The brewing facility is entirely gluten-free, and no gluten-containing items are allowed on the premises.

Glutens—proteins found in grains such as the aforementioned barley—are the malefactors in the autoimmune disorder celiac disease. It's believed that one in every 133 Americans (that's over 3 million people) are gluten intolerant, though it's estimated that as many as 95 percent of celiacs are not yet diagnosed. No wonder gluten-free food is almost a $4 billion industry. Locally, it's big enough that seven gluten-free bakeries have sprouted up. If there's one thing Portlanders like more than baked yummies, it's beer.

Hence, James Neumeister spent years home-brewing feverishly and developing a perfect pale ale devoid of gluten. It's no secret that most others that entered the market are unpalatable, but for those who can't handle the gluten, what's a body to do? Neumeister's recipes, built on a foundation of chestnuts grown thirty miles away, are enjoyable even to those without such sensitivity.

"We use the chestnuts the same way a conventional brewery uses barley," Neumeister said of the brewery tucked into an industrial neighborhood. "Chestnuts have nearly identical starch content by weight to barley and contribute to the gravity similarly. The chestnuts provide great flavor and character while the sorghum provides a malty base." Ground Breaker buys ground chestnuts and roasts them on-site. Having said that, back when Neumeister was developing the recipes,

Beers brewed: Year-round: Pale Ale, Dark Ale, IPA No. 2, IPA No. 3. Experiment Ale Series: Squash Ale, Raspberry Ale, Fresh Hop Pale.

The Pick: Even sans "malt backbone," this IPA gives gluten-intolerant hops lovers the lupulin they crave—Nugget, Cascade, Horizon, and Meridian—for a beer that packs 60 IBUs but tastes like it has more. In fact, it tastes like there must be hop cones floating in it, which of course appeals even to those of us without gluten issues.

he did the grinding himself on a grinder he literally found in a rubble pile out in Central Oregon and then restored.

Of course, their lineup possesses another saving grace: hops. Pale Ale medaled at the 2012 GABF. Too bad Ground Breaker didn't exist when the competition's gluten-free category debuted five years earlier. And they don't call Ground Breaker IPA an IPA for nothing. It boasts Nugget, Cascade, Horizon, and Meridian hops, boosting it to 60 IBUs. It arrived in 2013 and promptly earned GABF gold. I've witnessed gluten avoiders—ones who really miss hops—come in and buy these beers by the case.

Among their four year-round beers, the "pale" ones receive a light roast of the chestnuts—and a dark roast for the Dark Ale. The latter is not at all chocolaty or in any way reminiscent of a stout or porter; it just brings out a lot more of that "chestnuts roasting on an open fire" flavor. For celiacs, it's like a liquid Christmas gift year-round. The seasonal creations that make up the Experiment Ale Series are fun and tasty, too. Once the weather warms up, Raspberry Ale hits the streets, loaded with 80 pounds of local raspberry purée. Come fall, the Squash Ale is a hit among burgeoning pumpkin beer fans.

The adjoining space around the corner became available later, and while it's not huge and the bar isn't very long, Neumeister wanted to add a tasting room for draft beer. Brewer Tim Barr uses the space to make unique iterations such as an Apple IPA that even finds its way into the house mustard used in the trout salad on the Ground Breaker Gastropub's menu. The gastropub, by the way, debuted in late 2013 as the nation's only dedicated gluten-free brewpub.

Ground Breaker Brewing

Opened: 2011.

Owners: James Neumeister and John Dugan.

Brewer: Tim Barr.

System: 7-barrel.

Annual production: 1,200 barrels.

Distribution: Pacific Northwest and online (where allowed).

Hours: Wednesday, 4 p.m. to 9 p.m.; Thursday through Sunday, noon to 9 p.m.

Tours: By request.

Food: Chef Neil Davidson created a gluten-free menu with salads, sandwiches, entrées, cheese, and charcuterie.

Takeout beer: Bombers, growlers, and kegs.

Extras: Sunday brunch during the summer. The ice cream at the pub is made with their gold medal IPA.

Other location: Gastropub/Tasting Room (2030 SE 7th Ave.; 503-928-4195).

Hair of the Dog Brewing Co.

61 Southeast Yamhill Street, Portland, OR 97214
(503) 232-6585 • HairOfTheDog.com
Twitter @HairOfTheDog

The first time I visited Hair of the Dog's new digs—it relocated from the Brooklyn neighborhood to adjoining Buckman in 2010, sixteen years after opening—I didn't just sample many of the groundbreaking beers the brewery is regarded for, but also some nosh, since the new spot finally had a tasting room and a kitchen. Bringing me my plate of pastrami was none other than owner-brewmaster Alan Sprints. He had, after all, moved to Portland from his native LA to attend culinary school. It was an added treat that the man who made my fine beers made my tasty lunch, too. He's not the cook anymore, but he still oversees the menu and brings his gastronomic touch to his beers. Today, they're considered creative and dynamic. Back in the mid-nineties, they were a paradigm shift.

"As a teenager," began Sprints, who was born in 1959, "I didn't think people could own a brewery. When I moved to Portland the first year of the Oregon Brewers Festival . . . it brought [brewing] down to a scale that was imaginable." Hair of the Dog remains a 4-barrel brewery. "The people that exposed me to new things, as far as beer goes, I thought were normal, but it turns out they were unusual. I thought everyone was going to want to try new and different," Sprints explained. Hair of the Dog debuted with Adambier (at 10 percent alcohol, he couldn't legally call it "beer"), an old ale conjuring smoky toast and tobacco on top of dates and molasses. He named this first beer after the biblical first man (but thankfully, despite the portion of smoked malts, it's not reminiscent of ribs). However, most beer consumers weren't ready for it then. (The majority today wouldn't know what to do with such beer.) "It was quite frustrating at the time," Sprints lamented. "Now it's the opposite." The earliest vintages of that beer

Beers brewed: Year-round: Fred, Adam, Ruth Pale Ale, Blue Dot IPA. Seasonals: Greg (with winter squash) and Doggie Claws (barleywine). Series: Little Dogs and From the Wood.

The Pick: Fred. Loosely dubbed a strong ale, this rich and spicy beer contains light pilsner and peppery rye malts for a foundation spiked with Belgian candi sugar, and is hopped to the nth with ten different hop flowers for a marmalade effect. The result is a 10 percent ABV, 65 IBUs that masquerades as a Belgian Double IPA (Dubbel IPA?).

command triple digit prices. Recently Sprints made 12-ounce bottles of a beer called Dave—300 gallons of 1994 Adam that he'd freeze-distilled down to 100 gallons, hence tripling the alcohol content—available for two grand (proceeds benefit Guide Dogs for the Blind).

He knows he can make more beer (yet still not make enough). He can brew more often, add fermenters, offer draft beer outside the tasting room, or expand in other ways. "But somewhere along the path of Hair of the Dog, I looked at what I wanted," he said. "I never wanted to have a beer factory. I started it to make the kind of beers that I liked; having something unique that people could really enjoy was the goal."

The biggest intersection of beers that both Sprints and his consumers liked came in the form of another 10 percenter with rye malts and a whopping ten varietals of hops, for a beer that'd likely be described as an imperial rye IPA today but in 1997 was simply called Fred. It's named for Fred Eckhardt, the Portland beer writer, historian, and icon. Sprints consulted with him to build it around ingredients Eckhardt liked. Sprints relayed the story that once Fred (the beer) was available, the Dean of American Beer Writers penned a story called "The Curse of Fred" about how he went all over town trying to buy his namesake beer but everyone gave him a free pint. The uber-rich ale spends six months maturing in new American oak barrels, creating a real woody flavor that I love.

I also enjoy beers aged in spent barrels. Sprints was one of the very first craft brewers to use bourbon barrels for aging, over a decade before it has become de rigueur for breweries to run barrel-aging programs. Today Hair of the Dog's stockpile has nearly 200 barrels. Most of the results are labeled "From the Wood"; examples include Peach Fred and Cherry Adam. Beer geeks queue up on limited-release days.

The best way to enjoy several iterations and vintages of Fred and other beers is at FredFest, a mini but mighty beer festival held at the brewery in honor of Eckhardt's birthday. The fest began in 2006 on his eightieth birthday. Every year, Eckhardt, renowned for his charitableness, selects a different nonprofit for the bash's proceeds.

Even when not celebrating Fred (the man) or breaking into the stash of barrels, the pub's a great place to visit. The constant stream of sample glasses indicates it's on most beer travelers' itineraries. Tap offerings generally include beers ranging from the From the Wood Series to Little Dogs, low-alcohol or small beers made from the second runnings of (possibly) Fred or Adam. "If you want to have three beers," cracked Sprints, "there aren't many that I make that you can have three of," given their high gravity. Doggie Claws is his popular winter barleywine (11.5 percent ABV), and that's also when Little

Doggie Claws, wagging a tail a third as powerful as the original, becomes available.

Of course, given Sprints's background, the food menu holds its own. "We play around with local ingredients," he said, which is mostly standard for Oregon brewpubs now. What's not standard, however, is that they don't serve burgers and pizzas. The beer-braised brisket is a Sprints family favorite, just like young Alan's mom made growing up. The sausages, bacon, pickles, and more are made in-house. One seasonal special upped the classic Caprese salad by using creamy burrata cheese and heirloom tomatoes with apples and honey.

The pub, which seats seventy, is designed to be homey. Some brewpubs have beer books on a shelf. Here there are beer and dog books. The interior is bathed in unexpected colors—lime green, turquoise, and heather gray—but what really catches the eye is the collection of Chinook art. "I love the artist Roger Long, who's been an influence on me," Sprints said. The menu also features a vintage bottle section. A bottle of Matt aged in bourbon and apple eau de vie barrels goes for twenty bucks.

Clearly there's a naming convention at play. Adam. Fred. Dave. Furthermore, the first lager, a Maibock named Lila, honors Sprints's mom, and Ruth, an excellent pale ale, commemorates his grandmother. "Four letter names have served us quite well," he said. "These beers are individuals, just like people . . . Don't judge them based on what something else tastes like."

Hair of the Dog Brewing Co.

Opened: 1994.

Owner and brewer: Alan Sprints.

System: 4-barrel.

Annual production: 800 barrels.

Distribution: Oregon, Washington, California, New York, and Denmark.

Hours: Seasonal; check before you visit.

Tours: By appointment.

Takeout beer: Limited growlers and bottles.

Gift shop: Shirts, hoodies, and glasses.

Food: Meats, cheeses, sandwiches, and vegetarian options. Desserts include "beeramisu."

Events: FredFest, scheduled around the dean of American beer writing Fred Eckhardt's May 10 birthday, is a beer lover's paradise that feels more like a house party than a brewery festival.

Hopworks Urban Brewery

2944 Southeast Powell Boulevard, Portland, OR 97202
(503) 232-HOPS (4677) • HopworksBeer.com
Twitter @HopworksBeer

Hopworks Urban Brewery is known colloquially as HUB, but it might as well be HUBBBB. First and foremost, they're about the beer. But they're also about bikes, evidenced by the canopy of frames and bike repair equipment at the original brewpub on Powell Boulevard, plus the fact that the satellite pub on North Williams Avenue—replete with stationary bicycles that literally generate electricity for the building—is called BikeBar. Bands, of course, also play a starring role at their annual Biketobeerfest.

And as every mommy and daddy in town will tell you, this is the place to take your babies. There are play areas for the kids both up- and downstairs. Of course, my wife and I used to go even before we had a baby, but now that we're a "party of two and a half," we find ourselves here more frequently. Owner-brewmaster Christian Ettinger pointed toward his studies abroad in Cologne as the wellspring for his affinity for family-oriented pubs. Having said that, before creating Hopworks Ettinger was the brewmaster at Laurelwood, Portland's original kid-friendly brewpub, and admitted that even as he was building their play area, he asked owner Mike De Kalb, "Why would you want to take up seats?" That, naturally, was before the Ettingers had a pair of their own.

Spurred by his own parents to pursue a career in the craft beer industry ever since he took up homebrewing (before he was legally allowed to buy beer), his first brewpub experience came in Eugene, but he knew he was destined for Portland. "It's the culture," Ettinger said. "It's the prime place for brewpubs." He pushed that concept further by

Beers brewed: Year-round: HUB Lager, Hopworks IPA, Velvet ESB, Deluxe Organic Ale, Seven Grain Survival Stout. Seasonals: Abominable Winter Ale, Noggin Floggin Barleywine, Kentucky Christmas, Secession Cascadian Dark Ale, Ace of Spades Imperial IPA, Galactic Imperial Red Ale, Rise Up Red Ale, Abbey, Belgian Pale Ale, Belgian Apple, and more.

The Pick: Seven Grain Survival Stout. I'll catch hell for not picking one of their vaunted IPAs or other super-hopped ales, but considering how locally roasted coffee is equally as popular as craft beer, this rare, year-round, coffee-enhanced beer is no mere oatmeal stout. There's also wheat, amaranth, quinoa, spelt, and kamut, all combining to produce a chewy stout that features a pound of cold-pressed coffee per barrel. It's very rich, low acidity, and quite complementary to meat-topped pies.

setting out to create an "eco-brewpub." HUB uses only renewable energy (far beyond the pedal power at BikeBar). It's 100 percent carbon neutral, from rooftop barrels capturing rainwater for cleaning to the basement's biodiesel-powered brew kettle using HUB's fryer oil. The food, and of course the beer, are organic. Even the housemade root beer is sweetened with organic "evaporated cane juice" (sugar to you and me). "Our goal is to be *the* organic beer for Cascadia," Ettinger said.

The twin juggernauts in HUB's lineup are Hopworks IPA—a big, citrusy, American version—and HUB Lager—a dry German-style pilsner that is less likely to have you ride your bike all wobbly. As far as that goes, the two pubs often pour a traditional Radler, a cocktail of the lager and housemade lemonade. When I ride over for Biketobeerfest (notice it's pronounced "bike-to-beer fest"), I'll get samples of all the rarer offerings but then stick with the Radler for the rest of the day and night.

In true Oregonian fashion, Hopworks has built its reputation on converting British-style beers into super hoppy offerings that stretch beyond a handful of IPAs to include Galactic Imperial Red Ale and Abominable Winter Ale, which I'll call an IPA for sipping in front of a winter fire. I love Seven Grain Survival Stout, which, as the name implies, gets its fermentables from more than just barley. But it's more than a bass-heavy oatmeal-plus stout; local super-roaster Stumptown's Organic Holler Mountain blend coffee offers much-needed high notes. Ettinger informed me that after cold extracting for three days, the same coffee grounds are used as a coarse filter for fining, so the beer "comes out coffee-er, with lower acidity. We wanted the coffee to be an element but not the dominant flavor."

More recently, head brewer Tom Bleigh has been developing a Belgian beer program, which is technically only new to bottles. Their Belgian-style Apple beer, which hit shelves in late 2012, is a re-creation of a recipe from 2008, the year after they tapped their first beer. And Hopworks garnered the coveted People's Choice Award at the Portland Cheers to Belgian Beers Fest twice with an Abbey in 2009 and 2011. As for the bottled brands, they're "a perfect variety of Belgian beers that I like to drink," said Ettinger, which is how they opted to brew the Abbey and a Belgian pale ale.

The Abbey I'm happy to point out, is the "base liquid" for the first sour beer HUB ever made in 2010 called Piledriver. There are several barrels currently aging beers, but former head brewer Ben Love (who vacated the position to co-found Gigantic Brewing) was given carte blanche to experiment. Some of the liquid filled bourbon barrels. The rest, along with 60 pounds of sour cherries, filled Cabernet barrels.

After a dosing with *Brettanomyces* and serving eighteen months' time, the beer was blended and limited bottles of Piledriver were released during a special dock sale in 2012. Bleigh expressed to me his interest in creating an authentic Flemish Red ale, but I can't hold my breath that long.

As far as upcoming projects and products, Hopworks currently is only licensed to brew (hence why the Belgian Apple ale consisted of 49 percent juice and 51 percent malt, as mandated by law) but is obtaining a winemaking license to make hard cider. HUB's organic dry cider is bound for four-packs of pint-sized cans.

Still, it's all about the beer. Mostly. "I came at this from a long career in brewing," Ettinger said. "I viewed getting into the restaurant world as a way of creating a dynamic experience where you could put forth food that you're proud of, service that you think is remarkable," (I'll interject with patient, since kids can get boisterous), and a controlled environment. Regarding the latter, Ettinger explained that his father, the architect who designed the eco-brewpub, instilled in him an affinity for design and that he "took the design and aesthetic as seriously as the beer."

Hopworks Urban Brewery

Opened: 2008.

Owner: Christian Ettinger.

Brewers: Christian Ettinger (brewmaster) and Tom Bleigh (head brewer).

System: 20-barrel.

Annual production: 11,000 barrels.

Hours: Sunday through Thursday, 11 a.m. to 11 p.m.; Friday and Saturday, 11 a.m. to midnight.

Tours: Saturday at 3 p.m. Walk-ins welcome, but arrange in advance to guarantee space (limited to around twenty). E-mail Tours@HopworksBeer.com.

Takeout beer: Growlers, bombers, tallboy cans, and various keg sales.

Distribution: Cascadia.

Gift shop: The back wall features T-shirts, hoodies, bike jerseys of course, and extras including branded hydroflasks (stainless steel growlers).

Food: Pizza first and foremost; burgers, salads, and sandwiches also available.

Event: Biketobeerfest celebrating Portland's three B's: beer, bikes, and bands.

Extras: Ample parking (two lots). Play areas for kids. Three medals apiece from GABF and World Beer Cup.

Other location: Hopworks BikeBar (3947 N. Williams Ave., Portland; 503-287-MALT [6258]).

Lucky Labrador Hawthorne Brew Pub

915 SE Hawthorne Boulevard, Portland, OR 97214
(503) 236-3555 • LuckyLab.com
Twitter @LuckyLabPDX

When my wife and I were house hunting, I had one rule of thumb: Wherever we landed, it had to be a short walk from the Lucky Lab so I could go with Dunkel, our German shorthaired pointer, all the time. In the end, we got a place that's a long walk from the brewpub, which is actually better for both Dunkel and me since it's healthier that way. It's one of my favorite brewpubs, not because there's anything mind-blowingly monumental about it, but because it comfortably and amiably accommodates the jeans-and-T-shirt crowd, the flannelled and the furry.

Inside it's spacious, all timber and down to earth. The walls are bedecked with paintings of Labradors, both black and yellow, as well as thumbtack boards pinned to the hilt with customers' pooches, plus photos of patrons donning their Lucky Lab shirts in exotic locales around the globe. The wooden tables and chairs provide ample seating and the skylights keep it well lit even on the gloomiest of days.

The real tailwagger here is the back patio, where this public house transforms into a public doghouse when the weather's nice. It's a place where Fido and Fifi get to socialize as their masters play Battleship or any of the board games available inside. (It's probably best that the dartboards are on the opposite end from the game room and dog area.)

I don't know if cofounders Alex Stiles and Gary Geist played Battleship or Connect Four together, but the Lucky Lab is the product of these longtime friends who grew up together in Portland and became homebrewing partners. For a while, they put the fun and games away and "did suit jobs," said Geist, but after they hung up their ties, he worked at BridgePort Brewing behind the bar and Stiles brewed for them, though they didn't overlap. They'd talked about opening a brewpub of

Beers brewed: Year-round: Black Lab Stout, Blue Dog Pale Ale, Top Dog Extra Special Pale Ale, Hawthorne's Best Bitter, Super Dog IPA. Seasonals: Scottish Holiday, Solar Flare Ale, The Mutt, Belgian Canine Style Tripel, Bike Route Rye, Crazy Ludwig's Alt, Dog Day IPA, Got Hops?, Hellraiser ESB, Stumptown Porter, Winter Wonder Dog.

The Pick: Super Dog is a big, fluffy IPA with a wet nose and offers lots to love, especially for fans of grapefruity hops and ample malt body.

their own for ages, and with the help of some investors it all came together in 1994. I say brewpub, as does almost everyone, but as Geist puts it, "We're not a tavern and we're not a restaurant." No one would apply the label "gastro" anything to this spot. The Vegetarian's Nightmare, a sandwich with five luncheon meats, is the only menu item that tops eight dollars. "The focus has always been on the beer; it's the passion we came from," Geist said. As he and I sat at one of the communal tables inside, Stiles was in the back, brewing away as he's done for the last two decades.

"We're pretty lucky," said Geist.

"It's built into your name," I responded.

"We were originally Lucky Dog, but there was a Lucky Dog dog food," he said. "Alex suggested Lucky Labrador, and it stuck with me because I grew up with Labs."

The dog motif is everywhere, from beers named Black Lab Stout (as a stout lover, I think it's one of the finest in town), Top Dog Extra Pale, and the various canine-themed IPAs: British-style Dog Day IPA, Super Dog IPA, and Super Duper Dog. The regular Super is their bestseller and packs over 90 IBUs into a solidly built beer with 6.5 percent ABV (the pound of hops used for dry-hopping adds an extra floral fragrance but doesn't even kick up that big bitterness). The Super Duper takes Super's regular 12-barrel batch and squeezes it into a 7-barrel batch for a concentrated 8 percent alcohol and way over 100 IBUs.

Speaking of hops and hounds, one of the cooler if still low-key events hosted at this Lucky Lab—there's an even larger brewpub on Northwest Quimby with eighteen taps, compared to Southeast Hawthorne's mere twelve, and not to mention public houses in Multnomah Village and in North Portland—is the hop harvest party. Beer-loving green-thumbs are invited to bring their backyard hops in for a picking party where the hosts offer open taps from a jockey box and perhaps some hop-infused barbecue wings. Most of the cones, over 300 pounds last year, including some from the pub's own decorative bines growing next to the patio, wind up in the hop back (though some are thrown directly into the kettle) for a beer called The Mutt. "We never know what kind of hops they are," said Geist, but he noted that the result is an "adorable" beer of indeterminate style that throws a "crazy bouquet."

Their larger events include Dogtoberfest—"Alex and I came up with this stupid idea: 'How 'bout if we do a dog wash?'"—that began with a free little ad in *Willamette Week* offering a free dog wash and wound up bringing in about sixty pups. It has since grown into a fundraiser for DoveLewis Emergency Animal Hospital and draws over six hundred dirty dogs. Larger still, Tour de Lab sees about 1,700 riders rolling into, or at least past, all four Lucky Lab locales. Bikes are a big part of this ecoconscious company (Solar Flare Ale honors the solar panels atop the building that heat all of the brewing water), which partly explains why Lucky Lab bike jerseys are rather popular here and at larger retail outlets. But maybe those REI shoppers aren't into beer (hmph!) or conservation (double hmph!). Maybe they just love the lab logo. "There's no such thing as a mean Labrador," said Geist, who compared the sweet pets to their own sweet pub, taking note of the well-loved and well-worn décor and fixtures. "They're not regal like poodles." I can't imagine a brewpub called the Plucky Poodle being nearly as comfortable.

Lucky Labrador Hawthorne Brew Pub

Opened: 1994.
Owners: Alex Stiles and Gary Geist.
Brewer: Alex Stiles.
System: 15-barrel.
Annual production: 1,100 barrels.
Distribution: Oregon.
Hours: Monday through Saturday, 11 a.m. to midnight; Sunday, noon to 10 p.m.
Tours: By appointment.
Takeout beer: Bombers, growlers, and kegs.
Gift shop: The back wall displays T-shirts, bike jerseys, hoodies, and caps.
Food: Sandwiches, bentos, vegetarian-friendly, and snacks for you and your furry friend.
Events: Worst Day of the Year Ride in early February, scheduled to likely coincide with the worst weather, starts at the Hawthorne pub. The Annual Barleywine and Big Beer "Tastival" in early March offers over forty barleywines of various vintages and other strong beers. The Hop Harvest in late August is a hop-picking party for homegrown hops. Dogtoberfest, held each September, is a fund-raiser dogwash.
Extras: Dogs always allowed on back patio; minors until 9 p.m.

Portland U-Brew & Pub

6237 Southeast Milwaukie Avenue, Portland, OR 97202
(503) 943-2727 • PortlandUBrewAndPub.com
Twitter @PDXuBrew

I love the Sellwood neighborhood for many reasons: the tree forts in many a front yard, Oaks Bottom Wildlife Refuge, Sock Dreams retail outlet, and brunch spots that don't have long lines or expensive menus. The beer equivalent of all these things is the homebrew supply shop with the BOP (Brew On-Premise) and pub that make it a neighborhood hub.

Throughout Portland, there are several shops for the homesteaders and do-it-yourself fans, but as a beer lover there's none better than Portland U-Brew. In between the era of rudimentary Mr. Beer Kits and the enthusiast's Blichmann TopTier brew stands, BOPs were more prevalent, and part of Sellwood's charm is that it feels as if time stands still even though Portland U-Brew & Pub opened in 2011.

Jason Webb and his father, Cliff, are happy to sell you everything you need to make beer at home—supplies and ingredients are contained to the front room—but coming in to brew on the BOP's 15-gallon system makes it feel communal. And it'll be no more than a few weeks before you're rejoining the community when you return to bottle or keg your beer. Customers bring in everything from homegrown rhubarb to Snickers bars, so it's nice to have a pro on hand to help keep the results from turning into a total mess. (In the shop, there's a book of recipes, and because of the nature of homebrewers there are lots of cuckoo recipes like that Snickers Stout or peanut butter cookie ale.) Tackle one of the recipes for a high-gravity barleywine such as Webb-head or GnarlyCharlieWine, dubbed a Cascadian barleywine for its inclusion of dark roasted malt; you can even find proper nip bottles for when it comes time to rack it in the style's traditional packaging!

Beers brewed: Year-round: Grapefruit IPA, Loving Cup Milk Stout, Red-Eye Red, Golden Road Ale. Seasonals: With eight taps there are always occasional and one-off beers available.

The Pick: Grapefruit IPA. Take a super citrusy IPA enlivened with known grapefruit-imparting hops—Cascade and Centennial—and then push those flavors to eleven by adding liquefied whole grapefruits, peel and all, which marries perfectly with the West Coast hops. This ain't no half-juice radler; this is a refreshing and zesty IPA.

Jason's professional experiences read like random pages of this book copied and pasted onto one résumé: Portland Brewing, Cascade Lakes, and the McMenamins Lighthouse Pub. He began at long lost Saxer Brewing and inherited his love of brewing from his grandfather, who was a backyard brewer for forty years (in England, so it wasn't illegal like it was here).

One beer that originated as a kooky idea brought in by a homebrewer is Grapefruit IPA. Even though it may sound strange, grapefruits (including peel and pulp) augment the West Coast "C-hops"—Cascade and Centennial—that feature already-pithy accents. It's now the most popular beer they keep on their eight taps at the pub. I guess I'm only surprised that the bacon beer—the strips of porcine rapture were fried up in the tiny kitchen—didn't turn into a staple.

An ongoing source of inspiration for PUB's beers is the Portland Brewers Collective. It's a gathering of area homebrewers and enthusiasts who meet at the pub on the third Thursday of every month to drink and socialize, and if some homebrew critiquing takes place, then so be it. The pub has a living room vibe, albeit a living room with a full bar, and a huge, square hole in the floor enabling guests to peer down into the basement-level brewery. The kitchen looks like a bachelor pad and includes a panini press for the light bites they serve. If only there were bacon frying up all the time.

Portland U-Brew & Pub

Opened: 2011.

Owners: Jason Webb and Cliff Webb.

Brewers: Jason Webb and you.

System: Half-barrel with 4-barrel fermenters.

Annual production: 100 barrels.

Distribution: Sellwood.

Hours: Tuesday through Thursday, 3 p.m. to 7 p.m.; Friday and Saturday, 11 a.m. to 7 p.m.; Sunday, 11 a.m. to 6 p.m.

Tours: Just come on in.

Takeout beer: Growlers.

Gift shop: Shirts, hoodies, and homebrew supplies.

Food: A panini press and some personal pizzas.

Events: The Westmoreland/Sellwood Brewfest held mid-August is an annual fund-raiser for Fences for Fido, with a dog wash and games on the back patio.

Extras: Hosts the Portland Brewers Collective for area homebrewers every third Thursday.

13 Virtues Brewing Co. /
Philadelphia's Steaks & Hoagies

6410 Southeast Milwaukie Avenue, Portland, OR 97202
(503) 239-8544 • 13VirtuesBrewing.com • PhillyPDX.com
Twitter @13VirtuesBrew

In 1987, Steve Moore had a vision to support his family via cheese-steak sandwiches, just like the ones he enjoyed back home in Philadelphia. By then his family, including his one-year-old son, Cameron, lived in the suburb of West Linn yet Steve and his wife, Amelia, staffed the restaurant, actually down the block from its current space, by themselves. In 2001 they added a second Philadelphia's Steaks & Hoagies shop in West Linn, eight miles from the one in Portland's Sellwood neighborhood.

When Moore added a 3-barrel brewing system in 1994, it became the Beaver State's fourteenth brewing company. But were it not for the tiny neon "Brew Pub" sign in the window you'd likely never know there was a brewery in back. Now that Cameron has grown and become an avid homebrewer in his own right, he's helping to helm Philly's 2.0. Note: It's called 13 Virtues Brewing Co.

The name is connected to famous Philadelphian Benjamin Franklin, who quaffed a few tankards of ale from time to time. He is frequently quoted as saying, "Beer is proof that God loves us and wants us to be happy," but regrettably he's misquoted! Regardless, he extolled what he called the thirteen virtues. These include being silent, humble, and chaste—not things typically associated with beer consumption. Initially, beers took the names of each virtue. There was a session IPA called Temperance at only 4.5 ABV and Moderation Mild had less alcohol still. And let the name Chastity Cherry Wheat sink in. Alas, the father and son Moores quickly moved away from the naming gimmick. The current styles and brands include throwing shade at low-budget Milwaukee's Best with Milwaukie's Better Pilsner and You Down With OPP?, a pale ale that's zesty by nature given its use of orange zest.

Beers brewed: Year-round: Milwaukie's Better Pilsner, 45th Parallel IPA, You Down With OPP? Orange Peel Pale, Calypso Red, Cold Spice Habañero Ale, Rainy Day CDA, Mildfire, Ray Brown Porter, '77 Stout. Seasonals: Traverse Cherry Wit, Westmoreland White IPA, Hoptimal Results IIPA, Helles Having No Beer, Magic Mile Marzen, Defenestrator Doppelbock, Woozy Weizenbock, MAX Stout Imperial Stout, Patience Bourbon Barrel Imperial Stout, Springwater, Belgian Blonde, Baltic Porter.

For his part, Cameron is enjoying wrapping his head around going into the family business and adding a second-generation spin on things. For better or for worse, that starts with differentiating between the Philly cheesesteak shop and the brewery. I only got to see the new tasting room when it was under construction, but it will have a mellow, after-work vibe with thirteen taps behind the bar: one for each virtue, whether by design or not. He mentioned the addition of a food truck that will be parked outside—although I can't imagine that sandwiches can't be walked over through the adjoining back door—but noted the importance of keeping it 13 Virtues in the back and Philly's up front. At the same time, he prudently doesn't want to shun the heritage of being one of Portland's oldest surviving breweries. Only seven that opened before 1994 remain with us.

A good beer-and-cheesesteak pairing offers both contrasting sweet and spicy flavors. The right beer's malt and hops therefore complement the beefy sammich's sweet and spicy peppers. Philly's peppers (and pickles) are made in-house. Playing to the hot side, brewer David Vohden makes Cold Spice Habañero Ale with spicy rye malt (that the beertender will blend upon request if you can't stand the heat). To play off the sweet side, I suggested they make a Tastykake Stout. Tastykake, for the uninitiated (and I'm aware I'll be labeled a slanderer or miscreant for saying this), is Philadelphia's homegrown version of Hostess. Their individually wrapped chocolaty, creamy treats are certainly delicious and imported to Philly's, not that they'd actually use said snack cakes in the recipe. Cameron said he loved the idea. The design would be up to Vohden since he gets lots of leeway, though I'm sure the homebrewer in Cameron would love to mash in for that one.

13 Virtues Brewing Co. / Philadelphia's Steaks & Hoagies

Opened: Brewing since 1994; business opened in 1987.
Owner: Steve Moore.
Brewer: David Vohden.
System: 3-barrel.
Annual production: 300 barrels.
Distribution: Portland.
Hours: Friday, 4 p.m. to 8 p.m.; Saturday, noon to 9 p.m.; Sunday, noon to 4 p.m.
Tours: Taproom overlooks the "brewing arena."
Takeout beer: Growlers and dock sales.
Gift shop: Shirts, hats, glasses, and imported Tastykakes.
Food: Cheesesteaks!
Other location: 18625 Oregon 43, West Linn; 503-699-4130.

Alameda Brewing Co.

Pub: 4765 Northeast Fremont Street, Portland, OR 97213
(503) 460-9025 • AlamedaBrewing.com
Twitter @AlamedaBrewing
Facility: 4736 Southeast 24th Avenue, Portland, OR 97202

After fifteen years as a brewpub serving Beaumont Village along Northeast Fremont Street, in 2011 Alameda turned on the juice and built a separate production facility to occupy a chunk of beer shelves around town and throughout the Northwest. "If you looked at the Oregon Brewers Festival lineup from, say, '96, 50 percent of them aren't open anymore," said Carston Haney, the Grizzly Adams–looking brewmaster since 2008 who moved from the pub to the plant. Alameda is one of the seven breweries that opened in the nineties that's still brewing. "Making beer is profitable," added Haney. "If it isn't, you're doing something extremely wrong."

A big chunk of Alameda's equation is offering a solid lineup of hoppy beers, along with a knack for the super light and robust dark stuff. P-Town Pilsner and the Kolsch-style Siskiyou Golden handle the easy-drinking side and each weighs in at nearly 4 percent ABV. Representing the dark side, Black Bear XX Stout is so grizzly it won four GABF medals in a six-year span. Instead of boasting a big, roast flavor, the grain bill calls for unmalted black malts—rye and chocolate—creating a softer stout sans acrid notes. If you find it at the pub on the nitro tap it's chocolatier and silkier still. If Alameda deems Irvington Juniper Porter the stout's little brother, then the fall seasonal Stubs Old Crow Hazelnut Porter is the nutty brother. This porter

Beers brewed: Year-round: Black Bear XX Stout, El Torero IPA, Yellow Wolf Imperial IPA, Klickitat Pale Ale, P-Town Pilsner, Siskiyou Golden Ale, Irvington Juniper Porter. Seasonals: Stubs Old Crow Hazelnut Porter, My Bloody Valentine (saison with blood orange), St. Brigid Irish Red, Rose City Red, Bad Bunny Cream Ale, Huckleberry Hound Golden, Papa Noel's Olde Ale.

The Pick: Yellow Wolf Imperial IPA. This wolf packs 103 IBUs into an uber-hoppy beer that's pungent as all get-out, like a tropical daiquiri at a reggae concert. It also warms with an 8.2 percent ABV so while it's delicious, it just takes one lone Yellow Wolf to get me to my happy place.

features what Haney called "hazelnut press cakes," sourced from a family-owned company in the Mid-Willamette Valley. "The hazelnuts were a waste product—for them, not us—from their oil press," he explained. "What caught my interest in using these press cakes is that approximately 90 percent of the oil is removed during the pressing process, but the flavor and aroma is retained."

This brings us to Alameda's sweet spot, or actually the bitter spot, where a trio of hop-centered ales reigns, including Klickitat Pale and El Torero IPA. The leader of the pack is Yellow Wolf, an imperial IPA that howls with a piney, tropical aroma announcing its 100-plus IBUs. Haney originally designed it as an extra pale ale called Yellow Dog, but considering the surge in *Humulus lupulus* (the Latin designation of hops that not coincidentally translates as "wet, earthy wolf") the name is quite fitting, even if the beer is more of an orange-copper color. It's so popular there've been one-off versions—let's call them lone wolves—such as Green Wolf, Dire Wolf, and my surprising favorite, Yellow Wolves of Thailand. The latter was the same base IIPA with dried mangoes, flaked coconut, Thai basil, and ginger added (what I might call a ThaiPA).

Of course, the real experimentation takes place at the pub (I wish the Lemon Pepper Saison was permanent) where Marshall Kunz gets to let his homebrewer roots go wild. It's also where Matt Schumacher, originally just the chef until he bought out an original owner's share to become co-owner, still mans the kitchen, making each Black Bear Stout Turkey Pot Pie by hand. The kitchen is in back and the brewery's behind the bar, all under the high ceiling of the spacious, single room. To find it, just look for the humongous, dark bronze hop cone high above the front doors; such a decoration should be a staple of the trade across the land.

Alameda Brewing Co.

Opened: 1996.
Owners: Peter Vernier and Matt Schumacher.
Brewers: Carston Haney (production) and Marshall Kunz (pub).
System: 20-barrel (production brewery) and 5-barrel (brewpub).
Annual production: 3,000 barrels (production brewery); 700 barrels (brewpub).
Distribution: Oregon, Washington, Alaska, Idaho, British Columbia, and Alberta.
Hours: Sunday to Thursday, 11 a.m. to 10 p.m.; Friday and Saturday, 11 a.m. to 11 p.m.
Tours: By request at brewpub. Production brewery not open to the public.
Takeout beer: Growlers, bottles, and kegs.
Gift shop: Display case at entry with apparel and glassware.
Food: Apps, burgers, sandwiches, and pastas. The veggie burger uses spent grains.

Awesome Ales

Portland, OR
(503) 710-6417 • AwesomeAles.com
Twitter @AwesomeAles

Unlike our good friends in California and around New England, few in Oregon function as "tenant," "contract," or "gypsy" brewers. However, not long ago, MillerCoors contracted Full Sail in Hood River to make their Henry Weinhard brands (Portland's Weinhard brewery having shuttered in 1999). Neither Awesome Ales nor the brewery it contracted to make its initial ales, Seven Brides in Silverton (page 284), are quite on that scale, and maybe that's what allows them to be awesome.

The brainchild of David Lederfine, who operated the Portland beer bar-turned-music venue Snake and Weasel at the turn of the millennium, Awesome Ales expands on Lederfine's brewing experiences that started in 1995 with McMenamins and included stints at Oregon Trail Brewery (Corvallis), Astoria Brewing (Astoria), and Three Creeks (Sisters).

Awesome debuted with three beers: an IPA, a strong ale (7.9 percent), and Southern Sky, billed as a French pale ale or the "marriage of a French biere de garde and a Bohemian pilsner with Oregon sensibilities." Lederfine designed and brewed them and spends non-brewing days shoring up more accounts. Early adaptors included Plew's Brews among the North Portland beer haunts and NWIPA from the Southeast Portland set, while taphouses and growler stations around the state also went awesome. It helps that his prior gig was selling beer for a local distributor.

"We hope to continue to grow the brand and move into multiple Northwest markets over the next two years," Lederfine said. "In a few years, when we start approaching the 1,600-barrel mark, I would like to build a brewery, one that will have excess capacity that I can offer to somebody else so they can get their start."

Awesome Ales

Opened: 2013.
Owner and brewer: David Lederfine.
System: Tenant-brewed in 20-barrel batches.
Annual production: 800 barrels.
Distribution: Northwest.

Beers brewed: Year-round: The 4:19 Got a Minute IPA, Southern Sky French Pale Ale, Spike Driver American Strong Ale.

Breakside Restaurant & Pub Brewery

BREAKSIDE
◆ BREWERY ◆
PORTLAND, OR

820 Northeast Dekum Street, Portland, OR 97211
(503) 719-6475 • Breakside.com
Twitter @BreaksideBrews
Taproom and Brewery: See page 118.

The story of Breakside doesn't start in the North Portland neighborhood of Woodlawn, where it opened as a 3-barrel brewpub, but in Juneau, Alaska, where owner Scott Lawrence was enjoying some beers at Alaskan Brewing with some friends when he had his epiphany. "I just started smiling. I told every person I knew. I Facebooked it," he said, since we all know nothing is ever really legit until it's on the social media network. His idea: start a brewery. Nothing outlandish, "four or five beers," he figured. He also thought it'd take a few years to come to fruition when he conceived of this brewery in June 2009. Instead, Breakside opened in May 2010. I wouldn't call him impatient, just a committed risk-taker.

Lawrence didn't merely pull off his flight of fancy. If you were to line up a sample of every beer Breakside brewed in 2013, there'd be exactly one hundred beers in that tasting flight, ranging from a light summer lager to a bourbon-aged old ale to a passionfruit sour ale, from Ale to the Chief Braggot (ale blended with honey mead) to Weissbanger, a cocktail-inspired Bavarian hefeweizen infused with vanilla, orange peel, and anise. Furthermore, Lawrence pulled this off while initiating brewing operations at a brand-new, 30-barrel production facility in the suburb of Milwaukie for rapidly expanding draft and bottled distribution. Truly, he's ambitious, but he hardly did all this alone.

Perhaps his wisest executive decision was hiring then-twenty-eight-year-old brewmaster Ben Edmunds. The Great Lakes native went to Yale for undergrad before studying brewing at the Siebel Institute, followed by training at the Doemens Academy in Munich. It's the combination of traditional German training and Northwest pioneering spirit that inspires his myriad recipes. "Even though it clearly flies in the face of Reinheitsgebot," said Edmunds, referencing the Bavarian Beer Purity Law, "when we use chilies and chocolates and fruits and spices in beer, we do it with the same methodology that a German brewer would create their Helles . . . When we experiment, we do so with some sort of method—we don't just throw a bunch of random crap into the boiler or fermenter."

I'm compelled to mention that one of the hundred beers in 2013, called Duck Duck Drunk, started as a chocolate porter until they added duck carcasses. Here's Edmund's abridged explanation: "I thought that the most effective way of getting a meat flavor into beer would be to treat the entire wort as a stock. We bought 100 pounds of Muscovy duck carcasses and roasted them in the wood-fired oven at Nostrana," he began, referencing their friends at Portland's acclaimed Italian restaurant. "We wanted a rich, umami, gamey duck aroma. I took the ducks and started adding them to the kettle as we ran off the lauter. Rather than bringing the wort to boil, I held the kettle between 195 and 200 degrees Fahrenheit for seventy-two hours, imitating how you would simmer a stock. After the 'duck rest,' I pulled [out] the carcasses and brought the wort to boil, then hopped, cooled, and fermented it. Two weeks later, and voila: *biere de canard*."

I don't know what kinds of yeast you use in a duck porter, but I'm sure they flocculate together. By the way, Edmunds added, "I always like to point out that we make a lot of 'normal' beers, too." As proof, Breakside's topsellers are their IPA and Pilsner. Three of their GABF medals were awarded for their classic British ESB, an English-style mild called Session Brown, and for their flagship Irish Dry Stout.

Like its vaunted collaborators, Breakside has achieved the perfect amalgamation of neighborhood pub and destination restaurant. Speaking of acclaimed restaurants, the Breakside brewpub, with its fire-roasted jalapeño poppers as one of the more popular appetizers, doesn't aspire to be a Michelin star restaurant. Portlanders ain't fancy; they're comfort food gourmands. Breakside brewed wildly different beers for several of Portland's most esteemed eateries as part of a Restaurant Collaboration Series. The restaurants range from James Beard Foundation Award–winner Beast to instant-hit Podnah's Pit BBQ and a pizza

Beers brewed: Year-round: IPA, Wanderlust IPA, Woodlawn Pale Ale, Pilsner, Irish Stout, Aztec (amber with habanero and serrano chilies and cacao nibs). Seasonals: Safe Word Triple IPA, Old World IPA, Newport Summer Ale, Passionfruit Sour, Salted Caramel Stout, India Golden Ale, Toro Red, Big Country (winter ale), Pool Party Session, Post Time Kolsch, La Tormenta Dry Hopped Sour, Session Brown, Savory Stout, Newport Summer Ale, French Fennel Farmhouse, Smallwares Saison, Apizza Alt, 1911 Vienna Coffee Beer, Just the Tip Spruced Wheat, Beach Saison, Pumpkin Bicre de Garde, Coconut Pumpkin Stout, Smoked Apple Ale.

The Pick: Passionfruit Sour. Tart, Lacto-fermented Berliner Weisse is rapidly gaining popularity around here, in part because of its easy-drinking, low alcohol content (4 percent). Breakside eschews adding a sweet fruit syrup like most others. Instead, this one is conditioned with the tropical punch that only passionfruit can add. The GABF judges who awarded it a bronze medal were almost spot on.

joint called Apizza Scholls where foodies queue up daily. "We created a list of 'ideal' restaurants that we wanted to work with, and then we approached the chefs," Edmunds said. "Amazingly, everyone said yes—a testament to the way that Portland chefs value beer." The participating chefs pitched their ideas for elixirs that would pair with their respective styles of cooking, which is how sister restaurants Le Pigeon and Little Bird wound up with a French Fennel Farmhouse ale.

Breakside Restaurant & Pub Brewery

Opened: 2010.

Owner: Scott Lawrence.

Brewers: Ben Edmunds (brewmaster), Sam Barber (senior brewer), Jacob Leonard (director of brewing operations), Will Jaquiss (brewer), and Seth Barnum (brewer).

System: 3-barrel.

Annual production: 550 barrels.

Distribution: Oregon, Washington, Idaho, British Columbia, and Japan.

Hours: Monday through Thursday, 3 p.m. to 10 p.m.; Friday and Saturday, noon to 11 p.m.; Sunday, noon to 10 p.m.

Tours: Not available.

Takeout beer: Growlers, limited bottles, and keg dock sales.

Gift shop: Shirts, hats, glasses, and other gear.

Food: Sandwiches, salads, and snacks.

Extras: Cellar Reserve Club offers exclusive bottled beers but is currently limited to eighty members.

Burnside Brewing Co.

701 East Burnside Street, Portland, OR 97214
(503) 946-8151 • BurnsideBrewCo.com
Twitter @BurnsideBrewco

The star in any brewpub should always be the beer. That's why it's called a brewpub and not a pubbrew. Yet co-owners Jay Gilbert and Jason McAdam (who doubles as the brewmaster) either brag or confess that food sales slightly outpace beer sales on-premises. They boast a fantastic lineup of brews, yet the food menu, to some, takes center stage. I call that a selling point.

The iconic staple is a starter called the Cohiba, duck confit rolled in collard greens in the shape of a cigar and actually served on a handsome ashtray replete with "ashes" (crushed malt) for dipping. The burger? It's seared in duck fat. As for those beers to pair it all with, yes the IPA is tasty, but where else are you going to find an award-winning wheat beer made with apricots and Scotch bonnet peppers? Sweet Heat earned GABF gold in the Experimental category in 2012. Not that they'll stop you from simply enjoying several pints of the Lime Kolsch—they hand zest 40 pounds of the little green guys per 15-barrel batch—on the front patio.

With McAdam's experience as the brewer and cofounder of Portland's defunct Roots Brewing and Gilbert's background in beer sales at Full Sail, Burnside is constantly expanding, but as Gilbert put it, "Growth is a byproduct of what we really want to create. We'll continue putting [fermentation] tanks in so we can continue being creative." As is the case with nearly all Oregon breweries, the moneymaker is the IPA—it does the most volume on draft and represents 30 percent of bottle sales. But I've seen four different IPAs on draft—including an imperial, a session, and a smoked one—at one time. They've also made tart Berliner Weisses, including one made with marionberries, and they continue working on barrel-aged and sour beers.

Beers brewed: Year-round: Sweet Heat, IPA, Oatmeal Pale Ale, Alter Ego Imperial IPA, Stock Ale, Couch Select Lager. Seasonals: Lime Kolsch, lowercase session ipa, Prime Meridian Fresh Hop, Berliner-Weisse, Gratzer, Permafrost, Oyster Strong Ale, and more.

The Pick: Sweet Heat. An anomaly of a flagship brand, this honey orange-hued wheat beer incorporates apricot purée as well as Scotch bonnet peppers sourced from the Dominican Republic to create a beer that is simultaneously fruity sweet and full of chili heat but also fully delicious paired throughout a meal and not just as a sample-sized oddity.

Referring to his own beers and those from around the community of Portland brewers, McAdam commented, "There's a handful of us that really like to eat and cook . . . We've got a different take on beer." Beers that illustrate this point have listed beef hearts and bull balls as ingredients. Uni Ale, like the sushi item from which it derives its name, used sea urchin along with tomato water and smoked sea salt.

Augmenting this aspect on the pub side, Chef Nate Yovu came to Burnside from New York after gigging at a Michelin-starred restaurant, not to mention acclaimed Captain Lawrence Brewing. "Chef Nate uses every last piece of everything that comes through here," Gilbert remarked, such as rendered pork fat for the fried pork nuggets, so I had to put in an order. Far from regular meatballs, they're breaded in panko and ladled with a sauce reminiscent of honey mustard, in which whole mustard seeds are made to resemble caviar, and garnished with pickled watermelon. The multi-textural plate-scape—crunchy, chewy, and gooey—snaps and pops in your mouth in a delicious miasma of tangy and umami flavors.

Most brewpubs—all good brewpubs, I'd say—cater to their own neighborhood, but Burnside, aided by its central location on one of Portland's busiest thoroughfares, is also a true destination. And while they welcome folks who drive from all over, the parking lot relinquishes a few spaces to its front patio with eight picnic tables that are covered in the rain so guests (and their pooches) can stay dry. Same goes for the giant branded grain silo out front that now serves as a landmark for those looking for the brewpub, as well as a manifestation of their designs for the brewery's growth.

Burnside Brewing Co.

Opened: 2010.

Owners: Jason McAdam and Jay Gilbert.

Brewer: Jason McAdam.

System: 15-barrel.

Annual production: 3,500 barrels.

Distribution: Oregon, Washington, and British Columbia.

Hours: Monday and Tuesday, 3 p.m. to 10 p.m.; Wednesday and Thursday, 3 p.m. to midnight; Friday and Saturday, noon to midnight; Sunday, noon to 10 p.m.

Tours: By request.

Takeout beer: 22-ounce bottles, growlers, and dock sales.

Gift shop: Apparel and glassware.

Food: Next level pub grub. The burger seared in duck fat in a hop-studded bun is out of this world. Seasonal entrées and small plates keep the restaurant always packed.

Columbia River Brewing Co.

1728 Northeast 40th Avenue, Portland, OR 97212
(503) 943-6157 • ColumbiaRiverBrewpub.com
Twitter @CRBrewCo

When Rick Burkhardt and his wife, Lynn, opened the Columbia River Brewpub in 2010 in the Hollywood District, there were over 1,700 craft breweries operating in the United States. The American Homebrewers Association reported there were a million active homebrewers by that year. So imagine how bewildering it is to him that thirty-seven years earlier, when he got bitten by the homebrewing bug, he had already dreamed of the day that he'd open his own brewery.

"If only we'd known those magical two words: micro brewery." This is the first sentiment shared by Lynn, who's a staple behind the bar. It was while visiting her family back in England where she was born— "a small village with a pub on every corner," she remarked with no trace of an accent— that Rick not only discovered the world of ales, so different from the industrial stuff back home, but also learned to brew. He was so taken with making beer that her family sent them packing with trunks full of the raw ingredients: hops, malts, and dry yeast.

Consider that in America in 1973, five years before President Carter signed the Cranston Bill legalizing homebrewing, at best one could hope to find canned malt extract, possibly augmented with hop extract. Rick brewed in his garage outside San Jose, just south of Anchor Brewing in San Francisco and New Albion Brewing in Sonoma, which Jack McAuliffe opened in 1977. If the Burkhardts had acted sooner while in the cradle of craft brewing, they'd be synonymous with its genesis. As such, that just meant that Rick had a longer time to hone his chops, and his recipes.

The Burkhardts put their idea of opening a microbrewery on hold for two reasons. First, Rick had great job security working for Sears. Secondly, the first of their three kids was born in 1977.

Beers brewed: Year-round: Rose City Raspberry Wheat, Sandy Blonde, ESB, Columbia River Brewing Pale Ale, Hop Heaven IPA, Stumbler's Stout. Seasonals: War Elephant Imperial IPA, Paddler's Porter, Rye IPA, Hollywood Hefe, Double Vision.

The Pick: Stumbler's Stout. This classic oatmeal stout rewards drinkers with the richness of cocoa nibs and vanilla beans that, despite the extra body and smoothness from the oats, doesn't strike you as overly sweet. At 6 percent ABV it's my go-to for playing darts.

"We decided the risk was better taken after our kids are grown," Rick said. Not to spoil the ending, but Heather, their middle child, now works at Columbia River. And her eldest son, one of the Burkhardts' seven grandkids, washes dishes at the pub when he wants to earn some moolah.

The Burkhardts relocated to Bend in the late eighties, back when there were only two small brewpubs (one of them was Deschutes). After Bend, Rick's job moved them to Idaho. Before long, his benefits would kick and a second career as a brewmaster-publican made the lure of "retirement" so appetizing. They craved moving back to Oregon, but Rick said, "Everyone thought I was crazy because of the number of existing brewpubs." So they eyed the East Coast and even took a trip to Florida. But the economic downturn at the time had decimated the Sunshine State's brewpub population. (Rick said it went from forty to three; I'll leave it to *Florida Breweries* author Gerard Walen to research that.) Besides, Rick pointed out, the "clientele" there is rather different. Let's just say a huge factor in the success of Portland breweries is that the demographic here is youthful, receptive to new flavors, and partial to ales, whereas Florida's is . . . not.

That's when it happened. While Rick was traveling for Sears, his real estate agent called. The space vacated by the Laurelwood Pizza Co.—which had been Laurelwood Brewing Co. prior to that, and was previously the Old World Pub and Brewery—became available. Two days after the Burkhardts bought it in July 2010, original 7-barrel brewhouse and all, Columbia River Brewing opened for business. Referring to the basement-level brewhouse visible from the ground-level restaurant, Rick noted that "The Old World had quite a vision when they cut the hole in the floor . . . and the original owners still come in here."

By August, the beers flowing from the taps weren't homebrews but Rick's professional beer. But he didn't ditch his 10-gallon system—he still uses it for test batches when brewing new recipes, though with nearly four decades of experience and recipe development under his belt, he said that doesn't happen very often. "I had sixty homebrew recipes I'd perfected over the years . . . I've reproduced all but five here," he said.

You'll always find at least ten house beers on tap, maybe as many as twelve depending on seasonals. A key to this wide range is pitching six to eight yeast strains. One mainstay is Rose City Raspberry Wheat, even though Rick would never have done a fruit beer given his druthers. Heather pushed for it and even helped with the brewing.

At the 2012 World Beer Cup, the auspicious, biennial competition in which entries from around the globe are judged blind, Columbia

River garnered two medals, both silver and both for stouts. One went to Stumbler's (Oatmeal) Stout, which clocks in at 6 percent alcohol. The other was for Drunken Elf, and only Rick knows if he'll brew that one again. Originally created for the Holiday Ale Fest (one of Portland's best fests), this 9 percent imperial stout got 10 pounds of Belgian chocolate and some very expensive Kona coffee, but sold for a mere five bucks a pint from the bar. I implored Burkhardt to bring it back, or at least have more dark beers on tap, but he responded, "First and foremost, Portland is an IPA town, no getting away from that." Hence, you'll always find three, maybe four different IPAs on tap. The first two beers they bottled were Hop Heaven IPA and War Elephant Imperial IPA.

Rick said he'd like to bottle more, if his plans for a production facility come to fruition. Considering the Burkhardts had no prior pub experience and their staff already calls them Mom and Dad (not just Heather), Lynn said with a smile, I like their chances of running a successful second brewery as part of this retirement plan.

Columbia River Brewing Co.

Opened: 2010.

Owners: Rick and Lynn Burkhardt.

Brewer: Rick Burkhardt.

System: 7-barrel.

Annual production: 600 barrels.

Distribution: Oregon's Northwest quadrant.

Hours: Sunday through Thursday, 11 a.m. to 10 p.m.; Friday and Saturday, 11 a.m. to 11 p.m.

Tours: Any day, as long as Rick isn't busy brewing.

Takeout beer: Growlers, bombers, and dock sales of half-barrel kegs or corny keg fills.

Gift shop: Shirts and hoodies line the back wall.

Food: Their Reuben, fish and chips, and vegan pot-pie are the most popular. The Stout Burger (made with Stumbler's Stout) and housemade veggie burger are also delicious, and the beer-battered fries are the best in town.

Extras: Minors allowed. Patio dining and drinking off the parking lot.

Ecliptic Brewing

825 North Cook Street, Portland, OR 97227
(503) 265-8002 • EclipticBrewing.com
Twitter @EclipticBrewing

John Harris's uncle gave him a telescope as a teenager. Eventually the amateur astronomer put it away and caught the homebrewing bug. It might seem obvious today that one would go into brewing as a career and keep the cosmos as a hobby, but in 1986 being a professional stargazer seemed as unlikely as being a professional brewer. Yet that's when Harris was hired as an original brewer at McMenamins, Oregon's first brewpub. Then a new brewpub in Bend opened, which is how he came to create beers such as Deschutes Black Butte Porter and Mirror Pond Pale Ale. Next, Full Sail, where he became a co-owner.

Afterward, rather than going quietly into that dark night, figuratively speaking, he is going into it on his own terms with the launch of Ecliptic Brewing. "I haven't been written out of history yet, huh?" he said to me self-deprecatingly. Not coincidentally, Ecliptic opened during the autumnal equinox 2013. About a decade earlier, he'd dusted off that old telescope. If there's one thing astronomy has taught him, it's that, "Looking at other galaxies makes you realize how small we are." So whereas stars and suds were literally night and day for Harris, he devised a way to make them align. Ecliptic, named for our astral (and perhaps his occupational) journey around the sun, burst to life like a protostar.

At Ecliptic, all the beers are named after stars, nebula, galaxies, and other astronomical themes. Procyon Pale Ale is his Northwest pale ale, rife with Cascades and named for the "Little Dog Star" in the Canis Minor constellation. Arcturus is an orange giant some 36.7 light-years away, but it's also Ecliptic's first IPA, exploding like a supernova of C-hops: Cascade, Centennial, Chinook, and Columbus. I say "Ecliptic's first" rather than house or flagship because, as he explained to me, if the stars in the sky never stay put throughout the year, why should his beers?

Beers brewed: Year-round: Arcturus IPA, Procyon Pale Ale, Spica Hefepils, Capella Porter, Mintaka Stout, Rigel Sparkling Ale. Seasonals: Filament Winter IPA, Orange Giant bourbon barleywine.

The Pick: Arcturus IPA. Within the ever-expanding universe of IPAs, its "constellation of C-hops" (Cascade, Centennial, Chinook, and Columbus) still shines brightly thanks to notes of citrus zest, resin, and Northwest pine-scented goodness.

Fittingly, Ecliptic is the newest point in the Boise neighborhood constellation including Lompoc, HUB Bikebar, StormBreaker, and Widmer Bros. Ecliptic is Harris's way of getting "back to small . . . back to fun." With a brewpub, his emphasis is on being experimental (culling from vast experience) and he deemed a 15-barrel system the best way to achieve that. "There's no reason to work your butt off," working hard for little volume, he said, recollecting his first 3-barrel brewhouse. With his previous brewery, the focus was "production, production, production." Here, he works closely with his chef and designs food-friendly beers. "I want Ecliptic to be a brewer's brewery," he added.

Just like Harris, the brewing system has a bit of history behind it. He miraculously purchased BridgePort's old mash tun, which had been collecting space dust in a land far, far away. (OK, it was in Dogfish Head's warehouse in Delaware. But after all, Betelgeuse doesn't belong in Andromeda, it belongs in Orion, amIright?) Continuing the space theme, the semi-orb lights overhead are arranged in an analemma, the figure eight-like shape representing the sun's perceived path overhead. Not every square inch of the 14,000-square-foot warehouse and 1,000-square-foot patio resembles a planetarium, but the wall sectioning off the pub's dining area isn't just full of random holes—they're in the pattern of northern hemisphere constellations so you'll see the Big Dipper, Orion's Belt, and others. On the other hand, the photos on the walls weren't captured by Hubble's Wide Field and Planetary Camera: they're portraits of beer snapped through an electron microscope.

Portlanders don't need a theme to cluster around great beer; they're simply drawn to its inescapable gravity, as evidenced by the crowds when Ecliptic opened. It's a given that the celestial sphere and earthly beer are both heavenly. But for this veteran brewmaster, they hold much in common. "Creating a new beer is a cosmic thing," Harris said. "[You're] combining ingredients and bringing it to life."

Ecliptic Brewing

Opened: 2013.
Owner and brewer: John Harris.
System: 15-barrel.
Annual production: 2,000 barrels.
Distribution: Portland.
Hours: Sunday to Thursday, 11 a.m. to 10 p.m.; Friday and Saturday, 11 a.m. to midnight.
Takeout beer: Growlers and bottles.
Gift shop: T-shirts and growlers.
Food: Salads, sandwiches, seasonal entrées, kids menu, and Lunation Dinner Series.

Ex Novo Brewing Co.

2326 North Flint Avenue, Portland, OR 97227
ExNovoBrew.com • Twitter @ExNovoBrew

Ex Novo is a brewing company but that's its stealthy disguise, the nerdy glasses (and beard) covering up its true identity as a nonprofit corporation. It joins Oregon Public House as a distinctly Portlandish way of not just crowdfunding, but brewed-funding.

When I first met founder Joel Gregory at a backyard crawfish boil serving up his homebrew, he told me about planning a nonprofit brewery called Ex Novo, meaning "out of nothing," or moreover "from scratch." Slogans like "Blending together a love for our craft with a love for our neighbor" and "A better beer for the greater good" aren't platitudes since 100 percent of their net profits will benefit four nonprofits: Impact NW (assisting families living in poverty), Friends of the Children (mentoring at-risk kids), Mercy Corps (providing international humanitarian aid), and International Justice Mission (fighting to liberate enslaved children around the world).

Head brewer Ian Greene brings worldly brewing experience with him, having studied brewing in Scotland and set up a brewery in Norway, not to mention mashing in at West Coast heavies such as Stone Brewing in San Diego and Bend's Boneyard Beer. Beyond the core beers, Joel said Greene gets carte blanche on the brew deck.

Not only does Joel have a young daughter who'll be a staple at the pub, but also given its location across from a park, I'm sure we can expect many pint-sized philanthropists accompanying their do-gooder parents, since drinking here is basically liquid altruism.

Ex Novo Brewing Co.

Opened: 2014.

Owner: Joel Gregory

Brewer: Ian Greene.

System: 10-barrel.

Annual production: 700 barrels (goal).

Hours: Monday, 3 p.m. to 9 p.m.; Tuesday through Thursday, 3 p.m. to 10 p.m.; Friday, 3 p.m. to 11 p.m.; Saturday, noon to 11 p.m.; Sunday, noon to 9 p.m.

Takeout beer: Growlers.

Food: Snacks and entrées including yam fry bread with pancetta, beer-braised brisket, and twice-baked purple potatoes, plus vegan options.

Beers brewed: Pale, IPA, Session IPA, Scottish, Saison, Stout, Pilsner, Mexican Lager, and barrel-aged and sour ales.

Fire on the Mountain Brewing Co.

3443 Northeast 57th Avenue at Fremont, Portland, OR 97213

(503) 894-8973 • PortlandWings.com

Twitter @Portlandwings

In the "Beer and" world, the couplet can be completed by innumerable things. Beer and burgers, pizza, cheese, football, music, philosophy, you name it. But in the "wings and" world, there's only one natural pairing: beer. OK, wings and beer and sports, but here's the kicker—visit the Fire on the Mountain location in Fremont, the third in the local restaurant chain, and you'll find just one flat screen in the corner behind the bar, installed almost as an afterthought. Everything else is well thought out.

Begun on New Year's Day 2005 by Sara Sawicki and Jordan Busch (partners but not a couple), the first Fire on the Mountain opened on North Interstate Avenue in North Portland's Overlook neighborhood. A second, larger, more central spot followed on East Burnside Street. The third Portland location opened in 2012, adding a 7-barrel brewhouse to the mix and taking the central concept one step further. That concept, in Sawicki's words: "Wings and beer go really well together."

From day one, they've always had a great draft list, tapping a variety of styles from mostly local breweries. Varying degrees of wing sauce heat call for different styles of beer. With the third restaurant, Sawicki said they had talked about having their own brewery for awhile. "We never had the opportunity to do it before, but the new space lent itself to [having] it there."

Beers brewed: Year-round: Wanderin' Rye, Lefty Lager, Hoosier Amber?, Shocks of Sheba IPA, Electric Mud Oatmeal Stout, seasonals.

In lieu of a wall of TVs behind the full bar, ceiling-high windows display the brewing system and tanks where the house beers—served at the other locations as well, of course—are born. Brewer Ben Nehrling, who spent seven years cutting his teeth at McMenamins, generally keeps four beers on tap. They're mostly traditional styles, though you might find a honey-milk stout served on nitro or a Cherry Bruin. And plenty of what are now guest taps remain.

The Pick: Shocks of Sheba, named after the reggae program on local KBOO whose hosts were early regulars, is the one beer guaranteed to stand up to the various wing sauces. And it's not too heavy, which you'll appreciate if you also get any of the fried appetizers.

The flight of four is a good value at $4.25, but not as good as the $2.50 pints all Monday long. But what I really like? At the front of the house, since they can't very well do a "flight" of each of the dozen wings they have available, you'll find a tray akin to a mini-cupcake pan, with all twelve sauces available for dipping. The plate of celery sticks guarantees eating *something* healthy here, and diners can ensure they order the right level of spiciness for the classic buffalo hot sauces, or discover that the lime-cilantro might just be the best sauce Fire on the Mountain makes, or realize that signing up for the El Jefe Challenge is a bad idea.

El Jefe, by the way, is the name of their insanely hot wing coating. It ain't no Hooters' Three Mile Island sauce that's basically butter with a pinch of capsicum and a dash of vinegar; it's habanero to the hilt. My first time here, a group of us ordered some and I think I "won" by downing the most: two. The other El Jefes went half uneaten. The challenge began as fifteen in five minutes, but ever since Busch accomplished the feat in 3 minutes and 45 seconds, patrons are now required to suck 'em down in three and a half. The winners get their Polaroids affixed to the wall. I asked about a theoretical wall of losers, those who'd attempted the challenge but failed, and was told that it would easily fill up the wall past the bathroom.

Fire on the Mountain Brewing Co.

Opened: 2012.
Owners: Sara Sawicki and Jordan Busch.
Brewer: Ben Nehrling.
System: 7-barrel.
Annual production: 900 barrels.
Distribution: On tap at all three Fire on the Mountain restaurants.
Hours: Sunday through Thursday, 11 a.m. to 11 p.m.; Friday and Saturday, 11 a.m. to midnight (Burnside open until midnight daily).
Takeout beer: Growlers.
Gift shop: A few shirts and apparel available behind the cash register, along with bottles of most of their sauces.
Food: Wings! Yeah, there's also pizza, burgers, sandwiches, and an array of fried apps, but make sure you order some wings. Of the twelve sauces, I like the Hot (Buffalo) and the Lime-Cilantro.
Extras: Parking lot. Family-friendly (except at the bar). Outdoor seating.
Other Portland locations: 1708 East Burnside, (503) 230-WING; 4255 North Interstate, (503) 280-WING.

Humble Brewing

Portland, OR
HumbleBrewing.com
Twitter @HumbleBrewing

Shortly after Humble Brewing debuted at Winter Beer Fest at Plew's Brews (a dive-turned-beer bar in North Portland), the Concordia neighborhood brewery quintupled production. That meant graduating from a 10-gallon to a 1.5 barrel brew system. With the cheeky tagline, "Competing for the title of Portland's smallest brewery," Humble produced a half barrel by EOY 2011, meaning breweries that barrel-age lost more beer to evaporation. In 2012 Humble rose to Oregon's eighth smallest brewery. As cofounder Scott Davis said, "If it takes ten years to build our brand, we're prepared for that . . . But it's a pain."

Davis's partner, Chad Freitag, a mechanical engineer by day, hosts the nanobrewery behind his house. The pair met through their wives and became homebrewing buddies. "Above all, we want this to be fun," Davis said. "We're brewing a lot of different styles based on the season and types of beers we like to drink."

Or, as I wisecracked, beers they *would* like to drink. They sold their first keg to NePo42 for sixty-five dollars, but friends requested a growler, which set 'em back fifteen dollars, so as Freitag lamented, there went their profit margin.

Among their myriad beers are Humble IPA, Ryemin' & Stealin' (a lower-alcohol rye beer), and Gonzilla IIPA, featuring 20 pounds of hops per batch. That's nothing to most brewers, but remember that's over 13 pounds per barrel, with late additions of Centennial and Cascade, and it's then dry hopped with Columbus and Centennial. It's 8.1 percent alcohol and a monstrous 93 IBUs.

Beers brewed: Year-round: Humble IPA, Chinook Pale Ale, Saaz Saison, Centennial Session Ale. Seasonals/recurring: Ryemin' & Stealin' Rye, Gonzilla Imperial IPA, Brett Saaz Saison, Cascade Session Ale, Fall Farmhouse, and more.

Humble Brewing

Opened: 2011.
Owners and brewers: Scott Davis and Chad Freitag.
System: 1.5-barrel.
Annual production: 25 barrels.
Distribution: Portland.

The Pick: Saaz Saison. A bit grassy, a bit lemony, and sure, a bit lemongrassy, this easy-drinking ale has become the staple among Humble's single-hopped beers.

Laurelwood Public House & Brewery

5115 Northeast Sandy Boulevard, Portland, OR 97213
(503) 282-0622 • LaurelwoodBrewpub.com
Twitter @Laurelwood1

On Laurelwood's tenth anniversary in 2011, regulars who routinely down a couple of pints of the best-selling Workhorse IPA were treated to all that cumulative hoppy goodness in a single glass with their celebratory Imperial Workhorse. They kicked the alcohol content up from 7.5 percent ABV to 10 percent, 1 percent alcohol by volume for each year (since candles are passé).

They also tapped other unique kegs, including Mexican Mocha made with South American malt, cinnamon, chocolate, and serrano chilies. The rare offerings seemed to serve a dual purpose. The first, ostensibly, was to show that in Portland, where people sometimes fall victim to the "New Sexy More is More" mentality, a relative brewing veteran hadn't lost a step in concocting contemporary and boldly dazzling beers. It also subtly insinuated that the pub is a place for serious beer drinking when perhaps its broader reputation is that it's one of the most family-friendly brewpubs in town. It's a well-deserved reputation at that, as the bona fide play areas indicate. Yep, two of them, one in each of the main dining areas.

Owner Mike De Kalb and his wife, Cathy, had a ten year old and a three year old at the time. "We were looking to market to people like us," he said. Parents don't want animatronic mascots; they want good food, beer, and atmosphere, too. Verily, the frequency with which my wife and I come here has increased tenfold since we became parents. When I hit the pub child-less, I head up to the rooftop patio if it's nice out. Many patrons don't even know it exists, but my dog surely does.

Creating atmosphere is a funny thing. Prior to being brewpub owners, the De Kalbs's experience as restaurateurs situated them at the airport.

Beers brewed: Year-round: Workhorse IPA, Mother Lode Golden Ale, Organic Pale Ale, Organic Free Range Red Ale, Hooligan Brown Ale, Organic Tree Hugger Porter, Space Stout. Seasonals: Portlandia Pils, Organic Portland Roast Espresso Stout, Deranger Imperial Red Ale, Vinter Varmer, Organic Moose & Squirrel Imperial Stout, Stingy Jack Pumpkin Ale, and more.

The Pick: Tree Hugger Porter. Go easy, Workhorse fans. With a dearth of dark beers year-round, Tree Hugger is a reliable dry porter offering balanced roastiness and, at 5.6 percent, is one of their most sessionable beers during the rainy season and the other one.

Portland International Airport, PDX, is routinely ranked the best airport in the United States by *Condé Nast Traveler* and part of the equation includes amenities. So how perfect that there are Laurelwood outposts in two PDX concourses? They're even past security, meaning travelers are free to fill growlers or take bombers on the plane, a regrettable nickname for 22-ounce bottles as far as the TSA must be concerned.

The company has since expanded and currently includes an additional outlet some six miles south in the Sellwood-Moreland neighborhood renowned for its family atmosphere. Mike De Kalb had also eyed building a production brewery but ultimately wound up contracting with Widmer Brothers (Craft Brew Alliance) to brew and bottle some top brands in order to extend distribution beyond Oregon and Washington into Northern California, Montana, Nevada, and Idaho.

The main brewpub, the first to offer certified organic beer in Oregon, actually opened eleven blocks down Sandy Boulevard in a space vacated by the now-defunct Old World Pub and Brewery. Old World's brewer, Christian Ettinger, newly devoid of a brewing gig, then created Laurelwood's brewing program. He and Laurelwood were recognized three years later, earning World Champion Small Brewpub and World Champion Small Brewpub Brewmaster honors at the biennial World Beer Cup. The first five of Laurelwood's dozen GABF medals are also to Ettinger's credit. Ettinger went on to create Hopworks Urban Brewery in Southeast Portland. His assistant, Chad Kennedy, helmed the brewery until leaving to establish Worthy Brewing in Bend, which is how current brewmaster Vasilios "Vasili" Gletsos landed the gig in July 2011, right after Laurelwood's tenth anniversary.

A quick word on Gletsos's background: When it comes to folks in the industry, brewing professionally isn't always first on their résumé. There are often more staid jobs prior to this occupation that most people consider exotic. Even in comparison, his previous work is unique. Gletsos was a professional puppeteer. We're not talking Muppets or marionettes, but "parade performance . . . radical theater" puppets. The career change occurred when, upon relocating from his native East Coast to Portland, he asked himself: "What am I going to be more successful at?" So it was after a fruitful string of jobs at BJ's Brewery, Rock Bottom, and MacTarnahan's that Gletsos took over the brewing program.

"Like any brewpub, our primary concerns are quality and freshness," he said. And Laurelwood offers a fantastic range among their eight core beers and beloved seasonals. Still, he noted, "Sometimes I want to expand the horizons of our drinkers. There's an itch to make something fun and geeky. Mike trusts me with the brewing operation."

Sitting by Gletsos's side, De Kalb neither bragged nor defended this: "In all these years, I've never told any of our brewers 'No.'"

Laurelwood Public House & Brewery

Opened: 2001.

Owners: Mike De Kalb and Cathy Woo-De Kalb.

Brewers: Vasilios Gletsos (brewmaster) and Shane Watterson (head brewer).

System: 15-barrel.

Annual production: 7,500 barrels

Distribution: Oregon, Washington, Idaho, Montana, and Pennsylvania.

Hours: Monday through Thursday, 11 a.m. to 10 p.m.; Friday, 11 a.m. to 11 p.m.; Saturday, 10 a.m. to 11 p.m.; Sunday, 10 a.m. to 10 p.m.

Tours: By request. (De Kalb says he gives the nickel tour while Gletsos gives the "buck-fifty tour.")

Takeout beer: Bombers, growlers, and kegs (with advance reservation).

Gift shop: There's a wall of merchandise up front with loads of shirts and hats, glassware, and other odds and ends, including their line of beer-imbued condiments.

Food: Wide range of pub fare from salads to entrées, including loads of burgers and other sandwiches, plus a kids menu of course.

Other location: Sellwood-Moreland pub (6716 SE Milwaukie Ave., Portland; 503-894-8267).

Lompoc Brewing

Fifth Quadrant/Sidebar
3901 North Williams Avenue, Portland OR 97227
(503) 288-3996 • LompocBrewing.com
Twitter @LompocBeer

Lompoc Brewing owner and original brewer Jerry Fechter says he subscribes to the brewing industry mantra, "If you're not growing, you're dying," but I'm not sure I believe him. Yes, he has grown his Portland empire to four pubs since he bought the business in 2000, and has increased production from the initial 7-barrel brewery he built for the original owners in 1996 to a 15-barrel system. But he once told me he envisioned opening a new pub at least every couple of years. And he figures he could be selling 5,000 barrels worth of heavy hitters like Proletariat Red and C-Note Imperial Pale Ale instead of producing just over 3,000 barrels, but he knows it'd be "no fun" for Lompoc's brewer, Bryan Keilty, if he had to make "the same five or six beers day after day." Then again, Fechter did mention that he could see opening another two locations, including one in Southwest Portland (the only quadrant Lompoc's not in). And he'd consider expanding distribution to California, but only the Central Coast town of Lompoc.

Fechter had worked in the Alphabet District at a brewpub called The Old Lompoc, which he bought along with iconic publican Don Younger (R.I.P.) of Horse Brass Pub notoriety. He explained that Younger put in some money, and business meetings mostly consisted of going to the Horse Brass to listen to Younger pontificate. After purchasing the Old Lompoc and turning it into the New Old Lompoc—the first taste of Fechter's tongue-in-cheek naming conventions, even though he credits Younger with the idea—they realized that they could open additional pubs and use their small brewery to service the additional locations.

They opened the Hedge House in 2003, not knowing how trendy Southeast Division would

Beers brewed: Year-round: C-Note Imperial Pale Ale, Proletariat Red, L.S.D. (Lompoc Special Draft), Stout Out Loud, Fool's Golden Ale, Kick Axe Pale Ale, rotating IPA. Seasonals: Monster Mash Porter, C-Sons Greetings, Batch 69 Baltic Porter, Old Tavern Rat Barleywine, Heaven's Helles, Cellar D'or Saison, Franc'ly Brewdolph, 8 Malty Nights, and dozens more.

The Pick: C-Note Imperial Pale. When your flagship is that half-step between a pale ale and an IPA, it's gotta be the crowd-pleasing sort. Toffee notes in the malt bill provide just enough malt base (6.9 percent ABV) to anchor this beer while letting the citrusy and spicy hop regimen (100 IBUs) steal the show.

become. It's my favorite of the Lompoc pubs, primarily because it's a short walk for me, but also because it's small and cozy, and I can hang out on the patio with my boys (son and dog). Oaks Bottom came along two years later, along with Jim Parker, who briefly served as a business partner, the result of Younger being out of the country at the time when the opportunity arose. Fechter credits Parker for introducing Oregon to the "Totcho" (nachos on a bed of tots, as basic and brilliant as sliced bread) that he thinks Parker picked up somewhere back in Colorado.

That same year, up in the Boise neighborhood, the final—and ultimately largest—puzzle piece fell into place. Much like the Hedge House opened in Richmond before this Southeast neighborhood started popping, this section of Portland's Northeast quadrant was not commercially developed the way North Williams is now. An Old Lompoc employee nicknamed Boozanne dubbed the newest pub The Fifth Quadrant (5Q for short), riding that Lompoc tongue-in-cheek whimsy again. Within a year they added a 15-barrel system that's now Lompoc's only one since the New Old Lompoc location shut down. (It reopened in 2013 in the same location, sans brewery, in a new LEED Gold building).

The brewpub is by far the biggest of the Lompoc pubs, offering plenty of indoor and outside seating. (What's better than chowing down on a burger and quaffing a pint with the smell of hot wort in the air?) Then in 2009, it upped its game. Sidebar opened in the attached space around the corner. Those barrels completely lining the walls of the tasting room? Yep, they're aging a number of fun projects under Keilty's reign that are frequently only tapped on-premises. Maybe you'll find a Belgian-style ale wherein they're experimenting with currants. Or you might happen upon a vintage of one of their eight holiday beers even in the middle of summer. One of my favorite lineups featured various iterations of Black Dawn Imperial Coffee Stout in which they played with different blends or single-origin coffee beans from Ristretto Coffee Roasters across the street.

The tasting room, Fechter told me as we sat there chatting, was intended to be "an awesome space and sit right among what we're doing." He followed this statement by drawing my attention to the extra touches, like the fireplace, or moreover the portrait hanging above it. It's of Don Younger, painted by the *Oregonian's* beer writer John Foyston just before Younger passed away in 2011. (I'm not saying Foyston missed his calling, but I've never seen a painting of a beer character that's as good or captivating.) It's one of the many things at the heart of Lompoc Brewing.

Remember Fechter said only sticking to a few core beers would be no fun, and you'll know why anywhere from twenty-five to as many as forty seasonal offerings come out of the brewery. Fechter said the spring release of Batch 69 Baltic Porter is a personal favorite of his, which pours a cola brown and opens with dark roasted coffee notes before warming to something akin to an imperial nut brown ale. Beyond these, he noted that his pubs are neighborhood gathering places where patrons catch a Timbers soccer game on TV or watch as their pint glasses fill and then empty. The variety, the events, and the vibe all speak to his mission: "We just wanna have fun, man."

Lompoc Brewing

Opened: 1996.

Owner: Jerry Fechter.

Brewer: Bryan Keilty.

System: 15-barrel.

Annual production: 3,500 barrels.

Distribution: Oregon and Washington mostly.

Hours: Monday through Thursday, 11 a.m. to midnight, Friday and Saturday, 11 a.m. to 1 a.m.; Sunday, 11 a.m. to 11 p.m.

Tours: By appointment only.

Takeout beer: Growler fills, bombers, and kegs.

Gift shop: Shirts and stuff on the wall.

Food: Comfort food. The meatloaf sandwich made with sirloin and bacon and topped with fried onions is the winner. At the Oaks Bottom location, get the Totchos (nachos made with tater tots)!

Extras: "Tightwad Tuesdays" feature $2.50 pints. Patios at all the pubs. Specialty beer tastings at Sidebar throughout the year. Annual "Chowder Challenge" held at 5Q in February.

Other locations: Lompoc Tavern (1620 NW 23rd Ave., Portland; 503-894-9374; 16 taps). Hedge House (3412 SE Division St., Portland; 503-235-2215; 12 taps). Oaks Bottom (1621 Bybee Blvd., Portland; 503-232-1728; 10 taps).

The Mash Tun Brewpub

2204 Northeast Alberta Street, Portland, OR 97211
(503) 548-4491 • TheMashTunBrewpub.com

The Mash Tun Brewpub (named for every brewery's top four most important piece of equipment) has been open since 2005, making it a veritable veteran of Beervana. It gets little lip service but has something better than blog-love: patrons. The place with no sign above the entrance, just around the corner on Northeast 22nd Avenue from its Alberta Street address, is usually packed by evening, with patrons either in the beer garden during pleasant weather or inside on a chilly night.

The interior is mostly wood (well, obviously the brewhouse, visible through picture windows and recently expanded from 3.5 to 7 barrels, is stainless steel) and there's a pool table in the center, plus a dartboard tucked behind the front door. Numerous hanging plants are a nice, lively touch.

Two hallmarks of a good neighborhood spot are a friendly, attentive wait staff and reasonable prices—hence the unwavering local support. The fact that regulars can enjoy seeing their barroom scribbles in beer coaster or bathroom chalkboard formats is a fun bonus. And speaking of art, the Mash Tun is at the epicenter of the Alberta Arts District, a Boho if gentrifying neighborhood where "Last Thursdays," an unpermitted art crawl, brings in Portlanders in droves. So while the brewpub may not be a local or tourist foodie darling like Aviary restaurant and the original Salt & Straw ice cream shop that has made this part of Alberta very hip, it doesn't pretend to be trendy.

First and foremost, it's about the house beer. I know I've always opted for the IPA on tap, like Keelhaul IPA. It's billed as "herbal and citrus" hop flavors with "sweet and nutty" maltiness, but I get lots of lemon and don't mind the lack of ballyhooed malt backbone (though at 7.2 percent ABV it's there). My wife, the dark beer fan, always gets the Penfold Porter, then gets it again. It's got good,

Beers brewed: Year-round: Alberta Pale Ale, Concordia Cream Ale, rotating IPAs (including Summit, Broken Rudder, and Keelhaul), ESB, Penfold Porter, Kilgore Stout. Seasonals: Many, such as Scottish Ale, Razorback Red, and Punkinhed Ale.

The Pick: Concordia Cream Ale. At 4.5 percent ABV, this is a true session beer with flaked corn that makes it light (but not too light) and a touch sweet (but not too sweet). Sufficient local aroma hops make it palatable to beer lovers and/or lightweights.

malt-driven cocoa flavor. Because the IPAs are not drink-all-night beers, at least for me, I also like to go for the Concordia Cream Ale, named after the neighborhood. It's "sessionable" at 4.5 percent and emulates the clean starkness of a light lager, but with sufficient flavor so it appeals to lightweights like me. Best and most unusual of all, The Mash Tun does pitchers. The cream ale is the portrait of a pitcher beer.

All in all, The Mash Tun is a good snapshot of how far brewpubs have come since the early to mid years of craft brewing, yet is quaintly frozen in time before the recent epoch. Maybe it's the caveman in me, but I think this analog brewpub is a pretty good respite in this digital age. And the fact that it's always crammed proves we Neanderthals travel in packs.

The Mash Tun Brewpub

Opened: 2005.
Owner and brewer: Christian Bravard.
System: 7 barrel.
Annual production: 200 barrels.
Hours: Daily, noon to midnight.
Takeout beer: Growlers and corny kegs filled.
Food: Lots of burgers. The food is often organic, with many vegetarian-friendly options.
Extras: Minors until 9 p.m. Free wi-fi, pool, darts, and jukebox. Awesome patio.

McMenamins

Headquarters: 430 North Killingsworth Street, Portland, OR 97217
(503) 223-0109 • McMenamins.com
Twitter @CaptainNeon

Sometimes I think about who'd be on the Mt. Rushmore of this-or-that, the people who are most historically significant in a particular field. It's a fruitless exercise, but fun to think about. The problem with who'd go on the Mt. Rushmore of Oregon beer (Henry Weinhard and Don Younger, for starters) is that there are more than four "musts," and it's all the more challenging because Mike McMenamin and his younger brother Brian are two different people whom we conveniently lump together as the McMenamins. They are so monumental in the history, as well as the modern landscape of Oregon beer, that maybe the company gets its own Mt. Rushmore: Brian, Mike, Ruby, and Hammerhead. Ruby's not a brewer; she's a bewitching raspberry ale. And Hammerhead, even though he can be seen marching en masse in the annual Oregon Brewers Fest parade in his trademark denim overalls, is a Northwest pale ale. In many ways, their story starts in 1985 with a crucial bill that legalized brewpubs in the state, but that was the main event they'd been training for.

"Our dad drank beer. We always liked beer," Brian said, sitting down with me in the Chapel Pub, their headquarters in Northeast Portland since 2006, to talk about the company's past, present, and future. As Portland natives and self-described "beer freaks," Brian and Mike "snuck up to Washington and tried different beers that Oregon didn't have. We decided to open a pub together and sell every beer we could get." As one of the original owners of Produce Row in industrial Southeast Portland, founded in 1974, he recalled carrying around one hundred beers in bottles, cans, or draft. Brian officially came on board in 1980 when he turned twenty-one, and three years later he and Mike opened their first joint venture: The Barley Mill Pub. When the fifty-year-old space with a colorful history as various taverns became available, they took their first step toward building a regional empire. The barley mill that greets all guests—no longer just barflies but families, too—is the same one used by Chuck Coury at his ephemeral but groundbreaking Cartwright Brewing Co. (1979–1982) in Portland, Oregon's first post–Prohibition brewery. Preserving history, supporting the neighborhood with a gathering place, and imbuing it with their personal favorite music by the Grateful Dead (among the characters gracing the pub's mural, you'll find Jerry Garcia standing behind Mike and Brian) have become the three cornerstones of their business.

By 1985, they had several pubs selling everyone's beer they could get in stock. Together with the Widmer brothers, the Ponzis (Bridge-Port), and Portland Brewing's Fred Bowman and Art Larrance (now of Raccoon Lodge and Cascade, respectively), they wrote a bill that created the law legalizing brewpubs in Oregon. "It was fun going through the process," Brian says now, perhaps clouded by thirty years of house beers. By everyone else's account it was an arduous process, yet for every entrepreneur who opens a brewpub today as quick as greased lightning, it's because of that law that has barely changed since passing.

It's important to note that the McMenamins don't operate a brewery but rather twenty-four brewing facilities across Oregon and Washington (and they view Northern California as a natural extension in the future). Seventeen of those are in Oregon, beginning with the Hillsdale Brewery in Southwest Portland that opened in 1985. What's more, they now run fifty-eight total pubs across Oregon, meaning each of the breweries provides kegged beer to a couple additional locations. "The pub's only as strong as your community is," Brian said during the Oregon Public Broadcasting special *Beervana*, and continued, "Your community has to support you. So if you're not there for your community, then you're not going to do very well."

The good thing about having so many properties is that no matter where in the Pacific Northwest you find yourself, there's likely a McMenamins nearby. The bad thing is that I still haven't made my way to all of the ones even in Oregon. I particularly enjoy the Chapel Pub HQ on North Killingsworth. The anteroom features a potbelly stove for fragrant warmth in the wintertime and inviting patio/beer garden during bouts of sunshine. It's cavernous, with all the rooms spilling off of rooms. It was initially both a wedding chapel and a mortuary, built circa 1932, and it's a fitting metaphor for what they do. Most of their locations started out as something splendid and beautiful—these include a grand ballroom, a Masonic Lodge, a Methodist church, and a Southern Pacific Railroad depot—but died as all living entities do. McMenamins renovates them and marries their love of beer and community to revive them as new hubs for the neighborhood. They're never just about the beer, and they're each unique. Many host live music; some present concerts by national acts. Four of the breweries are embedded into hotels because what better way to do a beercation in Oregon than crash at an old Catholic school or county poor farm and enjoy a house-brewed nightcap down the hall or in your room itself?

As for those beers, there are four standard, company-wide brands that every brewer must make. Hammerhead is a pale ale mostly marked by Cascade hops. With the McMenamins' Irish roots they loved Guinness, so the dark beer category is covered by chocolaty Terminator Stout (but March sees the return of their seasonal Irish Stout). And obviously there's an IPA, although within that realm the individual brewers get some leeway. As a matter of fact, each brewer gets plenty of space to flex his or her artistic muscles. "Fearlessness," said Brian, has been the bedrock of their brewing aspirations from the beginning. "You can't be afraid to fail." It sounds utterly absurd today, but there used to be a government-approved list of ingredients for making beer—fruit wasn't on it. There's an entire Fruit Beer Festival in Portland now, but in 1985, when blackberries or rhubarb found their way into different batches in Hillsdale—to say nothing of the Mars bars sacrificed in another brew—it was radical bordering on heresy. Ruby ("It was originally Ruby Tuesday but we had to change it because of the burger chain") was first brewed in 1986 and uses 42 pounds of puréed Oregon raspberries. Collectively, it's the best-selling beer of the bunch.

The reason I didn't nominate a brewer for the McMenamins Rushmore is because there's never been one primary person. The first to hold the honor was Ron Wolf, whose brewing résumé included the vaunted original craft brewery Anchor in San Francisco. He only brewed a total of thirteen batches in Hillsdale, but they included that first fruit beer (he plucked blackberries off the back fence) and Terminator. Today, he's a sommelier at The Painted Lady, the esteemed restaurant in the heart of the Willamette Valley wine country.

Over the last thirty years there have been several dozen brewers. Some move from brewpub to brewpub within the McMenamins empire. Some have gone on to found their own. Legendary Oregon brewer John Harris was among the first at Hillsdale in 1986, then moved to Bend to work at a little brewpub called Deschutes before moving back to Portland, where he was enlisted by Full Sail; in 2013 he created his own Ecliptic Brewing. Jack Harris (no relation) moved up the coast from Lincoln City's Lighthouse Brewery to start Fort George in Astoria, and fellow Lighthouse alum Jason Webb now helps people brew their own at Portland U-Brew. After Steve van Rossem's gig at High Street in Eugene, he helped kickstart Block 15's success in Corvallis, and more recently christened Planktown's brewery in Springfield. Jason McAdam started at the Crystal Brewery on West Burnside and presently slakes thirsts at his Burnside Brewing on East Burnside. And Alex McGaw honed his chops at the Fulton Pub before earning a gold medal at the World Beer Cup for his Two Kilts Brewing Scottish Ale.

"We have a great legacy of our ex-brewers out there in the Oregon industry and beyond," Brian said, which is why the four best-known beers don't really begin to tell the story. There are over one hundred different beers on tap each day across the chain of pubs. Brian reflected on Crystal's European focus, Concordia's British traditions as well as "Northwest big beers," and how the Cornelius Pass Roadhouse "does the crazy ones." But in my experience, they all tinker to some degree. Possibly the biggest beer geek destination of late is Edgefield, the sprawling campus acquired in 1991 in Troutdale between Portland and Hood River. It's the largest of all the breweries, hence the bulk of their 25,000 total barrels brewed each year originate there, and It's also where the McMenamins winery and first distillery are based (they recently added a second distillery at the Roadhouse in Hillsboro). Wine-making began in 1990 and the small on-site vineyard supports their estate-grown Poor Farm Pinot Gris. Plus, the winery license means they get to make their own ciders, crafted entirely from Oregon and Washington fruit. They started distilling house spirits in 1998. Hogshead is their most popular whiskey but they make several, including Monkey Puzzle, dry hopped with Teamaker hops (that contain 0 IBUs) and sweetened with blackberry honey from hives kept on the estate. (As a side note, there's also a McMenamins Coffee Roasters located in Portland's Irvington neighborhood that services all the pubs with fair-trade beans.)

Thanks to having access to the freshest wine, whiskey, brandy and other barrels, the cask-aged beers coming out of here are fantastic. A rum-aged chocolate stout with vanilla beans sampled during my last trip to Edgefield still haunts me. "Beer, wine, spirits . . . yeah, I like it all," said Brian through a grin. This also presents them the opportunity to pour sample flights of beers alongside the whiskeys they were aged in. Naturally, used barrels make their way to other facilities. Despite the occasional intra-company competition like the Hillsdale Brewfest, where the winning beer gets to represent the company at the Oregon Brewers Festival, there's certainly a fraternity/sorority of McMenamins brewers.

"Mike would never allow one central brewing facility," said Brian. "That would kill the whole thing." Likewise, none of the breweries are the same, even if the early ones all feature grundy tanks shipped from England. Grundies have been dubbed the Model T's of the first wave of craft breweries, and the McMenamins ones are generally adorned with their classic style of art, many of which feature characters that are part of the company's lore. Lyle Hehn, who's been a full-time member of the staff for over twenty years, is one of the three full-time contracted artists. Hehn and his colleagues tell the stories of each property through pictures painted on walls, ceilings, fermentation tanks, exposed plumbing, and virtually any surface they so desire. The Black Rabbit appears all over Edgefield as a semi-unofficial mascot. People would abandon all sorts of pets near the farm, and Brian explained that the gardeners loved to take in the strays. Most iconic among McMenamins characters, of course, are the Ruby Witch and Hammerhead. "Those came from Lyle. And if you ask him about them ten times," said Brian, "he'll give you ten different answers."

Even though McMenamins is a chain, it's clear that every property has its own history (Tim Hills is the official company historian), character, and distinctive features. "We're anti-cookie cutter," Brian said earnestly. "Even the fact that we're a chain wrangles me." Some locations have movie theaters; some have spas. The Gearhart Hotel & Sand Trap Pub includes one of the oldest eighteen-hole courses west of the Mississippi and, being Irish, Brian professed, "Yes, we grew up playing that silly game." Perhaps sillier still is the disc golf played with proprietary Frisbees—the Grand Lodge in Forest Grove offers a ten-hole course.

It's a wide-ranging concept that is as funky as the brothers themselves. From the smallest pubs to the largest hotel properties, each acts as its own communal utopia with garden-fresh food when possible; beer fresh from the outbuilding, basement, or wherever there's room for a brewery; and colorful characters painted on the walls and usually straddling bar stools. There are more than two thousand employees (brewers, painters, a historian, and hundreds of servers among them) but it maintains a family vibe, and in fact Mike's three kids work within the company. (Neither of Brian's does at the moment.) An organization like this could and should exist in every region of the country, yet there's only one on this scale. And gradually, as the right opportunities present themselves, they'll continue to scale up. "We're pretty stubborn old Irish guys," said Brian. "We keep working on them . . . If it feels good and it's fun, we'll keep adding places."

McMenamins

Opened: 1983.

Owners: Brian and Mike McMenamin.

Brewers: 30-plus.

Annual production: 25,000 barrels across the board.

Distribution: Fifty-eight pubs from north to south.

Hours: See individual entries.

Gift shop: Yes, huge ones.

Food: Wide-ranging menus of pub staples.

McMenamins Concordia Brewery at Kennedy School

5736 Northeast 33rd Avenue, Portland, OR 97211
(503) 249-7459 • McMenamins.com/KennedySchool
Twitter @CaptainNeon

Fun, funky Kennedy School offers fifty-seven rooms, some of which are former classrooms from when the McMenamins renovated this elementary school, built in 1913 but expelled in 1975. Twenty-two years after the school closed, they fashioned it into an epic complex with guest rooms, a great indoor-outdoor restaurant, a World War I victory garden (now a community garden), four proper bars, and the Concordia Brewery, named for this residential neighborhood.

The brewery is tucked into what used to be the little girls' room. No jokes necessary. Equally humorous: The cigar bar is fittingly called Detention. The Honors Bar is smoke-free. The Boiler Room (in the actual boiler room) is the coolest, most ornate of the campus's bars, all of which are off-limits to kids (like those displayed in the historic photos). This otherwise family-friendly locale hosts "Mommy Matinees" where kids can run amok Tuesdays through Thursdays. All other screenings are perfect for relaxing on homey sofas with fresh beer.

McMenamins Concordia Brewery at Kennedy School

Opened: 1997.
Owners: Mike and Brian McMenamin (see page 92).
Brewers: Matt Carter and Dave Kosanke.
System: 7-barrel.
Annual production: 1,675 barrels.
Hours: Daily; bars and restaurant hours vary from 7 a.m. to 1 a.m. (Friday and Saturday until 2:30 a.m.).
Tours: Walk-in tours when the brewer is available.
Takeout beer: Growlers.
Gift shop: Loads of apparel, souvenirs, and bottles of house-brand beers, wines, and spirits.
Food: Burgers, sandwiches, and salads. Try the A+ Pastrami with Hammerhead braised onions on a house pretzel bun with Terminator mustard.

Beers brewed: Year-round: Hammerhead Pale Ale, Terminator Stout, Ruby, IPA. Seasonals: King's Landing IPA, Oatmeal Porter, Concordia Pale Ale, and a Concordia Barrel Series that includes Whiskey Widow.

Migration Brewing Co.

2828 Northeast Glisan Street, Portland, OR 97232
(503) 206-5221 • MigrationBrewing.com
Twitter @MigrationBrew

The Twenty-Eighth Avenue corridor gets paid short shrift around town. Maybe Twenty-Eighth's lack of goodly, hoodly identity explains the oversight when people list the city's top destinations. But in my opinion, the businesses—predominantly outstanding restaurants and cafés—that stretch from Northeast Glisan Street to Southeast Pine Street qualify as Portland's best kept secret for a walking street. How excellent that it's bookended by Migration Brewing on the north end (in Kerns) and Coalition Brewing on the south end.

Having said that, roll into Migration on a sunny day, or during a Blazers broadcast or Timbers game, or some live music, and it's clear this is no unknown hole in the wall. The year-round Terry's Porter is obviously a porter, and it commemorates the former Blazers point guard. During soccer season, Timbers Ale is a spruced-up version of Clem's Cream Ale and that's not figurative—they literally add spruce tips.

Four friends—Salt Lake City native Colin Rath, his Wisconsin-bred roommate Mike Branes, and Portland natives and brothers McKean and Eric Banzer-Lausberg—brought Migration to life in an abandoned radiator shop destined for greener pastures. Well, the hop bines that grow in and around the beer garden during the summer add some greenness, but it's mostly cement topped with enough wooden picnic tables to seat around sixty. "Having a patio was our dealbreaker. It was crucial," Rath told me as the summer sun beat down. Good thing I had Clem's Cream Ale in hand. I opted for the regular draft version, though the cream was also available on nitro. The story behind the name is that Clem was Eric and McKean's dad, who sadly passed away as they were opening the brewery.

"No one's from Portland," said Rath, though of course some folks like the Banzer-Lausberg

Beers brewed: Year-round: Migration Pale Ale, Terry's Porter, Clem's Cream Ale, Luscious Lupulin IPA, Glisan Street Dry Hop, Old Silenus Strong Ale. Seasonals: Cross Pollination, four seasonal IPAs (Life O'Rye-ly Spring IPA, 503 Summer IPA, Better Off Red Fall IPA, and Black Hearted Winter IPA), PDX Kolsch, and a Migrator Series of rotating world beer styles.

The Pick: Clem's Cream Ale. Always on draft and often on nitro, Clem's Cream is super refreshing and befitting the amazing beer garden when it's sundrenched and you don't want those rays skunking your hoppy Luscious Lupulin IPA.

brothers are exceptions to that rule. "Migration just sums up Portland." But Rath threw in the fact that this bike-happy pub also respects those who commute by bicycle as a form of daily migration.

Whether you ride in, walk in, or—ack!—drive up, you'll find this airy spot frequently packed. Luckily, it's made even roomier since they annexed the adjacent address, hence the name "Annex" for the additional 2,000 square feet of indoor-outdoor space. People play darts in the back, folks make sure they don't spill beer on their laptops (there's free wi-fi), and anyone who likes the idea of discounted pitchers during happy hour can enjoy those screened games. A pint and a meatball sub with fries are always ten bucks. I like it with the MPA (Migration Pale Ale).

That was Branes's first beer here, designed to appeal to newbies and hopheads alike. Branes is indeed the brainchild behind each of the house beers. Rath intuited that his homebrewing roommate would fill the role perfectly. "It was Mike's dream for years and he would've probably done this just further down the road," he said. "He was ready." Clearly.

Beyond the core beers Branes designed, he creates a new IPA each season. Don't let the 503 IPA summer release fool you into thinking it's some India Session Ale. It's got 7.3 percent ABV and 80 IBUs. Keep it in a shady spot if you're drinking it on the patio to avoid those prodigious yet delicate hops from getting light-struck (skunky). The Migrator Series is another seasonal rotation wherein a new ingredient or non-house yeasts might get called upon, but while they're experimentations, they're often nods to classic styles and never gimmicky. Migrations, after all, are designed as something to which you return.

Migration Brewing Co.

Opened: 2010.
Owners: Colin Rath, Mike Branes, Eric Banzer-Lausberg, and McKean Banzer-Lausberg.
Brewer: Mike Branes.
System: 7-barrel.
Annual production: 2,000 barrels.
Distribution: Self-distributed around Portland.
Hours: Monday through Saturday, 11 a.m. to midnight; Sunday, 11 a.m. to 10 p.m.
Tours: By appointment only.
Takeout beer: Growlers and limited bottles.
Gift shop: T-shirts, hoodies, a pint glass, and cozies.
Food: Snacks (pulled pork nachos!), burgers, and salads.

Natian Brewery

1321 Northeast Couch Street, Portland, OR 97232
(971) 678-7116 • NatianBrewery.com
Twitter @NatianBrewery

Founder Ian McGuinness used to brew on a 40-gallon system that produced 320 pints a pop. Put another way, the tiny Natian Brewery would've had to brew 580 batches just to give each of the 185,672 members of the Rogue Nation, the fan club of one of Oregon's largest breweries, a pint. Then came their 1,000 percent, three-year-long, overnight growth.

Natian was one of the earliest nanobreweries and was also, I'm pretty sure, the first brewery project on the crowd-funding platform Kickstarter. Back in mid-2009, a month and a half after Kickstarter launched, McGuinness and his girlfriend Natalia (they Brangelina'ed their names into the company's moniker, which was cute but now they're no longer an item) raised 20 percent above their $1,500 ask. Nanobreweries run on nanobudgets, and McGuinness doesn't talk about the "little financial boost" because at the time, beermakers turning to the arts-driven, crowd-sourcing site was being debated. (During the subsequent four years, well over one hundred aspiring professional brewers spare-changed for brewery bucks via Kickstarter.)

But there's only so much beer a nanobrewery can make on alms for the pour. Natian's nanobrewery didn't take up much room, so McGuinness got permission to tuck the apparatus into the corner of the bottling and canning company that is his daytime gig (he's the quality control manager). He found himself brewing daily so he upsized to a 10-barrel system in late 2012. Ironically, at the bank where he applied for a loan, the folks who control the vault grilled him: "So you just think magically, overnight, your business is going to grow tenfold?" The quote is his, uttered to me at the unveiling of the new system, though probably not the loan officer's verbatim.

After nearly a year of volleying with the financial institution that allowed Natian to grow, McGuinness announced the next step publicly, which was

Beers brewed: Year-round: Undun Blonde Ale, Lumberjane Stout, Big Block IPA, Old Grogham Imperial IPA, CuDA CDA. Seasonals: Makeshift Organic Golden, Autumn Chocolate Amber, Destination Honey Red, La Luz Summer Ale, Hint O'Mint, Pu-Pu-Pu Pumpkin Ale.

The Pick: Undun Blonde. I often find blonds bland, but this one's on the hoppy side for the style. The nice, light body allows the citric lemony goodness to carry the flavor beyond chewing hay.

actually what increased interest. "That's when I saw the biggest spike," he said of the surge in social media interest. Like their budgets, nanobreweries have nanofollowings. "When Burnside [Brewing] or Gigantic [Brewing] opened up, they immediately had more Facebook followers than I do." A primary difference is that Burnside, five blocks from Natian, opened as a brewpub and Gigantic premiered with a tasting room and patio. I include this not to taunt Natian, but to emphasize how far the brewery has come since tiptoeing into Portland's brewing scene. Most recently, McGuinness is looking for a space to open a tasting room.

In the meantime, Natian has dozens of taps around town and frequently concocts unusual offerings such as the spearmint-honey minty Hint O'Mint and Autumn Chocolate Amber, an amber-hued beer with some hop character (rather than a dark roasted stout) that was once poured at an Aquariva Restaurant Brewer's Dinner, paired with chocolate-braised rabbit drizzled with chocolate balsamic. Having said that, McGuinness focuses on the hoppy half of the brewing spectrum with a slew of IPAs including Big Block, Old Grogham Imperial (which began as a winter seasonal IPA aged on rum-soaked oak spires for added wintry warmth), and pitch-black CuDA (a Cascadian Dark Ale).

Furthermore, Natian's tallboy pint cans, filled with four year-round beers including some IPAs and Undun Blonde to lighten things up, pop up more now that he's not filling just sixteen cans a minute like in the early days. Some of his coworkers at the bottling plant laughed because the canning line is capable of filling eight hundred cans per minute. I asked why he couldn't just use it for a single minute and literally take care of an hour's labor that way. "Because we're honest," he half-lamented, explaining, "The federal government deems it illegal to transport bulk beer." The merits of one pallet of beer being "bulk" are debatable to some, but not to Uncle Sam. Brewers are inherently creative, and the creative solution, thanks entirely to his boss, is that Natian leases the building for a dollar a day. Loophole to the rescue.

Natian Brewery

Opened: 2009.
Owner and brewer: Ian McGuinness.
System: 10-barrel.
Annual production: 250 barrels.
Distribution: Oregon and Pennsylvania (where McGuinness grew up).
Tours: By appointment only.

Occidental Brewing Co.

6635 North Baltimore Avenue, Portland, OR 97203
(503) 719-7102 • OccidentalBrewing.com
Twitter @OccidentalBrews

My favorite destination in St. Johns on the eastern banks of the Willamette in North Portland—before Occidental opened in 2011, anyway—is the family-owned Tulip Pastry Shop, established in 1950. The neighborhood, in many ways, retains that era's aesthetic. Tulip's half maple, half chocolate-dipped, cream-filled bars aren't nearly as flashy or nouveau as the rest of Bridgetown's vaunted doughnut shops and are, in fact, some of my favorite doughnuts in town. My analogy, since this is a brewery guidebook, clearly points to Occidental, not just because it's a family-run company (Dan Engler runs it with his nephew Ben Engler), but mainly because their Continental-style lagers are top-notch and harken back to an earlier age in brewing.

Occidental is located in the shadow of the St. Johns Bridge, the last to cross the river before heading into Washington and the only one that feels like entering a gothic cathedral when driving (or bike riding) across. The brewery's taproom doesn't serve food (you're welcome to BYO) but it does offer a wide area adjacent to the brewhouse for friends (bipedal and furry) to savor the pantheon of Germanic lagers (and one brilliant Czech pilsner). In other words: no ales. Ergo: no IPA. If you need a lot of hops, your best option here is the Altbier with 50 IBUs, but in general, this is a house of balance and sessionability (although some of their seasonals top 6 percent ABV, such as the 7 percent Maibock and winter warmer doppelbock Lucubrator).

When Dan took up homebrewing in 1992, imperial IPAs and oddball adjunct beers weren't really a thing. After trying an imported bottle of Franziskaner circa '94, Dan attempted his first batch of wheat beer. "Hefeweizen interested me early on . . . I'd first traveled to Germany in 1994 and had the opportunity to sample other hefeweizens." As such, he explained, "I got more and more interested in German beers over time." Occidental's

Beers brewed: Year-round: Hefeweizen, Altbier, Kolsch, Dunkel, Pilsner. Seasonals: Maibock, Dunkelweizen, Schwarzbier, Festbier, Lucubrator Doppelbock.

The Pick: Dunkelweizen. Although the flagship Kolsch is a go-to for common beer-drinking scenarios, the return of Dunkelweizen each fall is an ideal way to celebrate the earth-toned season. This murky wheat beer offers similar banana esters to the Bavarian-style hefeweizen, but the toasty malts round out the banana bread-quality that's still a no-nonsense beer.

Altbier, he noted, has its roots "after reading about that style in 1994. I hadn't had it before." (His spin through Germany took him to Bavaria but clearly not Dusseldorf, where alts originated.) For nephew Ben's part, he credits Dan with turning him on to the range of German styles even though he'd worked at a brewpub up in Tacoma during college.

Since the word hefeweizen is somewhat synonymous with a beer that put Portland on the beer map, Widmer Hefeweizen (first sold in 1986), it bears distinguishing that Occidental's Bavarian-style hefe and Widmer's benchmark for American-style hefe are "different animals," said Dan. *Hefe* means "yeast" in German (and *weizen* or *weiss* means "wheat"). The Bavarian yeast lends banana and clove aromas and flavors, and perhaps bubblegum or cotton candy, too. Not so the American version. So really, the two Portland-brewed beers don't even compete. Not to mention Occidental brewed under 1,300 barrels in all of 2013 (capacity is 2,200 barrels) and Widmer's newest fermentation tanks hold 1,750 barrels apiece. In true Widmer fashion, Ben mentioned that Widmer's brewers, Ben Dobler and Doug Rehberg, have come over to help them pitch yeast and offer lab services.

A funny postscript is Dan's recollection of someone from another large brewery, name redacted, who came in upon Occidental's opening its doors and said, "German styles? Oh, good luck with that; we tried that." Craft beer drinkers today are well aware of the breadth of beer styles and explore the flavors and textures of each. Occidental's Kolsch is the bestseller—by a huge margin in the summer—while other brands level out when it's colder and darker. Thirteen percent of volume sells on-premises to regulars from NoPo and beyond, or to frequent tourists who return to the taproom, which is decked out in a large breweriana collection (vintage cans, steins, etc.), world currencies, and a sweet mosaic of their logo made from bottle crowns.

Occidental Brewing Co.

Opened: 2011.
Owners and brewers: Dan Engler (brewmaster) and Ben Engler (brewer).
System: 10-barrel.
Annual production: 1,250 barrels.
Distribution: Oregon, Washington, and British Columbia.
Hours: Wednesday and Thursday, 4 p.m. to 8 p.m.; Friday, 3 p.m. to 8 p.m.; Saturday, noon to 8 p.m.; Sunday, noon to 6 p.m.
Tours: By request.
Takeout beer: Growlers, some canned brands, and kegs from the dock.
Gift shop: An array of hats, hoodies, and tees.

Old Town Brewing Co.

5201 Northeast Martin Luther King Boulevard,
  Portland, OR 97211
(503) 459-4868 • OTBrewing.com
Twitter @OTBrewingCo

Old Town Pizza owner Adam Milne didn't have a hand in establishing the company back in 1974. He was just a kid then. The original location is the one in Old Town Portland, but the owners had opened a few others, now all gone. Little Adam held his ninth birthday party at one in Eugene. Imagine what you'd do if you found out a beloved place from your childhood was about to shut down. If you were in a position to save that place, you'd salvage it, which is what Milne did in 2003.

He wasn't alone. Many say the pizzeria is haunted by the ghost of a woman named Nina (rhymes with Dinah), who purportedly was an, uh, "employee" of the brothel run inside the former hotel built in 1880. And not so much an employee but a prisoner, so it makes sense that many have claimed to witness her, including a former manager and local residents.

Five years after taking over, Milne opened a second Old Town Pizza in Vanport Square in the King neighborhood (three blocks from his home). The space is replete with seating for 250 patrons upstairs or down, including by a fireplace, and on miraculous sunny days there are picnic tables on dual patios. The building was originally a Chevrolet dealership in the 1940s, on what was once Union Avenue some fifty years before it became MLK Boulevard. This one doesn't have a resident ghost, but it has something better: a brewery.

Milne installed a 7-barrel brewery in 2012 and renamed the restaurant Old Town Brewing. He'd actually wanted to open it as a brewpub but didn't want to bite off more than he could chew, he told me as I sipped an imperial pint of a Cascadian dark ale. (In addition to five core beers, there are always a rotating dark beer and a hop-forward beer available, so I'm not sure which handle this

Beers brewed: Year-round: Union Pilsner, Volks Wheat, Shanghai'd IPA, Paulie's Not Irish Red, Vanport Pale Ale. Seasonal: Rotating "dark selections," "hop handles," and "brewer's selection."

The Pick: Cents & Centsibility Fresh Hop Ale. Brewmaster Minister is not an over-the-top guy, so he created a fresh hop ale as a balanced pale ale using 50 pounds of Willamette-grown citrusy Centennial hops, to which the name alludes. This no-nonsense beer rightfully earned gold at the 2013 GABF in the Fresh Hop category.

black and hoppy beer flowed from.) The second restaurant was a big enough endeavor, but the longing for a brewery nagged at him. Now eight beers are available at both spots (and at retailers since they started bottling, beginning with Shanghai'd IPA).

As a matter of fact, the new brewery created a liquid tribute to the pizzeria's fortieth anniversary in 2014—a pre-Prohibition-style lager spiritedly named Nina. At the same time, Old Town received a tribute of its own. Following a 2013 GABF medal, they earned two medals at the 2014 World Beer Cup for Paulie's Not Irish Red and a Kolsch.

If you live within a two-mile radius of the brewery, they'll deliver beer (and pizza, of course) to your door—by bike. Old Town might just be the first brewery (though not the only one at this point) in America to deliver growlers by bicycle. Sooo Portland. Milne ran the growler courier idea by the OLCC, which shot down the idea. But then they checked and called back with the OK because, as his research had shown, there was nothing explicitly forbidding it. In fact, taphouses in the immediate area, like Saraveza Bottle Shop, get kegs delivered on two-wheelers. Another awesome aspect is that the 64-ounce portion costs ten bucks and the growler itself is a standard five bucks, yet they let you swap out your old one when you accept delivery of a new one. Alas, cleaning all the returns is one of brewer Bolt Minister's less glamorous tasks and one I imagine he has allocated to his assistant, Cory McGuinness.

Minister, (his first name, Bolton, is a family name) says his philosophy is, "Like what you drink, drink what you like." He's not one for crazy beers because drinking beer is something you should "enjoy with your friends, your community, [and] your barmates. It shouldn't be a self-indulgent activity where you take yourself too seriously." The philosophy carries over to all facets. He's a fan of classic country music, not steakless sizzling new country. (He organized a George Jones tribute beerfest as a wake for "The Possum.") His previous brewing experience at a few other Northwest breweries came from pubs that likewise emphasize community and casual dining. I agree with him that a pizzeria is not the kind of place you come to with your family or buddies only to ignore them while paying exclusive attention to what's in your glass. "When you geek out you miss out," he added.

Maybe that's why his ideal pairing, if you need to call it that, is an imperial pint of Union Pilsner (remember, this used to be Union Avenue) with the Margherita pizza: straightforward, classic, and nothing froo-froo about it. The wheat ale contains coriander and a touch of ginger. It'd go well with a meaty pizza, and I'll note that the sausage is made in-house. But really, he added, "Every beer goes with pizza!"

Old Town Brewing Co.

Opened: 2012.

Owner: Adam Milne.

Brewers: Bolt Minister (brewmaster) and Cory McGuinness (assistant brewer).

System: 7-barrel.

Annual production: 500 barrels.

Distribution: Two pizzerias and a few other accounts.

Hours: Sunday through Wednesday, 11:30 a.m. to 10 p.m.; Thursday through Saturday, 11:30 a.m. to 11 p.m.

Tours: By request.

Takeout beer: Growlers and half-barrel kegs.

Gift shop: Apparel.

Food: Pizza! Thick or thin. Try the Margherita.

Extras: Beer (and pizza) deliveries by bike.

Other location: Old Town Pizza & Taproom (226 NW Davis St., Portland; 503-222-9999).

StormBreaker Brewing

832 North Beech Street, Portland, OR 97227
(971) 703-4516 • StormBreakerBrewing.com
Twitter @StormBreakerPDX

Before Amnesia Brewing's brewer relaunched as StormBreaker, upon mentioning heading to Amnesia someone responded, "Who *wouldn't* want to go there on a Sunday afternoon?" It's on the south end of North Mississippi, an excellent patch of Northeast Portland. That wasn't the case when Amnesia opened in 2003. A decade later, the owner morphed it into a production brewery in Washougal, Washington, yielding brewer Rob Lutz and partner Dan Mallick this turnkey operation with a killer location—especially on sunny days if there's an open spot.

"Summers here are no brainers," Lutz said, but much of the year the sun makes like a unicorn and feels purely mythical. For those days, he said, "We wanted to have a cool bar that people would want to hang out at. We added beer and whiskey pairings and craft cocktails with beer ingredients." White Hopper uses vodka infused with citrusy Amarillo hops and entails puréed tangerines and peaches.

Lutz explained, "We tried to make [StormBreaker] more inviting," meaning a policy change from Amnesia by allowing minors (Mallick's a dad) and overhauling the menu from Amnesia's tasty but utilitarian grilled bratwursts to include a Minneapolis-style Juicy Lucy burger (the cheese is on the inside) and healthier fare including spiced lentils and charred cauliflower with hazelnut Romanesco, which pair well with dry-hopped Mississippi Red or the saisons Lutz is devising.

StormBreaker Brewing

Opened: 2014.

Owners and brewers: Rob Lutz and Dan Mallick.

System: 7-barrel.

Annual production: 800 barrels (planned).

Distribution: Oregon.

Hours: Sunday and Monday, noon to 10 p.m.; Tuesday through Thursday, noon to 11 p.m.; Friday and Saturday, noon to midnight.

Takeout beer: Growlers and bottles coming soon.

Gift shop: Shirts, hoodies, and growlers.

Food: Stormburgers and sandwiches, salads, and finger food aplenty.

Beers brewed: Year-round: Mississippi Red, Cloud Ripper IPA, Savage Nimbus DIPA, Opacus Stout, Total ReKolsch, Right as Rain Pale.

Upright Brewing

240 North Broadway, Suite 2, Portland, OR 97227
(503) 735-5337 • UprightBrewing.com
Twitter @UprightBrewing

Upright Brewing began as a straightforward, farmhouse-slanting brewery with four core beers. But owner-brewer Alex Ganum has taken his affinity for jazz to the next level by improvising dozens of rare beers—often riffed as part of the Sole Composition series. In true freeform style, Upright's beers now span beyond Franco-Belgo inspirations to classic German ones such as a Leipzig-style Gose, the year-round, draft-only Engelberg Pilsner, and various British bitters, among others. Musically, their beers have paid tribute to Frank Zappa, The Clash, the Bad Brains, and Captain Beefheart, the latter quite literally with a beer brewed with grilled beef hearts. Fear not, no others contain offal. But if you can find a bottle of peachy Fantasia, made to resemble a peche lambic, it's awfully good. Ganum said their affinity for diverse brewing styles mirrors their love of music. "We're huge jazz fans, but we listen to everything. We don't want to limit ourselves or get too hung up on our brand. We're just having fun down here."

"Down here" refers to being shoehorned into the basement of the Leftbank Building, centrally located in the Rose Quarter. (Note: There's no sign out front.) The below-level tasting room is in the same space as the brewery with its open fermentation tanks, where stacked barrels aren't mere decoration but always have something intriguing maturing inside. The colorful bass clef painting honors Charles Mingus, the upright bass player (hence the name Upright.) "Mingus is really special to me," Ganum said. "I'd call him one of the best American composers of the century, no question. He wasn't just a bass player—he was a really phenomenal composer." Rounding out the musical vibe, where other tasting rooms would've built an actual bar, bartender Brent Small often spins vinyl and a live bluesman jams on Sundays. Maybe if free jazz were something you drank, it'd taste like Upright beers.

Beers brewed: Year-round: Four, Five, Six, Seven, Engelberg Pilsner. Seasonals: Fantasia, Billy the Mountain, Fatali Four, Oyster Stout, Late Harvest, Gose, and the Sole Composition series of one-off creations.

The Pick: Sole Composition. For something new and exotic, look to the Sole Composition series, typically composed of barrel-aged versions of the numbered beers such as Four (saison) or Six (rye saison), with added fruit and wild yeast for results that are approachably tart, refreshingly novel, or both.

As for the beers—and please allow me to riff off the musical motif—sometimes Upright plays it straight, a la Wynton Marsalis, when they're making Engelberg Pils, and other times they improvise like they're Miles frickin' Davis, exemplified by the soulful De La Six. Using their quotidian Six—a darker rye ale—as their launching pad, safflower, lemon peel, and rooibos tea are blended in before aging the whole she-bang in gin barrels for a mellifluous aroma and semi-tart taste. Likewise, Four—a light, bready saison with notes of key lime zest and banana peel—gets treated to various ingredients ranging from fatali chili peppers (Fatali Four), wherein the heat dissipates as it ages in wine or gin barrels, to cherry purée (Four Play), soured for a year in Pinot Noir barrels with wild yeasts. They throw in whole cherries, stems and all, for a similar beer called Cherry Four.

Beyond popping into the tasting room and discovering what one-off beer is on draft, a chunk of the excitement emanates from finding something equally obscure in bottles. Upright always has 50 to 60 barrels going, and each one Ganum called a labor of love, which is why there's often a two-bottle limit "just to get them around." It's fair to say that anyone in Portland who maintains a personal beer cellar has some space dedicated to Upright.

Finally, because it's Upright's tasting room and not a pub, I recommend heading over to Grain & Gristle (1473 Northeast Prescott Street) a couple of miles away in the Sabin neighborhood, which Ganum co-owns. The fried egg burger is a true classic and pairs quite well with Five, one of Upright's hoppiest offerings. Or partake of Portland's most important meal of the day, the weekend brunch, and ask if they've got any bottles left of the red wine-aged Coffee Stout to go with those bacon pancakes.

Upright Brewing

Opened: 2009.

Owner: Alex Ganum.

Brewers: Alex Ganum, Gerritt III, and Bobby Birk.

System: 10-barrel.

Annual production: 1,250 barrels.

Distribution: Oregon, Washington, British Columbia, Northern California, and Paris.

Hours: Friday, 4:30 p.m. to 9 p.m.; Saturday and Sunday, 1 p.m. to 6 p.m.; open pre-Blazers home games, 6 p.m. to tipoff.

Tours: The brewery is in the tasting room.

Takeout beer: 750-milliliters and growlers.

Gift shop: T-shirts, hoodies, and hats.

Widmer Brothers Brewing

929 North Russell Street, Portland, OR 97227
503-281-2437 • WidmerBrothers.com
Twitter @Widmer_Brothers

When brothers Kurt and Rob Widmer founded their eponymous brewery in 1984, the United States was home to only forty-four brewing companies, an all-time low. By the time they started selling beer in early 1985, "The Big Six" brewers (now down to two) controlled 90 percent of the beer market. The terms "microbrewing" or "craft beer" hadn't been coined, considering fewer than two dozen such goofy breweries had sprouted up (a few of which had already failed). Still, with capital investments topping $50,000 from friends and family, including their father Ray who was easily lured out of retirement, the Widmers sensed they could turn their homebrewing avocation into a professional vocation.

"Our original business plan was to have an on-premises pub and only ten additional accounts, draft only," said older brother Kurt, born in 1951. "The two of us could live off of that." Rob, five years his junior, contrasted this with a glimpse of where their business is today by adding, "We now have 700,000 accounts nationwide." Those accounts are spread across Craft Brew Alliance (CBA), the 2008 merger of Widmer Brothers and Seattle's Redhook, before Kona Brewing came into the fold two years later. Anheuser-Busch InBev owns about a third of CBA via its distribution and equity alliance, though Widmer beers were coming off Budweiser trucks before the Belgian conglomerate bought AB.

Considering Widmer Brothers' beers are nationally available thanks to multiple brewery expansions soaring deep into the millions of dollars, the saga of their early, serendipitous success is a fun one. It's not pegged to their maiden beer, Widmer Alt, created to honor their mother's heritage rooted in Düsseldorf, altbier's provenance.

Beers brewed: Year-round: Hefeweizen, Alchemy Pale Ale, Drop Top Amber Ale, Upheaval IPA, Pitch Black IPA, Nelson Imperial IPA. Seasonals: KGB Russian Imperial Stout (winter), Old Embalmer Barleywine (winter), Columbia Common (spring), Green & Gold Kolsch (Timbers season), Citra Blonde (summer), Okto Festival Ale (fall), Brrr and Brrrbon (fall), Marionberry Hibiscus Gose.

The Pick: Marionberry Hibiscus Gose. Talk about Americanizing German-style wheat beers. This one starts with the resurrected style of a salted weissbier with lactic acid tartness augmented with Oregon's native berry then deepens the magenta hue with dried hibiscus flowers for a phenomenal, sharp treat. Stock up on this seasonal release.

Nor does it stem from their follow-up offering, Weizen, since that was actually a filtered beer that poured crystal clear. At least, it was intended to be. Rob set up the story. "Our filtration was really rudimentary. If the Weizenbier was hazy, people would call and say, 'There's a problem with your beer.' They didn't even taste it, they'd just say it wasn't right."

As we all know, it's their hefeweizen that perpetrated—and cemented—their success, but it came about by a simple request from a Portland bar owner who had requested a third style of beer to offer their patrons particularly keen on bottled hefeweizen imported from Germany. *Hefe* means "yeast" in German, and *weizen* means "wheat," so the beer is characterized by its haziness resulting from leaving all that yeast in suspension. It caught on in Bavaria centuries earlier, but Americans were drinking straw-colored, transparent lagers. "So with the prospect of putting out a beer that looked almost like a glass of orange juice, our concern was that it wouldn't fly," Rob appended.

This was 1986, and there was one other problem. "We only had two fermenters. A third beer was physically impossible to do," said Kurt, before explaining they simply racked a few kegs of Weizen before filtering it at all. "We just gave it to them and said, 'Are you sure you wanna do this?' We thought they were potentially destroying our reputation."

The inverse was true. Widmer Hefeweizen became one of the biggest single-brand success stories in the industry. Kurt shared some stories, funny in hindsight, about upstart and corporate espionage. "There were a lot of people who now have breweries that paraded through our brewery just to see what we were doing. We had guys coming in and videotaping . . . One [brewing company] hired one of our brewers just to explain it to them."

As such, the story of Widmer Brothers Brewing is inextricably linked to wheat beer. I will clarify that the cloudy beer known as hefeweizen, a.k.a. weissbier, is a traditional Bavarian style noted for its banana and clove aroma produced by the particular yeast strain. But the Widmers used their house yeast, which doesn't produce those quintessential banana esters and clove phenols. So hefe purists held a grudge. However, many American palates still enjoyed or even preferred this new "American-style Hefeweizen." My dad's a primary example. Like many, Widmer Hefeweizen served as his gateway craft beer and remains so. Also like many, he butchers the pronunciation. Though he left New York decades ago, he pronounces it "hefer-why-zen" and most just call it "heff," but the Widmers would like one Germanic aspect to carry over: it's pronounced "HAY-fuh-vy-tsen."

As for the copper-colored, hoppy Alt, it can still be found at the Widmer Brothers Pub. Upon moving to their current location, they did eventually open a pub in 1996, the same year they put Hefeweizen in bottles. It looked like a mid-nineties casual-dining restaurant until 2014 when they sharply remodeled it to commemorate their thirtieth anniversary. The brick walls remain, but there's now a communal table. Behind the handsome wood bar, twenty-four taps provide for more specialty beers, their Square Mile brand cider, and draft root beer. The unique beers aren't brewed on-premises. The small batches, Alt and all, come from their 10-barrel pilot brewery tucked into a nook or cranny at the Rose Garden Arena where the Trailblazers (and twelve-time Western Hockey League champion Winterhawks) play.

From producing around 800 barrels their first year in operation to earning Mid-Size Brewing Company of the Year in 2004 at the GABF, to cranking out three-quarters of a million barrels of CBA brands today (a third of which are Widmer beers), it's phenomenal that Hefeweizen accounts for some 40 percent of the brewery's production on the main 250-barrel system with its massive 1,500-barrel fermenters.

But they brew many more styles than that. The recent annual production schedule boasted nearly thirty brands, even with being back down to one year-round Northwest IPA, Upheaval. I dug when they replaced their original, Broken Halo, with the Rotator IPA Series. I don't know how popular they were, but some of my favorites were the Spiced IPA, which incorporated chai tea spices (hence why I couldn't help calling it a ChaiPA), and Shaddock IPA, which complemented the Citra hops already evocative of bitter citrus pith with actual grapefruit peel. I recall speaking with the brothers in 2005, shortly after they'd launched the first in their W Series, an India Pale Ale, which Kurt explained was packed with hops and popular with a niche group of drinkers they called beer geeks. Funny what a difference a handful of years makes.

One other line worth mentioning is Omission, their gluten-free beers or, more accurately, low-gluten beers. For gluten-free "cerevisaphiles," there are finite options, and let's be honest, if you've tried those sorghum-based ones, most suck where flavor is concerned. The kicker with Omission is that these beers are made from traditional ingredients including barley, then deglutenized enzymatically. Food labeled as gluten-free cannot exceed 20 parts per million (ppm) gluten. For comparison's sake, when Widmer Brothers sends beer out for testing, the pale ale comes back showing gluten levels as high as 50–100 ppm, whereas Omission beers indicate 5–6 ppm. Widmer isn't the first to use this process—they're just the first to do it commercially in the United States. Some people with gluten sensitivities scoff, but CBA's CEO, Terry Michaelson, and brewmaster Joe Casey's wife are both diagnosed celiacs. (Michaelson became director at Widmer in 1994, but his diagnosis came six years later.) Omission beers instantly became the best-selling gluten-free beers, and the key lies in the fact that they taste good, even to those of us lucky enough to imbibe all the gluten we want.

Speaking of evolving palates and trends, Widmer Hefeweizen wasn't the first American wheat beer, but deserves credit for its widespread appeal. Their use of wheat hardly stops there. The brothers told me about brewing a tart Berliner Weiss in the early nineties, and I got to try their Lemongrass Wheat Ale (a boozy wheat wine ale) they'd released in 2011. Marionberry Hibiscus Gose began as a one-off in 2012—goses originated in Leipzig roughly a millennium ago—and is brewed with salt, hibiscus flowers, and Oregon-grown berries. It tastes as delicious as it sounds strange.

In the end, it comes back to what beer you find refreshing and simply enjoyable. "I've gone from wanting a flavorful beer, to 'It can't possibly be too bitter,' to going back to wanting it to be more balanced," said Kurt, who's now CBA's chairman of the board. (He and Rob still work five days a week in a shared office with desks facing each other.) "I usually have two beers when I'm drinking beer. If it's too high alcohol, then one and done is no fun. Beer shouldn't be an accomplishment. If the best thing you can say after a pint is, 'I got through that,' where's the pleasure or enjoyment in that?"

At that, Rob, the more social beer geek whose title is Director of Quality, brought up a quote he recalled from a beer blog: "I climbed beer geek mountain and now I'm coming down the other side." And that's where these two position themselves, waiting with full pints and open arms.

Widmer Brothers Brewing

Opened: 1984.

Owners: Kurt Widmer and Rob Widmer.

Brewers: Joe Casey (brewmaster), Doug Rehberg, Ben Dobler, and Matt Licklider.

System: 250-barrel and a 10-barrel pilot, plus breweries in Washington and New Hampshire.

Annual production: 252,000 barrels (Widmer); 726,000 barrels (CBA).

Distribution: National.

Hours: Sunday through Thursday, 11 a.m. to 10:30 p.m.; Friday and Saturday, 11 a.m. to 11 p.m.

Tours: Friday at 2 p.m. and 3 p.m.; Saturday at noon, 1 p.m., 2 p.m., and 3 p.m.; Sunday at 1 p.m. and 2 p.m.

Takeout beer: Growlers, kegs, and cases/six-packs.

Gift shop: Doubles as the reception area, with tons of swag.

Food: American and German favorites, including burgers and schnitzel.

Ambacht Brewing

1060 Northeast 25th Avenue, Suite N, Hillsboro, OR 97124
(503) 828-1400 • Ambacht.us
Twitter @AmbachtAle

Co-owner and brewer Tom Kramer neatly summed up Ambacht's mission: "To do Belgian-inspired ales that are very flavorful but light in body." Not only is Belgium a muse for their rich beers, but so is Hair of the Dog Brewing, way closer to home. The conflux of the two just might lie in a beer called G++. The name is a play off C++ programming language since Intel's Hillsboro offices are down the street. But in the case of the beer, while Ambacht already has a 6.5 percent Golden Farmhouse Ale, G++ is an 8 percent Strong Golden Ale aged in bourbon barrels procured from Hair of the Dog owner Alan Sprints after he has used them to age his Cherry Adam From the Wood.

"We don't like really hoppy beers," Kramer crowed. "We're the only Oregon brewery without an IPA." Well, not the only, but you can count Oregon's IPA-less breweries on one hand.

Kramer's love of Belgian ales stems from his time living in Maastricht, a beautiful Dutch town near Belgium. *Ambacht* is Dutch for "to craft" or "handmade." Funny story: He toyed with calling the brewery Aardvark, another Dutch word that translates to "earth pig." Then he considered Aambacht, adding an extra "A" simply so the brewery would always top alphabetical lists of breweries.

Kramer not only homebrewed all-grain batches but also brewed professionally at the now-defunct Tuck's Brewery, which explains how Ambacht procured a 5-barrel system. (They recently increased to 20 barrels.) He shares brewing duties with Brandy Grobart, his cousin thanks to marrying into Grobart's family. Grobart had brewed extract batches but Kramer got him into mashing with the

Beers brewed: Year-round: Golden Farmhouse Ale, Dark Farmhouse Ale, Golden Rye Farmhouse Ale, Golden Rose Farmhouse Ale, Ginger Farmhouse Ale, Pie Cherry Pale Farmhouse Ale, Pie Cherry Dark Farmhouse Ale. Seasonals: Matzobraü, G++ Belgian Golden, Honey Triple.

The Pick: Ginger Farmhouse Ale. Building on the base of many of Ambacht's beers, the Golden Farmhouse Ale is a honeyed saison and benefits from less-than-subtle fresh ginger for an aroma that's spicier than the swallow but is equally refreshing on its own.

good stuff. The two specialize in Belgian-style farmhouse ales, and in fact it's safe to say that their whole lineup consists of a lighter, golden version and a darker iteration. Beyond the Golden Farmhouse and Dark Farmhouse ales, rye is added, naturally, to Golden Rye Farmhouse, rosehips to Golden Rose, and ginger to Ginger Farmhouse.

I feel confident in proclaiming that there's one farmhouse ale that has never been attempted in Belgium or in any other commercial brewery: Matzobraü. Playing off the breakfast dish *matzo brei*, basically scrambled eggs with matzo and cinnamon, the dark farmhouse ale has been reviewed in the pages of non-beer publications such as *Bon Appétit*. In Kramer's best New York Jewish accent, he explained the beer's genesis: "We were making beer. We [had] extra matzo. We're tired of eating it. Let's throw it into the mash." Some 150 pounds of matzo—now donated by friends and family after Passover because there's only so much of the unleavened crackery bread that one can consume during that week—add extra graininess akin to biscuit malts, and the result can be described as a Belgian-style Dunkelweizen.

Ambacht is all organic—North American Organic Brewers Festival is as big a fest for them as Cheers to Belgian Beers—and they rely on low mash temperatures for added dryness which, even if it seems counterintuitive, is further assisted by incorporating local honey in each beer, including using blackberry honey for bottle conditioning. Kramer originally used his own honey in Honey Triple, but the recipe calls for 25 percent honey, which his four hives can't service; hence, they use their friend's wildflower honey. Despite having the most honey content, after the sugars ferment out Honey Triple actually tastes less like the nectar than the Golden Farmhouse, to which the honey is added at the end and results in it tasting more like bee labor.

Beyond those apian efforts, Kramer and Grobart labor over filling bottles; despite the increased brewery size, their beer gun fills them one at a time. Visit their new tasting room and save them the effort by drinking draft beer and lazing around with Pearl, the brewhouse poodle.

Ambacht Brewing

Opened: 2008.
Owners and brewers: Tom Kramer and Brandy Grobart.
System: 20-barrel.
Annual production: 120 barrels.
Distribution: Portland metro (they joke that they don't deliver to Gresham).
Hours: Tuesday through Friday, 4 p.m. to 8 p.m.; Sunday, noon to 5 p.m.
Takeout beer: Bottles only.

Boring Brewing Co.

13503 Southeast Richey Road, Boring, OR 97009
(503) 793-1382 • BoringBrewing.com
Twitter @BoringBrewing

John Griffith's road to becoming a nanobrewer began in 1989 when he grew obsessed—his word choice—with homebrewing, thanks to the likes of Charlie Papazian and others who were writing about and championing the DIY approach to better beer. After years of dreaming about starting his own brewery, a little fate and a lot of paperwork allowed Griffith to brew commercially in an accessory building on his own property. Visitors have to look for the little sign he sets up out front on the sleepy street. Upon exiting your car, you might first notice his goats and chickens, who are happy beneficiaries of his spent grains. But alas, it's where the property is located that excites people most. That's because it's Boring.

Named after William H. Boring, a Union Army veteran who moved here after the Civil War, the town adopted its name in 1903 before he died in 1932. Griffith "without a doubt took advantage" of the appellation—I doubt Estacada or Damascus Brewing Co. would work as well. On that note, Boring (population 8,000) is the sister city to Dull in Scotland. Griffith is considering making a Dull Scottish Ale, so I suggested a collaboration beer with Dull Brewing Co. until I learned the Scottish city has a population of 80, as in 1 percent of Boring's residents, and a church but no brewery—proof that Boring is way more exciting.

By day, Griffith is a radiology administrator, having worked in health care since 1983. It took him five years to take up homebrewing, and his most formal training is a weekend course in brewing science at University of California, Davis. The first Boring beer, RyPA, went into fermentation tanks in late 2012 and debuted in early 2013. It's a burgeoning style today, but he's been making this hoppy rye ale since the twentieth century.

Beers brewed: Year-round: Boring RyPA, Big Yawn IPA, Boring Brown, Hoppy Blonde, Oatmeal Pale Ale. Seasonals: Fresh Hop, Hot Scotch (Scottish ale with Scotch Bonnet peppers), Oatmeal Stout.

The Pick: Boring RyPA. In an era when new hop varietals abound to lend beers different hop spice characteristics, rye pale ales like this one extract a complementary spicy bite from peppery malted rye, making this an ideal pairing for grilled meats.

Inexplicably, he hasn't turned his porter that earned a first place ribbon at the state fair circa 1993 into a commercial beer.

Hoppy Blonde, a true light-bodied blond with just enough of a floral kick to keep it from being, hm, uh . . . banal, has become his bestseller thanks to having more permanent tap handles than the others. Riffing off the name, Griffith introduced Big Yawn IPA as an even hoppier option. "I got feedback on the RyPA," he said with an implied scratch of his head. "It didn't have a big enough hop character for the Portland crowd." For the sake of comparison, Big Yawn makes folks open wide for its 7.5 percent ABV backed with 75 IBUs, while Boring RyPA clocks in a skosh under that at 6.5 percent and 70 IBUs.

Nearby, you'll likely find Boring pouring at Nuts on Sports (Boring), Tippy Canoe (Troutdale), and even the local golf course while in Portland proper. Sellwood Public House and high-minded destinations such as Belmont Station and Apex are among the solid supporters.

"I made a personal commitment to not rush my beer out the door," Griffith explained from inside his impeccably clean brewery. "I want to take the proper time like I did in homebrewing. It really optimizes the beer and cleans it up." Certainly he doesn't rush much of anything. There's no timetable, but he's exploring taking Boring Brewing up to a 10-barrel system and turning it into his day job. That'd be a thrill.

Boring Brewing Co.

Opened: 2013.

Owner and brewer: John Griffith.

System: 5-barrel.

Production: 200 barrels.

Distribution: Much of Oregon.

Hours: Irregular hours. Check Facebook or call ahead.

Tours: Whenever open. Call to schedule tasting.

Takeout beer: Growlers.

Gift shop: Shirts, stickers, and Boring SiliPints (unbreakable pint cups made from Silicone).

Breakside Taproom & Brewery

BREAKSIDE
→ **BREWERY** ←
PORTLAND, OR

5821 Southeast International Way, Milwaukie,
OR 97222
(503) 342-6309 • Breakside.com
Twitter @BreaksideBrews
Brewpub: See page 70

When Breakside's original brewpub opened in North Portland's Wood-lawn neighborhood in 2010, it debuted as the second smallest brewery in Oregon and the stress of hemorrhaging money literally gave owner Scott Lawrence an ulcer. A year and a half later the company expanded in a big way with a 30-barrel brewery thirteen miles south in a 7,700-square-foot warehouse in a Milwaukie industrial park. By their fourth anniversary, they'd already drawn up plans to annex 10,000 additional square feet across the parking lot and had taken delivery on some of their new 120-barrel fermenters that propelled Breakside into the top twenty largest Oregon breweries. It seems Lawrence heeded his own advice that he'd uttered to me back in 2011: "You'll never get rich as a brewpub owner."

With the new and ever-enlarging production facility, Breakside focuses on its four flagships—IPA, Wanderlust IPA, Woodlawn Pale, and Pilsner—as well as dual "seasonals" every other month. More space also equals more room for barrels (mostly bourbon) and blending projects. This is what enables there to always be a handful of sour ales and other barrel-aged beers among the taproom's twenty-four taps.

A standard among the spent spirit-casked beers is Bourbon Barrel-Aged Aztec, which begins as an amber ale with habanero and serrano chilies as well as cacao nibs from Mana Chocolate, Portland's bean-to-bar chocolatiers. Aging in Jim Beam barrels allows the chili spice to mellow and the sweet cacao flavor to combine with the vanilla and bourbon flavors from the wood. Another local

Beers brewed: Year-round: IPA, Wanderlust IPA, Pilsner, Woodlawn Pale Ale. Seasonals: Summer Float, Irish Stout, Salted Caramel Stout, Bourbon Barrel-Aged Aztec, Old Whisky Dick, India Golden Ale, Passionfruit Sour, Post Time Kolsch, Toro Red, Safe Word Triple IPA, Old World IPA, Pool Party Summer Ale, and more.

The Pick: Wanderlust IPA. Breakside does so many attention-grabbing beers, but Wanderlust's hop bill contains Mosaic, Simcoe, Cascade, Summit, and Amarillo, which are easily five of my favorites, and each of their characteristics shines through: grapefruit pith, pineapple rind, fresh guava, and some of that stuff they legally sell across the border in Washington, courtesy of Summit. In a word: delectable.

producer, Random Spirits, makes one of the few barrel-aged gins, which gives some Oregon breweries the rare opportunity to experiment with aging beers on gin. The floral kick from hops complements rather than battles the botanical punch from gin and gives a beer like Breakside Gin Barrel Citra IPA a fragrant, unique payoff. Once their bottling line is in place, which will introduce 12- and 22-ouncers beyond the current 750-milliliter ones, we can look forward to seeing more of these rarities outside the two brewery locations.

As for drinking Breakside's freshest IPA, Pilsner, or wood-aged beers, the Milwaukie tasting room is sectioned off from the industrial stainless steel by a reclaimed-wood-paneled wall. It becomes a lively place after quitting time on weekdays (work whistles seem to blow around 4 p.m. on Fridays), when good music plays semi-loudly, whereas Saturday is "sampler city," according to brewer Ben Edmunds, meaning beer pilgrims from near and far make it a point to visit this suburban location and geek out, since there's usually a brewer behind the bar to talk shop.

Breakside Taproom & Brewery

Opened: 2012.

Owner: Scott Lawrence.

Brewers: Ben Edmunds (brewmaster), Sam Barber (senior brewer), Jacob Leonard (director of brewing operations), Will Jaquiss (brewer), and Seth Barnum (brewer).

System: 30-barrel.

Annual production: 8,000 barrels.

Distribution: Oregon, Washington, Idaho, British Columbia, Japan, and Scandinavia.

Hours: Monday through Friday, 3 p.m. to 7:30 p.m.; Saturday, 2 p.m. to 8 p.m.

Tours: By appointment.

Takeout beer: Growlers, limited bottles, and keg dock sales.

Gift shop: Shirts, hats, glasses, and other gear.

Food: Sandwiches, salads, and snacks.

Extras: Cellar Reserve Club offers exclusive bottled beers but is currently limited to eighty members.

Bunsenbrewer Fermentation Laboratory and Public House

31   1.042

Bb

Bunsenbrewer

16506 Southeast 362nd Avenue, Sandy, OR 97055
(503) 308-3150 • Bunsenbrewers.com

Located at the base of Mt. Hood, the city of Sandy was something of a brewery jinx. Lucky for Aaron Hanson he's a man of science and doesn't believe in curses.

The Bunsenbrewer nanobrewery—or "fermentation laboratory" as Hanson thinks of it—was conceived in 2011 and grandly opened in January 2014. In between, Hanson presented at the World Brewing Congress on "Enzymatic production of gluten-free beers from conventional grains." In other words, reducing gluten in beer made from barley. As such, his father-in-law and others who are gluten-sensitive will be able to enjoy beer here, but so will the gluten tolerant.

I snuck in during build-out to observe the middle school science lab aesthetic, billed as "OMSI plus beer." There will be science experiments for kids and adults alike under the encouraging gazes of past and future geniuses, namely Einstein and Mr. Spock. The beers—named after scientists ranging from the Polish-French pioneer of radioactivity Madame Curie, to Albuquerque's kingpin chemist Walter "Heisenberg" White—will have a chem lab feel since each batch will be conducted a bit differently and sampled in 150-milliliter beakers. (I suggested using Erlenmeyer flasks for glasses, but we'll see.) Oh, and servers wear lab coats.

Rather than aiming for consistency, Hanson said his emphasis is experimentation. "Each brew will get a method sheet, because I'm a nerd." Patrons can see how the grain bill, yeast, or temperature changes batch to batch, and comparison beer reviews will earn Nobel Prizes . . . er, I mean discounts.

Beers brewed: Madam Curie's Radioactive Red, Heisenberg IPA, Planck Oatmeal Brown, Feynman Amber, Hawking CDA, Faraday Vanilla Porter, Bill Nye the Science Rye, de Duve Belgian Wit, Verbeek 2 Imperial IPA, Pasteur Sweet Brown, Kelvin Triple Pale, Fahrenheit Habanero Belgian Red, Tesla Coffee Stout.

Bunsenbrewer Fermentation Laboratory and Public House

Opened: 2014.

Owner and brewer: Aaron Hanson

System: 1.5-barrel.

Annual production: TBD.

Distribution: Sandy.

Hours: Sunday through Thursday, 11 a.m. to 11 p.m.; Friday and Saturday, 11 a.m. to midnight.

Tours: By appointment.

Takeout beer: Growlers.

Gift shop: Shirts and pint, er, 500-milliliter glasses.

Food: "Simple, unashamedly cheap pub food" (i.e. giant pretzels and hot dogs).

Captured by Porches Brewing Co.

35851 Industrial Way #D, St. Helens, OR 97051
(503) 757-8359 • CapturedByPorches.com
Twitter @CapturedbyPorch

Portland's food carts, clustered in "pods" across Bridge-town, open so frequently that there are reportedly around seven hundred of them. That's enough for over a dozen to moor outside every brewery in the city. But Captured by Porches Brewing (CbP) isn't one of those. Based in St. Helens, roughly thirty miles north, CbP first made a splash around PDX when they received special permits to pour beer on-the-go from "mobile pubhauses."

Founded by Dylan Goldsmith and his now-ex-wife Suzanne Moodhe after some short-lived commercial brewing stints, the unusual name stems from the seeming result the Goldsmiths' porches surrounding the brewery had on friends. Under the name Beer Porches, Moodhe runs the pubs-on-wheels, and CbP beer is readily found at markets and beer retailers via returnable, swingtop bottles. Considering the dollar deposit, you better believe people are more apt to return them compared to other packages' nickel deposits.

Invisible Alchemy is a kombucha company that leases space and equipment from Goldsmith and their delicious, fruity kombuchas also come in returnable bottles.

Beers brewed: Year-round: Invasive Species IPA, Yggdrasil Imperial Pale Ale. Seasonals: Apricot Ale, Pumpkin Ale, Rebecca's Divine Wit, Emma (amber), Punctured by Corpses (porter), Two Cats Kolsch.

Captured by Porches Brewing Co.

Opened: 2007.
Owner and brewer: Dylan Goldsmith.
System: 9-barrel.
Annual production: 750 barrels.
Distribution: Greater Portland Metro.
Hours/tours: None.
Food: Several food trucks parked around the mobile pub outlets.
Extras: Roll up to three "mobile pubhauses" around Portland. $1 refundable swingtop bottles.

The Pick: Undead Pumpkin. Much like the beautiful mélange of chocolate and peanut butter served in one cup, ordering a pint of Undead Porter and their other Halloween seasonal, Pumpkin Ale, is the cultish order for a remarkably smooth, creamy beer that marries the porter's chocolate flavors and fresh pumpkin goodness.

Cascade Brewing & Raccoon Lodge

7424 Southwest Beaverton-Hillsdale Highway,
    Portland OR 97225
(503) 296-0110 • RacLodge.com
Twitter @CascadeBrewing

Founder Art Larrance's history in Portland's beer community includes acting as one of the major players in changing the law in Oregon (1985) to allow breweries to serve beer in their own pubs (or pubs to brew their own); cofounding Portland Brewing (1986) with childhood and lifelong buddy Fred Bowman; and creating the Oregon Brewers Festival (1987) that attracts over eighty thousand beer lovers each July. He also started Cascade Brewing (1998), tucked in the first floor of the Raccoon Lodge, which introduced beers like Apricot and its somehow-apricotier counterpart, Noyaux. Fermented with wild bacteria that create and embellish sour flavors, these are similar to yet distinct from—Lambic ales from Belgium's Payottenland. The appellation is uniquely ours. They are "Northwest-style sour ales."

Larrance grew up in Portland before any craft beer revolution but always drank local suds, or "Western beer" as he calls it. Beer from St. Louis was Eastern beer. In February 1995, after parting with Portland Brewing, he signed the option for the building that's now the Lodge. By the time Cascade Brewing launched in December 1998, "the market had really changed," he said.

He hired brewmaster Ron Gansberg away from Portland Brewing, as well as Grant Ritchie, who's now Cascade's GM, er, Goodwill Ambassador. Their standards are Portland Ale, Cascade IPA, and Razberry Wheat. Larrance said his favorites are the raspberry and Portland ale. The latter is an easy-drinking, dip-your-toes-in light-bodied ale that's neither treacly sweet like an amber nor overly bitter like a Northwest IPA, and it's the one he keeps on tap at home a mile from the brewpub, where he's lived since 1969.

Beers brewed: Year-round: Portland Ale, Red, Pale, Cascade IPA, Kellarman Red Pale Ale, Razberry Wheat, Kriek, Apricot. Seasonal sours: Blueberry, Strawberry, The Vine, Sang Noir, Honey Ginger Lime, Vlad the Imp Aler, Bourbonic Plague, Noyaux, more. Others: Stouts, saisons, more.

The Pick: Kriek. Unlike the traditional Krieks, or cherry beers, of Belgium, Cascade Kriek uses Bing cherries and is fermented with a house blend of critters including *Lactobacillus* and *Pediococcus* so it has more lactic acid and less farmhouse funk. It was their first sour beer—local cherries made the choice obvious—and the bright red, exceptionally juicy, pucker-inducing ale was deemed the best sour beer in the world by the *New York Times*.

The Raccoon Lodge is in the Southwest Portland suburb of Raleigh Hills (practically Beaverton). In 2010, he opened the Barrel House (see page 41) in the Southeast Portland neighborhood of Buckman, decidedly more of a beer mecca.

What came next, a handful of years into Cascade Brewing's existence though something he and Gansberg had discussed since the beginning, was a means to reinvent the brand. "The first one to get to a style owns that style," he began, directly alluding to the way Deschutes is synonymous with porter thanks to Black Butte, or how Widmer Bros. is synonymous with wheat beer thanks to Hefeweizen. "Out of default, we picked this style because there was nothing else left, but it's the most difficult style . . . We'd been looking for our magic elixir."

The Lodge and the Barrel House are only seven miles away yet light years apart. I value both elements. As a beer geek, I appreciate that the Barrel House provides a reverential platform for the complex sour ales. The Barrel House sells 75 percent beer and 25 percent food, the opposite of the Raccoon Lodge's larger kitchen and emphasis on the family. As a father, I like that the Lodge is spacious and provides kids with crayons and a raccoon mascot coloring page (the best ones are proudly displayed). There's also a large beer garden so during the nice hundred days of the year, they set up an open mic on Sunday afternoons where even young, budding musicians step up. Having said that, the downstairs Raccoon Den is what Larrance calls "a whole 'nother market" with video poker, pool tables, and no minors allowed since who wants kids around when you have your first beer at 10:30 in the morning watching football? It may not scream pigskin, but if I'm drinking at that hour, I'll take their Oblique White Stout, a strong, blond ale infused with oatmeal and Oblique Roasters coffee beans.

Cascade Brewing & Raccoon Lodge

Opened: 1998.
Owner: Art Larrance.
Brewers: Ron Gansberg and Preston Weesner (lead blender).
System: 10-barrel.
Annual production: 1,500 barrels.
Hours: Sunday through Friday, 11:30 a.m. to 11 p.m.; Saturday, 11:30 a.m. to 11:30 p.m.
Tours: By request.
Takeout beer: Bottles and growlers.
Gift shop: Many shirts, sweatshirts, caps, and more.
Food: Starters, burgers, pizzas, and a healthy menu including kale salad.

Columbia County Brewing

164 South 15th Street, Saint Helens, OR 97051
(503) 896-7776 • ColumbiaCountyBrewing.com

Mount St. Helens stands 8,365 feet tall. Thirty-nine miles to the west, the city of St. Helens rises a less menacing 39 feet above sea level. In fact, there's nothing really menacing here at all. That's part of the draw for the nearly fifty thousand residents and visitors who come for fishing, boating, and windsurfing along the Columbia River. The drive from Portland usually takes thirty-nine minutes.

Trent Dolyniuk and his wife, Kelly, moved to Saint Helens in the mid-nineties. Their daughter, Samantha, grew up here, as did Ed Rosenlund, who's now her husband. When Ed—a handy pipefitter by trade and amateur brewer with more than a decade of experience—and his father-in-law, Trent—a chef with his own catering company—decided the town needed its own brewpub, it took a year to hatch their idea.

"Columbia County Brewing is made by, for, and in Columbia County," Dolyniuk said. "We have no ambition to bottle or can." This means kegs may end up as far as Portland, or Woodland, Washington, which is closer since it's just over the river. They serve delicious hot food and cold beer; one of the beers Dolyniuk described to me, Aldern (an American pale ale with barley house-smoked over their own alder wood charcoal), sounds like a very food-friendly beer.

Columbia County Brewing

Opened: 2014.
Owners: Edwin and Samantha Rosenlund; Trent and Kelly Dolyniuk.
Brewer: Edwin Rosenlund.
System: 7-barrel.
Annual production: 250 barrels (projected).
Distribution: Columbia County.
Hours: Wednesday through Saturday, 4 p.m. to 10 p.m.
Tours: Available upon request.
Takeout beer: Growlers.
Gift shop: Shirts, mugs, etc.
Food: Barbecued meats and grilled vegetables.

Beers brewed: Year-round: Westy Wheat, Aldern Smoked Pale Ale, Hard Hat IPA, Edwin's Ale (American reddish-pale ale).

Feckin Irish Brewing Co.

415 South McLoughlin Boulevard, Oregon City, OR 97045
(503) 880-5608 • FeckinBrew.com
Twitter @FeckinBrewing

Lest you think the traditional, family-friendly Maher's Irish Brew Pub is no place for such language, realize that if the OLCC and TTB don't have a problem with it, why should anyone else? "It's not a harsh word in Ireland," said co-owner and brewer Mark Maher. "My grandmother uses it."

Why call it the Feckin Brewery? Why the feck not? That was their attitude toward starting it in the first place, explained Maher. "We know what we're up against with Ninkasi [and the bigger Oregon breweries]. But we just want to be a part of [the beer community]." So Maher, his dad Dave, and their partner Mike Vessely—who had worked in quality control for Blitz way back—decided, "Feck it, we're doing it either way!"

"We're looking to take the old traditions [of Irish beer styles] and put Northwest twists on them," Maher said. "All my family's from there. My dad brewed in Ireland." Note: Dave was a professional chef there, not a pro brewer. Still, in terms of beer, that means brewing an IRA (the name may seem indelicate to some, but it stands for Irish Red Ale) and Northwesting it up with lots of locally grown hops, doubling the IBUs (usually 37) of a traditional Irish Red.

Additionally, they're building a tasting room right above Willamette Falls, which, at 1,700 feet wide with a 42-foot drop, is the second largest in America after Niagara.

Feckin Irish Brewing Co.

Opened: 2013.
Owners: Dave Maher, Mark Maher, and Mike Vessely.
Brewers: Mark Maher and Dave Maher.
System: 7-barrel.
Annual production: TBD.
Distribution: Northern Oregon.
Hours and tours: Friday and Saturday, 3 p.m. to 9 p.m.
Takeout beer: Growlers and dock sales.
Gift shop: Feckin swag.
Food: Pasties (meat pies).

Beers brewed: Year-round: IRA (Irish Red Ale), IPA, Irish Oatmeal Porter, Pirate Blonde, Dublin Pale. Seasonals: Fresh Hop.

Krauski's Brewskis / The Hoppy Brewer

328 North Main Avenue, Gresham, OR 97030
(503) 328-8474 • OregonsHoppyPlace.com
Twitter @TheHoppyBrewer

The sign says The Hoppy Brewer, but the nano-brewery behind the curtain is called Krauski's Brewskis. The former opened in 2011 as a home-brew supply and bottle shop because owner Steve Krause tired of having to head to Portland. The shop became cramped once he added six taps. He took over the adjacent store, which he described as a detox shop, so he could "retox" them. Now there are a dozen taps, including one or more from Krauski's Brewskis.

Krause isn't just playing off his nickname. Meadows Ski Resort is less than an hour's drive up Mt. Hood, so his beers are also named after ski runs. Gun Barrel is an Imperial IPA (9.7 percent ABV) named after his favorite black diamond at Heavenly in Tahoe. The Plunge is his double imperial IPA (12.4 percent ABV), named after the double diamond trail of the same name in Telluride where the huge moguls serve as an apt metaphor for the monstrous hops. As one customer quipped, "This is the smallest brewery in Gresham making the biggest beers."

On what Krause calls "cook days," you'll find him mashing on the 1-barrel system—scaled up since the 10-gallon system Krause used for classes—on the adjacent courtyard, which serves as the great beer garden, replete with hanging planters adding the garden vibe.

Krauski's Brewskis / The Hoppy Brewer

Opened: 2013.

Owner: Steve Krause.

Brewer: Ricardo "Rico" Alvarez.

System: 1-barrel.

Annual production: 40 barrels.

Distribution: On-premises.

Hours: Monday through Thursday, 11 a.m. to 8 p.m.; Friday, 11 a.m. to 9 p.m.; Saturday, 9 a.m. to 9 p.m.; Sunday, 11 a.m. to 5 p.m.

Tours: Peek behind the curtain.

Takeout beer: Growlers.

Gift shop: A case displays shirts, stickers, and more on the homebrew shop side.

Food: None, but you can enjoy takeout in the beer garden from nearby eateries.

Beers brewed: Year-round: Powder Stash Imperial Pale Ale, Midnight Rye'dr Cascadian Imperial Dark Ale, Glissade IPA, Gun Barrel IIPA, Plunge IIIPA, Bushwhacker Barleywine, Poacher Imperial CDA.

Max's Fanno Creek Brewpub

12562 Southwest Main Street, Tigard, OR 97223
(503) 624-9400 • MaxsFannoCreek.com
Twitter @FannoCreekBrew

It sounds like a subject for that old Mike Myer's skit, "Coffee Talk," on *SNL*, where hostess Linda Richman might say, "Max's Fanno Creek is neither Max's nor is it a creek. Discuss." And she'd be at least half right. Overlooking Fanno Creek, the brewpub was opened in 2007 by Marvin Bowen and brewmaster Max Tieger, whose Tuck's Brewery in Hillsboro went dark. Tieger soon bolted, but his first name remains on the front awning. Everyone in Tigard knows it as Max's. Perhaps to alter the reality, there's a portrait of a ridiculously adorable Boston terrier framed near the entrance with a nameplate that reads "Max," implying this very family-oriented brewpub with the game stations in the front is named for a beloved, pint-sized mascot.

While most of the pub is designed for kids (there's an extensive children's menu) and their parents, the bar area with three TVs overhead is where you can dive into a six-sample flight selected from ten house beers on tap so as to try topsellers like the grassy IPA and sweet, clove-inflected, Belgian-style Reverend's Daughter. The latter is one of the few original recipes Tieger brought with him; another was Vanilla Cream Porter, a sweet, creamy beer that'd make a good float. Wistfulness for the early days of Oregon craft brewing is manifested in the homage to the state's first microbrewery, Cartwright, displayed near the entrance. To the right, large windows exhibit the 10-barrel brewhouse. Directly opposite is a trio of Nintendo Wiis, reinforcing the family vibe, but even those are underneath a mural—one of many found indoors and out—of pints and mugs of beer and giant hop cones.

I'd like to mention, if somewhat randomly, that they sell a selection of T-shirts (like all brewpubs have for sale), but some of these super basic tees were also only three dollars. That's basically a free brewery shirt minus three bucks, and I needed a

Beers brewed: Year-round: Pagan Pale Ale, X IPA, Reverend's Daughter Belgian, Vanilla Cream Porter, Dry Hopped Pacific Red, Ivan the Imperial IPA, Bull Mountain Stout, Old Town Ale, Kicking Back Kolsch, Golden Ale.

The Pick: Dry Hopped Pacific Red. I don't normally lean toward beers named for their color, but this is no middle-of-the-road red. At 5.7 percent ABV and a hefty 45 IBUs, the dry-hopping compensates for the caramel malt body with a savory quality that complements any pizza and leaves a sticky mouth coating to appease lupulin lovers.

green shirt. I wish more places would follow their lead, since fans essentially become walking billboards.

Anyway, as the hub of Main Street, the picnic tables out front make for an appealing place to feast on pizza and sip creations from current brewer Craig Gulla, who cut his teeth at McMenamins. And maybe because the owners know that Tigard is a bit off the beaten path for Portlanders, and as a way to celebrate those for whom Max's is their local, they host an annual three-day, music-filled celebration of small batch beer from area nanobreweries called Nano Fest (www.nanobeer fest.com).

Max's Fanno Creek Brewpub

Opened: 2007.

Owners: Marvin and Connie Bowen.

Brewer: Craig Gulla.

System: 10-barrel.

Annual production: 350 barrels.

Distribution: About a dozen taps around Tigard.

Hours: Monday through Thursday, 11 a.m. to 10 p.m.; Friday, 11 a.m. to 11 p.m.; Saturday, 9 a.m. to 11 p.m.; Sunday, 9 a.m. to 10 p.m.

Tours: By appointment.

Takeout beer: Growlers and various sizes of kegs.

Gift shop: Growlers, hats, and T-shirts. Some of the shirts are a mere $3, which is brilliant.

Food: Sports enthusiast and kid-friendly pub grub, including fried finger foods, pizzas, and sandwiches such as the Mad Max Burger with gruyere, bacon, "frizzled" onions, ham, and a fried egg.

Events: Nano Fest started in August 2009 and features twenty super small batch breweries from around the area.

McMenamins Cornelius Pass Roadhouse Brewery

4045 Cornelius Pass Road, Hillsboro, OR 97124
(503) 640-6174 • Mcmenamins.com/CPR
Twitter @CaptainNeon

Cornelius Pass Roadhouse became an early McMenamins property in 1986 but was built by Robert Imbrie in 1850, predating Oregon statehood. Stroll through the six acres and you'll happen upon the Octagonal Barn, where livestock has made way for catering events but it's said five white barn owls roost inside. They inspired White Owl Whiskey, unoaked and made in the antique Alambic still from Cognac now perched in the granary barn. Beer-wise, seek out Barn Owl Bitter.

The brewers are Brady Romtvedt and Chris Oslin. Romtvedt, whose Uncle Mike actually brewed for McMenamins early on, designed one of Oregon's earliest Cascadian Dark Ales, appropriately called Dark Star, a nod to the McMenamin brothers' affinity for that Grateful Dead opus.

The Roadhouse Brewfest sets up in Imbrie Meadow (though I also love lazing in the apple grove where they should host a cider fest) in mid-July. The idyllic meadow is made for romping (or lounging with a beer).

McMenamins Cornelius Pass Roadhouse Brewery

Opened: 1986.

Owners: Brian and Mike McMenamin (see page 92).

Brewers: Chris Oslin and Brady Romtvedt.

System: 6-barrel.

Annual production: 1,700 barrels.

Distribution: Hillsboro vicinity.

Hours: Sunday and Monday, 11 a.m. to 11 p.m.; Tuesday through Thursday, 11 a.m. to midnight; Friday and Saturday, 11 a.m. to 1 a.m.

Tours: By request.

Takeout beer: Growlers, mason jars, bottles, and kegs.

Gift shop: Ample apparel, glassware, and branded souvenirs.

Food: McMenamins burgers, salads, pizzas, and specials.

Beers brewed: Year-round: Hammerhead Pale Ale, Terminator Stout, Ruby, IPA. Seasonals: Barn Owl Bitter, Dark Star CDA, Nehalem Lager, Silvercone IPL, Oatmeal Vanilla Stout, Palmer Lift Porter, and more.

The Pick: Dark Star CDA. Carafa is the black malt among the recipe's four types of malted barley but it's the Centennial and Simcoe hops that shine through, escaping the high gravitational pull—it's 8 percent ABV—for citrusy top notes to temper the roasty and astringent malty bottom.

McMenamins Edgefield Brewery

2126 Southwest Halsey Street, Troutdale, OR 97060
(503) 667-4352 • Mcmenamins.com/Edgefield
Twitter @CaptainNeon

After relaxing in the heated soaking pool, amble past the glassblower making ornate vases or wine stoppers and pick up a cigar to enjoy by the brick fireplace in the cozy Little Red Shed while sipping a Moroccan Coffee made with house-distilled coffee liqueur. Then tiptoe through the herb garden, used by on-premises chefs; if you're winded, rest beneath the weepy Mulberry tree. It's understandable you'd be tired from strolling across the seventy-four-acre parcel that was formerly the Multnomah County Poor Farm. Disparate features include golf courses—a twenty-hole course and a twelve-cup that each cost a mere buck-a-hole—and a grassy concert venue where I've enjoyed artists from crooner Tony Bennett to the hipster band fun. The winery has its own vineyard and hosts nightly live music. The veritable resort and spa includes over one hundred guest rooms (starting at a reasonable $70 a night plus hostel-style rooms for even more frugal travelers). One of Edgefield's coolest elements is the nonstop artwork painted throughout every hallway, stairwell, and imaginable canvas. Look for the Black Rabbit to spring up here and there, inspired by folks who abandoned pets near the poor farm. Those hares' heirs still hop around today.

Oh yeah, and there's a brewery.

For seven decades, from 1912 until 1982, those who needed "a leg up" were sent to the poor farm. Artists, outcasts, and hundreds of others who'd fallen on hard times—over six hundred during the Great Depression—sought refuge (and were put to work in the fields) until the grounds were vacated of all residents, inmates, and patients. After years of disrepair, the grounds and its structures were bound for demolition until Mike and Brian McMenamin read an article in the *Oregonian* and were struck by a vision. The banks didn't see it, and for a few years, the brothers didn't see any income from it, but now this suburban Troutdale location makes an ideal hub for those slurping up the

Beers brewed: Year-round: Hammerhead Pale Ale, Terminator Stout, Ruby, IPA. Seasonals: Black Rabbit Porter, Black Widow, Thundercone Fresh Hop, Jam Session ISA, Edgefield Wheat, Edgefield Extra Barley Wine, Percolator Coffee Stout, and more.

The Pick: Black Rabbit Porter. An Edgefield creation, this falls somewhere between a dry Irish and a robust porter with serious roasted coffee and chocolate tones atop the nutty crystal and chocolate malt base.

excellent beer culture of Portland. It's only a twenty-minute drive west to downtown, and twenty minutes east is breathtaking Multnomah Falls in the Columbia River Gorge, with the brewery hotspot of Hood River a short push farther.

But no one would blame you for not leaving Edgefield's grounds, especially since wherever you explore, you can have a pint in hand. The brewery is the largest in the company's chain, with a team of five brewers producing 19-barrel batches (though it's a 25-barrel system). McMenamins doesn't distribute bottled beer outside of their own shops, but those bottles come from Troutdale.

Since there's also a distillery and a winery (which means they make their own cider and brandies), the brewers get to experiment with barrel aging beers. Maybe that means barleywine rounded out in Hogshead Whiskey barrels or Black Widow Porter spun through a barrel of Three Rocks Spiced Rum. I had a rum barrel chocolate stout aged with vanilla beans that was pretty epic, and Percolator is basically Terminator Stout with McMenamins' own roasted coffee added and then ameliorated with cocoa nibs soaked in Three Rocks Rum. Insanity. New barrel-aged beers are tapped inside the Distillery Bar every second Thursday at 5 p.m.

In July, the Sasquatch Brew-Am golf tourney benefiting the beery Glen Hay Falconer Foundation pairs amateur golfers with pro brewers. Anyone partnered with Jeff Cooley, recently the Edgefield brewery manager but now McMenamins' district manager, shouldn't get their hopes up about his home course advantage since he's no Bubba Watson.

McMenamins Edgefield Brewery

Opened: 1991.

Owners: Mike and Brian McMenamin (see page 92).

Brewers: Nathan Whitney, Lloyd "Drew" Phillips, Bruce Loux, Will Gaither, and Matt Bergfield.

System: 25-barrel.

Annual production: 1,000 barrels.

Hours: Ten bars open daily.

Tours: Just ask.

Takeout beer: Growlers, bottles, and kegs.

Gift shop: More of a country store, with beer, shirts, and glasses, but also local wares, honeys, books, crafts, and house spirits, wines, and brandies.

Food: The Power Station is casual: pizzas and burgers, including a Hammerhead Garden Burger. The Black Rabbit Restaurant is more upscale; entrées include salmon with salmon caviar, cold-smoked wild boar, and wild mushroom flan.

Events: Celebration of Syrah (April), Sasquatch Brew-Am golf tournament (July).

McMenamins Old Church & Pub

30340 Southwest Boones Ferry Road, Wilsonville, OR 97070
(503) 427-2500 • Mcmenamins.com/Wilsonville
Twitter @CaptainNeon

Although its name is the Old Church, this is actually the newest McMenamins brewpub in Oregon, opened in 2011 right on the centennial of the church's construction by the Wilsonville Methodist Society. It's so new it even features a rarity for the company: a brand new brewhouse. In fact, it's the only one with a "hop rocket" (think Randall from Dogfish Head Brewery) that propels beer through a barrel of hop cones for intense hoppy freshness. What a fittingly pioneering feature for a McMenamins brewery on Boones Ferry Road, named for Alphonso Boone, who settled here in 1846 and was the grandson of frontiersman Daniel Boone.

The combination of old and new makes for interesting experiences and flavors. Some couples who were married in the church—deconsecrated in the mid nineties—still return for Valentine's Day dinner. The grounds are now surrounded by strip malls, but inside the décor takes on a nautical theme, replete with wooden hulls and images of riverboats. And the original brewer, Mark Goodwin, swears he's seen and heard ghosts, mostly kids from when the brewery was in the century-old church's basement nursery. Many on staff, none of them crazy, confirm those stories.

Current brewer Justin Azevedo carries on Goodwin's tradition of highly experimental barrel-aged and sour beers for the thirteen taps. Goodwin once made a sour version of Ruby with *Lactobacillus* and a Maple-Vanilla Terminator Stout garnished with griddled bacon. But I must record here that Goodwin also made one of the best beers I've had, which he created after all the McMenamins brewers received Mosaic hops to play around with. His single-hopped Mosaic Pale Ale reminded me of days gulping guava nectar. The Old Church is definitely the branch in the McMenamins tree to discover forward-thinking concoctions.

Having said that, for nearby residents or anyone a good fifteen minutes south of Portland just

Beers brewed: Year-round: Terminator Stout, Ruby, Hammerhead Pale Ale, and an IPA. Seasonals: Thirteen taps, so nine ever-changing lagers and ales.

The Pick: Livin' La Vida Mocha. Azevedo's porter indulges in cold-pressed McMenamins' house-roasted coffee as well as a heap of chocolate for a mocha porter that provides plenty of bitterness but, served on nitro, achieves the silkiness and creaminess of an iced mocha.

off I-5, the central area of the grounds features a patio surrounded by a grassy amphitheater perfect for lying out on warm days and when bands perform. I won't say it's a religious experience, but with over a dozen beers to choose from, ranging from simple and sessionable lagers to more extreme ales, and coupled with "The Almighty" burger topped with smoked gouda, pancetta, charred onion jam, and roasted garlic aioli, plus a healthy dose of sun, it's heavenly.

McMenamins Old Church & Pub

Opened: 2011.

Owners: Brian and Mike McMenamin (see page 92).

Brewer: Justin Azevedo.

System: 7-barrel.

Annual production: 850 barrels.

Distribution: On-premises and at some other McMenamins pubs nearby.

Hours: Sunday through Thursday, 11 a.m. to 11 p.m.; Friday and Saturday, 11 a.m. to midnight.

Tours: Walk-ins when the brewer is available.

Takeout beer: Growlers.

Gift shop: Limited apparel and gift items.

Food: McMenamins menu of salads, sandwiches, burgers such as The Almighty, rice bowls (including "munchkin bowls" for kiddoes), and the devilishly delicious Stella Blue Fries, fresh-cut fries with blue cheese sauce and bacon.

Extras: You can book your wedding in the old church. The annual Boone's Ferry Autumn Ale Fest is a McMenamins-only brewfest held the first Saturday of November.

Red Ox Brewing

9795 Southwest Murdock Street, Tigard, OR 97224
(503) 310-8033 • RedOxBrewing.com
Twitter @RedOxBrewing

Portland area natives and brewing brothers Adam Amato and Matt Shelby—they were Theta Chis together at University of Oregon—conceived of Red Ox Brewing over a decade before it materialized. Amato served as best man at Shelby's kid brother Brett's wedding where, as Shelby said, "Red Ox provided the beer, of course." They filed in 2014.

The brewery's name is a nod to their fraternal origins. Theta Chi's colors are red and white, and the Greek letters are ΘX. "The red ox," Amato explained, "was always an unofficial mascot." There were no oxen harmed in the making of this nanobrewery (which is based in a garage, so no visitors), nor were there any slapstick scenes of a live ox or cartoonish mascot costume being stolen by a rival fraternity, but that didn't stop Shelby from calling the operation "all very sitcom-like." He described Amato as the mad scientist of the brewery and himself as "a pretty good navigator of red tape."

The 55-gallon "hand-me-down" brewing system takes up the bulk of the Shelby family's garage, proving how supportive his wife, Tabitha, truly is. "She's resigned to the fact that our three-car garage has no space for her to park, and that my Sundays are often spent watching water boil," he said.

As a self-financed venture, Shelby proudly stated, "If we want a new fermenter, we better sell enough beer to pay for it." Beer will range from an approachable blond to a barrel-aged stout "and all the hoppy goodness in between," he said. Look for it at the Tigard Farmers Market and other local accounts.

Red Ox Brewing

Opened: 2014.
Owners and brewers: Adam Amato and Matt Shelby.
System: 1.5-barrel.
Annual production: 50 barrels.
Distribution: Tigard Farmers Market and area taps.

Beers brewed: Year-round: Sun Porch Pale Ale, Brickhouse Blonde, Anger Zone IPA. Seasonals: Amazon ISA, Housekeeper Red, Moontower CDA, Dubba Bubba Imperial Stout.

Short Snout Brewing

Milwaukie, Oregon
ShortSnoutBrewing.com • Twitter @ShortSnoutBrew

Buster and Bella snored away by the "taproom," brewer Brian VanOrnum's living room in his suburban Portland house. A 10-gallon homebrew system resides in the garage, Short Snout's brewhouse. The name is an homage to Buster and Bella, his extremely cute pugs. VanOrnum funded his commercial brewing aspirations via Kickstarter when he surpassed his $15,000 goal by $1,366.

VanOrnum isn't an extreme brewer in some sort of Dogfish Head/ Russian River Brewing sense—his extremes come from cyclocross racing and when he and his wife compete in mixed martial arts.

Finding Short Snout on tap is extremely difficult. Your best bet is probably the Sellwood Public House (8132 SE 13th Ave., Portland). Milwaukie is to the south, adjacent to Portland and a couple of miles from Portland's Sellwood hood.

VanOrnum said he's a few years away from getting to brew as his full-time occupation, though he's come a long way since his Mr. Beer Kit in 1999. His first step toward capitalization came from Pub Grub for Pups, his "doggie bakery" business making puppy treats from his spent grains. More lucrative, one of Short Snout's 182 Kickstarter backers—and contributor of $5,000— was "a brother of one of my wife's best friends and has been a supporter of mine for as long as I can remember. He has always encouraged me to chase my dream." With small-batch brewing, whenever there's a beer festival, be it fresh hops or rye ales, VanOrnum's usually up for creating a beer.

Beers brewed: Year-round: Beelzebella, Dank Nugs Fresh Hop Ale, Rugged Pug CDA, Mt. Olympug Imperial Pale Ale, Blackberry Sage Porter, Harvest Wheat (with Riesling grapes), Kettlebell Blonde.

The Pick: Kettlebell Blonde. This beer is either free or expensive depending on how you look at it. Created as a "recovery beverage" for nearby microgym The Warrior Room, a keg is available (post-workout). It's a light, golden ale that, after a kettlebell workout, is the most delicious thing in the world.

Short Snout Brewing

Opened: 2012.
Owner and brewer: Brian VanOrnum.
System: 1.5-barrel.
Annual production: 5 barrels.
Distribution: A few kegs around town.

Stickmen Brewery & Skewery

40 North State Street, Lake Oswego, OR 97034
(503) 344-4449 • StickmenBeer.com
Twitter @StickmenBeer

It's a gospel fact that the best way to soak up the glory of summerlike days is in the sanctuary of a beer garden. Praise be for Stickmen Brewery & Skewery in the tony Portland suburb of Lake Oswego where Oswegans can soak up the sun and lakefront views while sipping fresh beer.

I doubt anyone on the overwater deck takes their gaze off Oswego Lake, but if they did crane their necks, the 7-barrel brewery is visible through the windows. The "skewery" half of this Izakaya-style pub—meaning it serves Japanese-style food on sticks and other small plates—brings out the sake and shochu fans. And since they already hybridize Japanese and Lake Oswego culture, they've done limited batches of Sake Beer, a strong, fruity ale fermented with sake yeast.

Although the IPA as well as the imperial honey Kolsch are crowd favorites, so are the seasonal saisons. The most recent Spring Saison was fermented with Belgian Ardennes yeast, highlighting this delicate beer's lemony and spicy aromas and flavors. This made pairing it with a variety of meat or vegetable bites almost effortless. But why stop there? The pub on its own private lake also has done a Meyer-Bay Saison created for Portland Cheers to Belgian Beers festival.

The brewpub is the dream of Tim Schoenheit and Jon "JT" Turner, who are both locals but met while working for a software company in Tokyo and hanging out at Izakaya bars. They intuited that a convivial atmosphere with small plates and shochu would be well received back home, although the industrial lager beers would have to be nixed. Turner had been homebrewing for nineteen years and turned Schoenheit on to it about

Beers brewed: Year-round: Big Honey Imperial Kolsch, F-Bomb IPA, Iron Mountain DIPA, Angela's Alt, Porter. Seasonals: Spring Saison, Fall Saison, The Bitter X Triple IPA, All Rye'm No Reason Rye IPA, Madame Molly Irish Red, Amelioration Belgian Dark Strong Ale, Brown Dn'Unda, Buona Mattina Coffee Porter, Oatmeal Stout, Cordially Chocolate Cherry Porter.

The Pick: Meyer-Bay Saison. Taking the already lemony Spring Saison, Stickmen enhanced it with Meyer lemon peel and bay leaves, creating an interesting set of flavors that toggles from heavily sweet citrus to more robust Italian seasoning as it warms in the tulip glass.

three years before they started plotting to go pro. Legally, they sort of had to—they were brewing practically every week and it's a little-known fact that the government only permits making 200 gallons of beer at a home with two adults. Certainly they're not the only ones who push exceeding the legal limit in their homes. When they attended a panel titled "Going Pro" at a National Homebrewers Conference in 2011, Schoenheit recalled one of the panelists asking if anyone in the room was planning on going pro. "Nearly every hand rose."

Indeed, since Stickmen opened its doors in 2013, several hundred breweries have opened, not all of them in Oregon even. But I have to believe that this is the only one with such a beautiful lake vista from a back patio. It seats 240 people (with room to expand) and has a separate backbar, which is great for families since minors aren't allowed near the front bar. If you're in a hurry and don't have time to enjoy a casual pint, it's very likely this is also the only brewery that does growler fills and dock sales from an actual dock.

Stickmen Brewery & Skewery

Opened: 2013

Owners and brewers: Tim Schoenheit and Jon "JT" Turner.

System: 7-barrel.

Annual production: 225 barrels.

Distribution: Portland area.

Hours: Monday through Thursday, 11:30 a.m. to 10 p.m.; Friday, 11:30 a.m. to midnight; Saturday, 11 a.m. to midnight; Sunday, 11 a.m. to 10 p.m.

Takeout beer: Growlers and dock sales (from an actual dock).

Gift shop: T-shirts.

Food: Izakaya-style Japanese pub grub, including Yakitori skewers such as pork belly, roasted beets, and bacon-wrapped cheese, plus filled buns and sandwiches.

Three Mugs Brewing Co.

2020 Northwest Aloclek Drive, Suite 108, Hillsboro,
  OR 97124
(971) 322-0232 • BrewBrothers.biz
ThreeMugsBrewing.com
Twitter @3MugsBrewing

For the do-it-yourself hunter or militiaman, there's an arms and ammo store in Suite 102 of the Cornelius Pass Business Park. For the DIY beermaker, you want the business next door, Brew Brothers. What started as a garage-based business to help local, all-grain homebrewers get grain for cheaper has morphed into an all-in-one supply shop, bottle shop, taproom, and now Three Mugs brewery. There's even a pub in the works for "down the road" said Chris Jennings who, along with his father, Jay, and brother, Josh, are the cartoon mugs adorning the beer-mug logo. It's no Van Gogh, nor do the yellow faces in the steins pass for Matt Groening, but they strike an uncanny resemblance to the actual family given Chris's red Amish-style beard, Jay's dangling cigar, and the Gene Simmons–esque tongue unfurled from Josh's mouth. Just peek at the photograph of the trio that hangs in the supply shop surrounded by homebrew competition ribbons.

Before the brewery, before the shop, heck, even before the kids, Jay started homebrewing courtesy of a Mr. Beer kit, a Christmas gift his folks bought him from their local Fred Meyer in 1978. Although his brewing equipment collected dust during his twenty-one years in the air force, when he retired in 2005 out came the mash paddle and all the rest. By that point, he shared his hobby with Chris, who in turn grew so enamored with it that he prompted Jay past extract brewing and into all-grain brewing.

Fast forward to the present again, where Brew Brothers is in its fourth location in the eight years since its founding, and it's fun to see how the Jennings keep making the space homier even though they moved it out of their house. Enter Brew Brothers from the front, which faces Cornelius Pass Road, and you may be greeted by Finnegan the family Labrador (well, she might be half lab, half something bigger like Great Dane), who will then escort you through the backdoor that leads to the brewery and tasting room.

Beers brewed: Year-round: Northern English Brown, Amber Ale, Imperial NW Red, Imperial IPA, IPA.

Or enter from the east side of the building—the Three Mugs side where the 1-barrel system resides (Chris aspires to scale up to 10 barrels)—and plunk down at the bar or order your first beer as you make your way to the foosball table. Where initially there were only five taps, now there are twenty (including a beer engine for cask-conditioned ale). Chris aspires to have around eight taps, possibly even double that, flowing with house brews ranging from light pilsner to bodacious barleywine, from zesty wheat beers to roasty dark ones, and from "hoppy to something else hoppy" (his words). Chris said he likes to brew to style, noting, "If I say this is gonna be an ESB, it's a [traditional British] ESB." He then noted that he also enjoys making German and Belgian styles, but that there will always be a tap devoted to "experimental brews." Vegans stop reading here.

"I like to make blood sausages." Thus began Chris's response when asked what he had in mind as far as experimental recipes. Enumerating the ingredients he stuffs into hog casings, he then queried, "Why can't you add blood to beer?" It wasn't rhetorical. "After a month of toiling over temperatures and pH to make sure I wouldn't introduce botulism," he spiked his first attempt with 3 gallons worth of the frozen, congealed stuff. Then he upped it to 7 gallons the next time. After putting the sanguine Scotch Ale on tap, Jay insisted, "Everyone loved it."

Or, y'know, you can always order an IPA, where the weirdest thing added might be a new New Zealand hop varietal.

Three Mugs Brewing Co.

Opened: 2014.
Owners: Jay, Christopher, and Joshua Jennings.
Brewers: Christopher and Jay Jennings.
System: 1-barrel.
Distribution: On-site mostly.
Hours: Tuesday through Friday, 2 p.m. to 8 p.m.; Saturday, noon to 8 p.m.; Sunday, noon to 6 p.m.
Takeout beer: Growlers.
Gift shop: Everything for the beer lover and homebrewer, from mugs to mini mash tuns to Mosaic hops.

Two Kilts Brewing Co.

Two Kilts Brewing Co.
Sherwood, Oregon

14841 Southwest Tualatin Sherwood Road,
 Suite 501, Sherwood, OR 97140
(503) 625-1700 • TwoKiltsBrewing.com
Twitter @TwoKiltsBrewing

You won't find co-owners and brewers Alex McGaw and Chris Dillon donning a pair of kilts at Two Kilts while brewing their Scottish Ale, but you will spot their tartan-wrapped forklift in the brewery. Dillon admitted it gets a bit tedious when people ask, "Where's your kilt today?" But they're usually happy to play the name up at beerfests. I asked why they didn't at least have branded kilts available on the shelves o' swag that line the brewery's tasting room. McGaw said they're working on some, courtesy of a local kilt manufacturer. But here's the name's story so we can get on to the beer.

"We were drinking beer at Fulton," began McGaw, who sports a jutting, bushy, red beard. "We needed a name," he continued, referring to the brewery they were developing in 2009. "My dad's from Glasgow. All of Chris's relatives—although he was raised in Beaverton—are from Ireland. We had a list of fifty names but none evoked a mutual 'Yes, that's great!' Then I got a text: 'Two Kilts Brewing Co.'" That text elicited the emphatic affirmative, and they've been hailed and haunted by it ever since.

The Fulton Alex referenced is the McMenamins brewpub where he'd been brewing when he met Dillon, who owned a detail shop across the street. When word spread about an IPA McGaw had concocted, Dillon came over and started asking him questions. "A lot of questions," McGaw stressed. In fact, Dillon, seven years McGaw's elder and with a slightly graying beard to prove it, had been homebrewing for seventeen years.

"Chris is a go-getter. I'm the laid-back guy," said McGaw. "Chris made all the magic happen." After filing, they Frankensteined together their initial brewery that included an old 10-barrel, food-grade mix tank, repurposed as a 6-barrel mash tun with a false bottom. The boil kettle was a decommissioned surge tank from Jim Beam that found its way to Hood River. Two fermenters were previously

Beers brewed: Year-round: Scottish Ale, IPA, Pale Ale, Oatmeal Stout, Cocoa Porter. Seasonals: Scotch Ale, Russian Imperial Stout, Double IPA, Pumpkin Ale, Heather Ale, Beet-Nik Beet Ale.

The Pick: Scottish Ale. Hints of rye spice from the crystal malt make this beer not sweet nor bitter but medium bodied and flavorful. The best part is how it gets smokier as it warms.

bright tanks from a brewery in California's Redwood Forest. Two years later, however, they sold that equipment to Uptown Market and ramped up to a new 15-barrel system. They're aiming for rapid growth.

Although Two Kilts premiered with a hoppy pale ale and a hoppier IPA, as McGaw explained, "We talked about how the industry was moving into everything being too hoppy. So we talked about making our pale a classic American pale ale using Northwest hops that have been handed to us." (By "handed to them," he meant by virtue of this majestic locale, not from some sketchy hop dealer's truck.)

But today, the bestseller is their Scottish Ale, which in 2014 delivered the first World Beer Cup gold medal to Sherwood. They make a Scotch Ale too, but it may take a Level 4 beer nerd to discern the differences in the styles. McGaw was able to summarize their related offerings nicely: "For Scotch Ale, after playing with the peet, we pulled off just the right amount so it doesn't offend anybody. Scottish is lighter than Scotch at 6 and not 8 percent."

Furthermore, they make over twenty playful beers that rotate among the tasting room's eleven taps. Pumpkin beers are the most popular seasonal style, so Two Kilts doesn't take theirs lightly. Five hundred pounds of jack-o'-lantern—not the canned kind—are added to each batch, along with cinnamon, vanilla, brown sugar, and molasses. "We refuse to use anything less than the real deal," he said, pointing out that vanilla beans are used in their Vanilla Cream Ale. Seventy-five pounds of raw beets get tossed into the boil of Beet-Nik, though they add a few shakes of organic beet powder for aroma.

The taproom is the best bet for finding one of these numbers. It's just off Highway 99, a little hard to find, but locals in Sherwood, which previously was one of the few brewery-less cities in Portland Metro, have no problem finding it.

Two Kilts Brewing Co.

Opened: 2011.

Owners and brewers: Alex McGaw and Chris Dillon.

System: 15-barrel.

Annual production: 500 barrels (with a larger system, the goal is 2,500 barrels).

Distribution: Portland metro and Willamette Valley.

Hours: Monday through Saturday, 3 p.m. to 10 p.m.

Tours: By request.

Takeout beer: Growlers and bombers, with dock sales coming soon.

Gift shop: Shirts; working on kilts (from Stumptown Kilts).

Food: None, but they'd eventually like to add a kitchen. For now, you can BYO.

Uptown Market Brewery

6620 Southwest Scholls Ferry Road, Beaverton/Portland, OR 97223
(503) 336-4783 • UptownMarketPDX.com
Twitter @UptownMarketPDX

The small, unassuming shop on the bend of Scholls Ferry Road—a commuter road between Portland and Beaverton—that made a business out of selling beer to go is now making beer to enjoy while hanging out. There've always been eighteen rotating taps for patrons while they chill or shop for bottles, but as of January 2014 the owners finally gained approval to give Beaverton its first brewery.

"I describe it as the Bermuda Triangle of Portland," said co-owner AJ Shepard, "because we are in unincorporated Washington County, the city of Beaverton, with a Portland address, and Tualatin water." Fun side note: Three of the most populous Oregon cities are suburbs of Portland but shockingly Beaverton, unlike Gresham and Hillsboro, was dry of local suds.

Uptown Market is a one-stop shop for homebrew supplies and coffee. Over a thousand beers fill the chillers, painstakingly arranged along the beer spectrum with dark stouts and porters on the left gradually sliding to pilsners and other light lagers on the far right. Beer geeks looking for whatever's new head straight to the chiller marked "Top Shelf" on a handwritten sign. Now add to this spectrum ultra-fresh beer. Among Uptown's community you'll find distributors discussing new releases, with beer nerds standing aside as business suits pick up a bottle of something special for dinner.

Uptown Market Brewery

Opened: 2014.
Owners: Brothers AJ and Chris Shepard, and Stuart Faris.
Brewer: Jason Rowley.
System: 7-barrel.
Distribution: Portland metro.
Hours: Monday through Saturday, 10 a.m. to 10 p.m.; Sunday, 10 a.m. to 8 p.m.
Takeout beer: Growlers and dock sales.
Gift shop: T-shirts and swag, bottles, and homebrew supplies.
Food: Food carts.

Beers brewed: Year-round: USA (Uptown Session Ale), Stop Work Stout, Otis Reddin' (Imperial Oatmeal Red), Bitter Brunette ESB.

Vertigo Brewing

VERTIGO BREWING
HILLSBORO, OREGON

21420 Northwest Nicholas Court, Suite D-7,
Hillsboro, OR 97124
(503) 645-6644 • VertigoBrew.com
Twitter @VertigoBrew

Mike Haines painted Vertigo Brewing as their "exit strategy from Intel," the semiconductor company they met at when he and fellow co-owner and brewer Mike Kinion both worked there. Of course, they got paid to work there. Kinion lamented that Vertigo was initially something "we dumped our savings into."

To get to that point, the Mikes first had to get hooked on making beer. Haines's wife gave him a gift certificate to a now-defunct brew-on-premises. That led to them continuing to hone their skills in Haines's garage for the next seven years. After nearly sixty years at Intel between them, they launched Vertigo as a commercial entity in 2008 and took turns "retiring" to work at the brewery full time.

They originally continued to brew in single-barrel batches. "Long days," said Kinion, describing brewing the same recipe seven times in a row just to fill their sole 7-barrel fermenter. Behold, since 2010 they've had a 7-barrel system and even ordered a 20-barrel fermenter beyond the four bright tanks that serve the tasting room.

The taproom opened in June 2012 in the industrial park suite adjacent to the brewery. Brewers everywhere probably field one question more than anything else: What's new? The taproom allows them to always offer something new, frequently in the form of a barrel-aged beer. Fortuitously, a spirit blender (they don't actually distill their own bourbon) named Big Bottom moved into a neighboring suite. There was a great Big Bottom Bourbon Barrel-Aged Milk Stout on during a recent visit.

I suspect the second most popular question is: What IPAs have you got? "We brewed so many IPAs as homebrewers," said Haines, "so we keep experimenting." Nearly their entire current lineup started as homebrews (notable exceptions are their two fruit beers: Razz Wheat and Apricot

Beers brewed: Year-round: Schwindel Alt, Razz Wheat, Apricot Cream Ale, Arctic Blast Vanilla Porter, Smokestack Red, Friar Mike's IPA. Seasonals: Barrel-aged beers (all one-offs), Left Nut Brown, Harvest Hefe, T.B.D. Blonde, High Dive Rye.

The Pick: Friar Gone Wild Imperial IPA. This brother (of Friar Mike's) from an imperial mother is lush to the point of corpulence, ensuring balance for this 100-plus IBU dish, if possibly listing on the malty side. And yet that hoppy side delivers the pine and resin notes needed.

Cream). Friar Mike's IPA is named neither for Haines nor Kinion but a third Mike. Their friend got ordained as an online friar—it was a mere five bucks more than the reverend ordination—in order to marry off some friends. As Kinion sort of lamented, "Friar Mike's not a good name because it implies it's a Belgian IPA, but the name has such good recognition that we can't change it."

Just as Friar Mike's isn't a Belgian IPA, Friar Gone Wild IPA is not a wild-bacteria inoculated beer. Of their imperial IPA, Haines mentioned, "Our mash tun will only let us turn out about 8 kegs per brew session, so we don't have a lot to offer other places." That should be reason enough to head to Vertigo for this rare and delicious brew. Whereas Friar Mike's is 6.1 percent alcohol and 67 IBUs, going wild means a 50 percent boost in each metric.

Of course, one newer beer, The Closer Pale Ale, is also exclusive— to Hillsboro. When a Short Season-A baseball team announced they were coming to the Portland suburb, there was a level of excitement. The hardball team, the Hillsboro Hops, enabled Vertigo to step up to the plate by creating this sessionable pale ale perfect for summer game days, and the stadium is just five minutes away.

Zooming in from the community, they like to keep things in the family. Haines's wife and sister-in-law help out, as has his oldest son since he was old enough to drink Dad's beer (and therefore old enough to clean kegs). His younger daughter, he said, is "chomping at the bit" to work in the taproom.

Oh, and in case you're wondering if the name is in any way an homage to the classic Hitchcock film, the answer is no, but that didn't stop the Mikes from hanging a poster of it next to the picnic tables inside.

Vertigo Brewing

Opened: 2008.

Owners and brewers: Mike Haines and Mike Kinion.

System: 7-barrel.

Annual production: 450 barrels.

Distribution: Northwest Oregon.

Hours: Wednesday through Saturday, 4 p.m. to 9 p.m.; and an hour before Hillsboro Hops home games (usually 7:05 p.m.).

Tours: Upon request.

Takeout beer: Growlers, bottles, and dock sales.

Gift shop: Glassware and shirts to wear.

Food: Rotating food trucks. BYO is OK.

Coastal

The Oregon coast stretches 363 miles from the Columbia River to the Califor-nia state line. Where spruce and fir forests flow along plentiful rivers to the mighty Pacific, the coast is abundant in beauty but had always been deficient in beer. After 2010, the tide finally turned.

As with most coastal towns, the population surges in the summer, offering the best in cycling, sand castle building, surfing, and sunsets. But why let all that spectacular coastal real estate go to waste in the winter? As giant swells overtake the shoreline, winter storms generate thunderous waves on the sandy or rocky coast, providing a free waterworks display courtesy of Mother Nature that no Hollywood director could replicate as dazzlingly. Not to mention, after the tidal fury passes, it often leaves party favors from the sea strewn across the beach. And while there's something to be said for sipping hot coffee or cocoa, storm-watching havens happen to host ideal beer spots.

Starting from the north, Astoria isn't on the true coast but it's near the mouth of the Columbia, so it pretty much feels like it. Be sure to bring your dog or your kite to run around with on *Clatsop Spit in Fort Stevens State Park*. It's the northernmost point of Oregon, and feels like the top of the world.

Seaside is a family destination with an old boardwalk vibe. Just below it, Cannon Beach takes on a more elegant tone, and its *Haystack Rock* (probably the most famous among the three on the Oregon coast alone) entrances people (and shelters plenty of starfish for unique stargazing during low tide) for hours. From there, Tillamook attracts kayakers, not to mention turophiles—cheese lovers—who visit the famous *Tillamook Cheese Factory*.

As a brewery guidebook, it demands mentioning here that the beachiest, sandiest, most wave-kissed brewery is Pelican in Pacific

Beach. Hike up the sandy dune to the top of **Cape Kiwanda** to gaze out upon another Haystack Rock. Since 1959, the annual **Dory Days Festival** celebrates the fleet of doryboats (when not out at sea they can be seen floating on the sand, protected by the cape) and tradition of dorymen, and yes, includes a fish fry.

As for fresh sealife, the entire coast offers excellent crabbing opportunities year-round. In **Depoe Bay**, resident pods of gray whales have earned this central coast town the honor of "Whale Watching Capital of the Oregon Coast." Newport, famous among beer lovers for Rogue Ales, occupies the awe-inspiring Yaquina Bay and boasts plenty of natural wonders such as **Devil's Punch Bowl State Park**, where the tide pools are captivating and the winter storm action is mesmerizing. If being outdoors when it's miserable sounds, well, miserable, you can spend hours at the **Oregon Coast Aquarium**. If one of the largest cities on the coast—home to around ten thousand residents—is too bustling, head down to Yachats. Fewer than a thousand people call it home year-round, which means gazing into the orange and purple starfish-inhabited tide pools at **Cape Perpetua** is hardly ever crowded though it's growing as a tourist destination, in part for its underdeveloped beauty.

What comes next as you venture south along the ocean-hugging Highway 101 is forty miles of natural, shifting sand dunes. Dune buggies are the prevalent method of transportation and available for rent to enjoy the **Oregon Dunes National Recreation Area**. It's also the inspiration for Frank Herbert's best-selling sci-fi novel *Dune*, which began as Herbert's writerly method of procrastination while researching a story for a magazine about the dunes in the town of Florence.

The largest coastal community is Coos Bay and it finally, once again, has its own brewery in 7 Devils. This is a popular spot among cyclists, crabbers, and clammers. A bit farther south, cranberries rule the day in Bandon (aka Bandon by the Sea). The **cranberry bogs** are such a big business that you should expect to sample unusual berry treats ranging from cranberry ketchup to cranberry wine. As a nod to the ingredient harvested here, Salem's Gilgamesh Brewing makes a sour cranberry ale called A-Bandon. Incidentally, Bandon is also home to the third of the coast's Haystack Rocks.

And finally, near the California border, making it popular among Oregonians and Californians alike, Brookings is the most temperate of the beach destinations and hosts great events such as the **Azalea Festival** over Memorial Day in the thirty-three-acre Azalea Park (since 1939), the **Southern Oregon Kite Festival** in July, and the fun-loving, family-friendly **Pirates of the Pacific Festival** in August that boasts a beer garden that should be a grog garden.

Arch Rock Brewing Co.

28779 Hunter Creek Loop, Gold Beach, OR 97444
(541) 247-0555 • ArchRockBrewingCompany.com
Twitter @ArchRockBrewing

Larry and Marjie Brennan gave the Southern Coast its first brewery where the Rogue River runs into the ocean. Thanks to ProBrewer, the classifieds for professional and aspiring brewers, they found James Smith, who traded Salt Lake City for salty sea air. Smith segued from award-winning Uinta Brewing in his native Utah, where as head brewer he worked on a 45-barrel system, to Grand Teton Brewing and their 30-barrel system at the feet of the Grand Tetons, then happily downsized to Arch Rock, where the Brennans replaced their cabinet shop with a 15-barrel brewery a half mile from the shore. It's not that they are diehard beer geeks who left their home in Phoenix for a more hospitable climate in terms of weather and beer appreciation. They just intuited that Curry County needed a brewery (though a pair of pocket-sized nanobreweries soon followed down Highway 101 in Brookings).

Smith instantly turned Arch Rock into another award-winning brewery, earning gold at NABA for his State of Jefferson Porter. The medal casually hangs above the taps, where you can sample their beers and fill growlers or half-growlers but not order full pints. For that, you've got to hit the Hunter Creek Bar & Grill directly adjacent. The porter name, I should point out, is in reference to the Jefferson Movement that swept this region of Southern Oregon and Northern California with the intention of forming a breakaway state. Supporters were incensed that the capitals of Salem and Sacramento were guilty of taxation without representation. There were plans for an elaborate State of Jefferson rebellion to occur on December 8, 1941. The bombing of Pearl Harbor gets the thanks/blame for this nonexistent fifty-first state. But the roasty porter named for it is all Smith's doing.

During my visit, a steady stream of tourists and locals sampled the beers—Arch Rock Lager, Pistol

Beers brewed: Year-round: State of Jefferson Porter, Pistol River Pale, Gold Beach Lager. Seasonals: Single-Batch Series, brewer's choice.

The Pick: State of Jefferson Porter, the gold-medal–winning beer, pours a chocolaty brown hinting at the deep chocolate flavor buried under the mocha aroma. Yes, there is a robust maltiness that suggests molasses and brown sugar, but it's not syrupy on the tongue, just rich from the roasted malts, and holds up from first sip to last, then back to first.

River Pale, the porter, and a single-batch seasonal that happened to be 28 Fingers Wit—and each walked out ordering a different growler as a testament to the quality of each one. Smith calls Pistol River a pale since it's only 35 IBUs, but it's dry hopped with Bravo, Nugget, Centennial, and CTZs so it's piney and pungent. "I didn't want to do an over-the-top, 100-IBUs IPA," he explained, favoring hop flavor and aroma to full-on bitterness. It came very close to earning a medal at NABA, and I won't be surprised in the slightest if it garners some hardware soon. Then again, it's more deserving of glassware.

You can also find these back-to-basics beers self-distributed from the actual Arch Rock in Brookings up to Florence, where we recently lost Wakonda Brewing.

Arch Rock Brewing Co.

Opened: 2013.

Owners: Larry and Marjie Brennan.

Brewer: James Smith.

System: 15-barrel.

Annual production: 500 barrels.

Distribution: Southern Coast.

Hours: Tuesday through Friday, 11 a.m. to 6 p.m.; Saturday, 11 a.m. to 5 p.m.

Tours: It's very compact. Walk in and you've gotten the tour.

Takeout beer: Growlers, half-growlers, and kegs.

Gift shop: One green T-shirt.

Extras: Belly up to the Hunter Creek Bar & Grill adjacent to the brewery to enjoy a proper pint. Fill ten growlers, get one free.

Astoria Brewing Co. / Wet Dog Café

144 11th Street, Astoria, OR 97103
(503) 325-6975 • WetDogCafe.com

I'm a sucker for family businesses that maintain a feeling of being more family than business. Owners and husband-and-wife team Steve and Karen Allen have a Brady Bunch Plus situation of having seven kids between them, so it's no wonder they number among the forty or so employees behind the bar or somewhere on the floor. Even those not directly related feel like part of their brood. Steve is a dead ringer for Steven Spielberg, which is only tangentially significant since his film *The Goonies* was set and filmed here in Astoria. Allen bought the Wet Dog Café in 1997 (the café had opened two years earlier) and immediately knew he was going to add a brewery to make it Astoria's first modern brewpub. Initially called the Pacific Rim Brewery, it segued into Astoria Brewing Co. in 2005.

Brewmaster John Dalgren, who grew up in Astoria, is given free rein to brew whatever he wants beyond the wide array of core beers, so the twelve-strong menu is a good indicator of what you'll find on tap. Sometimes the popular kegs kick; oftentimes a new seasonal appears. Maybe instead of Strawberry Blonde (brewed with over 100 pounds of fresh strawberries per batch) you might find Brewberry Wheat Ale on tap (made with marionberries, not blueberries as you might expect from the name). Although there's some ebb and flow with the taps, there'd be hell to pay if they ran out of Bitter Bitch Imperial IPA. Here I should add that all of the beers have either pooch-themed names or artwork to complement the Wet Dog aspect.

Speaking of the motif, only the riverfront deck—open all summer and, weather permitting, autumn too—allows canine companions. When we came with our dog, Dunkel, we were pleased that he could order a kiddie (not a kitty) burger patty for a buck.

Beers brewed: Year-round: Old Red Beard Amber, Da Bomb Blonde Ale, Strawberry Blonde, Volksweissen, Stone Cold Strong, Solar Dog IPA, Bitter Bitch Imperial IPA, Bad Ass Imperial Stout, Poop Deck Porter, Trolley Stop Stout, West Coast Lager. Seasonals: Astoria ESB, Brewberry Wheat, Golden Hopportunity Fresh Hop, Honey Cranberry Cream, Kirby Kolsch, Killer Whale Pale, and more.

The Pick: Bitter Bitch makes no pretense at being balanced, so if you're looking for a sensation like sucking on a hop cone—the beer is labeled as containing "100+ IBUs" because the alphas tip their brew calculator past 130 on top of its 8.2 percent ABV—this is a fun one to try.

Inside, the saloon is clustered with beer neons and license plates, but you still get a view that's no less awesome. It's as close to the Columbia River as you can get without getting wet. When I caught Allen inside the pub with Buddy, one of his Yorkies who modeled for the Volksweissen logo, he declared Buddy not a patron but an employee. Yes, the 1974 V-Dub Bug that the Bavarian-style Hefeweizen is named after is also his. And yes, his other Yorkie, Kirby, is the inspiration for Kirby Kolsch, heaven forbid he felt left out.

In 2013, Astoria Brewing added a 15-barrel brewing system to its 4-barrel pub system. Responding to demand from around Oregon and Washington (visible across the river), they began canning four brands: Bitter Bitch, Poop Deck Porter (a great, chocolaty brew), Old Red Beard Amber Ale (for those who lean toward caramel malts over bitter hops), and a new one called Trolley Stop Stout.

A visit to this town near the coast seems like a summer plan, which it no doubt is, but along with the winter stormwatching—a real pastime—the best time to soak up Astoria and Astoria Brewing Co. is probably late February (schedule a whole week to include Fort George Brewery's Festival of Dark Arts if possible), when the FisherPoets Gathering takes over, as it has since the late 1990s. The Wet Dog is one of the prime venues to listen to fishermen and fisherwomen recite fisher poems and spin fisher yarns.

Astoria Brewing Co. / Wet Dog Café

Opened: 1997.

Owners: Steve and Karen Allen.

Brewers: John Dalgren (brewmaster) and Chris Olsen (assistant brewer).

System: 15-barrel production and 4-barrel pub.

Annual production: 800 barrels.

Distribution: Oregon and Washington.

Hours: Monday through Friday, 11 a.m. to 10 p.m.; Friday and Saturday, 8 a.m. to 10 p.m.

Tours: By appointment only.

Takeout beer: Growlers, 12-ounce cans, and dock sales.

Gift shop: A formidable gift shop features its own café with snacks as well as odds and ends like non-housemade beer jelly and Beanie Babies.

Food: Beyond the expected items on this extensive menu, there are whole sections for seafood burgers and four catch options for fish and chips.

Events: FisherPoets, a three-day gathering at the end of February. Live music Wednesday through Sunday.

Other location: Tasting room around the corner at 1196 Marine Drive, Astoria.

Bill's Tavern and Brewhouse

188 North Hemlock Street, Cannon Beach, OR 97110
(503) 436-2202 • BillsTavernAndBrewhouse.com

Bill's Tavern existed on this spot before the modern incarnation of Bill's Tavern and Brewhouse. But gone is Bill Gallagher. Gone is Bill Moore. Owner Ken Campbell bought the bar in one of Oregon's most visited and charming coastal towns in 1982, but fifteen years later, after completely leveling it, rebuilt it and added a brewery in 1997 upon meeting business partner Jim Oyala. Some of the original fixtures remain, as does a framed menu from an earlier incarnation, the Imperial Grill, back when a T-bone would run you a buck fifty and something called a Liberty Steak cost just fifty cents. And the brewpub has changed little since the revamp.

Visitors are drawn to Cannon Beach for its unfettered coastal charm. The primary attraction is Haystack Rock, a monolith that juts out of the sea, and the surrounding tide pools offer the chance to get up close and personal with purple and orange starfish and aquamarine sea anemones during low tide. Afterward, it's back up to the main drag, Hemlock Street, making the brewpub one of the few that receives most of its foot traffic from those with sandy feet.

Upon entering, the family side is to the left, the adults-only side with the bar is to the right, but if you look up you'll see the 7-barrel brewhouse. With no elevator or dumbwaiter, getting 2,000 pounds of malt upstairs turns into quite a chore.

A stop at Bill's while in Cannon Beach is compulsory, and it has been a pleasant discovery that the quality in the beers seems to inch up each time. No shame in that—there's always a curve, especially considering I learned that brewer Dave Parker started out here behind the bar, not brewing above it. When Jack Harris, now up the coast at Fort George Brewing, initiated brewing duties, he scored a pair of bronze medals at GABF in 1999, including one for Blackberry Beauty, a wheat beer with blackberries and marionberries. In 2004,

Beers brewed: Year-round: Asa's Premium Blonde, Duck Dive Pale Ale, Blackberry Beauty, American Bilsner, Foggy Notion Weissbier, Rudy's Red, 2x4 Stout, Ragsdale Porter, Evil Twin IPA. Seasonals: Cherry Porter, The Stranger Rum Barrel-Aged IPA, Oatmeal Imperial Red.

The Pick: Oatmeal Imperial Red. Unlike their classic Rudy's Red, this imperial version is spicy to the point that it seems like the grain bill contains rye instead of velvety oatmeal. It definitely appeals to IPA fans, but even the bitter averse should dig it.

Bill's Tavern struck gold with Duckdive Pale Ale. Both of these beers remain staples and the two bestsellers. They're pretty straightforward and reliable.

One new development with their liquid offerings comes thanks to outside forces. When Cannon Beach Distillery opened in late 2012 a mere block from the brewery, the two businesses struck an agreement, and ever since some mighty fine beers have resulted. Upon my last visit, I tried the rum barrel-aged Stranger IPA. Ordinarily, I wouldn't expect an IPA's bitterness and citrus notes to gibe well with the sweeter vanilla notes found in a rum barrel, but since it spends only a few weeks in the barrel to condition, you still get the bright, hoppy notes up front followed by a sweet and spicy oak finish that warms not from fusel burn but from a touch of boozy throat coat.

Another development in the literal sense, though not new at this point, is the Warren House Pub, located a couple of miles south in Tolovana Park. It's a less built-up part of town so you almost get it to yourself, depending on the time or weather. It's got a great deck with a garden, and on nice days sea breeze and beer—the same ones on tap at the main pub—are a killer combo.

Of course, besides the actual brewery, the pub has another big attraction, at least on Thursday nights. House band the Floating Glass Balls jams what they call "authentic Oregon beach bum music" (think bluegrassy folk tunes) since you can't work on your Oregon tan by night.

Bill's Tavern and Brewhouse

Opened: 1997.

Owners: Ken Campbell and Jim Oyala.

Brewers: David Parker (brewmaster) and Rich Amacher (assistant brewmaster).

System: 7-barrel.

Annual production: 600 barrels.

Distribution: Cannon Beach area only.

Hours: Daily, 11:30 a.m. to 10 p.m.

Tours: By request, when available.

Takeout beer: Growlers.

Gift shop: A few shirts and glasses by the bar.

Food: Burgers, fish and chips, plus more pub grub.

Other location: Warren House Pub (3301 S. Hemlock St., Cannon Beach; 503-436-1130).

Buoy Beer Co.

#2 Seventh Street, Astoria, OR 97103

503-468-0800 • BuoyBeer.com • Twitter @BuoyBeer

The trolley along the Astoria Riverfront carries passengers directly past—and preferably to—the fourth brewery in this town of fewer than ten thousand people located near the mouth of the Columbia. Buoy Beer's objective is to lure more beer lovers to Astoria and bring the flavor of Astoria to beer lovers. Initially, the beer program focused on traditional European lagers and Northwest ales. It's why founding brewer and co-owner Dan Hamilton, who not only had thirty years' experience as a homebrewer but also was head brewer at BridgePort in Portland, launched with two pilsners: a bready German and a spicy Czech.

Equally important to the brewpub is the seafood, which they hit on several fronts. The brewery and taproom occupy part of the 44,000-square-foot building that was once Bornstein Seafood. Andrew Bornstein, another co-owner, moved that business down to Piers 1 and 2, but the restaurant still gets his freshest catches for Chef Eric Jenkins (formerly the executive chef at Oregon State University's Seafood Cooking School). The brewpub retains a seafood cannery aesthetic—fittingly, they plan to can beer—and the Oregon walnut wood bar curves around a fish ladder, giving those perched at the bar amazing river views.

Buoy Beer Co.

Opened: 2014.

Owners: Luke Colvin, David Kroening, Andrew Bornstein, Dan Hamilton, and Jerry Kasinger.

Brewers: Kevin Shaw (head brewer) and Dan Hamilton (founding brewer).

System: 20-barrel, plus a 3-barrel pilot.

Annual production: TBD.

Distribution: North Coast initially, then up to Seattle.

Hours: Sunday to Thursday, 11 a.m. to 10 p.m.; Friday and Saturday, 11 a.m. to midnight.

Tours: Inquire at the taproom.

Takeout beer: Growlers and kegs.

Gift shop: Various clothing, glassware, stickers, coasters, etc.

Food: Buoy poutine, Buoy oysters (fried with jalapeño jam), and a Buoy Bison Burger.

Beers brewed: Year-round: German Pils, Czech Pilsner, Pale Ale, NW Red, Oatmeal Stout, Dunkel, Helles, ESB.

Chetco Brewing Co.

Brookings, OR
(541) 661-KEGS (5347) • ChetcoBrewery.com
Twitter @ChetcoBrew

Chetco Brewing debuted on a high note. The nanobrewery opened on April 20, 2013, with an IPA hopped with local Willamette and New Zealand-harvested Nelson Sauvin for a beer called Willa Nelson, tapped at the Vista Pub. Look for Lilly Centennial-hopped IPA at the PC Tavern (nobody in this seaside town of seven thousand calls it the Pine Cone Tavern), located on Chetco Avenue a half mile from the Chetco River.

Owner-brewer Mike Frederick loves brewing single-hopped IPAs. "I just think it's a fun thing," he said to me over an IPA. "You get those particular characteristics." One such characteristic of some of Chetco's beers that no other brewery has is that they boast Frederick's homegrown hops. He and his wife, Alex, have eighty bines in their backyard, eleven varietals strong. Within three weeks of his first homebrewed batch from the kit Alex gave him, he had not only graduated to all-grain brewing but also ordered hop rhizomes so he could grow his own.

The brewery is rooted in their DIY ethos and was self-financed. Even the system comes with a good nano-story, which Mike sports on the back of his T-shirt: "A good friend lends you his awesome homebrewing system. A great friend lets you open your microbrewery with it." The protagonist is James Smith from Arch Rock Brewing up Highway 101.

The South Coast joined the brewing community later in the game, but it's got the right spirit. Chetco beers are available at the farmers market, where you can pick up a growler of viscous, chocolaty Block & Tackle Stout or, if you're a hop head, Thunder Rock IPA. The honey-orange elixir has good clarity, impressive considering Chetco's beers are unfiltered. A thick head props up a piney aroma, translating instantly on the tongue

Beers brewed: Year-round: Willa Nelson IPA, Chetco Effect, Chetco Logger, Thunder Rock IPA, Lilly Single-hop IPA, Raymond's Red, Very Berry Porter, Block & Tackle Stout.

The Pick: Thunder Rock IPA. The honey-orange elixir has good clarity, impressive considering all of Chetco's beers are unfiltered, with a thick head that props up a piney aroma translating instantly on the tongue, joined with candied citrus peel. Warming reveals danker notes.

and joined with candied citrus peel. Considering it's a demonstration of what Brookings-grown hops can do, you can also walk around the farmers market with a farm-fresh glassful.

It makes a fitting bookend to their first year in business that the Fredericks held a one-year anniversary party marked by a tap takeover at the place where Chetco's commercial beers all started, the Vista Pub. Naturally one of them had to be the World Beer Cup award-winning Block & Tackle Stout. They were understandably excited, but took the honor in stride. They didn't attend the conference and competition, which was held in Denver, in person. Instead, they found out the good news via text—many texts, including one from me. I ribbed that because they run a nanobrewery Alex can't let Mike get a megahead. She texted back, "They don't call Mike 'Mr. No Frills' for nothing."

Chetco Brewing Co.

Opened: 2013.
Owners: Michael and Alexandra Frederick.
Brewer: Michael Frederick.
System: 1.5-barrel.
Annual production: 40 barrels.
Distribution: Southern Oregon and true Northern California.
Hours: No public tasting room.
Gift shop: T-shirts, pint glasses, stickers, hats, and an iPhone case.

De Garde Brewing

1909 Second Street, Tillamook, OR 97141
(541) 301-8109 • DeGardeBrewing.com
Twitter @DeGardeBrewing

Biere de garde is a French style of farmhouse ale historically brewed in winter, or sometimes as late as spring, but
intended to be served to farm hands during summer when
hotter temperatures make fermentation impossible to pre
dict. (Yeast, like some people, gets crazy from the heat.)
Biere, of course, means "beer," but *de garde* translates to
"for keeping" or "guarding." This De Garde Brewing's beers
are certainly keepers, and you may just find their limited bottles guard-
ed behind the counter at select bottle shops.

Brewer Trevor Rogers is keenly aware that the fan base for his beers
is primarily Portland beer geeks, not locals in coastal Tillamook . . . yet.
He previously worked at nearby Pelican Brewery, which is known for
consistently winning awards for approachable beers, but the dapper
gent who dons a vest and newsie cap doesn't focus on the consistency
of De Garde's beer profiles or awards. He speaks
scientifically yet passionately. He makes the wort
but never pitches any yeast or bacteria, instead letting the onshore and offshore winds spontaneously
introduce fermentation. "I just try to get out of the
way of the yeast," Rogers said. "I want to let wild
ale be wild . . . We strongly believe that this particular area is uniquely suited to this type of brewing.
We love the character and vigor of the local popula-
tions and have fostered a 'relationship,' if you will,
in which we can coax particular characteristics and
desired acidity through temperature and ingredients, while letting them lead the process."

Step one was delivering kegs to Portland
before building a tasting room—sort of like bringing the mountain to Muhammad. Maybe that's
why Portland is often called a beer mecca?

From De Garde's 2013 debut during Portland
Fruit Beer Fest, this 7-barrel brewery made waves
with Belgianesque beers, starting with infinitely sessionable Bu Weisse. (Berliner Weisse is Germany's

Beers brewed: Year-round:
Bu Weisse, Imperial Bu
Weisse. Seasonals: Ever-
changing lineup including
Cran Bu Weisse, Blu Bu
Weisse, Imperial Blackberry
Bu Weisse, Soleil d'Or,
Rougie, Brun Marron, Corne-
lio Nunez Porter, and Saison
Desay blends.

The Pick: Bu Weisse. There
are seemingly infinite variations of this beer, but start
with the base Berliner Weisse.
This hazy yellow ale crams so
much character into its light
body that it startles your
tongue with a prickly acidity
and keeps you salivating till
the last lemonade-like drop.

Belgian-inspired style.) The name is a nod to the Moroccan word *Bu*, meaning "my," and also the cat of owner Linsey Hamacher, who'd lived in Morocco. (Rogers proposed to Hamacher at De Garde's meet-the-brewer premiere at The Beer Mongers taproom, so Bu is *their* cat.) Bu Weisse is a 2.2 percent tart ale Rogers described as a beer you can drink six pints of in an hour and not get too drunk. Having said that, he also makes an imperial version that's 5.5 percent ABV.

They're ramping up production because more Bu Weisse and Imperial Bu Weisse "allows us to produce a wider variety of the fruited iterations," said Rogers, referring to the blueberries, boysenberries, or blackberries that routinely find their way into barrels. This means new kegs and bottles of these refreshing beers on a monthly basis. He also added that wild saisons, blended from their stock of used barrels from various wines and even gin, will also arrive monthly.

Grapes from statewide vineyards—Rogers and Hamacher love wine as much as beer—also feature frequently. For example, Tempranillo Desay is brewed with small, black Tempranillo grapes from Abacela Estate Winery, which introduced these Spanish grapes to the Umpqua Valley.

Beyond grapes, beers are influenced by Oregon itself. "Ultimately," said Rogers, "we have to cater to what will work seasonally . . . When it's spruce tip time, I may want to make a hoppy beer, but I'd be foolish not to take advantage of such a great local ingredient."

By that reasoning, seek out Cran Bu Weisse, with cranberries harvested down the coast. The fruit promotes secondary fermentation and the naturally tart flavor and gentle acidity created one of my favorites of their beers. And I'll never get to try it again. Give Rogers a touch of credit for the way he brews, blends, and ages his beers. But there are natural factors, such as each year's cranberry harvest and differences in wind currents that, combined, all mean De Garde's beers capture—or "keep"—time and *terroir* in a bottle.

De Garde Brewing

Opened: 2013.
Owner: Linsey Hamacher.
Brewer: Trevor Rogers.
System: 7-barrel.
Annual production: 150 barrels.
Distribution: Oregon.
Hours: Thursday and Friday, 4 p.m. to 8 p.m.; Saturday, noon to 8 p.m.
Takeout beer: Bottles.
Gift shop: T-shirts, key rings, patches, buttons, and glassware.

Fort George Brewery + Public House

1483 Duane Street, Astoria, OR 97103
(503) 325-7468 • FortGeorgeBrewery.com
Twitter @FortGeorgeBeer

Fort George Brewery makes a savvy ode to Astoria's setting as the hometown in the movie *The Goonies* by selling a T-shirt adorned with "suspenders" in the style of Sloth. But whereas that character was disfigured, their Vortex IPA is truly delectable, with a perfect body. I'd say having the freshest possible pint is reason enough to visit, but throughout the year the location in general, and the brewery in particular, make stronger arguments.

First, Jack Harris was a journeyman brewer working at Bill's Tavern down the coast, though he lived in Astoria. Astoria Brewing is where Chris Nemlowill brewed. Together they envisioned opening a little brewpub in town. They didn't imagine it'd turn into something where only about 12 percent of their beer is sold via the pub and the rest goes to dominating canned beer shelves around the Pacific Northwest.

Visit in the fall for the almost-sacred experience of enjoying a Fresh Hop Vortex. Harris revealed to me the ever-tweaked hops bill. He did so over a pint of the good stuff out on the patio, where it actually pained him watching my glass be fully exposed to the harmful sunrays. UV light doesn't just cause cancer—it also breaks down the alpha acids in hops, causing light-struck beer to become skunked. (So maybe I'll skip over what's best about visiting in the long, warm days of summer.) "We're still working on the recipe, tweaking it and making it better," said Harris, adding that while they outwardly boast of the Simcoe, Centennial, and Amarillo hops, each batch may contain as many as seven different varietals. "We focus a lot of our attention on it because it's our most popular and we package it so often." The tallboy pint cans are a glorious thing.

Visit in the winter—short, dark, chilly days generate thunderous storm waves along the shoreline,

Beers brewed: Year-round: Vortex IPA, Cavatica Stout, 1811 Lager, Sunrise Oatmeal Pale Ale, Quick Wit, Divinity, Nut Red Ale, Working Girl Porter. Seasonals: Tender Loving Empire NWPA, Suicide Squeeze IPA, 3-Way IPA, Next Adventure Black IPA, North VII DIPA, Java the Hop IPA, Coffee Girl Porter, Kentucky Girl, Drunkin Pumpkin, Spruce Budd Ale, Spank Stout, Sweet Virginia Series.

The Pick: Vortex IPA. This juicy IPA bursts with Amarillo, Simcoe, and Centennial hops for a huge trop(ical)-hop bomb that smells as good as it tastes despite, not because of, its 97 IBUs.

providing a free waterworks display that no Hollywood director could replicate—for the equally stunning Stout Month. This February-long celebration of dark roasted malts actually predates Fort George, since Harris put on Highway 101 Stout Month while working at Bill's Tavern, featuring guest taps of all the locally brewed stouts. In fact, the Oregon native has done similar onyx tap takeovers at the McMenamins breweries of his past, dating back to the Hillsboro Pub in 1990 and including the Lighthouse Brewery even farther south in Lincoln City. "Stout is remarkably conducive to experimentation," Harris said of his stout obsession. "IPA is so strongly flavored. It wouldn't make sense to do a Black Walnut IPA." He paused for a split second. "Maybe it would?"

That experimentation has led to iterations of Cavatica Stout, their year-round American stout showcasing the aforementioned black walnut, as well as chili, pumpkin, and of course whiskey-aged versions. One of the most popular—and a personal fave—is Coffee Girl, "dry hopped" with 8 pounds of ground Rwanda Huye Mountain Coffee. Its drunken big sister, Kentucky Girl, is matured in bourbon barrels.

The culmination of Stout Month is the annual Festival of Dark Arts. The emphasis is on fermented liquid art of course, but there are a host of visual, musical, and performance artists also on display. They estimate that over two thousand people attend and try to sample as many of the fifty-five different stouts as they can. Over half of the brews are from participating breweries. If you love black ales, consider this event a must.

Whatever the season, Fort George is inviting. The dream of a "little brewpub" is, in reality, a humongous public house occupying a former auto dealership. Games and books are provided inside the taproom, along with sports to watch on the big screen and play, such as foosball and shuffleboard (yes, when you're drinking beer, those are sports). Originally the pub only included the downstairs, packed with thirsty patrons, some noshing on snacks and sandwiches. Now the upstairs, after major renovations, is open and provides spectacular panoramic views of Astoria while serving up wood-fired pizzas and giving the bands they book more breathing room than previously offered downstairs.

As for the brewery, there are actually two different systems—the 30-barrel production brewery dubbed "Little Miss Texas" since they procured it from St. Arnold Brewing in Houston, and the original 8.5-barrel system nicknamed "Sweet Virginia" that now serves as the pilot for the pub-only Sweet Virginia Series of beers.

If you take the weekend tour, note that some breweries lead guests to a hospitality bar afterward; Fort George doesn't, but at least they do let you buy a pint to take on the short tour, which most breweries don't allow. And the grotto pub in the detached brewhouse always pours something unique, even if it's unlisted. Don't forget to ask someone to snap your picture in front of the hot liquor tank that's painted like a large, red pig.

A new feature of the tour is the canning line—packaging a pint at a time—thanks to one of the more novel sources of crowdfunding: state lottery dollars. Harris described how they applied to Business Oregon for a $100,000 loan, unaware that Oregon Lottery contributes to this economic development program. In exchange for the forgivable loan, the brewery created several new jobs. The Lottery featured Fort George in an ad campaign, which Harris said was "unexpected." He added that "It was kind of like winning the lottery."

Incidentally, the Pacific Fur Company established a post and fort in Astoria in 1811, six years after the arrival of Lewis and Clark. The fort temporarily fell under British rule in 1813 and was, for the next five years, named after reigning King George III. The brewery's 1811 Lager marks the town's bicentennial. And though it's all American now, the brewery runs a British-inspired firkin program that introduces a new cask ale each week. "The beers are usually dry hopped with something," noted Harris. One of the brewers, Packy Coleman, "owns a farm and brings in fresh stuff to use in his firkins" because they get carte blanche to brew and enhance anything they want. Or rather, make that got. "They were putting in Skittles and Twinkies," Harris said with a hint of eye-rolling and head-shaking, "so I had to restrict them a little."

Fort George Brewery + Public House

Opened: 2007.

Owners: Jack Harris and Chris Nemlowill.

Brewers: Jack Harris, Michal "Polish" Francowicz, Jason Palmberg, Piper Gladwill, and Packy Coleman.

System: 30-barrel.

Annual production: 10,000 barrels.

Distribution: Oregon, Washington, and Idaho.

Hours: Monday through Thursday, 11 a.m. to 11 p.m.; Friday and Saturday, 11 a.m. to midnight; Sunday, noon to 11 p.m.

Tours: Weekends at 1 p.m. and 4 p.m.

Takeout beer: Growlers, cans, and dock sales.

Gift shop: Wearables for adults and kids, glasses, stickers, and koozies.

Food: Quality pub grub in the ground level of the pub, including housemade sausages, and gourmet pizzas upstairs, plus truffle mac and cheese.

Events: Festival of Dark Arts/Stout Month. "Firkin Fridays" year-round.

Full Sail Brewing Co.

506 Columbia Street, Hood River, OR 97031
(541) 386-2247 • FullSailBrewing.com
Twitter @FullSailBrewing

Hood River isn't one of Oregon's crown jewels, it's two of them, thanks to the emerald Columbia River Gorge and sapphire water that courses through it. It also wears the crown of most breweries per capita, given that it's home to five breweries among some seven thousand residents (and that's not counting the ones directly across the river in Washington or up the road toward Mt. Hood, which majestically looms over the town). Among them, Full Sail Brewing—opened as Columbia River Brewing in 1987—generated this beer-rich empire. Although you can call cofounder and president Irene Firmat the queen and her husband and brewmaster Jamie Emmerson the king, the brewery is employee owned, which only partially explains why it landed on *Outside* magazine's list of Best Places to Work. It doesn't hurt that Hood River is renowned for its kitesurfing, with the gorge creating perfect conditions on the river that attract "boardheads" the world over. The pub at the brewery offers a spectacular view overlooking the river and all those kiteboards at full sail.

Their story may start with beer. The Amber Ale they introduced in 1988 earned gold at the 1989 GABF (the first of six different styles to medal there) as their first of 130 gold medals across competitions. From world beer competitions to county fairs, they've amassed over three hundred awards and accolades.

We know this story is set in a gorgeous land. But what really drives their story is the cast of characters. Firmat was one of the first women in the modern brewing industry and remains at the head of one of the largest in the country. Emmerson drives

Beers brewed: Year-round: Amber, IPA. Pub Ale Series: Nut Brown Ale, ESB, English Pale Ale, Wassail Winter Ale, Old Boardhead Barleywine. LTD Lager Series: Bohemian Pilsner, Pale Bock, Vienna Lager, Black Bock, Oktoberfest. Session Lagers: Premium, Black, Fest Red. Brewer's Share Series. Brewmaster Reserve: Cascade Pilsner, Fresh Hop Pilsner, Bourbon Aged Imperial Stout.

The Pick: Bourbon Aged Imperial Stout. Considering Full Sail's workhorses are light- to medium-bodied, easy-drinking ales and lagers, you might not expect their bourbon barrel-aged imperial stout to strike such a mesmerizing chord, but the robust, chocolaty base, once matured for a full year between Maker's Mark, Four Roses, and Heaven Hill casks, folds in sensuous vanilla bean flavors and spirited oak, making it a serious seasonal treat.

a biodiesel car as part of the way he lives sustainably. Barney Brennan, the supervising brewer, isn't just special, he's the "B" in the spring seasonal Extra Special Barney. I honestly don't know if the tour guide who conducts the four daily tours was joking when he said that, thanks to his ownership shares, he's due $400,000 when he retires, but he's part of the fabric. And let's not forget Meura. She's in charge of filtration. When other breweries expend as many as 10 or brag about using as few as 5 gallons of water to make 1 gallon of beer, Meura, the vertical leaf pressure filter, enables Full Sail to have a water use ratio of 2.5:1. That's just one part of how far their conservation efforts have come.

In 1987, Firmat saw the new brewery as a way to bring a slower, more flavorful slice of Europe back to America because at the time, domestic brewers mostly had only European beers to revere and emulate. Between Widmer Brothers, BridgePort, and Portland Brewing, Portland had a dizzying three breweries; clearly a fourth would've been too many, right? Her ability to be very wrong wasn't just a boon to Hood River, it affected her personal life, too. Her corporate background taught her that you don't fraternize with people at work, but in April 1988 Full Sail got a new brewmaster, a Siebel Institute alumnus, Jamie Emmerson. As she phrases it today, "Jamie really was my employee. We broke every rule." She added that there have been a few other marriages brought together at Full Sail. "Everything was so crazy back then; it was a great way to fall in love."

The craziness she alluded to was the independent brewing industry growing as quickly as an awkward Mastiff puppy. Full Sail's premier bottles on the market held Golden Ale, but after Emmerson came aboard, his first specialty beer was an imperial. By 1989, he introduced the aforementioned Amber, a medium-bodied blend of crystal, pale, and chocolate malts for more than a hint of toffee. Full Sail experienced some decade-long growing pains, which, fast-forwarding through them, nearly caused Firmat and Emmerson to lose the company when original investors wanted to sell their shares. In 1999 when the sale was finalized, Firmat and Emmerson managed to keep the brewery instead of it falling into the hands of a lesser-known yet international beer and spirits conglomerate.

"We won," said Firmat, "but what we won into was the beginning of the decline of craft [brewing]." The craft beer biz was going through an infamous retraction. "What we wanted to do was acknowledge that we didn't build it alone. It's a team effort and requires a lot of people to care," she added. The 47 in their logo symbolizes the number of employees who worked at Full Sail at the time and who became co-owners. Today there are 108, not an insouciant employee-owner among them, including 10 of the original 47.

A great manifestation of that sense of ownership is the Brewer's Share series wherein any Full Sailor—that's an internal name for their brewers—can create a one-off beer of his or her design. (A portion of the proceeds benefits a local charity of their choosing). These have included the aforementioned ESB from supervising brewer Barney Brennan, as well as other eponymous beers like Francisco Farias Martinez's Farias Clara Helles, Wendell Bryant's Vendell Veizen, and Jason Muñoz's Big Daddy J's Malt Liquor. The latter may not be a style of beer typically associated with craft brewing, but it is a malt-based strong ale.

"We love malt and hops and yeast and water," Firmat responded when I asked about Full Sail's refusal to make what I sometimes call "pie beers," ones designed to taste like something such as fruit pie or shepherd's pie (but not specifically to taste like beer). "When you add so many elements, you're starting to get away from the real creativity of beer, which is the discipline of doing this extraordinary breadth of palate with four ingredients."

She spoke those words as we chatted over a couple of Black Session Lagers, the onyx sibling to Session Premium Lager, a pre-Prohibition-style beer that debuted in 2005 (before the word "session" was all the rage) and sells in throwback stubby bottles by the case for comparatively cheap. She noted the schwarzbier's coffee and chocolate background, but I particularly find those notes striking in a beer called LTD 06 Black Bock from their LTD Lager Series that kicked off a year later in 2006. It's the winter holiday release from the line of five seasonal lagers, and the chocolate malts make you swear there are real cacao nibs and coffee beans in the beer, but that's just an example of the "elegance and clarity of flavor" she referred to in relying simply on beer's four main ingredients. Beer is liquid music. Consider the myriad genres of music that can be played with just a guitar, bass, drums, and vocals.

Continuing with the music metaphor, the brewery's pub in Hood River is a grand arena, with one of the best views from any brewery anywhere. But Firmat and I sat in the Pilsner Room, their satellite pilot brewery inside McCormick & Schmick's Harborside Restaurant at Portland's RiverPlace, the equivalent of an intimate listening room. Yes there's a river view of the Willamette, but it includes the Hawthorne Bridge I-5 overpass so it's not as spectacular. The system is the brewery's original one now that the Hood River brewhouse boasts a 200-barrel system and a whopping twenty-three fermenters as large as 600 barrels deep. The 15-barrel system where the Brewmaster's Reserve beers are made is where there'd been an 837-square-foot dance floor that helped lend the former Shanghai Lounge its reputation as a meat market (until the transition in 1992).

I guess Firmat and Full Sail got their Portland brewery after all, but it's not widely known, perhaps because it's one of the Rose City's five dozen breweries at this point. Better that they went to the riverside paradise that is Hood River. And over the years, Full Sail has become the area's de facto brewery incubator. Of those other breweries in town mentioned at the start, the company's original brewmaster, David Logsdon, formed the yeast manufacturer Wyeast Labs a year later before opening Logsdon Farmhouse Ale in 2010. In 2007, former assistant brewmaster Matt Swihart embarked on creating Double Mountain, and brewer Josh Pfriem never would've opened Pfriem Family Brewers in 2011 had Full Sail not lured him to town. There are others like Solera and Everybody's Brewing, of course, but it shows how much of an impact Full Sail Brewing has had on the lives of owner-employees past and present. And it proves a point that Irene made about investment in people and equipment—"Execution really matters; consistency really matters"—but it applies to their beer as well.

Full Sail Brewing Co.

Opened: 1987.

Owners: Irene Firmat, Jamie Emmerson, and employees.

Brewers: Jamie Emmerson (brewmaster) and Barney Brennan (supervising brewer).

System: 200-barrel (Hood River); 15-barrel (Portland RiverPlace).

Annual production: 120,000 barrels.

Distribution: Oregon and twenty-eight states.

Hours: Daily, 11 a.m. to 9 p.m.

Tours: Daily at 1 p.m., 2 p.m., 3 p.m., and 4 p.m. Tours last at least thirty minutes; kids must be at least twelve.

Takeout beer: Bottles, growlers, and dock sales.

Gift shop: Tucked inside the pub; everything from shirts and other apparel to dog bowls.

Food: Snacks, salads, burgers, and sandwiches.

Other location: Pilsner Room at McCormick & Schmick's Harborside Restaurant (0307 SW Montgomery, Portland, 97201; 503-222-5343).

Hondo's Brew & Cork

2703 Marine Drive, Astoria, OR 97103
(503) 325-2234 • HondosBrew.net
Twitter @HondosBrewCork

Hondo's opened in 2005 as a homebrew supply shop, then transitioned into Hondo's Brew & Cork by adding a bottle shop for 250-plus beers, as well as cider and wine. (I scored a bottle of Deschutes's The Dissident long after it disappeared from Portland shelves.) Owner RJ Kiepke further augmented it by installing a dozen rotating taps for mostly local beers such as brews from Fort George Brewery and kegs from up in Washington or down in California. (After all, it's a healthy walk over to the Fort George Brewery from here.)

When selling acidulated malt, whole-leaf Nugget hops, P.E.T. carboys, and other supplies wasn't enough, Kiepke got licensed to sell the beer made on the nanosystem, which was already being used for homebrewing classes. In fact, the system was just doubled in size, meaning they can now brew a full barrel at a time. Given that Hondo's produces, on average, a barrel's worth of liquid a month, that means only two taps are usually devoted to house brew. "We have a hard time keeping up with the demand for our beers," Kiepke confirmed.

Brewer and manager Robert Rand said expanding two-fold, while still not a lot, gives him some freedom to fit in new recipes. "But we are trying to increase that number to six of our own beers on tap," he added.

Hondo's Brew & Cork

Opened: 2013.
Owner: RJ Kiepke.
Brewer: Robert Rand.
System: 1-barrel.
Annual production: 15 barrels.
Distribution: On-premises.
Hours: Daily, 10 a.m. to 9 p.m.
Tours: By request.
Takeout beer: Growlers and a great bottle shop.
Gift shop: Glassware, plus caps and shirts.
Food: Short list of "munchies."
Extras: Brew-on-premises. Open mic Friday nights. Minors not permitted.

Beers Brewed: Year-round: Runnin' Late Pale Ale, Chocolate Porter, Cit Wit, River Bar Imperial Stout, Imperial IPA, Ho Ho Hondo's (winter ale), Pacifica Pale.

McMenamins Lighthouse Brewery

4157 North Highway 101, Lincoln City, OR 97367
(541) 994-7238 • Mcmenamins.com/Lighthouse
Twitter @CaptainNeon

The Lighthouse Brewery is near the ocean, not on it, because it's not in an actual lighthouse, to my chagrin. Rather, it's in the Lighthouse Square Shopping Center, but the scent of sea air carries to the upstairs balcony. Still, it's the oldest brewery on the Oregon Coast and third in the McMenamins Empire.

Doug Ashley is the twenty-fifth person to helm the "fishbowl brewery," so named because guests can (but shouldn't) tap the glass wall as he floats to and fro concocting liquids better suited to drinking than swimming in. Of his house beers, he said he enjoys brewing the gamut, from wheat and fruit beers to imperial stout. I found his latter, Black Pearl, super chocolaty with a roasted quality that made it both astringent and delicious.

Each August, the Lighthouse Brewfest welcomes brewers from all twenty-two McMenamins breweries in Oregon and Washington. To determine what beer they'll pour, styles are simply pulled out of a hat. Alienator is reserved for another McMenamins beerfest, the UFO Festival held at the company's Oregon Hotel in McMinnville. I expected it to be a doppelbock because they traditionally have an "-ator" suffix, but for some unearthly reason it's an IPA.

McMenamins Lighthouse Brewery

Opened: 1986.

Owners: Brian and Mike McMenamin (see page 92).

Brewer: Doug Ashley.

System: 7-barrel.

Annual production: 769 barrels.

Distribution: On-premises and local McMenamins pubs.

Hours: Sunday through Thursday, 11 a.m. to 10 p.m.; Friday and Saturday, 11 a.m. to 11 p.m. Extended summer hours.

Tours: Walk-ins when the brewer is available.

Takeout beer: Growlers.

Gift shop: Threads and McMenamins swag up front.

Food: McMenamins salads, sandwiches, pizza, and more.

Beers brewed: Year-round: Hammerhead Pale Ale, Terminator Stout, Ruby, and an IPA.

The Pick: Cascade Head. Named for nearby Cascade Head headlands, you'd think this golden ale would feature Cascade hops, but the Sterlings and Chinooks lend a pronounced spiciness to this light sipper first brewed here in 1986.

Newport Brewing Co. / Bier One

bier one

NEWPORT, OREGON

424 Southwest Coast Highway, Newport, OR 97365
(541) 265-4630 • Bier-One.com

Half a mile from Rogue's Public House and a mile and a half from their 100-barrel brewery, Luke Simonsen and his wife, Christina, made Newport a two-brewery town when they founded the Newport Brewing Co. Luke brews 2 barrels at a time, and that beer is the proprietary domain of their Bier One homebrew supply and bottle shop that already contained fifteen taps. The local hangout, offering an outdoor patio and billiards, darts, and foosball (all indoors, naturally), has been a hub for beer lovers since 2009.

Those handles always feature popular Northwest styles, so it's not surprising that their house beers are generally in the same vein, including two IPAs, a traditional Northwest style and a blond, and a stout and a barrel-aged imperial. One of their specialties is the Berliner Weisse—the German-style ale much more common in America than in Berlin nowadays—that forgoes the traditional red raspberry or green woodruff syrups and instead comes in flavors like blood orange, pineapple, and ginger (and yes, raspberry). "Our Berliner is a lot more high octane than the German ones," mentioned Christina, pointing out that theirs is 6 percent alcohol instead of the conventional 2 to 4 percent.

Newport Brewing Co. / Bier One

Opened: 2009 (Bier One); 2013 (brewery).

Owners: Luke and Christina Simonsen.

Brewer: Luke Simonsen.

System: 2-barrel.

Annual production: 100 barrels.

Distribution: Available on tap at Bier One.

Hours: Monday through Sat, noon to 11 p.m.; Sunday: noon to 9 p.m.

Tours: None. The actual brewery is in the Simonsen's garage and not open to the public.

Takeout beer: Nope.

Gift shop: Bier One is a taproom, bottle shop, and homebrew supply store.

Food: Among the snacks and sandwiches there's a baked Monte Cristo, baked brie, and German sausage corndog.

Beers brewed: Core beers: Smooth Hoperator IPA, Max Stout, Berlinerweisse, Lukecifer Imperial Barrel Aged Double Stout, Conde Blonde IPA, and Alsea Amber, though everything rotates.

Pelican Brewing Co.

33180 Cape Kiwanda Drive, Pacific City, OR 97135
(503) 965-7007 • PelicanBrewery.com
Twitter @ThePelicanPub

Finding a brewery in a beach town isn't uncommon. Finding one directly on the beach is a better treasure than anyone swinging a metal detector could ever hope for. In that sense, Pelican is a gold mine both for its location—one visit and you won't stop talking about it either—and its thirty-two medals earned at the GABF since opening in 1997.

If nature calls while visiting, the walk down the hallway to the bathrooms is like visiting Graceland, except replace the gold records with medals and swap the King, Elvis Presley, with the Master, Eugene-native Darron Welch. His framed GABF honors for Small Brewpub of the Year in 2000 and 2005 were succeeded the following year by Large Brewpub Brewer of the Year, reclaimed again in 2013. In perhaps the more propitious competition, the internationally focused and biennial World Beer Cup, Welch and the Pelican were crowned champion brewery in the Large Brewpub category in 2008 and 2012; in 2014 they took home the Small Brewing Company championship since Pelican added a larger production facility in neighboring Tillamook.

Those blind tastings by expert beer judges prove that a mesmerizing view doesn't make beer taste better. But sit and sip al fresco on the pub's back patio, lulled by the view and the sound of rolling waves, and maybe the beer is more delicious. Buy some bottles or fill a growler and head to Cape Kiwanda State Park, a short, sandy stroll from the brewpub, for an equally awesome view of Haystack Rock just off the coast. I should mention that on the north coast, sometimes waves don't

Beers brewed: Year-round: Imperial Pelican Ale, Kiwanda Cream Ale, Doryman's Dark Ale, Tsunami Stout, MacPelican Scottish Ale. Seasonals: Winter: Bad Santa CDA, Red Lantern IPA, Mother of All Storms, Stormwatcher's Winterfest. Spring: Nestucca ESB, Winema Wit. Summer: Surfer's Summer Ale. Fall: Ankle-Buster Belgian Pale Ale, Elemental Fresh Hop Ale, MacPelican's Wee Heavy, Le Pelican Brun.

The Pick: Mother of All Storms. One of Oregon's most sought-after (and traded) beers, this bourbon-soaked beast is murky and imposing enough to frighten King Neptune, but once this bodacious barleywine warms and opens up a medley of overly ripe fruit, booze-soaked vanilla beans, and cane syrup sweetness give way to woody tannins to help savor the calm after the storm. This is an ideal beer for storing and revisiting a few years later.

roll—they crash during winter storms, making this an ideal spot for the popular sport of storm watching.

Summer days call for the excellent, grapefruity Imperial Pelican Ale—no trace of India on this stretch of the coast colonized by Jeff Schons and Mary Jones, whereas dark nimbus clouds call for rich Tsunami Export-Style Stout to keep toasty. Pair it with the clam chowder, or better still the chili made with Tsunami. Arrive during the off-season and make sure you try Stormwatcher's Winterfest, a malty, English-style barleywine that only arrives with the weather.

Most of the pub's menu, created by executive chef and former homebrewer Ged Aydelott, offers beer cuisine well beyond their beer-battered fish and chips, down to the beercakes with MacPelican Scottish Ale right in the batter (pancakes, shmancakes) served at breakfast. Even the popular burgers come on a pub-baked bun made with spent grains that also appear in the veggie burgers themselves.

Because you could easily spend the entire day and evening here—though I'd advise sticking with the lighter beers such as Kiwanda Cream Ale as a nice alternative to a pilsner or other light lager, or the Surfer's Summer Ale with biscuity malts and apricoty hops—consider booking a room across the street. The Inn at Cape, also owned by Schons and Jones, offers ocean views from every room (with only the Pelican pub in the bottom half of the frame). Reserve well in advance for their coveted annual release of Mother of All Storms—a bourbon barrel-aged version of Stormwatcher's—into a package deal called "Mother's Day" (held in November, not May), wherein a case of this limited release is delivered like room service.

In 2013 Schons and Jones set their sights beyond Pacific City. The $1,300,000 expansion that earned them the Small Brewing Company award added a larger production and bottling facility just up the highway in Tillamook. By more than doubling capacity, Pelican turned the brewpub's system into a pilot brewery where brewer Whitney Burnside gets to let her creativity run free as well as do more barrel aging. This means they can package core brands more and expand distribution (considering for sixteen years there was hardly any). The production facility includes a forty-seat tasting room and small pub, but it doesn't have quite the same view, nor the ocean breeze blowing through your hair that makes the brewpub the worst place to rush a beer.

Pelican Brewing Co.

Opened: 1997.

Owners: Darron Welch, Ken Henson, Jeff Schons, and Mary Jones.

Brewers: Darron Welch (brewmaster), Whitney Burnside (pub head brewer), and Waylon McAllister (production facility lead brewer).

System: 30-barrel, plus a 15-barrel at the pub.

Annual production: 2,500 barrels. Goal: 10,000 barrels.

Distribution: Oregon and Western Washington.

Hours: Brewpub: Sunday through Thursday, 8 a.m. to 10 p.m.; Friday and Saturday, 8 a.m. to 11 p.m. Taproom: Daily, 11:30 a.m. to 9 p.m.

Tours: Tillamook brewery tours on Saturday or by appointment. Pacific City brewpub tours by appointment or by request at the pub.

Takeout beer: 32-ounce, 64-ounce, and bombers to go.

Gift shop: Ample merchandise in the hut outside the main entrance.

Food: Extensive menu including many dishes cooked with beer, such as Tsunami Stout Chili, the eye-catching Tower of Rings in Doryman's Dark batter, clams and mussels steamed in Kiwanda Cream Ale, and breakfast beercakes made with MacPelican Scottish Ale since it's one of the few brewpubs open in the morning. At the Tillamook Tap Room, look for Fried Tillamook Cheese Curds.

Extras: Winner of thirty-two GABF medals (and counting), three resulting Brewpub of the Year honors, fifteen World Beer Cup medals (and counting), plus another three resulting Brewpub of the Year honors. Three Brewers Dinners spring, fall, and winter. Annual Mother's Day held in mid-November for the release of Mother of All Storms.

Other location: Brewery/Tap Room (1708 First St., Tillamook; 503-842-7007).

Rogue Ales

ROGUE

2320 OSU Drive Newport, OR 97365
(541) 867-3664 • Rogue.com
Twitter @RogueAles

Some of Brett Joyce's first jobs at the Rogue River Brewing Co. in the Shakespeare-oriented town of Ashland included cleaning brewing tanks and making pizzas. His father, Jack, was an executive at Nike—yes, the Fortune 500 Company—until 1988, when he co-founded the little brewpub directly on the headwaters of its namesake river. That year, according to stats gleaned from the Brewers Association and veteran beer writer Stan Hieronymus, became the beginning of the "micro" brewery boom, when the number more than doubled to 136 in America. Rogue River Brewing produced 1,000 barrels its first year, good enough to be the fiftieth largest brewer in the country. I remember talking to Jack years ago and asking him what he and his partners, some old fraternity brothers of his, had hoped to achieve with the business. "We didn't think about it," he quipped. "The plan was to not go broke."

Of the microbreweries that have survived, many remain some of the largest brewing companies in the country—names like Brooklyn Brewery, Great Lakes, and Deschutes. I say survived, yet it's not a story of survival but rather of evolution. Rogue is now nation- and worldwide and owns eleven public houses across the Pacific Northwest (and ties to one in the South Pacific). But that might not be the case had Brett, once we fast-forward seventeen years to 2005, not received The Call. At the time, Brett worked in marketing for Adidas—the Miller to Nike's Budweiser—but one of Jack's old fraternity brothers implored him to quit. "I would not risk the friendship that I have with my son, so my partners called him," Jack said.

That's how Brett became the president of Rogue Ales. When they moved the bulk of their

Beers brewed: Year-round: Dead Guy Ale, American Amber, Beard Beer, Brutal IPA, Cap'n Sig's Northwestern Ale, Dad's Little Helper, Dry Hopped St. Rogue Red, Hazelnut Brown Nectar, Juniper Pale Ale, Mocha Porter, Morimoto Imperial Pilsner, Morimoto Soba Ale, Morimoto Black Obi Soba, New Crustacean Barleywine, Shakespeare Oatmeal Stout. Voodoo Doughnut beers: Bacon Maple Ale, Chocolate, Peanut Butter & Banana Ale, Pretzel, Raspberry & Chocolate Ale. XS Series: XS Imperial I2PA, XS Old Crustacean Barleywine, XS Dead Guy Ale, XS Russian Imperial Stout. Rogue Farms beers: Dirtoir Black Lager, Good Chit Pilsner, Single Malt Ale, OREgasmic Ale, Roguenbier Rye. Seasonals: Chipotle Ale, Chocolate Stout, Double Chocolate Stout, Irish Lager, Mom's Half-E-Weizen, Santa's Private Reserve, Yellow Snow IPA, Rogue Farm Honey Kolsch, Wet Hop Ale, Pumpkin Patch.

brewing operations to Newport along the coast, they soon pulled the stakes from the Ashland tent after it flooded in 1997, hence the name change from Rogue River Brewing. They play up the alternate meaning of the word: a tradition-bucking, mischievous scamp. Jack's title became Chief Wisdom Officer. A pioneer among the first wave of craft brewers, his passing in May 2014 at age seventy-one saddened the industry that still benefits from the collective wisdom of its forefathers.

Of course, the story of Rogue isn't just about Jack. Or Brett. Or legendary brewmaster John "More Hops" Maier, who was pegged for the job after he was named the American Homebrewer Association's Homebrewer of the Year in 1986, aided by having attended the Siebel Institute of Technology. His wife, Stacey, is an equally indispensable character in the cast of Rogue (as was their big, black Labrador, Brewer, the inspiration for their dog-friendly Annual Brewers Memorial Fest held inside the brewery). Many folks stand in the Rogue limelight, but one guy deserves a share of the credit, and he's dead.

Dead Guy Ale embodies the Rogue ethos. They call it a Maibock, which should mean it's a bottom-fermented lager, but it's top-fermented with the house Pacman ale yeast, so a true Maibock it is not. Traditionally, Maibocks are brewed in winter and lagered (stored) in ice caves, then brought out in May (*Mai* means "May" in German). It's their flagship, but instead of putting all their muscle behind the brand to make it such, Brett explained that John originally made a beer called Maierbock that, frankly, did not sell. Later, recounted Brett, "We made a beer for [the] Casa U-Betcha chain of Tex-Mex restaurants, for the Day of the Dead." Guess what they called it. "People liked the beer and loved the name." That beer was infused with chilies to pair with the cuisine. They kept the name, but replaced the recipe with Maierbock's, the malty beer seemingly tinged with caramel with a peppery hint of hops that would go on to convert masses into craft beer fans. The imperial version, Double Dead Guy, is chewier, hoppier, and altogether deadlier, and is released only in time for Dia de Los Muertos.

But Brett still gives all the credit to Maier. "John's the hero. He's a man of few words, but by not saying a lot he's being iconic." After all, how many brewers' images grace their own bobblehead dolls? (His is available at the Newport brewery's colossal gift shop, which you have to walk through to get to the on-premises, two-story pub, Brewer's on the Bay, which overlooks Yaquina Bay.) Most importantly, Brett added, "He designed every recipe" and is approaching two thousand batches so far.

Rogue has almost thirty year-round brands and a healthy handful of seasonal ones for which they've won twenty-nine GABF medals over the years. Oddly, the beer with the most wins is Smoke Ale, a rauchbier that set the judges' hearts en fuego nine times in blind taste testings between 1990 and 2011, but has since been retired.

"We fight for the beer drinker," said Brett. "Does the beer drinker want limited options?" We all know the answer. "Consumers and retailers want variety; they don't want just two beers. We had that insight early on, but it's not efficient, smart, or profitable." Rogue produces well over 1,000 barrels a year, and has climbed from the fiftieth to the twenty-second largest craft brewery in the country. So that notion is debatable, but I certainly understand his point. They don't just push Dead Guy and Brutal IPA. They know not everyone reaches for a hazelnut-flavored beer all the time, but if you're looking for one, Hazelnut Brown has medaled four times in the Specialty category—the catch-all for miscellaneous beers that don't fit a true style—including back-to-back golds in 2011 and 2012. Despite that, Brett said that beer has experienced a "significant drop-off. Then a significant drop-off again." Hmmm. That indeed doesn't sound like a formula for profitability, but I hope they don't retire the hazelnut.

Certainly that is what makes for loyal fans, who can become card-carrying citizens of the Rogue Nation. That's not just figuratively speaking: my dog, Dunkel, has photo ID, meaning he's one of the 185,672 citizens (at the most recent count), but unlike the other 185,671 he can't get member benefits like a buck off pints at Rogue public houses. That citizenship, Rogue's team calculated, makes the Rogue Nation the fifty-third smallest nation in the world—there are over three times as many Rogues as there are Greenlanders (population 56,483).

There are so many facets to the Rogue story, it's deserving of its own book. It actually got one, though it's primarily dedicated to Rogue's GYO (Grown Your Own) efforts, resulting in their microhopyard in the once "Hops Capital of the World," Independence (see page 236), and barley farm out on the slopes of the Tygh Valley in Eastern Oregon. The book, *Rogue Farms 1880–2012—Three Centuries: a Short History*, is a pretty hilarious read and indicative of their style.

But reading about beer, be it in a history book or, uh, a guidebook, is no replacement for enjoying beer. In Newport, there's the forty-tap pub at the brewery, surrounded by a dozen towering conical fermenters, and there's the public house by the wharf—it "only" features thirty-five taps—that was the brewing location until 1992. Find yourself three Dead Guys to the wind and, if it's vacant, you can check into the apartment directly upstairs. Best of all, they allow pets if you make it to the Brewers Memorial Fest, where the Maiers get to play host along with their pooches, curly-coated retrievers named Mojo and Luna.

"Are you glad you accepted?" I asked Brett.

"I never once thought I was gonna get the call," he reflected, thinking back on the last several years. "Yep. It's been a great challenge, and a great honor."

Rogue Ales

Opened: 1988.

Owner: Brett Joyce.

Brewer: John "More Hops" Maier.

System: 100-barrel.

Annual production: 111,000 barrels

Distribution: All fifty states and over thirty countries.

Hours: Sunday through Thursday, 11 a.m. to 8 p.m.; Friday and Saturday, 11 a.m. to 9 p.m

Tours: Monday through Friday at 1:30 p.m., 3:30 p.m., and 5:30 p.m.; Saturday and Sunday at 11:30 a.m., 1:30 p.m., 3:30 p.m., and 5:30 p.m.

Takeout beer: Entire range of bottles from 12-ounce to 3-liter jeroboams, growlers, or any size container, and dock sales.

Gift shop: It's huge. Beers, shirts, bike jerseys, Brewshoes, Brewmaster John Maier bobbleheads, condoms, and more.

Food: Brewer's on the Bay, the on-site pub, features an ample menu of apps, soups, salads, sandwiches, burgers, dogs, and specialties such as Kurobuta Kurizo Tacos and a house-smoked salmon melt, plus a kids menu.

Fests: Brewer's Memorial Ale Fest is held in mid-May. The event (ages twenty-one and up) benefits various Lincoln County animal shelters and welcomes over three thousand people, many of whom come with their four-legged family members. It's twenty-one and up but dogs need not be the equivalent three in "human years." Includes guest breweries, live music, a dog wash, and competitions including a Brewer look-alike contest since the fest is in memory of Brewer, the Maier's big black lab.

Other location: Rogue Ales Public House (748 SW Bay Blvd., Newport; 541-265-3188).

Rusty Truck Brewing

4649 Southwest Highway 101, Lincoln City,
   OR 97367
(541) 994-7729 • RustyTruckBrewing.com
Twitter @RustyTruckBrew

This joint started as Roadhouse 101 directly on Highway 101 and certainly achieves the aesthetic, with road signs and car hoods on the wall and plenty of neon. But instead of Patrick Swayze (R.I.P.), you'll find families with kiddoes in tow. If you're looking for something more adult, stick to the subdivided saloon side of Rusty Truck Brewing (the one with the lottery machines). If you like your classic rock and like it loud, this is your spot. Live bands, mostly blues and classic rock covers, play Friday nights. The brewery is situated behind the restaurant, so unlike some brewpubs, guests won't smell the beer actually being made. But stick your nose in a glass of Road Wrecker and you'll smell those hops (that smell like citrus pith). Hops not your thing, or not looking for a beer that's almost 7 percent ABV? Try the Taft Draft Toffee Porter.

As the sign out front says, Rusty Truck specializes in seafood, and both the shrimp cocktail and fish and chips are popular items. But if you have your heart set on the blackened mako shark tacos on the menu, go fish for another pint because they're no longer available.

Rusty Truck Brewing

Opened: 2011.

Owner: Brian Whitehead.

Brewers: Brian Whitehead (brewmaster) and Jon Anderson (head brewer).

System: 10-barrel.

Annual production: 550 barrels.

Hours: Seasonal; check before you visit.

Tours: By request.

Takeout beer: Growlers and dock sales.

Gift shop: T-shirts and swag.

Food: Seafood, ribs, steaks, and pizza.

Beers brewed: Year-round: Beach Blonde Ale, Cherry Chocoholic, Fender Bender Amber Ale, Low Rider Lager, Moonlight Ride Blackberry Ale, Nelscott Reefer Hempeweizen, Pedal To The Metal Double IPA, Procrastinator Stout, Road Wrecker IPA, Slant 6 Pale Ale, Stupiphany Imperial Red Ale, Taft Draft Toffee Porter.

The Pick: Stupiphany. As an imperial red over an IPA, this malt-driven ale still finds a way to haul lots of hops.

Seaside Brewing Co.

851 Broadway Street, Seaside OR 97138
(503) 717-5451 • SeasideBrewery.com
Twitter @SeasideBrewery

Seaside the summer tourist destination has a boardwalk feel akin to Santa Cruz or the entire Jersey Shore. But Seaside the home is a "very blue-collar town where you better love to work," said Seaside Brewing cofounder Jimmy Griffin. Four blocks east of the beach along Broadway Street on the more, shall I say, mature end of this main drag, farther from the places that serve carnival foods such as elephant ears and deep-fried everything, is the new brewpub with quite a lot of history. Look closely and you can see the repaired hole in the brick wall above the main bar where a jailbreak had been attempted back when it was the drunk tank in this former City Hall. The actual prison bars have been restored, hopefully just for decorative purposes. It sat empty and fell into disrepair for twenty-three years. Today, if anything, it's become more captivating.

Founded by Griffin and partner Vince Berg, two former Rogue Ales GMs, the brewery has truly required lots of labor and tons of love to become a reality. It also necessitated battling a major beer brewing conglomerate that tried to derail their mission, as well as the most predominant coffee brewing empire, which had designs on this space. Afterward, the owners (and brewers) debuted their brewery in the summer of 2012 on a 10-gallon homebrew system, then transitioned to a single-barrel brewery they cobbled together, and finally realized their initial vision of a 15-barrel brewery to serve the coast, the Willamette Valley, and beyond.

The space is infinitely inviting, but let me start with the beers. It's almost funny that Griffin and Berg were managers and not brewers, because their beers rock as much as nearby landmark Haystack Rock. (Since it's in the ocean, would that

Beers brewed: Year-round: Lockup IPA, Lock Down Double IPA, Honey Badger Blonde, SS Imperial Pale Ale, Muther Hefei-Weizen, Shorties Oatmeal Stout (nitro) and Black Dynamite Vanilla Bean Chocolate and Bourbon Stout (nitro). Seasonals: 5 Mil Strong Ale, North Coast Red IPA, Breakout IPA, Spiced Porter.

The Pick: Black Dynamite lives up to its name in that it's pitch black and explosively tasty. This imperial stout with bourbon-soaked vanilla beans and cacao nibs (also getting the bourbon treatment), is a show-stopper from first chilled sip to last warmed drop. It has the sweetness to not just pair with dessert but replace it altogether, yet the bitterness and roastiness to enjoy snifter after snifter.

make it a watermark?) Maybe Griffin uttered to me in an off-the-record way or maybe not, but he said something about having hired some brewers who turned out to be divas. That doesn't fly here. So they take it on themselves.

From the clean, Bavarian-style Muther Hefer-Weizen that doesn't go deep into the field of phenols, to the imperial version of Lockup IPA called Lock Down Double IPA (remember, this is where town drunks wound up in the clink) that boasts huge pine notes boosted by dry-hopping with citrusy Simcoes, these guys have chops. Make sure you place your order correctly, depending on how burly you want your IPA. Berg mentioned that Lock Down may be a temporary name as it could cause confusion with its little brother Lockup, to which I suggested they could make the DIPA name even more confusing and call it Clock-up on account of its clocking in at 9.2 instead of 6.5 percent ABV and thereby maybe cleaning your clock . . . but we'll see.

Arrive in the winter and order a 5 Mil Strong Ale, named for the thickness of the wetsuits surfers need to don to not get hypothermia surfing the storm-driven waves (it snowed here in the winter of 2014), and the effect this beer has emulates the warming effect, just on the inside.

As mostly a summer destination, Seaside might feel chilly during the off-season but there's generally a warm vibe any time of year, especially during the weekly Yoga and a Beer nights held in the winter, proving that this is more than just a hangout for diehard surfers. With the dishes that all have a home-cooked meal quality—not that most families smoke their own meat or get fish as freshly delivered as the pub does—and both kid-friendly dining areas and patios or barfly-friendly bar, it's easy to see why folks enjoy doing hard time here.

Seaside Brewing Co.

Opened: 2012.
Owners and brewers: Jimmy Griffin and Vince Berg.
System: 15-barrel.
Annual production: 500 barrels.
Distribution: North Coast and Northern Oregon.
Hours: Daily, 11 a.m. to midnight.
Tours: By request.
Takeout beer: Growler fills.
Gift shop: T-shirts, hats, and stainless steel growlers.
Food: Menu heavy on the fresh fish specialties, but don't overlook the house-smoked meats like the brisket and the pizzas.

7 Devils Brewing Co.

247 South Second Street, Coos Bay, OR 97420
(541) 808-3738 • 7devilsbrewing.com
Twitter @7DevilsBrewery

Owners Carmen Matthews and his wife, Annie Pollard, sum up their mission in four words: "Peace, love, music, beer!" That last objective would've been enough for this coastal town that'd been brewery-less for a decade. But the nature of this brewpub—opened in 2013, when they were both thirty—is community. To their point, however, what's community without peace, love, music, and of course, beer?

Matthews is from Coos Bay; Pollard is a marine biologist but there's no marine life in her hometown of Salem. Both were homebrewers who dreamt of opening a brewpub before they'd even met. Kismet. Furthermore, they're both active with the Surfrider Foundation, Matthews as a chapter chair and Pollard as a volunteer coordinator.

The public house also functions as a gallery (check out the framed photos, sculptures, and more from local artists; Pollard crafted the blown-glass hop pendant lights and handmade all the ceramics, from the bowls down to the salt and pepper shakers). Even the botanical "rain" and beer garden is a communal green thumb project.

Seven Devils has plenty of ideas, from cask ale and fermented food programs to a homebrew club, but it's already a great hub where beer lovers, artists, kids, dogs (outside), and surfers can feel at home.

7 Devils Brewing Co.

Opened: 2013.

Owners and brewers: Annie Pollard and Carmen Matthews.

System: 7-barrel.

Annual production: 300 barrels.

Distribution: Local pubs along the coast.

Hours: Sunday through Thursday (closed Tuesday), 11 a.m. to 10 p.m.; Friday and Saturday, 11 a.m. to midnight.

Tours: Wednesdays and Saturdays during the summer, and by request.

Takeout beer: Growlers and kegs.

Gift shop: Shirts, hoodies, growlers, hats, and, yes, knitted "brewers' beards."

Food: Sustainable, seasonal specialties including poutine, black truffle mac and cheese, and 7 Devil's Food Cake made with Blacklock Oat Porter.

Beers brewed: Year-round: Groundswell IPA, Lighthouse Session Ale, Advocate NW Pale Ale, Arago Amber, Blacklock Oat Porter. Seasonals: Double Hop IPA, Shore Acres, seasonal spiced ale.

Tight Lines Brewery

625 Chetco Avenue, Suite 120, Brookings, OR 97415
(760) 885-9638 • TightLinesBrewery.com
Twitter @TightLinesBrewe

Tight Lines brewer and cofounder Nate Heath confessed, "My three-year plan is to get out of prison." He's not making hooch as an inmate—he's a correctional officer at a nearby state prison, having transferred here from his previous position at a prison in his native Southern California. He said he felt the southern coastal town of Brookings made for a better launching pad for his brewery. He and his wife, Nicole, partnered with his father-in-law, Dave Faires, to establish the brewery, though Faires is somewhat in absentia since he lives in the craft beer void of California's Palm Desert. Heath has always loved to fish, and since Brookings is a fishing mecca, "tight lines"—the "break a leg" of the angler world—felt right.

Heath's new side gig only allows him to brew 2 barrels at a time (though with 4-barrel fermenters). Dog Hair Porter earned its name when Faires (who had homebrewed in college before it was legalized) spilled malts in the garage where their Labrador shed heavily. But fear not, they don't replicate that part for commercial batches. RIP Pale Ale honors Heath's grandparents, who had enjoyed his homebrew. His inheritance partially funded the brewery. Furthermore, on account of his grandfather having been a veteran, Tight Lines concocted a light ale for the local VFW. (Heath even hooked them up with a kegerator.) But how to get non-veterans to discover and try the beer?

Within months of casting their tap lines around town, they expanded and opened a taproom where they introduce new styles. Heath said he was eager to develop this aspect of the brewery since Brookings is Oregon's southernmost beach town, meaning Tight Lines is the first brewery roadtrippers can visit when driving up from California. If it's a family trip, there's no need to leave the kids and dog in the car (which is never a good idea anyway), since everyone's welcome.

Beers brewed: Year-round: RIP Pale Ale, Dog Hair Porter, Siskiyou Kid IPA. Rotating: TL Amber, Piye (Pie-in-Your-Eye) Pumpkin Ale.

The Pick: RIP Pale Ale. The Cascade hops, practically a staple for pale ales, are what make this, if not a dead-ringer for Sierra Nevada Pale Ale, a worthy facsimile delivering just the right citrus and pine flavor that will have you hooked.

If you're not visiting during its limited hours, try the beers at the Black Trumpet Bistro, the Italian restaurant directly above the brewery. You might find a beer Heath's working on: a honey cream ale named Special Delivery, dedicated to his mom, who's a postal worker. I happened to meet her on my visit, too, and she said she's already dreaming of the day she'll retire and staff the taproom. The brew's Smith River honey, incidentally, is courtesy of a retired correctional officer-turned-beekeeper. Also look for Maxnificent, a Belgian Strong Golden named for Faires's grandson (Heath's nephew), Max; a Witbier named Quintessence; and a lemon IPA. And Heath has already picked spruce tips for a gruit spiced only with said local spruce.

Tight Lines Brewery

Opened: 2013.

Owners: Dave Faires; Nathan and Nicole Heath.

Brewer: Nathan Heath.

System: 2-barrel.

Annual production: 100 barrels.

Distribution: Brookings to Gold Beach.

Hours: Thursday through Saturday, 3 p.m. to 8 p.m.

Extras: Local events where you'll find Tight Lines include the Azalea Festival held over Memorial Day weekend, the Southern Oregon Kite Festival held mid-July, Gold Beach Brewfest, and a Brookings Artwalk the last Saturday of the month.

Twisted Snout Brewery and Public House / Pig Feathers BBQ

318 South Main Street, Toledo, OR 97391
(541) 336-1833 • TwistedSnout.com
Twitter @TwistedSnoutPub

In the realm of pairing beer with food, it's deliciously obvious why most brewpub menus focus on pizzas and burgers. For vegetarians, many a brewpub offers a veggie burger made with spent grains. But most beer-loving folks aren't vegetarians. We crave meat. And what cuisine is meatier than barbecue? None.

Enter Stu Miller, an Oregon State Grand Champion of barbecue. The story of his Twisted Snout Brewing actually starts with his Pig Feathers BBQ. Though they don't share an address (Pig Feather's address is 300 Main Street), they have the same phone number, devout customers, and master maker.

Stu said he learned to cook at age three, and luckily he kept picking up new culinary skills (not that a spaghetti-oriented brewpub couldn't work). He said he first made his own barbecue sauce at fifteen. "I'm fifty now, so it's been a while." That also means that according to the numbers and dates he gave me, he was nineteen when he homebrewed his first beer in 1982. That'll happen when you attend famed party school California State University, Chico, and your psych professor runs a homebrew supply shop. The Millers' sons have followed in his footsteps. His oldest, Robert, began apprenticing in the brewery with his dad before he even turned twenty-one. His younger son, Fulton, got his start cooking in the kitchen when he was twelve.

As for how Stu and his wife, Becky, launched their own tiny brewing empire, it resulted from a leisurely drive far from their home in Clackamas County, through Newport, seven miles west along the coast, when they spotted a sign for Toledo. Not the Ohio one 2,500 miles away, but the burg of

Beers brewed: Year-round: Gateway Golden Ale, Oops!, Wilbur's White Wheat, Twisted Snout IPA, Red-Headed Step Hog, Honey Oatmeal Porker. Seasonals: Holy Hog! Winter Ale, Spruce Hog, Dayle Earnhog Imperial Red, Raspberry Squeal, Savory Sow Basil-Tarragon IPA, and more.

The Pick: Honey Oatmeal Porker. The sweet and roasted notes of this porter play well with pulled pork as well as spice-rubbed ribs. Made with wildflower honey from the hills of Corvallis, the light body won't fill you up, leaving room for more meat.

around 3,500 people named after it (the founder's son was homesick for Ohio). Stu and Becky deemed this Toledo the sweet spot for the restaurant they'd spent years dreaming of opening.

Stu had won a few barbecue competitions, and in 1993 he became state champ. Focusing on pork ribs and chicken wings, the Millers dubbed their restaurant Pig Feathers in 2007. Travel guide bible Fodor's dubbed it "the best barbecue restaurant in the Pacific Northwest." Fodor's continued: "Owner and chef Stu Miller's sauces and rubs transform mere wings, pulled pork, and baby back ribs into tastes so rich and rare that they've brought grown men to tears."

Don't just take Fodor's word for it. Ask anyone in town, and he or she will be quick to tell you that Stu makes the best pulled pork, which, Becky mentioned, is oddly only the result of people walking in and kneejerk ordering pulled pork sandwiches despite such a delicacy not appearing on the menu. But the customer is always right, so now it's a staple and "goes gangbusters." The ribs, likewise, are delectable, though Stu pointed out their focus isn't on smoke. "It's about sauces and seasoning," he said, apropos of his salt-pepper goatee. So let's call it Toledo-style barbeque.

But this isn't a barbeque guidebook, it's a brewery guidebook. Twisted Snout premiered with a 1-barrel brewing system in the summer of 2011, then expanded threefold when the Millers bumped up to 3 barrels in the summer of 2013. There are always a dozen Twisted Snout beers on tap, half core recipes and half seasonals. Among the former, one of the most popular is the Gateway Golden Ale, essentially designed like a pilsner but fermented with ale yeast. Still, it's light, clean, and very easy to drink, just with a touch of tang that a lager yeast wouldn't have. Equally popular, naturally, is the IPA. In the Northwest fashion, it's a bit more red than pale, but those malts are doing what they can to support the hop bill of 2.5 pounds per barrel.

I didn't ask Stu how much tarragon and basil he adds to the Savory Sow IPA, a seasonal that's available quite often, but he explained that he adds the herbs at "flame-out," meaning just before the end of the boil so it's not technically dry hopped. The savory element adds a pleasant aroma of a Provençal kitchen and complements the spicing in the all-American meats in your basket. Another herbal beer I tried is the Spruce Hog, a pale ale base beer made more resinous with spruce tips that they pick right at the coast south of Newport; naturally, it's only available in early summer. Puzzlingly, while Stu has incorporated the spruce *terroir*—extra apt since the restaurant and pub are across the Yaquina River from a spruce saw mill—he hasn't done a smoked beer . . . yet.

Many a beer perfectly chases most barbecue, but don't overlook a particular pair. Raspberry Squeal is a golden ale with a pinkish hue from real raspberries. All respectable barbecue joints serve fruit sodas (strawberry and grape are my go-tos). This isn't nearly as sweet, but the fruit flavor and light body provide a great counterpoint to the dense, spicy, porky goodness. Moreover, Stu calls Honey Oatmeal Porker—a porter of course—"the best barbecue beer that we do." He's right. The honey's sweetness complements the sauce, the roast malts complement the hours of smoke, and the oatmeal provides just a touch of meatiness to chase like with like.

That's not to say you can't enjoy a pint of the Porker on its own in the adults-only tasting room that's separate from the restaurant, but why not at least get a half rack of ribs, just because you can? "We wanted the pub side to be something adults didn't have to have kids around, to be honest," Stu said. And as my own baby boy colored in his menu with their crayons, I can't argue with that reasoning or execution.

Twisted Snout Brewery and Public House / Pig Feathers BBQ

Opened: 2011.

Owners: Stu and Becky Miller.

Brewers: Stu Miller and Robert Miller.

System: 3-barrel.

Annual production: 130 barrels.

Distribution: Central Coast.

Hours: Sunday through Thursday, 11 a.m. to 9 p.m.; Friday and Saturday, 11 a.m. to 10 p.m. or later.

Tours: By request.

Takeout beer: Growlers.

Gift shop: Glassware, shirts, and of course, barbecue sauces and rubs galore.

Food: Barbecue! Ribs, wings, smoked prime rib, and fresh-ground burgers, including the "Stu-icidal Poblano" topped with chili verde.

Extras: Stay tuned to www.snoutfest.com for details on their plans for an annual Snout Fest, though other Toledo events such as the Annual Wooden Boat Show, Classic Car Show, and Summer Fest all pack 'em in.

Wolf Tree Brewery

SEAL ROCK, OREGON
BREWED IN THE WOODS

Seal Rock, OR 97376
(541) 961-2030 • Facebook.com/Wolf.TreeBrewery
Twitter @WolfTreeBrewery

When Wolf Tree Brewery debuted on the OLCC's October 2013 report of taxable barrels, it entered as the 166th largest brewery with 0.4 barrels. (There was no 167th place.) Hardly one of the state's big dogs. But perhaps everyone should watch their backs since owner-brewer Joe Hitselberger, a forester with the Oregon Department of Forestry, told me, "A wolf tree is a term used to describe the biggest tree in the forest."

Around Seal Rock, that's generally trees such as the Sitka spruce. Hitselberger grows or forages many of the ingredients on his cattle ranch that includes five hundred acres of coastal forest. Beyond the ranch-grown Cascade and Newport hops, he gathers spruce tips for the flagship Spruce Tip Ale. They come out in spring, but Hitselberger aims to make it a year-round beer by freezing the tips, much the way hops are preserved after the harvest.

The first in the brewery's Farm Dog series, with each beer named after a dog on the ranch, is Camille's Golden IPA (for his old golden retriever). Camille's clocks in at over 6 percent ABV and reaches 100 IBUs.

As for trying to make everything homegrown, there've been some test batches of barley, but Hitselberger said he isn't sure "the climate is well suited for that." He also does test batches of beers made with wild berries such as blackberries and huckleberries. "Using ingredients we harvest from the ranch is essential for our beer, and I think brewing with natural spring water makes the beer taste better," he said. "We also feed the cows the spent grain, and I think they appreciate it."

Wolf Tree Brewery

Opened: 2013.
Owner and brewer: Joe Hitselberger.
System: 20-gallon.
Annual production: 20 barrels.
Distribution: Lincoln County.
Hours: No visitors allowed.

Beers brewed: Year-round: Wolf Tree IPA, Spruce Tip Ale. Seasonal: Camille's Golden IPA.

Yachats Brewery, Market, and Farmstore

348 Highway 101 North, Yachats, OR 97498
(541) 547-3884 • YachatsBrewing.com

As with most coastal towns, the population surges in the summer, but for those who live in Yachats (pronounced "Yaw-hots") year-round, getting their own brewery will make it more spectacular. That's why Nathan Bernard and his wife, Cicely, are currently building a brewery within their new farm store, stocking farm and garden supplies as well as uber-fresh produce and other food goods from local farmers.

Construction has begun on the three-story structure that'll house the 10-barrel brewery. In it, Charles Porter from Logsdon Farmhouse Ales will occasionally be moonlighting to produce his planned beers, including Perpetua Belgian Pale Ale and a Coastal Dark Ale. Equally awesome are the designs for a tasting room on the top floor, which will offer epic views to pair with said beers, though it may not come to fruition until 2016.

Porter and Bernard are fishing buddies, so the brewery—over a decade in the planning and a few years in the building—is an extension, or what Bernard says is a way "to build Charles a playhouse." He and Cicely built their own, an actual house on five acres right up the Yachats River, where they brought to life their permaculture designs for "perennial polyculture." As Bernard further explained, because they select diverse species of plants and insects, their backyard forest produces amazing asparagus, artichokes, and more. With every aspect working together, "it's our philosophy of how we farm." And who doesn't work better when there's fresh beer involved?

Yachats Brewery, Market, and Farmstore

Opened: 2013.
Owners: Nathan and Cicely Bernard.
Brewer: Charles Porter (consulting brewmaster).
System: 10-barrel.
Annual production: 130 barrels (estimated).
Distribution: Central Coast.
Hours: Check before you visit.
Takeout beer: Growlers, and eventually cans and bottles.
Gift shop: Short-sleeve and long-sleeve T-shirts.
Food: Produce stand and deli case featuring local, organic items.

Beers brewed: Planned: Perpetua Belgian Pale Ale, Coastal Dark Ale, IPA, and barrel-aged beers.

The Gorge–Eastern

Let's address this grouping at the forefront. The breweries in Hood River and around Mt. Hood are closer to Portland than they are to Hells Canyon, but they are east of Portland and there's a shift—a change—that occurs the second you enter the **Columbia River Gorge**. It's like you've entered another world, a more gorgeous one. The canyon literally cradles you in this eighty mile stretch of land amidst the Cascade Range. And though the city of Hood River—human population, just over seven thousand, brewery population, five, plus four brewpubs right across the river in Washington—is only an hour's drive from the city, from there it's another two hours to the next brewpub, Prodigal Son in Pendleton, and a hypnotic five hours to the easternmost brewery in the state, Beer Valley in Ontario. It'd be easy to say that the eastern region looks and feels more like Idaho than Oregon, but there's no reason to be Western Oregon-centric. Besides, the breweries that dot the region are not to be missed, both for their excellent beer and their spectacular scenery.

As mentioned, it's only an hour's drive from Portland to Hood River, but it rightly should take several hours if you stop to enjoy some of the waterfall hikes. **Multnomah Falls** is the most popular and quite breathtaking (in the figurative and literal sense, since those switchbacks will get you) but there are well over one hundred such hikes in all, and who doesn't love going behind waterfalls like you can do on the Ponytail Falls trail?

Before the brewery boom that gave Hood River the highest amount of breweries per capita, the town was devoted to "boardheads," people who take advantage of the windy conditions and go kiteboarding. The low sky above the river is littered with said kites and even if you don't partake, it makes for a great spectator sport. For those who prefer to ride bikes rather than kiteboards, the **Historic Columbia River Highway State Trail**, the old U.S. Highway 30, is today reserved for those using only foot or pedal power.

Lastly, when in Hood River, whether if only for a day trip or an extended visit, check out the thirty-five-mile stretch of highway known as the **Fruit Loop** that traverses through orchards and vineyards and offers frequent vistas of Mt. Hood. There are not only breweries—Logsdon Farmhouse Ales is located just off Oregon Route 35 and Solera Brewery in Parkdale is at the far end of the Fruit Loop—but also a handful of **cideries** that have recently opened, taking advantage of all the varieties of apples and pears grown in the roadside orchards. Sure, cider is a great option for those with gluten allergies, but if there's one thing that unifies beer lovers it's an appreciation of the variety of flavors, which is why cider appears to appeal more to beer fans than wine lovers.

As for Northeastern Oregon, it's in Big Sky country, where you trade one majestic canyon for a series of them. Chiefly, there's the **Hells Canyon Scenic Byway**, 218 miles that bank from mountain passes to valley floors around the Wallowa Mountains. The small towns here retain their Old West vibe. Tumbleweeds and elk saunter down roads like bicyclists in Portland at dawn. The **Pendleton Round-Up** is the largest event that draws many thousands of rodeo fans, but after that it's off-season (stretching from Labor Day to Memorial Day). Hunting starts with elk season and concludes with turkey season. But when the days are warm and long, the wildflowers blooming, and the fish jumping, this corner is a haven for cyclists, bikers, hikers, anglers, and campers.

This corner of the state is home to just over 100,000 people. The influx of breweries here is all the proof you need that the entrepreneurial brewers are indeed Oregonians. The Eastern Oregon Visitors Association rolled out the **Brews Byways**, akin to the immensely effective Bend Ale Trail. You can't tackle the whole thing in a day, so rest your beer-soaked head at the historic **Geiser Grand** in Baker where the 1889 Café offers many Eastern Oregon beers on tap.

Oh, and the reason why no Southeast Oregon breweries are mentioned in this book? It's easy to dismiss that corner as "just" high desert, although it's a mesmerizing array of volcanoes and valleys, wildlife refuges, and windows into early western expansion. But towns are tiny and sparse, and there's nary a brewery.

Barley Brown's Brew Pub / Baker City Brewing Co.

2190 Main Street, Baker City, OR 97814
(541) 523-4226 • BarleyBrowns.com
Twitter @BarleyBrowns
Baker City Brewing: 2200 Main Street, Baker City,
   OR 97814

Barley Brown's used to be known for turning out very good beers from a very small pub in a very remote corner of the state. That is still true, only now they also turn out great beers directly across the street from the brewpub in a medium-sized brewery called Baker City Brewing. That's relevant because it appears Barley Brown's only won two medals at the 2013 GABF, when really they won five. In other words, Shredders Wheat's run of four straight GABF silver medals didn't end, it just earned its fifth medal under the Baker City name. But then again, it didn't win a silver medal; it took home gold. Having said that, it was the gold medal for the premiere of the American-style India Black Ale category—Cascadian Dark Ale, s'il vous plaît—in 2010 for Turmoil that really put Barley Brown's on the map. And for many an Oregonian, the part of the map where their Baker City location falls is the one they look at while making plans to drive to somewhere in Idaho. But that's changing now, so it's a good thing owner Tyler Brown built a larger taproom in the new brewhouse to accommodate the beer pilgrims and let the locals dine in peace and elbowroom.

The whole reason the Brown family landed in Baker City is that Tyler's parents were less than four hundred miles away from their destination, moving to Seattle, when the family car broke down (probably for the best since Seattle already has plenty of breweries). Staking their tent in this small town of some six thousand people over

Beers brewed: Year-round: Shredders Wheat, Tumble Off Pale Ale, Handtruck Pale Ale, Pallet Jack IPA, Forklift DIPA, Tank Slapper DIPA, Turmoil CDA, Chaos Double CDA, Disorder Stout, Don Vanuchi "The Killer" Russian Imperial Stout, Barley's Breakfast Stout (with coffee), Two Smoke (formerly Whiskey Malt Ale), Citra Hot Blonde, Point Blank Red (PBR), ESB, and more.

The Pick: Turmoil. Nothing against Pallet Jack, a phenomenal IPA, but Barley Brown has made its mark with this CDA, a.k.a. Black IPA. Turmoil is the best example of a beer that marries bodacious hops and roasted malts for dual bitterness from the pine and chocolate flavors.

thirty years ago, the Browns bought the building on Main Street that formerly housed a Baker City bakery and turned it into a Mexican restaurant. When a Mexican family opened another one a block away, the Browns' restaurant went out of business—even though Tyler purports that their competitor's dishes were less authentic and more American-Mexican—making way for Barley Brown's to open in the same spot in 1998. The menu is now straight-up American. I got the "Death Burger," a double cheeseburger with add-ons such as fried onions and ham. Another transition was switching the taps from regional craft brands to house beers. Tyler served as his own original brewer, though he didn't come from a homebrewing background.

"This was always intended to be a brewpub where you can serve beer to the locals. It was never part of our plan to take kegs to Portland, or even La Grande," said Tyler, referring to the city that's just forty-five miles up I-84. The fact that better beer places in Portland like Belmont Station and Apex started requesting kegs opened a can of worms.

Initially, Baker City residents wouldn't touch the IPA. The biggest seller was a Bavarian wheat beer. Now, Tyler runs a very adventurous beer program, as the brewery's seventeen GABF medals attest to. A key element was the hiring of a talented homebrewer named Shawn Kelso. Tyler knew Kelso since they were little. Not only did he stir up trouble with one of Tyler's three younger brothers, he happened to be in the same class as a girl named Corrina—now Tyler's wife. Kelso's now brewing at the 10 Barrel brewpub two hours away in Boise, but his recipe legacy remains and the new brewers, chiefly Eli Dickison who'd worked here in the kitchen a few years before returning as the brewer, keep racking up awards.

My favorite story about one of those early beers centers around the 2006 GABF, the same year they won gold for Tumble Off Pale Ale, but this is about a different hop-forward beer: the aforementioned Turmoil. "We had a bunch of guys from a well-known California brewery . . . come and hang out at our booth and drink Turmoil non-stop," began Tyler. "They'd get their glass, then go around the corner and talk about it. They make absolutely no claim to that, but the next year a brewer from Wasatch Brewing in Utah who was at our booth and knew who they were said, 'Hey, you guys gotta come try this beer. These guys copied your beer.'"

Here, Tyler mentioned that the brewmaster in question developed his above-referenced brewery's black IPA to commemorate their eleventh anniversary in 2007. That beer, in turn, became a year-round offering, which won the bronze in 2010, the first year American-style

India Black Ale was a recognized style. Turmoil won gold. When Turmoil took silver two years later in 2012, it became the first beer to return to the podium in the nascent category. When visiting, pray they have a beer on called Chaos that's essentially Double Turmoil. It's got such a crazy (and crazy expensive) hop bill, they've gone over a year without making it.

Another unique style visitors will always find at Barley Brown's is the rotating jalapeño beer. Kelso created the first one just as an experiment. Tyler liked the idea of a spicy beer to go with his pub grub and they thought it'd be the first and only batch, just to see if Kelso could make an actually drinkable form of the notoriously awful Cave Creek Chili Beer. (That's the one that comes with a whole jalapeño in the bottle, and that Tyler likened to "fizzy yellow hot sauce.") To their surprise, customers kept requesting it. Citra Hot Blonde, perhaps the most popular iteration, contains lime zest and lemongrass as well as the namesake tangy Citra hops.

The irony of Tyler admitting that they couldn't sell IPA in the early days is that Pallet Jack has become their top-selling beer. It's so nice it medaled twice at the 2013 GABF. Of course, one of those was the gold in American-style India Pale Ale (by far the most competitive category in terms of number of entries and stature) and the other was for the fresh-hop version of it. Given their location, they get the freshest hops from Oregon, Washington, and Idaho.

Those medals alone would've been impressive, but not enough to earn them Small Brewing Company of the Year and Brewers of the Year, a title crowned upon those who earn the most points. For that, Tyler beamed about such a "legendary" year during which they not only fired up the brand-new 20-barrel brewery as they continued to brew full time on the 4-barrel pub system, but also named the fourth-ever batch on the big brother Hand Truck, which would become the gold medal winner in the International-style Pale Ale category, though most beer marketers call it a session IPA for its light body and heavy dry-hopping. "It might be session IPA to some," cranked Tyler, "but I think that name is stupid." He hates the word "India" in reference to hoppy American ales. By that same token, he hates the word "imperial" applied to big beers, but he was happy that Don Vanuchi "The Killer," the new system's sixth batch and brewed to commemorate Barley Brown's fifteenth anniversary, earned silver in the Foreign-style Stout category, even though most people call Don Vanuchi an imperial stout.

So from now on, Barley Brown's and Baker City celebrate their anniversaries on the same day, albeit fifteen years apart. Some beers are brewed at the pub, some across the street, and a few at both, and as such visitors will always find roughly twenty-five different beers on draft between the pub's eleven taps and the taproom's twenty-two. Inside the former, family-friendly booths face the bright tanks and the bar area contains a dozen bar stools. Besides the growing number of awards, random décor such as vintage wooden skis and vintage cans of Billy Brew (Jimmy Carter's brother's notorious early microbrew brand) are displayed. In the taproom, which doesn't serve food so no minors are allowed, a beautiful, rustic bar made of walnut provides for capacity just under forty. (I'm not sure if that includes musicians on the stage they built.) As the beer geek community grows and is willing to undertake the long drive from Portland, I can see them needing to figure out a place to stash more folks.

Barley Brown's Brew Pub / Baker City Brewing Co.

Opened: 1998.

Owner: Tyler Brown.

Brewers: Eli Dickison and Addison Collard.

System: 20-barrel (Baker City Brewing) and original 4-barrel (brewpub).

Annual production: 1,500 barrels.

Distribution: Oregon.

Hours: Pub: Monday through Saturday, 4 p.m. to 10 p.m. Taproom: Daily, 2 p.m. to close.

Tours: By request when brewers are available.

Takeout beer: Growlers; 22-ounce bottles may come soon.

Gift shop: Shirts, hoodies, headware, and various merch.

Food: Burgers and sandwiches, pasta and Italian dishes, and a few Mexican dishes leftover from the early days.

Beer Valley Brewing Co.

937 Southeast 12th Avenue, Ontario, OR 97914
(541) 881-9088 • BeerValleyBrewing.com
Twitter @Beer_Valley

Ontario is in Oregon the way tomatoes are in the fruit family. Technically, of course tomatoes are fruit, but we consider them vegetables. (I admit it's a wonky metaphor.) The city of Ontario isn't just separated from Idaho by a sliver of the Snake River—people here actually set their watches to Mountain Time when the rest of the state lives in Pacific Time. But just like the fruit family is lucky to have the vine-ripened tomato, by claiming Ontario, Oregon gets to also lay claim to hop-centric Beer Valley Brewing. And that's the way owner and brewer Pete Ricks likes it.

Ricks grew up in Meridian, Idaho, due west of Boise, which itself is less than an hour from Ontario. His wife grew up in Boise. The fact that the Rickses have family here in the Treasure Valley is a big part of why they moved to Ontario in the first place; they'd previously lived down in Phoenix for over twenty years. On a related note, when he first started thinking about turning his homebrewing hobby into a second career after working as an information technology specialist (even though IT pays way better), they looked for a space in an area called Deer Valley in Phoenix's northernmost suburbs. Hence: Beer Valley.

Ricks has continued to brew every drop on the same system since day one. His wife tackles much of the business work. They even put their two daughters to work when possible, meaning the younger one fills bottles during summer break and the older one designed a few of the brewery's labels ("for free because we put her through art school").

Since I live in Portland, the two Beer Valley beers frequently on my radar are Leafer Madness (an IPA only in the sense that Ricks calls it an Imperial Pale Ale, though he does make a true IPA

Beers brewed: Year-round: Leafer Madness Imperial Pale Ale, Black Flag Imperial Stout, Owyhee Amber Ale, Pigskin Pale Ale, Delta 9 IPA, Half Mast CDA. Seasonals: Highway to Ale Barleywine (winter), Rosebud Imperial Red Ale (spring), Gone Fishin Mild Ale (summer), Oregonberry Wheat Ale (summer), Jackalope Imperial Pumpkin Porter (fall), Many Farms All Fresh Hop Ale (fall).

The Pick: Leafer Madness. I rarely opt for the lopsided, hop-sided boozy palate wrecker. Don't miss out on what those green, leafy monsters can do with this 9 percent imperial ale that has few peers. Available with fresh hops in September.

called Delta 9 that's also nice) and Black Flag, an American-style imperial stout. They're 9 and 11 percent alcohol, respectively, and brew calculators clock both at well over 100 IBUs. Naturally and wonderfully, he makes fresh hop versions of both during the late summer harvest. I liked how he said he loves Leafer but told me, "I don't drink much Black Flag because I got [stuff] to do."

Therein marks the dichotomy of Beer Valley's offerings. If Ricks only brewed to his own taste, he'd just make high-gravity beers. When he was learning how to homebrew, the guy at the supply shop asked him how much alcohol he wanted in his beer. He replied, "How much alcohol can I have in there?"

While he's aware and proud that he's known for big beers, he has added a few lighter styles to his lineup that fare better with locals, such as Owyhee Amber and Gone Fishin Mild. "There's not a lot of mid-spectrum. Our beers are either triple-digit IBUs or near-zero," he remarked, noting that his fruit and pumpkin beers had tripled in sales. His primary fruit beer is the summery Oregonberry Wheat, made with Oregon-grown plums, cherries, and blueberries. (I couldn't help but comment that plums aren't berries, but brewers rarely suffer restrictions.)

That brings up Beer Valley's Harvest Series. It includes Jackalope Imperial Pumpkin Porter, and fresh-hopped beers like Highway 19, which uses whole hops from Oregon's Willamette Valley, Washington's Yakima Valley, and Idaho's Treasure Valley, home to old-school C-hops like Cascades, Centennials, and so on. As a homebrewer, Ricks copped to doing a potato beer. Ontario is where the frozen potato company Ore-Ida is located. Did everyone know it's named for the Oregon–Idaho border town? (Fun fact: They invented Tater Tots in 1953.) Ricks continued musing about his Harvest Series and pointed out that Ontario's main cash crop is actually onions. "I want to do an onion beer . . . but we've been so slammed with our fresh hops. I'm just trying to keep up."

Beer Valley Brewing Co.

Opened: 2007.
Owner and brewer: Pete Ricks.
System: 15-barrel.
Annual production: 1,500 barrels.
Distribution: Oregon, Idaho, Washington, California, and a bit beyond.
Hours: Thursday and Friday, 2 p.m. to 6 p.m.; Saturday, 11 a.m. to 3 p.m.
Tours: First Saturday of every month at 1 p.m. and by appointment.
Takeout beer: Growlers and bombers.
Gift shop: T-shirts, branded knit caps, and there's a Black Flag flag listed online.

Big Horse Brewing / Horsefeathers Restaurant

115 West State Street, Hood River, OR 97031
(541) 386-4411 • BigHorseBrewpub.com

Years ago, Big Horse Brewing wasn't just *another* Hood River brewery, it was *the* other one. Having said that, when Horsefeathers Fine Food and Spirits opened in 1988, it didn't compete with Full Sail Brewing, which opened the same year just five blocks away. That's because Horsefeathers wasn't a pub at all, but an upscale dining restaurant that came to be known for making its own pasta, from a spinoff business called Justa Pasta directly under the dining area. Of course, it was certainly a hot spot for beer, considering chef-owner Randy Orzeck stated the beer menu ran 220 bottles long. The inventory clearance parties they'd have back when the restaurant would close for the winter were epic.

I should mention that Orzeck (originally an East Coast transplant) pointed to the third barstool as the one where he initially met his wife, Susan (formerly a Midwesterner), even if her recollection varied slightly. No matter which part of the bar, it's now a husband-and-wife operation. Orzeck served as chef for the first ten years but sold off the pasta business in 1995; it's now based in Portland. "I almost put the brewery in the first year, and I'd talked to Bert Grant at the time," Orzeck said, referring to the man famous for opening the first brewpub in the country back in 1982, two hours north in Yakima, Washington. But with Full Sail in plain sight, Orzeck faced the prevailing reality: "You can't have two breweries in town. That's ridiculous! How can this town support two breweries?" I laughed on cue. Hood River now boasts the highest breweries-per-capita in the country.

So in 1998, the 4-barrel Big Horse brewery moved into the vacated basement. (The Horsefeathers name stayed because, hello, that beautiful gold-leaf sign was already bought and installed.) Orzeck served as the initial brewer, with some tips from Dave Logsdon, the founding brewer at Full Sail long before he started Logsdon Farmhouse Ales.

Beers brewed: Year-round: Easy Blonde Helles, Pale Rider IPA, Paragon IPA, Nightmare Oatmeal Stout, and MacStallion Scotch Export Ale. Seasonals: Five on tap including Heather's Dark Secret (spiced dark farmhouse), Saison (brett farmhouse), Strictly Rude Rotating IPA, and my favorite, Red Zeppelin Imperial Red Ale.

The Pick: MacStallion Scotch. A flagship beer that is so lightly hopped? When Smith took over the brewhouse, he was told it's the one recipe he couldn't change since regulars live and die by the big, caramel malts that provide the horsepower.

Since Orzeck's five years of wearing the brewer's boots, there've been few guys down in the brewhouse. You can't see it from the pub, but it is easily viewed from behind a wall of glass doors a story below the pool tables. When brewer Jason Kahler left to start the Solera Brewpub, Darrek Smith took over, making his first professional brewing office one with a killer vista of the Columbia River.

That's on the list of reasons Smith said he loves brewing here. He leapt from homebrewer to pro, but said he likes that the 4-barrel system "is kinda like a big homebrew set up." He enjoys constantly playing around and getting to brew a wide range yet also hone his penchant for German lagers. Neither the Orzecks nor the regulars limit him (Save the MacStallion's Scotch Export Ale, the only holdout beer from when Orzeck manned the mash paddle). You'll likely find a pilsner and a helles on the lighter end of the spectrum and a couple of IPAs, including an imperial version, on the bitter end, but it's the seldom-seen Scotch Ale style that's the workhorse here.

Food-wise, beyond the extensive menu of burgers, salads (each with an interesting, housemade vinaigrette), and entrées, the daily specials are always fresh and lip-smacking. There are plenty of beers on that complement the grub, and whether you sit in the dining hall with a window overlooking the river (or the adjacent patio, if there's a free table) or the huge beer garden in the back, it's a welcome respite for tourists and local "board heads" alike. Part of that restful mentality explained the lack of a website until recently. Randy would rather be windsurfing than building and maintaining a web presence (which he farmed out), and he prefers to take the "it's just beer" approach.

Big Horse Brewing / Horsefeathers Restaurant

Opened: 1988; brewery added in 1998.

Owners: Susan and Randy Orzeck.

Brewer: Darrek Smith.

System: 4-barrel.

Annual production: 300 barrels.

Hours: Monday through Sunday, noon to 10 p.m.

Distribution: None off-premises.

Gift shop: Plenty of shirts, hoodies, and hats at the front.

Food: A creative list of organic beef burgers, sandwiches, and salads. There are always fresh salmon options.

Extras: Two pool tables on the middle level (with a great view). A "hidden" beer garden in the back where dogs and minors are allowed.

Bull Ridge Brew Pub

1934 Broadway, Baker City, OR 97814
(541) 523-5833 • BullRidgeBrewPub.com

Enter Bull Ridge and you're immediately greeted by Hamilton. Co-owner Julie Blank calls him their "mascot"—a huge stuffed bull elk the Blanks procured in Hamilton, Montana. As for the other elk, which are just trophy heads, customers brought those in since this is prime elk hunting territory. I figure Julie and her husband, Micah, are sort of bummed Baker City isn't the gold mining territory it started out as, if this is how regulars reward them.

Micah is a Baker City native and Julie has lived here since the mid-nineties. Together, they had no experience in the restaurant industry, but after Micah's contractor business nosedived during the recession, they spent six months with consultants to devise a business plan. That plan said Baker City could stand another brewpub, right around the corner from Barley Brown's. Bull Ridge opened as a pub in September 2011, though with only guest taps. Brewing began in 2012 on a 1-barrel system belonging to a homebrewer who'd moved out from Texas. However, third and current brewer Kerry Carpenter keeps seven taps flowing from the 7-barrel brewery. Pop in on Donut Thursdays to try his chocolaty Bear Claw Porter with chocolate donuthole sidecar. It's like the movie *Strange Brew* incarnate.

Bull Ridge Brew Pub

Opened: 2012.

Owners: Julie and Micah Blank.

Brewer: Kerry Carpenter.

System: 7-barrel.

Annual production: 100 barrels.

Distribution: Eastern Oregon.

Hours: Monday through Thursday, 11 a.m. to 9 p.m.; Friday and Saturday, 11 a.m. to 10 p.m.; Sunday, noon to 8 p.m.

Tours: By request.

Takeout beer: Growlers.

Food: Apps including "elkhorn" wings, burgers, sandwiches, salads, and pastas.

Extras: Near-nightly specials such as movie nights and live music.

Beers brewed: Year-round: Haymaker Hefeweizen, White Tail Pale Ale, Gunsight IPA, Bear Claw Porter, Rut Dust Amber, Lone Pine Lager. Seasonals: Frost Bite Winter Ale, Sugarloaf IPA, Kangaroo Killer.

Double Mountain Brewery & Taproom

8 Fourth Street, Hood River, OR 97031
(541) 387-0042 • DoubleMountainBrewery.com
Twitter @DoubleMountain

DOUBLE MOUNTAIN
BREWERY & TAPROOM
HOOD RIVER OREGON

Beer and pizza go hand in hand, we all know this. Make great beer and amazing pizza and you've got a surefire recipe for success. Alas, it's easier said than done, yet Double Mountain hit the bull's-eye. Credit founders Matt Swihart and Charlie Devereux, though only Swihart remains the owner and brewmaster. Double Mountain earned its reputation on the strength of hop-centric beers like Vaporizer dry-hopped pale, Hop Lava IPA, and Molten Lava IIPA, which, since bottling began in 2012, have helped grow the company into one of the state's largest breweries. But it's the location in picturesque Hood Valley that makes it a destination brewpub, serving incredible Neapolitan-style pizza (they call it New Haven-style pizza since Devereux grew up in Connecticut) marked by crispy, wood-fired crusts, with pies ranging from classic pepperoni to a white pizza with white truffle oil marinated portabella 'shrooms. Considering it's named for the views of Mt. Hood and Mt. Adams (across the Columbia River in Washington), it's only fitting that it's dually known for twin powerhouses in their beer and pizza.

Swihart left his post as assistant brewmaster at Full Sail Brewery (across the street), which has become Hood River's brewery incubator and drew the Indiana native here. He started in 1994 and first met Devereux on the line. Swihart's tandem desires to be his own brewmaster in charge of production and keep his kids in this natural playground replete with ski trails in the snowy months and hiking trails all other times meant "starting really small." But by offering new beers that

Beers brewed: Year-round: Kolsch, The Vaporizer Dry-Hopped Pale Ale, Hop Lava IPA, IRA India Red Ale. Seasonals: Molten Lava Imperial IPA, Black Irish Stout, Carrie Ladd Steam Porter, Killer Green IPA, Killer Red IRA, Devil's Kriek, Rainier (Tahoma) Kriek, Clusterf#ck Single-Hopped IPA with Clusters, Dapper Dan Nitro Brown Ale, Sinister 7 Bourbon Barrel-Aged Brown Ale, Jumpin' Jack Flash Heirloom Cider, On the Wagon table beer, Sacre Bleu Dubbel and more, plus a non-alcoholic Oh Man! Rootbeer.

The Pick: Killer Green IPA is essentially a fresh hop version of Hop Lava (much like Killer Red is a freshy version of the IRA). Experiencing the hop harvest is all about being in a singular place at the peak moment. This dazzling IPA boasts wet and sticky Brewers Gold, a versatile hop that pops with spicy and herbaceous notes that never topple out of balance.

weren't fully meeting the demand of Northwest palates in 2007, remaining small became a challenge.

Hop Lava IPA, accentuated with Cascade and Centennial, was his calling card for an "aggressive IPA that Portland drinkers really flock to." The mélange of citrus, floral, and resinous pine flavors make it a favorite Oregon IPA, even if I'm more apt to reach for a Vaporizer, a pale ale that's *only* 6 percent ABV to Hop Lava's 7 percent, yet one that many still consider an IPA. It's built on pilsner malts and dry hopped with Challenger, which I think gives it a scent of cologne. Swihart called the aroma "Jamaican herb," saying, "it reminds me of cannabis, hence the name Vaporizer." It all ties into his mindframe of arranging his hop bills according to "herbal and aromatic families of hops." Those notes of oregano and mint in the India Red Ale make it a good dinner beer and, with a solid Kolsch rounding out Double Mountain's four core brands, gives the company a solid foursome of year-round offerings.

But in my opinion—and I'm not alone—it's their dual pairs of fresh hop beers and cherry Krieks that shine the brightest. Killer Green IPA and Killer Red IRA are available only in September and October. "My favorite thing as a brewer is to select hops, maybe liking ones over in *that* field after rubbing some hops," Swihart said ebulliently, alluding to his partnership with Sodbuster Farms in Salem, where he goes to get a sense of each year's harvest while they're still on the bines. As such, the varieties that go into these beers fluctuate, but there's always 4 pounds of wet, whole hop flowers per barrel. The first pint of Killer Green to Oregon hopheads is like the first snowflake to Santa's elves.

A month earlier, Devil's Kriek and Tahoma Kriek, made with red Bing cherries and striking yellow Rainier cherries respectively (cherry-picked right from Swihart's own orchard), are a gustatory delight of late-summer beer drinking. Initially Swihart planted grapevines when he considered going into winemaking, but luckily we kept him on the beer side in all its facets. "Hood River should be a Lambic region," he said, referring to Belgium's famed Senne Valley that lays claim to the sour Lambic ale appellation. "We have the fruit, the breweries, and the knowledge source. This should be a destination for that." Ironically, every brewery that spun off from Full Sail makes Kriek beers except Full Sail. Swihart developed a *Brettanomyces*-based wild yeast culture to develop his Krieks' sourness rather than just using the cherries themselves. Devil's Kriek is a Flanders Red base where the cherries—pits and all—hang out in the barrels for a full year. Tahoma Kriek is the only one I know of that's not sanguine hued; it starts as a strong Belgian blond ale and the yellow cherries retain its golden appearance. I'm told we can expect more peche ales from his peach trees and he has already begun making cider from his apple orchard.

Both Krieks are now available in 375-milliliter "split" champagne bottles (so you can share it with just yourself), and several of their smaller batches or seasonal releases come in half-liter, reusable bottles. "We intended to bottle right away, but as soon as we opened our doors it was like floodgates," Swihart reflected. Making beer available draft-only is a great problem many Oregon breweries have faced and one Double Mountain conquered by expanding into the adjacent space, increasing brewing capacity and bottling capability and even providing room for additional seating. Guests enter the restaurant (unless there's room at an outside table) and find the bar just to the right. Past the bar area, visitors can step down into the newer lounge area that sometimes has a live band. Even though the beers are widely available in Portland and throughout the Northwest, you can't beat enjoying a fresh hop beer and pizza fresh from the wood oven.

Double Mountain Brewery & Taproom

Opened: 2007.

Owner: Matt Swihart.

Brewers: Matt Swihart (brewmaster), Kyle Larsen, and Greg Balch.

System: 20-barrel.

Annual production: 10,000 barrels.

Distribution: Oregon, Washington, and Vermont.

Hours: Opens daily at 11:30 a.m. Closing times change seasonally.

Tours: By appointment only, the first Saturday of the month.

Takeout beer: Growlers, 500-milliliter bottles, and keg dock sales.

Gift shop: Apparel, hats, baby onesies, vessels, stickers, and more on the wall above the bar.

Food: I call it "the best pizza in Portland." It's worth the drive. Try the Heirloom pizza with various heirloom tomatoes if you visit in late summer.

Extras: Family-friendly. Live music many Thursdays through Saturdays.

Events: Anniversary party on St. Patrick's Day weekend featuring special brews and brewmaster Matt Swihart on banjo in the bluegrass band Greenneck Daredevils.

Dragon's Gate Brewery

52288 Sunquist Road, Milton Freewater,
   OR 97862
(541) 215-2622 • DragonsGateBrewery.com

Walla Walla knows wine well. But when it comes to craft beer, they're just getting their feet wet (figuratively, of course, lest you were imagining winemakers stomping fresh hops). To test the waters in this area of Eastern Oregon just south of the Washington border, the husband-and-wife team of Adam and Jennifer Gregory—they love brewing together—launched Dragon's Gate, a King Arthur–inspired nanobrewery. They chose King Arthur because they participate in Renaissance Faires, and a nanobrewery because the 1-barrel system is not much bigger than the system they homebrewed on in their kitchen for years.

When they moved to Milton-Freewater and bought a house near Jennifer's folks, they immediately put some of their ten-acre plot to use by planting their own hopyard. Of the thirty bines, there are nine different estate-grown varieties, including Centennial, Cascade, Galena, Mt. Hood, Willamette, Magnum, Sterling, Saaz, and Hallertauer hops—a solid mix of European nobles and American aromas—meaning they never need to source from beyond their farm.

And when I mentioned testing the waters, that's more than just a figure of speech. The Gregory farm has a deep well and the water, even untreated, is perfect for brewing.

Dragon's Gate is a true farmhouse brewery, but farm life is a far cry from where and how Adam and Jennifer met in Southern California. He was a cop; she ran a bar. Don't get some *Hill Street Blues* vision of a gritty L.A. po-po falling for a misguided booze slinger. This actually took place on Catalina Island, a few hours sailing from the surf haven of Laguna Beach where Adam grew up. I doubt Catalina has a seedy underbelly, and if it has one, don't call on Adam. The way he put it, he was more of a nerd cop. Computer programming and graphic design were his beat.

He's a big bruiser whose surfer blond hair has grayed. But it's hard to look intimidating when he

Beers brewed: Year-round: Belgian IPA, Belgian Wit, Belgian Golden Strong Ale, Porter, Belgian Triple. Seasonals: Double Dragon IPA, Chi Saison, Le Morte d'Arthur Chocolate Stout, Pumpkin Ale.

The Pick: Belgian Wit. This traditional witbier's soft, wheaten body is embellished by enough orange peel to lend near orange juice quality, but the coriander and hops, grown right outside the brewery, rein in the sweetness with just the right spice as a counterweight.

and Jennifer don kilts to pour beer at fests and other events. They further play into the Ren Faire vibe with their imported Friesian horses—monstrous, black, Dutch horses like the ones knights used to ride during jousts—that they keep on their farm. Jennifer's sister happens to be a doctor of medieval literature, so she helps them keep the story straight.

Having said that, only one Dragon's Gate beer really plays into the imagery: Le Morte d'Arthur, their chocolate stout. They also brew an American porter, but everything else leans toward Belgian and farmhouse-style beers, even if they don't sound like they would be. "My IPA," Adam copped, "is a Belgian tripel hopped up." I guess a tripel masquerading as an IPA sounds like something you'd find at a Ren Faire. In any event, the homegrown Centennial and Cascade hops give it a Northwestern kick while the abbey yeast strain gives it an overriding spicy component that trails off to a pear-brandy flavor. Not that there's any pear in it. They save that for the Pear-Ginger Saison that's part of their experimental creations. Pumpkin beers are also big, but Dragon's Gate has the only one I know of that uses smoked yams. And as for the chocolate stout, Adam mentioned using smoked cardamom in a batch.

The point is, trek over the Blue Mountains to the Gregory's farmhouse brewery with its welcoming red patio furniture and you never know what you may discover. Adam perceives their current 1-barrel system as more of a pilot brewery and plans to install something larger one day. That's phase two. For phase three, Adam gave me one word: "glamping." Glamorous camping is a burgeoning industry. The area draws tons of visitors for the wine industry, and Jennifer is already a GM at a local winery, so visitors to the brewery will be able to camp in yurts right in a hop field and enjoy Dragon's Gate farmhouse ales around a bonfire. For a brewery inspired by the medieval era, I'd say that's part of a forward-thinking renaissance right there.

Dragon's Gate Brewery

Opened: MMXII (2012).
Owners and brewers: Adam and Jennifer Gregory.
System: 1-barrel.
Annual production: 25 barrels.
Distribution: Eastern Oregon and Eastern Washington.
Hours: Monday through Friday, by appointment; Saturday, noon to 4 p.m.
Tours: By request.
Takeout beer: Growlers and bottles.
Gift shop: Shirts, hats, jackets, stickers, glasses, and one day perhaps kilts.
Food: BYO, especially to picnic on the farm.

1188 Brewing Co.

141 East Main Street, John Day, OR 97845
(541) 575-1188 • 1188Brewing.com
Twitter @1188BrewingCo

Time well spent. That's the motto painted inside above the door to 1188 Brewing Co., making you reflect on it after you've spent some time inside. Sure, owners Ken and Jen Brown along with Jeremy and Shannon Adair want folks to spend money here, but time's a nonrenewable asset. Hence 1188 is the vision of how they want to spend their eventual retirement.

John Day, named after the pioneering trapper, is home to 1,700 residents and popular among Eastern Oregon hunters as the last stop in civilization. (The nearest brewery is eighty miles away!) Co-owner Ken hunts here but lives in Bend. He's a fire captain, and Jeremy is a Grant County lineman (cue Jimmy Webb's "Wichita Lineman"). The two are also brothers-in-law; co-owners Jen and Shannon are sisters.

Ken described their mission as the creation of something "small, with excellent beer, great food, and a fun atmosphere—somewhere you can bring the whole family and really enjoy your meal." There's no fryer. There are healthy sandwiches and soups made from scratch. The goal for the nanobrewery is to always have five to eight house beers on tap. Some batches result in multiple beers, such as the hefeweizen and the blackberry hefe, or the red ale and the smoked habanero red.

Jen and Shannon's father and Ken's dad were best friends (Ken and Jen were childhood friends) who raced snowmobiles together. Their bibs were 11 and 88 and their race photo hangs above "Time Well Spent."

1188 Brewing Co.

Opened: 2013.
Owners: Ken and Jen Brown; Jeremy and Shannon Adair.
Brewer: Jeremy Adair.
System: 2-barrel.
Annual production: 75 barrels.
Distribution: On-premises.
Hours: Seasonal; check before you visit.
Takeout beer: Growlers.
Gift shop: Shirts and caps.
Food: Starters, salads, paninis, and sandwiches of all manner.

Beers brewed: Year-round: Black Oak Instigator, Orney Hefeweizen, Leafdropper IPA, Rim Rock Red, Box Canyon Pale. Seasonals: Huckleberry Hefe, Lemongrass Lager, Habanero Red, Stout, seasonal IPAs.

Fearless Brewing Co.

326 South Broadway Street, Estacada, OR 97023
503-630-BEER (2337) • Fearless1.com
Twitter @FearlessBrewing

Estacada, thirty miles from Portland, is twelve miles off Highway 26 so it's no pit stop on the way up to Mt. Hood. "You have to be fearless to take your life savings and build a brewery way out in the sticks," said Bennett Johnson, cofounder and brewmaster Ken Johnson's wife.

That's reason enough to have named this brewpub Fearless. It services a town of fewer than three thousand people, sixty of whom can find seating in the pub. But the name derives from her husband's nickname during his corn farming days when he was growing up in Nebraska.

Johnson gave him a homebrew kit for Christmas, and he began entering competitions. "Ken entered three beers and returned home with four medals," said Bennett of the bonus hardware scored for earning best-of-show with an imperial stout. One award winner, Old Fearless No. 1 Barleywine, became the tenth anniversary beer, celebrating the pub set in a former Ace Hardware. During my visit, the sweetheart server called me—and everyone else—"My Friend." There are books and board games, and TVs above the bar (from an era before big flat screens).

"We have a Viking theme, honoring my Swedish ancestry," said Ken of the beer names. The exception is the smoky, sweet flagship Scottish Ale. Mjolnir ("Mule-ner") was Thor's magical battle hammer. The powerful imperial IPA is an iron fist in a velvet glove.

Fearless Brewing Co.

Opened: 2003.

Owners: Ken and Bennett Johnson.

Brewer: Ken Johnson.

System: 5-barrel.

Annual production: 1,100 barrels.

Distribution: Oregon and Washington.

Hours: Sunday, noon to 9 p.m.; Monday through Thursday, 4 p.m. to 9 p.m.; Friday and Saturday, noon to 10 p.m.

Takeout beer: Growlers and cans.

Food: Burgers and wraps.

Beers brewed: Year-round: Scottish Ale, Clackamas Cream Ale, Loki Red Ale, Porter, QUAFF ISA, Mjolnir IIPA. Seasonals: Strong Scotch Ale, Peaches & Cream, Old Fearless No. 1 Barleywine.

The Pick: Loki Red Ale. Named for the Norse mythological shapeshifter, this is a red ale hopped like an IPA, thereby shifting into an imperial red, if you will.

Hermiston Brewing Co.

HERMISTON BREWING CO.

125 North First Street, Hermiston, OR 97838
(541) 289-7414 • Facebook.com/HermistonBrewing

Eight years after Nookie's Sports Bar & Grill opened in 2005, owner Mitch Myers changed the name to Nookie's Restaurant & Brewery. The taps used to be dominated by national lagers and the mainstream Oregon brands, but when the first weekend house beers were tapped Myers said they set a new sales record. The people of Hermiston had been thirsting for their own brewery. The city's eponymous brewery became only the third in Umatilla County. Getting the rights to the name, surprisingly, proved tricky since Hermiston Brewing was registered some 115 years earlier. But because local Prohibition kicked in before the national Volstead Act of 1919, that original hometown brewery never came to fruition.

For many Oregonians who have Hermiston on their mental map, the town is synonymous with watermelons. Supermarkets stack cases of Hermiston Melons. "We released a Hermiston watermelon wheat beer called Melon Head," said Myers, adding that the first batch sold out in three days. Other local fruits gracing beers include peaches, strawberries, and blackberries, but fear not—among the fifteen beers there are also three different IPAs.

Hermiston Brewing Co.

Opened: 2013.

Owner: Mitch Myers.

Brewers: Craig Nichols and Brad Bledsoe.

System: 7-barrel.

Annual production: 200 barrels.

Distribution: Limited.

Hours: Monday to Thursday, 11 a.m. to 11 p.m.; Friday and Saturday, 11 a.m. to 1:30 a.m.; Sunday, 11 a.m. to 8 p.m.

Takeout beer: Growlers.

Gift shop: Shirts, caps, growlers.

Food: Burgers, fish and chips, sandwiches, and entrées.

Beers brewed: Year-round: Blue Mountain Hopped Up Blonde, Strawberry Blonde, Purple Ridge Imperial IPA, Thrill Seeker IPA, Nine Mile Pale Ale, Hermiston Hefe, Purple Haze Blackberry Hefe, White Mule, Tree Shake Peach Wit, Beshew Pale Face Porter, Rodeo Red, Black Bullet Stout, Roundup Redeye. Seasonals: Melon Head (watermelon wheat), Spider Bite CDA, Chubby Punkin Ale, Bad Santa Spiced Stout.

Laht Neppur Brewing Co.

Milton-Freewater, OR
(509) 337-6261 (Washington brewery)
LahtNeppur.com • Twitter @Lahtneppur

Laht Neppur Brewing Co. didn't originate in some exotic locale like the Malaysian capital, Kuala Lumpur, but in Walla Walla (which is equally fun to say). The Milton-Freewater facility, said owner Court Ruppenthal (spell his surname backward), is a production-only plant. Reasons for constructing a new brewery merely thirty miles south of Waitsburg, Washington, are myriad. "The biggest advantage is that our beer produced in Oregon can be self-distributed in Oregon and Washington," Ruppenthal said, whereas they previously needed a distributor outside Washington. He also cited Oregon's lower excise and corporate taxes, cheaper utilities, better access to major highways, and strong Oregon Brewers Guild.

Ruppenthal grew up in Portland suburb Vancouver, Washington, where his homebrewing led to winemaking. After completing the Enology and Viticulture Program at Walla Walla Community College in Eastern Washington's wine region in 2005, he started his brewery that same year. His love of working with fruit guides two of his beers: Peach Hefeweizen and Strawberry Cream Ale. Peach is a cult favorite at the Oregon Brewers Fest. "It's a little hard to believe that our Peach Hefeweizen has achieved such a following at OBF," Ruppenthal said, "and that last year [2013] for the first time, fruit beers outnumbered IPAs." Of course, Laht Neppur also makes an IPA and an imperial IPA. It's an Oregon brewery now, after all.

Beers brewed: Year-round: Peach Hefeweizen, Strawberry Cream Ale, Stout, Backseat Blonde, Mike's Golden Ale, Neddy's Brown Nut, Oatmeal Porter, Crop Duster Imperial IPA, IPA, Black Matt Imperial Witbier, Belgian Wit, Piper Canyon Scotch Ale.

Laht Neppur Brewing Co.

Opened: 2014 (founded in Waitsburg, Washington, in 2005).

Owner and brewer: Court Ruppenthal.

System: 30-barrel.

Annual production: 1,000 barrels.

Distribution: Oregon and Washington.

The Pick: Peach Hefeweizen. More American wheat beer than Belgian peche or German Weisse, this hazy, wheaty beer subs peachy overtones for a traditional hefe's banana and clove notes.

Logsdon Farmhouse Ales

4785 Booth Hill Rd., Hood River County, OR 97031
(541) 399-4659 • FarmhouseBeer.com
Twitter @FarmhouseAles

In the picturesque Columbia River Gorge, Hood River County is rife with so many farms that its scenic, thirty-five-mile Highway 35 is known as the Fruit Loop. So what better place to make authentic farmhouse ales than on Dave Logsdon's ten-acre family farm? The brewery is literally housed in a big red barn. In the mid-eighties, Logsdon cofounded neighboring Full Sail Brewery, then colaunched yeast industry giant Wyeast Labs, so naturally the beers he and partner Chuck Porter make are yeast-forward saisons. The certified-organic beers use only locally grown, whole hops. Spent grains are fed to their herd of Scottish Highlander cattle, the cartoonishly adorable cows that look more like long-horned, woolly buffalo than something you'd expect to see among Oregon vineyards and U-pick orchards. Maybe there's a connection: Logsdon Farmhouse ales stand out from the herd.

The use of the words "farmhouse" and "saison" are increasingly slapped on beer labels, albeit ones that emanate from breweries based in industrial parks and manufacturing zones. "It strikes me as odd," Logsdon deadpanned. "Almost all breweries have a house flavor," he iterated. "Regardless of how much cleaning and sanitizing of the equipment we do, there's a common thread that runs through our beers. It's not because of the yeast; we use multiple yeast strains." He concluded: "There's something that's coming from the farmhouse that's beyond my control."

This coming from the guy who helped revolutionize the craft-brewing industry by propagating isolated yeast strains (originally in the same barn his brewing system now occupies). On a related note, lots of people figure—or insist—that Seizoen (say-zoon) contains *Brettanomyces*, but Logsdon insists that's not one of the four cultures at work

Beers and ciders brewed:
Year-round: Seizoen, Seizoen Bretta, Kili Wit. Seasonals: Peche 'n Brett, Cerasus, Fresh Hop Seizoen, Far West Vlaming, Straffe Drieling Tripel, The Conversion, Oak Aged Bretta Wilde Appel, Bergschrund Signature Series.

The Pick: Seizoen Bretta. At once shapely yet amorphous, the complexity layers citrus zest with freshly baled hay, then heavily spiced peach butter, all while the *Brettanomyces* dries it out like a desert stone, which was good enough to earn gold in the Brett Ale category at the 2012 GABF.

in the earthy ale with hints of lemon zest and unripe nectarine. The funky Seizoen Bretta, naturally, is another story, one told through dry flavors of fresh-baked Southern biscuits as well as lemon pepper and sharp apple skin. Interestingly, Logsdon's father was a home winemaker and they're notoriously terrified of unruly brett. And his grandfather was a bootlegger during Prohibition, back on the family farm in Ohio. The logistics have changed, but essentially he's carrying on the family tradition of creating a beverage he really wants to drink. It's a bonus that others want to buy it.

The county actually limits the brewery's output, which they're presently not in danger of exceeding with 1,000 barrels per year. And the 750-milliliter bottles go for more than your average beer, sometimes topping $20 retail. But you have to act quickly if you want to find a bottle of, say, the World Beer Cup gold medal–winning Peche Brett, made entirely with organic fruit from the valley. Brimming with even more of the famous house flavor, Cerasus (another World Beer Cup gold medal winner) is a Kriek that takes the Flemish red ale, bottled separately as Far West Vlaming, as the base and adds cherries grafted from Sharbeekse trees, the only ones growing in America to Logsdon's knowledge. He's growing some four hundred trees on his property, and the unique sour cherries started making their way into Cerasus in 2013.

By the way, the Seizoens use pear juice for bottle conditioning. One fruit that's as abundant in the valley as cherries and grapes is apples, hence the six new cideries in the area. Thanks to having a winery license, Logsdon Farmhouse Ales is one of them, and their cider branch is ironically called Logsdon Farm Brewery. The first batch, Wilde Appel, is a tart, yet dry oaked cider fermented with saison yeast and brett.

For Porter's part, the brewery is run like a co-op, and he has his own Bergschrund Series that, to date, has seen the release of one beer, Aberrant, a funky golden ale that tastes like it's got a mix of secret herbs and spices, but that's just the power of the yeast. Among the brewery's other partners and collaborators, Dave's Belgian wife, Judith, mans the tasting room sometimes and serves as the "Belgian inspiration." Dave's cousin John Plutshack handles distribution and his wife, Jodie, puts her J.D. to work on legal matters. Finally, there's Seaberg Einarsson (the name's Icelandic), whom Logsdon calls a hobby painter; he created Logsdon's now-iconic label art depicting the snow off Mt. Hood melting into a tulip glass full of farmhouse ale behind a pastoral red barn. Here I'll mention that Logsdon's triplet daughters—Tamara, Katrina, and Alisa, the inspiration behind a new, spicy Belgian-style tripel called Straffe Drieling—help out here and there when they can (such as on bottling days). Tamara worked as a lab tech at Wyeast as her summer job, and now that she's in grad school finds herself in a lab full-time, so we'll see if Logsdon Farmhouse Ales turns into a second-generation brewery.

The latest news from the brewery is a welcome addition to beer tourists: a proper tasting room. It's a small room mere paces from the barn and overlooks a small pond on one side and field with the Scottish Highlanders on the other. The cows not only feast on all the spent grains, eradicating the biggest waste issue, but also, I hear, make for delicious sausages. And that'd call for a glass of Seizoen.

Logsdon Farmhouse Ales

Opened: 2011.

Owners: David Logsdon, his wife Judith Logsdon-Bams, Charles Porter, Seaberg Einarsson, John Plutshack, and his wife Jodie Ayura.

Brewers: David Logsdon and Charles Porter.

System: 15-barrel.

Annual production: 1,000 barrels

Distribution: Oregon, California, Washington, Arizona, Vermont, New York, British Columbia, Denmark, and Iceland.

Hours and tours: Thursday through Saturday, noon to 4 p.m.

Takeout beer: 750-milliliter bottles.

Gift shop: Shirts, hats, glasses, and label artwork.

Mt. Hood Brewing Co. (Ice Axe Grill)

87304 East Government Camp Loop Road, Government
  Camp, OR 97028
(503) 272-3172 • MtHoodBrewing.com
Twitter @MtHoodBrewing

Every ski town needs a brewpub, right? Take a winter vacation to the town of Government Camp to hit the slopes—Mt. Hood Meadows features over 2,100 skiable acres—or cross-country ski trails, or go snowshoeing. Visit in the snow-free months—the U.S. Ski Team trains on Mt. Hood in the summer thanks to Palmer Glacier, which is still a couple thousand vertical feet below Hood's peak, the highest point in the state at 11,249 feet—and hike the Timberline Trail, or strap on your brain bucket for superb and scenic single-track mountain biking along Gunsight Ridge. Any way you recreate, you deserve a liquid reward at the end of the day.

The original Mt. Hood Brewing from the turn of the twentieth century was actually down the mountain in Portland and had been subsumed by the Henry Weinhard Brewery. The unrelated new brewpub is one of eight restaurants operated by the Timberline Lodge, the ski lodge and retreat that opened in 1937 and has since been declared a National Historic Landmark. It sits six miles and a 2,000-foot elevation gain above Government Camp. Jeff Kohnstamm operates the lodge and its properties thanks to his father, Richard, who saved the Timberline Lodge from disrepair and financial ruin in the mid-1990s.

Brewing commenced in 1992 at Mt. Hood Brewing, located on the ground floor beneath the Ice Axe Grill, which opened a year earlier. One thing both incarnations of the brewery share, besides a name, is the advantage of using pure glacial water for its Pacific Northwest-style beers.

Complementing the appellation, the lodge features Cascadian flagstone quarried from an ancient lakebed, as well as pine and spruce timber throughout. When it's too chilly out, try to nab a seat by the fireplace with a bowl of three-bean

Beers brewed: Year-round: Ice Axe IPA, Cloudcap Amber Ale, Highland Meadow Blonde, Multorporter Smoked Porter, Cascadian Pale Ale, Hogsback Oatmeal Stout. Seasonals: The Double Bit (IPA and Barleywine blend), Broken Auger IPA and more, including a cask ale.

The Pick: Ice Axe IPA. The flagship ale is richly rewarding after a day of recreational exertion. The malt body is warming in the winter, while the hop bill is refreshing and floral in the summer. Not that there's ever a bad time for a classic pale pint of hoppiness.

chili. I recommend the Multorporter, a roasty, smoky porter that pairs perfectly with a toasty fire. Or go for the Hogsback Oatmeal Stout since the chocolate notes are the next best thing to enjoying s'mores. Arrive in good weather and head to the deck to sit and sip pints of Ice Axe IPA, the flagship ale, surrounded by Douglas firs. Not only are dogs allowed, there's even a menu specifically for them, replete with pub-produced dog biscuits made with spent grain. (And since it's Oregon, there are plenty of vegetarian and gluten-free options.)

Regardless of the weather, the Hogsback Stout can be ordered as a beer float. As a matter of fact, they'll make a float using any beer of your choice, but call me old-fashioned, I'm partial to an oatmeal stout float over an IPA float. For the kids or the truly old-fashioned, there's a regular float using the root beer brewed in-house.

Mt. Hood Brewing Co. (Ice Axe Grill)

Opened: 1991.

Owner: Jeff Kohnstamm.

Brewers: Tom Rydzewski (head brewer) and Jeff McAllester (assistant brewer).

System: 10-barrel.

Annual production: 1,150 barrels.

Distribution: Oregon.

Hours: Daily, 11 a.m. to 9 p.m.

Tours: By appointment.

Takeout beer: Growlers and 22-ounce bottles.

Gift shop: A display case at the front filled with garb, glasses, and more.

Food: Pizzas, burgers, brats, salads, and entrées such as Multorporter braised beef shortribs, plus a kids menu.

Mutiny Brewing

Mutiny is brewing

Mutiny Brewing Company
Joseph, OR

600 North Main Street, Joseph, OR 97846
(541) 432-5274 • MutinyBrewing.com
Twitter @MutinyBrewing

The Hells Canyon Scenic Byway that leads to Wallowa Lake at the south end of Joseph seemed like the obvious choice for Kari Gjerdingen to set up her brewpub after her year's stint brewing at Terminal Gravity, just five miles up the road. Sure, the town's only home to a thousand people, more or less (depending on the season), but oh what a haven it is. And you can't have a haven without fresh beer. Mutiny supplies it along with a beer garden to boot.

We sat in her brewpub, which is rife with wood, given Joseph's past as a lumber town. Local woodworker Steve Arment's ornate booths are artistic enough individually, but when you position yourself in the main entrance to view them in a row as if peering down a timber tunnel, the scene springs to life with native birds, fish, and woodland creatures. Gjerdingen could have gone for cheap and functional, but going the extra mile is always worth it and adheres to the brewer's ethos.

Gjerdingen, who hails from south-central Indiana, cut her teeth at Upland Brewing, although it wasn't yet the brewery renowned for exotic beers like Kiwi Lambic that it is now. She revealed that her father worked with the wife of Upland's brewmaster, and that was her "in" for a part-time job working on the bottling line. "I started coming in at 5 a.m. to help brew," she said, clarifying that it was on her own time, just to learn. After a year and a half of in-house training, she formalized her brewing studies at University of California, Davis, which has one of the best brewing programs in the world.

Degree in hand, she wound up at Terminal Gravity in 2006. And although she didn't stick around in Enterprise that long, she couldn't bring herself to leave the general area. She snowboards up at "Fergi" (Ferguson Ridge Ski Area) and in the summer hits the lake as often as possible. She said she knew, just knew, that if she didn't open a brewery in Joseph, somebody else would. That's

Beers brewed: Year-round: Ssswheat American Wheat Ale, Pale Ale, Super Pale Ale, Pi Dog Porter. Seasonals: "Beers that reflect the season on my whim."

The Pick: Ssswheat is light, refreshing, and drinkable for days, melding the American wheat ale style with the Belgian witbier by incorporating the latter's key spicing: coriander, orange peel, and chamomile.

how she picked the location. As for the name, she'd landed on that years earlier at Upland.

"A bunch of us [brewers] were standing around. Apparently we looked guilty," she said, though she hardly has the face of a mischievous devil. "We were, in fact, talking about increasing the alcohol in one of the beers"—at which point she feigned committing an intentional accident before continuing, "Someone walks over, sees us all, and asked 'Is there a mutiny brewing?'" With that, Gjerdingen looked over at her friend and coworker—they'd shared an industry-wide fantasy wherein apparently every brewer talks about opening up his or her own brewery—and said, "*That's* so good. Mutiny is brewing. So perfect."

That's why, although people say "Mutiny Brewing Co.," the handmade sign outside the brewpub reads "Mutiny is brewing." An added benefit is that Gjerdingen imagines it as a mutiny "against The Big Three [brewing concerns] or anyone making plain, boring beer."

For her part, Mutiny's most popular brew is the Ssswheat, pronounced the way you'd call something awesome "sweet." She calls it an American wheat beer, even though it contains the classic Belgian witbier ingredients orange peel, coriander, and chamomile, because the yeast strain makes it American. She doesn't even object to calling it a "lady beer."

For that matter, she proudly doesn't brew an IPA. For one, it's tough to sell as many high-gravity beers as sessionable ones. Furthermore, "As a brewer with little automation, [IPAs] are heavier. When you make an IPA, it's a workout," she explained, referencing the actual added weight of heaving malt bags for the bodacious body the beer requires to support the hop bill. Making low IBU beers is another form of mutiny.

Mutiny Brewing

Opened: 2009.

Owner and brewer: Kari Gjerdingen.

System: 4-barrel.

Annual production: 100 barrels.

Distribution: On-site.

Hours: Memorial Day through Labor Day: Daily, 11:30 a.m. to 9 p.m. (10 p.m. on weekends). Rest of the year: Wednesday through Saturday, 9:30 a.m. to 9 p.m. (10 p.m. on weekends).

Tours: When the brewhouse doors are rolled up in the summer, pop on in.

Takeout beer: Growler fills.

Gift shop: Shirts and caps behind the bar.

Food: Menu focuses on sandwiches: 6 Ranch beef for carnivores, vegetarian options.

Pfriem Family Brewers

707 Portway Avenue, Suite 101, Hood River, OR 97031
(541) 321-0490 • PfriemBeer.com
Twitter @PfriemBeer

Not only is Hood River's Waterfront Park an entry point for kiteboarders, its playground includes an awesome, kid-appropriate climbing rock (and equally adult-friendly wooden xylophone), making it an ideal place to hang out for all ages. Return visits generally yield added features. The same applies to the Pfriem brewery directly opposite the park. Okay, they don't have a climbing wall, but for kids there's a nook with toys and books, and for adults there's mighty fine Pacific Northwest-via-Belgium beer.

It's called Pfriem Family Brewers because the word "family" both honors the involvement of owner-brewer Josh's family and because the alliteration helps people know the "P" is silent (it's pronounced "Freem"). The Pfriems have two kids, daughter Sahale and son Watou, who, ideally, will carry on the family business way down the road. Since his preschool days, Watou has expressed his desire to be a brewer! And Sahale (pronounced "Sa-HA-lee" in this case) already has keen business acumen; if you think about it, a lemonade stand is sort of the craft brewery of the kid world. They are a large part of why the brewpub itself has a play area. Sahale got her name from Mt. Sahale in Washington, where Josh and his wife Annie first met as mountaineers. Watou was named after his dad's pilgrimage to the West Flanders town instrumental in Josh's brewing knowledge, though Josh has brewed at various breweries including Chuckanut up in Washington, where he's from, and Full Sail, which brought the Pfriem family to Hood River.

What's amazing is that prior to Josh and Annie (a.k.a. "Brewmama") opening the brewpub, this prime part of town was virtually undeveloped. Before the brewery reached its first anniversary, the pub proved so popular they knocked out part of a wall and added a beer garden with additional

Beers brewed: Year-round: IPA, Blonde IPA, Belgian Strong Blonde, Belgian Strong Dark, Wit, Pilsner. Seasonals: Belgian IPA, Double IPA, CDA, Belgian Stout, Super Saison, Little Saison, Tiny Saison, Schwarzbier, Mosaic Pale, Hoppyweizen, and more.

The Pick: Blonde IPA. A bright, hoppy IPA made with local hops that just tops the 6 percent alcohol mark (compared to their other four IPAs that ramp up the sweet and juicy factors and alcohol), it's one of the more refreshing, quaffable hop bombs around.

room for forty (and a firepit). When your view is the Washington side of the Columbia River Gorge and the river itself, coupled with Pfriem's amazing Belgian-inspired and Northwest-accented beers, there are fewer places in the world one would rather be.

Perhaps that best explains Pfriem's affinity for Belgian and Northwest beer styles, subscribing to the brew-what-you-like/like-what-you-brew philosophy. Two of my favorites are the Blonde IPA, a bright IPA that drinks like a hoppy lawnmower beer, and the Belgian Strong Blonde, which, unlike the IPA, derives its fruit and spice flavors from the yeast strain. And then there's the intermittent Belgian IPA, a hybrid Belgian Tripel and Northwest Imperial IPA that clocks in at 9 percent alcohol and combines local, spicy hops with foreign, differently spicy yeast.

While the twin blonds are among the brewery's bestsellers, the Wit and newer Pils are refreshing, sessionable, and flavorful popular choices, too. Josh said their goal for the first year of production was to hit 750 barrels. Instead, they reached 2,000. That they were able to do so and easily move in a pair of larger 45-barrel fermenters shows that they projected for growth in their initial business plan without having to experience the usual growing pains.

Speaking of growth, they expanded the brewery and kitchen and added a barrel (and tasting) room. Two of the first projects aging in French oak wine barrels were a Flanders Red and something Josh called a Flanders Blonde (instead of a Flemish brown because, per Josh's admission, he has a thing for blonds), but long term we'll see sour beers in the Lambic and Gueuze styles in large- and small-format bottles, which you can legally drink in Waterfront Park.

Pfriem Family Brewers

Opened: 2012.

Owners: Josh and Annie Pfriem.

Brewers: Josh Pfriem (brewmaster), Dan Peterson, and Gavin Lord.

System: 15-barrel.

Annual production: 3,000 barrels.

Hours: Daily, 11:30 a.m. to 9 p.m.

Tours: By request.

Takeout beer: Growler fills, dock sales, and bottles coming soon.

Gift shop: Apparel and glassware.

Food: Appetizers, seasonal salads, and sandwiches, plus steak frites and moules frites. (mussels with fries). Chef Thomas keeps the kid's menu unique and not fried.

Extras: New beer garden for even better river and gorge views. Very kid- and dog-friendly. Adding barrel and tasting room.

The Prodigal Son Brewery and Pub

230 Southeast Court Avenue, Pendleton, OR 97801
(541) 276-6090 • ProdigalSonBrewery.com
Twitter @ProdigalSonBrew

The Prodigal Son is a brewpub built into a former auto dealership, which explains why it's big enough to drive a truck through. The massive and eclectically designed space is ideal for family and community gatherings, with a total capacity of two hundred. There's even a built-in theatre that hosts everything from watching football and B-movie screenings to a Bible study and a knitting group. Cofounder Tim Guenther assured me it's not just the football fans who order beer.

As Pendleton natives, Guenther and co-owner Matthew Barnes (the head chef) named the pub after the biblical Parable of the Wayward Son (Luke 15:11–32) who returns to the land of his father and is surprised to be welcomed with generous, open arms. The day after graduation, Guenther recounted saying aloud, "We're f[reakin'] outta here" referring to Pendleton.

So it's a pleasant twist of fate that although he described himself as being an obnoxious youth, when he and his wife, Jennifer, returned for a visit to give his parents some time with their grandkids—who were just four and nine at the time—he knew he wanted to return home to start a business. Although he confessed, "I wasn't anxious for anyone to remember me; I let people confuse me with my three brothers," his pub has become a hub of family activity in town. One of the side rooms often hosts birthday parties and baby showers, while partitioned spaces along another wall include a playroom, a lounge, and a reading room. Incidentally, when I asked him if he hopes the brewpub will continue as a family business even though it's way too early to show his kids the ropes, he said both his daughters already know the whole brewing process and added, "I make 'em clean up the kids area." His younger daughter, Ella, is the namesake for Prodigal Son's Ella IPA.

Beers brewed: Year-round: A Beer Named Sue, Wheatstock Hefeweizen, Righteous Indignation Organic Red, Ella IPA, Max Power IIPA, Bruce/Lee Porter, Fatted Calf Sacrificial Coffee Stout (on nitro). Seasonals: Bob's Your Uncle British Mild, Sundown Saison, Cowboy Common, High 'N' Rye Pale, Christmas Carole, Splendor in the Glass single-hopped IPA series.

The Pick: Fatted Calf Sacrificial Coffee Stout. Sometimes brewed with locally roasted coffee and sometimes javaless, the beer upholds a strong roast component and mocha flavor and adds creamy texture with flaked oats beyond the seven-strong malt bill. Nitrogen imbues amazing smoothness.

"We're the first family-friendly brewpub here," Guenther said of his hometown of some eighteen thousand people that feels like walking back in time to the Old West. Saddle up for a visit in mid-September and take in the Pendleton Round-Up rodeo. Some locals had a hard time blurring the line between restaurants that are fit for families and saloons that are not. Along those lines, Guenther mentioned "We just bought the Packard Tavern." Located a minute's walk down Court Avenue, the classic tavern just got craftier, beginning with Prodigal Son beers on some of its eighteen taps, no doubt.

Geoff Engel brews those killer beers. His résumé includes Pyramid Brewing. There are generally eight on draft that exhibit a broad scope of styles, from those on the lighter end such as A Beer Named Sue golden ale and Wheatstock Hefeweizen (named after a nearby music festival and served with a grapefruit wedge because lemon and orange were already taken), up to Bruce/Lee Porter and Max Power Imperial IPA.

While you can get an imperial pint for only four bucks, several glass sizes are offered down to half-pints and 5-ounce samplers because you don't want to miss a stitch if you're pounding pints while knitting. But if you're parking it for a while, say, while listening to come live music, consider ordering a flight. That way you also get any seasonals.

While the bulk of the porcine goodness served in the pub hails from Hill Meat, Pendleton's natural pork processor, Guenther informed me that they have their own pigs, Prodigal Pork, fed a diet of spent grains. Chef Barnes turns them into bacon (both American and Canadian style), pork chops, rillettes, or other specials. Any time you return to the Prodigal Son is an occasion worthy of feasting on fatted calf . . . er, pig.

The Prodigal Son Brewery and Pub

Opened: 2010.

Owners: Tim and Jennifer Guenther, and Matthew Barnes.

Brewer: Geoff Engel.

System: 10-barrel.

Annual production: 500 barrels.

Tours: By appointment.

Distribution: Mostly Eastern Oregon.

Hours: Tuesday through Thursday, 11 a.m. to 10 p.m.; Friday and Saturday, 11 a.m. to 11 p.m.; Sunday, noon to 9 p.m.

Takeout beer: Growler fills.

Food: Finger foods and some British-oriented pub grub, plus burgers and sandwiches.

Events: Communal events including a Halloween horror movie fest, "Beer & Braaains."

Solera Brewery

4945 Baseline Drive, Parkdale, OR 97041
(541) 352-5500 • SoleraBrewery.com
Twitter @SoleraBrewery

Solera is a quaint brewpub in a community of a few hundred people, located midway between Hood River and the glacier-covered slopes of Mt. Hood, naturally making the view one of its stunning selling points. Before Jason Kahler founded Solera, he'd been trying to buy what was then Elliot Glacier Public House. Patience, as we all know, is a virtue. And it's a good thing Kahler is patient, because the beers he built his dream around require years of it: Kahler uses a process called "solera," which entails continuously blending vintages of beer in barrels. It's an on-going process of filling barrels, pulling about half the product out, topping it with new beer, aging, and repeating "until the barrel says it's done."

Kahler's first brewing gig was back home in Duluth, Minnesota. After attending the Siebel Institute, Full Sail Brewing brought him to this region (like most other brewers around Hood River). That was in 2000. He next worked at Walking Man Brewing on the Washington side of the Columbia River, then at Big Horse Brew Pub in downtown, where he had carte blanche to experiment with sour beers.

Kahler introduced Solera Brewing with two of his favorite expressions among the brewer's palette. "Just IPA and Berliner Weisse—everything else would be seasonals," he said. "I found I couldn't make Berliner Weisse fast enough . . . They weren't drinking anything else."

And Kahler takes advantage of the local bounty. Parkdale, off Highway 35 at the far end of the Hood River Valley's so-called "Fruit Loop," is convenient for making a wild kriek ale during cherry harvest (I suggested that he host a fest for krieks and cherry ciders . . . fingers crossed) and adding fresh peaches and apricots to the Berliner Weisse to embellish the tartness. He mentioned that regulars took to calling a powerful sour apricot beer (that he simply

Beers brewed: Year-round: Hedonist IPA, Berliner No Weisse. Seasonals: French Tickler Grisette, Kwazy Wabbit DIPA, Shortstop ISA, Puppy's Poison ISA, New Breed ISA, Lapin Lover Kriek, Peche Bier, Azacca Wheat, Old Droopy Drawers Scotch Ale, Good Smoke, The Fez sour farmhouse ale, Back Door Blonde, and more.

The Pick: Shortstop ISA. I look forward to trying the wild kriek, but until then, I enjoy Solera's India session ales. Apollo hops make this beer dance and punch like Apollo Creed—all-American and super alpha. Citrusy and floral flourishes pack a gentle wallop, rounding it out at 4 percent ABV and 45 IBUs.

calls Sour Apricot) Tie Me to the Bedpost, but if he knows the derivation, he didn't let me in on it. (The 9 percent alcohol may have influenced it.)

Other than locals, Solera welcomes plenty of "Portland beer nerds." Yeah, it's the beer, but the back patio is also like living in a postcard. It faces Mt. Hood and seats 150, soon to be expanded.

Hop fiends are a blessing and a curse because, Kahler commented, "The last thing I wanted to do was make IPA all the time, and unfortunately it's turned out that I'm making IPA all the time." Hedonist IPA is a mouthwatering cornucopia of tropical fruit flavors, but I'm a fan of his India session ales. He makes multiple low-alcohol yet hoppy beers with names like Shortstop, Half Pint, and Puppy's Poison. He also brews in the other direction with beers like Kwazy Wabbit DIPA.

Possibly as early as Solera's second anniversary in May 2014, Kahler said he expected to have his dream beers available in 750-milliliter bottles. He had to get the brewpub up and running and the brewhouse is quite confined, but when one of the area's new craft cideries, Hood Valley Cider Co., opened across the street, Kahler fortuitously found a basement to house used wine barrels for aging his beers. As for the liquid that goes in the barrel, Kahler is always experimenting. Full Sail taught him how to manage a yeast lab and propogate cultures. Of the *Brettanomyces* strains, he's a fan of the "pineapply, refreshing" Brett C (the one that isn't dubbed "horse blanket" and "barnyard," and I'm in full agreement that those are not desirable traits).

Speaking of desirable and undesirable flavors and aromas, when you enter the cozy brewpub and get a huge whiff of buttered popcorn, that's not diacetyl you're smelling. It's an actual popcorn machine, harkening back to the building's original use as a movie theater in 1930.

Solera Brewery

Opened: 2012.

Owners: Jason Kahler and John Hitt.

Brewer: Jason Kahler.

System: 7-barrel.

Annual production: 350 barrels.

Distribution: Self-distributed between Hood River and Portland.

Hours: Seasonal; check before you visit.

Tours: Upon request.

Takeout beer: Growlers; bottles coming soon.

Gift shop: Shirts and hoodies.

Food: Paninis and easy bar food. Grilled brats when weather permits.

Events: Annual Solera Ski Party (eighties ski outfits encouraged) in early February.

Tandem Brewing

298 South Oregon Street, Ontario, OR 97914
(541) 889-4166 • TandemBrewingCo.com

Honestly, I didn't visit Tandem Brewing. And it wrecks me. It wasn't because I couldn't bother to trek all the way to Ontario, which might as well be in Idaho since it's on the Ore-Ida border and on Mountain Time, but precisely because I *did* schlep out there and didn't know about this sub-1-barrel brewery. I reprimanded Beer Valley's Pete Ricks (by email) for not tipping me off to them and he responded, "Sorry Brian, thought you knew about those dudes. Real nice people that opened up a nano to service their coffee shop/café."

Those dudes are Todd Heinz and Carl Crume. They're old, old friends, and their coffee shop, founded in 2001, is called Jolt's & Juice. It's literally a café and smoothie bar. (Yes, you can get coffee smoothies.) It seems they figured, "Hey, we roast our own coffee on-site, so why not make our own beer, too?" Apparently they'd discussed it for years since the retail space is actually three stores in one and the closing of a spice business left a vacancy the size of a 25-gallon system.

Most of the beers have a bike theme going, much like the brewery itself, which is billed as "two heads above the rest." The most frequent beers are Road Rash Red (named for Crume's bike accident) and Chain Ring Double IPA, but these elder statesmen have some young tricks up their sleeves when it comes to incorporating the local *terroir*. The Espresso Porter uses their own roasted beans, naturally. And Crank'n'-Tater offers suds and spuds in one pint, made with real Ore-Ida–grown taters, and goes "like fire cakes" at the three-stage Tour of Ontario bike race in late March. Crank'n'Tater is actually a throwback to World War II potato beers.

Tandem Brewing

Opened: 2012.
Owners: Todd Heinz and Carl Crume.
Brewer: Todd Heinz.
System: 25-gallon.
Annual production: 25 barrels.
Food: Paninis, muffins and baked goods, and fresh fruit smoothies.

Beers brewed: Year-round: Road Rash Red, Chain Ring Double IPA, Espresso Porter, Stoker Whiskey Stout, Boneshaker Bourbon Rye Stout, Blueberry Pale Ale, Doubble Ebenezer Holiday Ale, Brown Ale, No Name Beer, Bunny Hop & Through the Rye IPA, Crank'n'Tater.

Terminal Gravity Brewing

803 Southeast School Street, Enterprise, OR 97828
(541) 426-3000 • TerminalGravityBrewing.com

The Wallowa Lake Highway (Route 82), part of the Hells Canyon Scenic Byway, leads directly to Enterprise, a town where the brewery to resident ratio is less than 1:2,000 per capita.

There's one brewery. Terminal Gravity is plunked down on a little idyllic spot that has a serene stream running through aspen trees. (Sorry, it's actually just a drainage ditch, but don't let that diminish the tranquility. Nor should you confuse it with the town's excellent water source.) This place teems with locals and tourists during the summer, when the beer line could easily take an hour. As such, the owners opened a kiosk for extra taps in the front beer garden.

Funnily, Enterprise wasn't their first choice for the brewery, named after beer's final gravity. Specifically, final, or terminal, gravity is measured as a result of the original gravity showing how much sugar is contained in the brewing wort. A beer reaches final gravity once the yeast consumes those sugars, and the specific gravity bottoms out when the beer has stopped fermenting. I think we can agree that Final Gravity wouldn't have sounded as cool as Terminal Gravity. Co-owners Steve Carper and his then-brother-in-law Dean Duquette looked in areas from Alaska to Colorado, but Eastern Oregon beckoned as a nice place to raise their families while building a business. Technically, there was a third business partner at the time, who was from Enterprise and more the money guy than a beer guy, and was how Ed Millar made the prudent switch from Bank of America to Terminal Gravity and came aboard as CFO.

Carper, whose title includes executive brewer, already had experience brewing at larger Portland and Seattle breweries and was ready to do something more his own speed. Duquette, whose title also includes plant manager, explained that he'd helped build their initial 5-barrel brewery, albeit for another brewing company that soon folded, which is how they came into a system for a quarter of the

Beers brewed: Year-round: IPA, ESG, Breakfast Porter, Bar X Stout. Seasonals: Festivale, Triple, Weed Whacker Summer Session Beer.

The Pick: IPA. One of the most quintessential Northwest IPAs, this one pours burnt orange instead of "pale" colored ale. Its ample citrus and grilled stonefruit flavors from the generous hop bill provide great balance to its almost 7 percent alcohol content.

price he'd originally sold it for. Part of business acumen has always been fortunate timing.

Initially the brewing operation, housed in an actual house built over a century earlier, was small enough to co-exist with a bakery and a sausage factory. (Duquette called the trinity "The brewer, the baker, and the sausage maker," perhaps overlooking that one of the three men in the nursery rhyme tub was already a butcher.) Terminal Gravity has since grown from a 5-barrel to an 18-barrel brewery. Bottled offerings like IPA and ESG (Extra Special Golden) are easily found in Portland.

The IPA is Terminal's moneymaker, and has been since 1997. That's when the *Oregonian's* beer writer, John Foyston, deemed it the beer of the year. The recipe has scarcely changed since, although Duquette admitted it alters when necessary because of "hops availability." I enthusiastically enjoyed a glass straight from the bright tank's zwickel (tap). Beyond that freshest possible pint, I also got a taste of Vienna. Naturally, it's a Vienna-style lager. "We're not making up cute, fancy names like Wallowa Lake Whatever," Duquette said. "Steve's always been pretty adamant about that. If it's an IPA, let's call it an IPA."

Beers like the lager, or anything that doesn't get distributed, make stopping in at Terminal Gravity a treat. The setting alone is incredibly welcoming. Besides darts and foosball inside, the real gem is enjoying beer outside beneath the aspens. When snow doesn't cover the ground and there are enough people willing to put their beers down, there's a volleyball court. Personally, I stick to brewery games like washers or bocce that you can play one-handed. No one would want me on their team since I'd never hustle—I'd be too afraid to spill my beer.

Terminal Gravity Brewing

Opened: 1996.

Owners: Steve Carper, Dean Duquette, and Ed Millar.

Brewers: Steve Carper (executive brewer), Frank Helderman, and Chris Hudson.

System: 18-barrel.

Annual production: 8,000 barrels.

Distribution: Oregon and Idaho.

Hours: Wednesday and Thursday, 4 p.m. to 9 p.m.; Friday and Saturday, 11 a.m. to 10 p.m.

Tours: Arrange in advance.

Takeout beer: Growlers, bottles, and kegs.

Gift shop: Shirts and plenty of apparel hanging on the pub's wall, plus bottle openers locally made from willow wood.

Food: Pub fare including 6 Ranch grass-fed beef and Stangles buffalo meat, nachos, salmon sandwiches, and salads, plus soups in snowy winters.

Thunder Island Brewing Co.

515 Northwest Portage Road, Cascade Locks, Oregon 97014
(971) 231-4599 • ThunderIslandBrewing.com
Twitter @TIBrewing

It used to be that if you were making the drive from Portland to Hood River for a day of hiking, wine tasting, berry picking, wind surfing, or of course brewery hopping, your only option for a beer to break up that grueling hour-and-a-quarter drive was an early pit stop at McMenamins Edgefield in Troutdale. But now, after visiting (and ideally hiking) Multnomah Falls, the Columbia River Gorge's most popular waterfall, you can visit the new nanobrewery option in the tiny town of Cascade Locks, almost halfway down I-84 before reaching Hood River.

Beer, scenery, and ideally some sun are a winning trifecta that would make any spot a worthy destination, especially when you throw in picnic tables and a few Adirondack chairs for al fresco quaffing. While it's easy to drive to Thunder Island, do what co-owner and brewer Dan Hynes would rather do: ride in along the Historic Columbia State Highway Trail that now connects Portland to Cascade Locks, the lowest point along the Pacific Coast Trail. If that's too strenuous, there's a new eighteen-hole disc golf course that opened on the opposite side of town around the same time. The only basket you'll find at the brewery is for fish and chips, courtesy of Pirate's, a food truck docked at the brewery. From the golf course to the brewery two and a half miles away, I'd call that a par 100.

Thunder Island Brewing Co.

Opened: 2013.
Owners and brewers: Dave Lipps and Dan Hynes.
System: 2-barrel.
Annual production: 75 barrels.
Distribution: Gorge to Portland.
Hours: Seasonal; check before you visit.
Tours: By request.
Takeout beer: Growlers.
Food: Pirate's Fish and Chips food truck.

Beers brewed: Year-round: Pale Ale, Scotch Porter, IPA, Kolsch, Mosaic Pale. Seasonals: TBD.

Willamette Valley

Lewis and Clark paddled down the Columbia River to the Pacific, but only Clark took the time to bank south and discover the fecundity of the Willamette Valley between the Cascade and Coast Mountains. It wasn't long before pioneers blazed a trail westward to see and feel the lush, fertile land for themselves. Situated at the North 45th Parallel, the rainy, cool climate constitutes excellent growing conditions similar to that of Bavaria, Bohemia, and Kent in the United Kingdom, all of which famously lend themselves particularly well to cultivating hops. Some pioneers went south in 1849, but others became homesteaders. The Willamette Valley is now America's second largest producer of hops. Gold rush, schmold rush: dry-hopping with gold nuggets does nothing to improve the taste of a pint of fresh IPA.

Until recently, the valley mostly drew visitors to its wine country, where Oregon Pinot Noir reigns. Individuals who love both grape and hop juice, or perhaps couples split between their affinity for Syrah and saison, can turn a sojourn through vineyards and hopyards into an enchanting weekend getaway.

The Willamette River runs for 187 miles along the valley floor, from Eugene northward to the Columbia. Far from being entirely rural, the valley is home to the state capital, Salem, and both major universities: *University of Oregon* in Eugene and *Oregon State University* almost fifty miles up the road in Corvallis. Whether you're a Duck, a Beaver, or neither, the energy around here during The Civil War—one of the most intense college football rivalries in the country—is electrifying and makes for excellent beer specials pitting the eight breweries from around Corvallis against the dozen that have surfaced in the Eugene area. For brewery pilgrims, this means there are four breweries within four blocks of each other in Corvallis's **Central Business District**, while Eugene's **Whiteaker neighborhood** is now hopping with five within a single mile walk over a few blocks, giving it the nickname the "Brewery District." In the battle of brewpub and public house crawls, the spoils go to all visiting victors.

To appreciate the local flora, **Oregon Garden** in Silverton offers eighty tranquil acres of plants, trees, flowers, and a few water features. Also nearby is **Silver Falls State Park** with incredible hiking along the fairly tame **Ten Falls Canyon Trail**. So named for its ten breathtaking waterfalls, this is a great trail for those with kids (or fur children). Speaking of pet-friendly destinations, **Minto-Brown Island Park** in Salem is a nine-hundred-acre oasis that feels like nine thousand.

Best of all, after the healthy hiking or palate fatigue from wine-tasting, not only are there breweries in twelve different cities throughout this part of the valley, but also several of the most destination-worthy taphouses. Eugene is probably leading the charge with the newly redesigned **Bier Stein**, featuring over twenty well-curated taps and more than a thousand bottles, so showing restraint while shopping is futile. Also in town are the two locations of **16 Tons**. Both their taphouse and café have fewer than twenty taps, so they have quality over quantity down pat.

Agrarian Ales

31115 West Crossroads Lane, Eugene, OR 97408
(541) 510-4897 • AgAles.com
Twitter @AgrarianAles

The aptly-named Agrarian Ales is an authentic farmhouse brewery situated in Oregon's fertile Willamette Valley and established by brothers Ben and Nate Tilley. Their parents, Ben Sr., and Debbie Tilley, founded Crossroads Farm in 1984. It feels more like it's in rural Coburg than Eugene, probably because you have to drive down country roads to reach it.

Upon arrival, the first thing you see, if they're in season, are the trellises with ten varieties of organic, Pacific Northwest hops the Tilley brothers planted back in 2006, anticipating the start of their own brewing company. And the big, red dairy barn is where the brewery resides. Since they're tied to the land, there are no year-round beers and brewer Tobias Schock prefers it that way. One of my visits yielded a beer called Dandy, a porter into which they tossed roasted dandelions. If it grows on the land—even if it's a weed—it's waste not, want not.

Belgene is the name of their series of hoppy saisons. The name is a tip-off—nay, a warning—that you won't encounter Northwest-style hop bombs but instead Belgian- and French-influenced numbers that showcase a different variety of estate-grown hops. The saison yeast ensures that these beers are brighter and earthier than the hop-forward IPAs one might expect.

Before hops were harvested, one the Tilley family's main cash crops was chilies. Twenty-five varieties, grown on the twenty-five-acre farm, made Crossroads a hot commodity at the local farmers market. Nowadays, there's always a chili beer on draft that changes with each season. Poblamo! was the first they made and featured roasted poblano peppers infused into a base of a malty amber session ale, wherein the poblanos dominated the aroma. While having a lively tingle on the tongue, the heat level remained subdued and pleasant the whole glass through. A subsequent one, Espelette,

Beers brewed: Seasonals: True saisons, farmhouse ales, and field beers, including Belgene, a rotating hoppy saison, and a new chili beer each season.

The Pick: Chili beer. Agrarian makes chili beers like no one else. There's always one on but it rotates, featuring (at least) one of the twenty-five varieties of chilies grown on the farm. But is it roasted, dried, or thrown in fresh? Is the base beer a saison, red ale, or perhaps a pumpkin ale? Whatever the case, expect something creative and flavorful.

was a smoky red ale made with the dried chilies famous in Basque Country. Agrarian beers are always full-flavored yet low on the Scoville scale (used for measuring the spicy heat of chilies, akin to the way hop bitterness is measured in IBUs). Not only do the chilies change, but so does their treatment, including drying, roasting, or perhaps fresh off the vine.

All of these may sound summery, but come the colder months the ambient temperatures allow them to brew lagers, or a particularly amazing winter saison called Apricity. The obscure word means "the warmth of the winter sun." The saison was built on a clean base of organic pilsner and pale malts, and the yeast lent a significant aroma of apricots.

Visits to the brewery are family-friendly. Kids can enjoy the play structure or a line of unique sodas, sweetened only with local honey, that Schock developed just for them. Having said that, even as a beer lover of legal age I enjoy the sodas so much that I bought a half-growler of one to take home. Cherry Cherry Bomb Bon was made from a neighbor's cherries for the first part of the name, plus cherry bomb chili peppers bursting with sweet and savory notes with a mild heat. Any number of fruits, herbs, or chilies—and even barley—is fair game.

Also on the play side, there are plenty of hula hoops for the big kids. And what's a farm without horseshoes? It's a great drinking game because you can pitch with one hand and hold your beer in the other. If you have a pint too many, ask 'em if you can crash in the yurt out in the field. You won't be the first.

Agrarian Ales

Opened: 2012.
Owner: Ben Tilley Jr.
Brewers: Tobias Schock and Nate Tilley.
System: 7-barrel.
Annual production: 300 barrels.
Distribution: Mostly mid-Valley draft accounts.
Hours: Friday, 3 p.m. to 8 p.m.; Sunday, noon to 8 p.m.
Tours: By request during open hours.
Takeout beer: Growlers and growlettes available.
Gift shop: Batik tie-dye shirts.
Food: Seasonal cheeses, plus a meat and veggie dish.
Extras: Hang out on the farm and play games such as horseshoes and cornhole while listening to a live band. There's also a playground to entertain kids.

Block 15 Restaurant & Brewery

300 Southwest Jefferson, Corvallis, OR 97333
(541) 758-2077 • Block15.com
Twitter @Block15Brewing

For their part, Nick Arzner and his wife, Kristen, were surprised to discover Corvallis didn't have a homegrown brewpub. By early 2008 they had rectified that. Next thing you know, there are now four brewpubs in a four-block radius, with a fifth one eyeing a spot a block away. Maybe one day there will be a fifteen-block brewpub crawl.

It all starts with Block 15. Arzner grew up a short drive away in Albany and was a dedicated but not devout homebrewer. Right from the start, he hired a fifteen-year veteran of the Oregon brewing industry, Steve van Rossem, who is now brewing at Planktown down I-5 in Springfield. Their intentions from the start were twofold: offer locally sourced pub food that wouldn't put a major dent in locals' wallets, and pair it with fine, fresh beer. It has worked. "We're half popular because of our food, half popular because of our beer," Arzner said. (I say it's vice versa.) The last monthly special I noted was a kimchi burger! There's even a handwritten list of everything from pork to salad greens, informing guests where the respective farms are located.

You'll have a tougher time deciding what to drink since there are fourteen taps (including a few guest taps) and a cask ale. No matter what style of beer you prefer—hoppy numbers such as Sticky Hands Double IPA, fruity ones like Fruit Wheat with raspberries, dark ales like Nebula "naked oat" stout, or Belgianesque beauties such as Wandelpad—you will find a new favorite beer here.

Of course, Block 15 is increasingly heralded for its wild ales that rampage with the microorganisms breezing through downtown Corvallis.

Beers brewed: Year-round: Alpha IPA, Aboriginale, Glo Golden Lager, Ridgeback Red, Nebula Naked Oat Stout, Fruit Wheat Ale, Print Master's Pale Ale, Wandelpad Belgian Pale. Seasonals: Sticky Hands IPA series, Reporter London Brown, Pomegranate Pappy's Dark, Super Nebula, Golden Canary, Framboise White, Strawberry Fields, Enchantment, Figgy Pudding, and several more.

The Pick: Framboise White. This is possibly the best raspberry beer in Oregon and has the word "white" in it for a reason. It starts as an imperial Belgian wit fermented with witbier yeast, *Lactobacillus*, and *Brettanomyces* before maturing in Chardonnay barrels with delicate golden raspberries. It pours a light honey color, is delectably fragrant, and balances tartness with just the right pinch of sweetness.

The brewery may not receive the same online hype that accompanies the new class of experimental brewers, but that has more to do with the fact that 90 percent of their beers are sold on-site, not found online. One of the coolest features—albeit a bit cruel if you're just passing through—is the chalkboard listing barrels undergoing extended cellaring down in the basement-level brewery and barrelroom. For instance, I had to sign up for their newsletter so that I'll be notified when Gin & Juice, a wild golden ale aged in gin barrels with kiwi fruit, becomes available.

Coming up sooner were two of my all-time favorite yet disparate beers: Framboise White and Super Nebula. The former, unlike some framboises, doesn't pour or taste a syrupy red but rather uses golden raspberries, a yellowish fruit that is definitely a raspberry, just subtler, and perfectly espouses the Chardonnay-aged witbier base. As for Super Nebula, it's aged in bourbon barrels and is one of the most stellar representations among a galaxy of imperial stouts. This one often becomes the actual or de facto people's choice at various stout festivals. No mere imperial version of Block 15's Nebula oatmeal stout (6.8 percent ABV), Super Nebula is augmented with roasted cocoa nibs and molasses, and a segment gets blended with a portion aged in top shelf bourbon barrels, finishing at 11 percent ABV.

Some of their rarities are bottled. What I love about these limited releases is that they're packaged in 375-millileter "half"-bottles, thus serving the dual purpose of halving the price and doubling the availability. Plus, if you score a bottle, you can selfishly and easily enjoy it by yourself.

Somewhat surprisingly, Arzner felt none of this was a sure thing. "I said to myself, I'll be happy if I get to brew one batch of beer and then go out of business." That was 2008, when he was twenty-eight and Kristen was twenty-four. She's now in charge of front-of-house, or what Nick calls "all the really important s[tuff]."

He joked that the IPA and fruit wheat ale "subsidized our barrel program." Those two beers account for the bulk of draft beer sold at the pub. Everyone, it seems, local or not, digs hops and/or fruits in their beer. He calls Sticky Hands his "hop experience ale project," offering a distinct iteration monthly, both on draft and in 750-milliliter bottles. They only make fifty cases of it. "If you still have one when next one comes out, you held onto it too long," Arzner said.

Arrange a tour in advance and you can explore the cavernous basement beneath the pub and see their twenty-seven tanks (up from the four they started with) and over 150 barrels aging unique beers at all times. That number is more impressive when you consider it's all managed by hand. They couldn't get a forklift down there if they tried. Hence, it's like playing Cask Tetris when it comes time to move them around.

The other salient point about the beers aging down in Block 15's beer cave is that despite their popularity, or because of it, they aren't producing any of them at full throttle. "We wanna grow quality, not quantity," noted Arzner. He and Kristen had contemplated expanding the brewpub, but instead opened a gastropub directly adjacent called Les Caves. The food menu is (more) upscale. The beer menu— a tome, really—contains 130 bottles, but don't miss the fluctuating Caves Saison brewed exclusively for the tavern. Touring the grotto with Arzner, he treated me to a tart taste of Caves Anniversary, the result of holding back some of each batch, then blending them back together and allowing the brew to naturally pick up some *Brettanomyces* and *Pediococcus*. He explained that the funky elements weren't manually inoculated but had naturally picked up, in his word, "terroir." Seeing as it's below street level, I believe that would make it *sub-terroir*.

Block 15 Restaurant & Brewery

Opened: 2008.

Owners: Nick and Kristen Arzner.

Brewers: Nick Arzner (brewmaster) and Matt Williams (lead brewer).

System: 7-barrel.

Annual production: 1,100 barrels.

Distribution: 90 percent sold on-premises. Eugene and Portland get the rest.

Hours: Sunday through Wednesday, 11 a.m. to 11 p.m.; Thursday through Saturday, 11 a.m. to 1 a.m.

Tours: By appointment only.

Takeout beer: Growler fills and limited bottles.

Gift shop: Apparel and glassware in a case in the back.

Food: Elevated pub grub, locally sourced. Try the Smoked Pork Chili Cheeseburger or the "Brewben" sandwich.

Events: Bloktoberfest block party with liter steins the first weekend in October without a home game, and Brewers Brunch.

Brewers Union Local 180

48329 East First Street, Oakridge, OR 97463
(541) 782-2024 • BrewersUnion.com

Don't expect anyone to call you guv'ner. Don't look for packets of crisps behind the horseshoe-shaped bar. And don't expect to find a chippie shop next door. But make no mistake: Brewers Union Local 180 is in fact *the* local, motivated by British pub culture, for everyone in Oakridge. The town of 3,200 people is in the Cascades, roughly between Eugene and Bend, completely engulfed by the Willamette National Forest along the north fork of the Willamette River. As such, it's a mecca for mountain bikers.

This public house and brewery is packed in every chamber during the summer, where you'll find blokes—er, folks—playing games, music on the guitar or upright piano, or shooting pool. There's even a mini billiard table for wee ones, since real public houses are by nature family-friendly. Guests are welcomed and encouraged to enjoy themselves, unhurried. Whether it's someone quietly plugging away on a laptop or a boisterous group on their fourth round, Brewers Union offers the epitome of whatever you deem comfy. There are no tabs crammed in your face to rush you out after just five hours.

Founder-brewer Ted Sobel has lived in Oakridge since 1991 and watched it become known as the "Mountain Biking Capital" of the Northwest. However, he actually doesn't seek out the single tracks. "Walking is the pace that I think," said the fervent hiker whose goatee is gray but ponytail isn't. His dream of brewing real ale professionally at his own proper pub materialized in 2008, making Highway 58 as desirable for beer hounds as for mountain-biking fiends. It's also popular among skiers in winter.

Sobel's affinity for brewing real ale developed long before opening his pub. He hitchhiked across England with his wife, where he fell in love with British bitters and pub life in general. He even got to brew there and tries to return annually. Upon returning stateside, Sobel, who had twenty-five years of homebrewing experience, built his own

Beers brewed: No core beers or recipes, but the six cask engines typically feature a mild, a bitter, an IPA, and probably something dark and/or strong.

The Pick: Wotcha Best Bitter. Ordering a "pint of bitter" from a pub that serves real ale is a treat. This one, bittered with Calypso hops, is a little fruity, a little earthy, and at 4.3 percent ABV, an ideal sipper. Repeatedly.

pub, which juxtaposes Britannia and Cascadia. He brews two imperial barrels at a time, which by U.S. measurements is just shy of 90 gallons, or 2.8 U.S. barrels, meaning each batch yields 8 firkins.

Naturally, Sobel serves his cask-conditioned real ales in imperial pints (20 ounces). Each beer is served from one of the six hand pumps used to dispense the living ales (unlike the guest kegged beers). Following tradition, he checks on them daily to evaluate when they're at the peak of vitality; nary a pint shall they fill until said moment. Sobel's ales condition in the firkins, ever so slightly cooled to cellar temperature, before the pumping action draws the beer into the waiting glass.

I tried a bunch of beers. I dug the Cwrw Bach Welsh Dark Mild, brewed with a touch of peated malt. *Cwrw bach* means "small beer" in Welsh and is as close to a Russian kvass—the very low-alcohol malt beverage that drinks almost like a soft beverage—as you're likely to find. On the opposite end, the Oaky Bumpkin stout finished on bourbon-soaked oak chips was a tasty treat, even if not one I could drink several pints of in quite the same way as the bitter.

Having said all that, Sobel didn't go into a dissertation about upholding tradition from an era in brewing before mega-corporations sped up and dumbed down beer manufacturing. His rationale for his real ale obsession is all of two words long: "It's yummy!" He's not alone in his appreciation. "It's working," he reflected. "People are being taught what a public house is." He's looking at opening a satellite pub down in Eugene, or maybe another one farther north like McMinnville, but said that'd require building a second brewery since he suspects a Eugene spot would max out capacity. That's actually in keeping with the British model of public houses with breweries. And in the reiterated words of a British visitor, "Damn, this is bloody spot on!"

Brewers Union Local 180

Opened: 2008.
Owner and brewer: Ted Sobel.
System: 2-barrel imperial.
Annual production: 118 barrels.
Distribution: On-premises.
Hours: Seasonal; check before you visit.
Tours: By request.
Takeout beer: You can fill growlers but I don't recommend it since cask beer doesn't travel well.
Fests: Keg & Cask Festival in early August.
Extras: Live music, movie nights, and book and game libraries. Families welcome.

Calapooia Brewing Co.

140 Hill Street Northeast, Albany, OR 97321
(541) 928-1931 • CalapooiaBrewing.com
Twitter @DrinkCalapooia

It's neither downtown nor adjacent to a university. There's not even a tourist draw in Albany. Calapooia is a brewpub on the edge of a residential neighborhood (and new housing is coming across the street that will fully envelop the pub). Yet it's so crowded here, especially on weekends, that I can't understand why more brewpubs don't set up in residential areas if they're able to swing the zoning.

"Albany has really embraced us. Most of our customers live within a half mile," said Mark Martin, the amiable, goateed publican who bought the brewery with his wife, Laura Bryngelson, in 2006. It first opened as Oregon Trader Brewing in 1993 and is now in the hands of its third owners. As such, in 2013 they threw a seventh anniversary party, but it has been in continuous operation for twenty years. Calapooia has grown so much since they took it over that they now brew on a 15-barrel system, up from the 6-barrel originally in place.

There have been so many people wearing Calapooia shirts each time I've visited that I wondered if there were forty brewers who had all just ended their shift. One such patron was an older woman who regularly comes in for beer and darts. There are always people using the three dartboards, and Martin said many come in with their own (but the heavily pocked wall proves not everyone's an ace thrower). This particular woman informed me the pub sits in the Periwinkle District, though Martin chimed in that they're attempting to rebrand it as the "Pooia District." Such regulars would hardly argue with that.

"My head brewer, Joe, before he worked here, was a semi-regular," Martin shared. "He just walked in and met this girl. He met his wife here at that table by the front door." (Many of the

Beers brewed: Year-round: White Water Wheat, Santi-Amber Ale, Big Aft Pale, Riverdog ESB, RIPArian IPA, Paddle Me IPA, 'Pooya Porter, Devil's Hole Stout, Chili Beer. Seasonals: Simcoe Springs IPA, Yeti Blackberry Wheat, Fresh Hop Rye, Ol' Lickspigot Barley Wine, Kringle Krack Strong Ale, Undertow Imperial Stout, Pacific Pilsner, Rip Tide Rye, Shipwreck Imperial IPA, and one-offs.

The Pick: Chili Beer. Featuring fresh jalapeño, serrano, anaheim peppers (seeds and all), and even a kick of habaneros in there to boot, to the tune of about 10 pounds of chilies per barrel, this is clearly a beer with some serious heat.

tables, I'll point out, are made from maple or black walnut and built by a local regular.)

It'd be impossible to say that each and every frequenter is as integral a part of the brewpub or vice versa, but the vibe isn't far from that. That's precisely what Martin and Bryngelson hoped for. "I always knew I'd own my own bar," Martin said. He mentioned that he and his buddy since fifth grade, Brian Bovee, now of Sky High Brewing, drove around Corvallis in 1991 as roommates at OSU looking for a place to open a bar. It's amazing what a couple of decades can bring about. "When [Laura] and I found out [the brewpub] was for sale, we just rolled the dice."

Other than the name, the couple hasn't made changes, per se, just enhancements. It started with a new coat of paint, then the bigger system and more fermentation tanks. Some of the beers are holdovers from Oregon Trader with recipes "modified to our liking," Martin said. Furthermore, they also own the Siletz Brewery (some sixty miles west near the coast) and brand and plan to reintroduce those long lost beers, giving Calapooia an additional brand of packaged beer to sell.

This being Oregon, naturally Calapooia's biggest seller is their Northwest IPA, RIPArian, and they're transitioning Paddle Me into a flagship IPA with the recipe designed by Martin himself. Number two is Chili Beer. We are witnessing the rise of chili beers around the state, beers with quite a different bite than ones with spicy hops, but this is probably Oregon's oldest since the recipe came from Oregon Trader, which, again, Martin and Bryngelson bought, the whole enchilada, chilies and all. Martin said it has started selling "through the roof" since they started bottling it in 2011.

The beer goes into the Chili Burger (and the chili itself) that Martin created. When they say it's "generously swathed in our homemade Chili Beer chili," I'd say it's almost less burger than it is bowl of chili with a patty swimming in the middle afloat betwixt a sodden bun. It's not just recommended that you eat it with a fork instead of your hands, it necessitates it. It's got some kick but doesn't pack nearly the heat that the beer does. If heat is what you're burning for, there's the El Fuego Burger made with diced jalapeños mixed into the patty and smothered in three-alarm cream cheese featuring puya and serrano peppers. Folks here clearly love their chilies. As the Chili Beer's label reads, "It's got some heat, but it won't burn your face off. Unless you're a whuss. Seriously."

Calapooia Brewing Co.

Opened: 1993.

Owners: Mark Martin and Laura Bryngelson.

Brewers: Mark Martin (brewmaster) and Joe Clark (head brewer).

System: 15-barrel.

Annual production: 1,200 barrels.

Distribution: Oregon-wide, plus Alaska, Washington, Idaho, and Montana.

Hours: Sunday through Wednesday, 11:30 a.m. to 10 p.m. (9 p.m. November to March); Thursday, 11:30 a.m. to 11 p.m.; Friday and Saturday, 11:30 a.m. to midnight.

Tours: By appointment.

Takeout beer: Growlers, bombers, and dock sales.

Gift shop: Some T-shirts on hangers on the back wall. And darts.

Food: Lots of burgers and more. Get the Chili Burger "swathed" in their Chili Beer.

Extras: The back patio, called the atrium, fills up in nice weather and is smoke-free. Kids are allowed until 8 p.m.

Chatoe Rogue Farmstead Nanobrewery

3590 Wigrich Road, Independence, OR 97351
(503) 838-9813 • Rogue.com
Twitter @RogueHopFarm

Rogue created an ultimate 360-degree hop-head-farmstead opportunity. Reserve one of the six rooms or even the whole house (but don't expect one of those fancy bed-and-breakfasts) for a unique, rural beercation. Non-overnight guests are welcome, too.

Independence, southwest of Salem, enjoyed a half-century run as the "Hop Capital of the World." Today, Rogue Farms grows forty-two acres of aroma hops that get processed on-site and sent to brewmaster John Maier at the main brewery in Newport. But Josh Cronin, who helms the 25-gallon Chatoe Rogue Farmstead Nanobrewery, gets enough to brew 200-pint batches. He also makes ciders and perries (pear cider) and is the beekeeper, ensuring the sweet nectar needed for Rogue's new meads. Maybe he'll find inspiration in the pumpkin patch (where all of the gourds for Chatoe Pumpkin Aie grow) or search around the fruit and hazelnut orchards that visitors can stroll through.

Everything is Chatoe Rogue Farm–grown and exclusively tapped on the tasting room's twelve lines, hence their "farm to table" bludgeoning expression, "Kernel to Urinal." Enjoy beers in the field or sprawled out on the lawn. Don't miss visiting the potbellied pigs Voo and Doo, or the free-range chickens that get free rein of the farm.

Chatoe Rogue Farmstead Nanobrewery

Opened: 2011.

Owners: Brett Joyce.

Brewer: Josh Cronin.

System: 25-gallon (almost 1-barrel).

Annual production: Not much.

Distribution: Nanobrewed beers only available on-site.

Hours: Seasonal; check before you visit.

Tours: Saturdays and Sundays at 3 p.m. or by scheduling ahead. Call (503) 383-9813 or email ncronin@rogue.com.

Takeout beer: Nearly everything that Rogue bottles.

Gift shop: Large and extensive collection of Rogue swag.

Food: Snacks, barbecue, and burgers.

Beers brewed: Head brewer Josh Cronin, as well as homebrew clubs the Heart of the Valley and Capitol Brewers, create Farmstead collaboration brews that change seasonally.

Chehalem Valley Brewing Co.

2515-B Portland Road, Newberg, OR 97132
(971) 832-8131 • CVBrewing.com

Even if you're actively looking for Chehalem Valley Brewing while cruising down Highway 99, you're still liable to roll right by since it's set far back behind Ye Olde Pizza. So take note and use that as the landmark instead of the rather small sign alerting westbound drivers only to the presence of a "Brew Pub." But once you make a few passes and pull into the parking lot, there exists this single-barrel brewery and tasting room with a great hop canopy by the patio, where those who have arrived are in no rush to depart.

Paul Looney's and John Price's wives were friends who realized their homebrewing husbands should meet. Paul had about six years of experience under his belt, while John had been actively brewing for nearly ten years. All of the beers brewed at Chehalem Valley were originally created in their amateur days, though the scale isn't much bigger at the moment.

"It's kinda difficult to keep our beers on tap," said Looney from behind the bar. (Price, it seems, cottons to manning the brewhouse more than the taphouse.) That's why, after three years in business, they're planning on scaling up to a 10-barrel system and probably bottling in 22s, too. In fact, the augmentation doesn't end there. While presently patrons can bring a pie from Ye Olde Pizza (they don't do slices), Chehalem is adding a kitchen and will extend hours to 10 p.m. and likely midnight on the weekends.

For now, the initial improvement of adding the patio has been a major boon, and Looney said the crowds have been bigger than he and Price ever expected. "We wanted a laid-back outlet. Not loud, no ruckuses. Somewhere people can [converse] without having to yell." Add to this the fact that my (well-behaved) dog Dunkel can accompany me at the bar—which I'm sure will change once there's food—and it's my kind of place. The whole space is very clean and no-frills. They're just not into frilly. There are some flatscreens and

Beers brewed: Year-round: Broken Bottle IPA, Hop on Pop Double IPA, Blackridge Stout, Northern Porter, Summit Amber, Naked Blonde, Citra Blonde. Seasonals: Pacifica IPA, Fresh-hop Cascade Pale Ale, Snowmelt Golden Ale, Hazelnut Brown, Bald Peak Black Ale, Hard Cider.

The Pick: Hop on Pop Double IPA. Malty, hoppy, malty, hoppy. A pint of this makes for a happy Mommy or Poppy. And since minors aren't allowed, hire a sitter and drink this double IPA 'til you're sloppy.

a dartboard for Monday dart/game night, and Price's wife books live music, but the sole emphasis is on the beer-drinking experience. (Although there are some local wines available because Chehalem Valley is still wine country.)

Among the taps, they try to keep at least five house beers on at a time, and that will kick up to around eight with the larger system. Looney said the IPAs are in highest demand but so is Citra Blonde, thereby sating both types of beer drinkers. Citra Blonde is 100 percent Citra hopped (including dry-hopping), coupled with its petite 4 percent alcohol body, and is loaded with character from one of the most popular, newer hops. On the darker end of the spectrum are Blackridge Stout and Bald Peak Black Ale. The latter is brewed with a blend of American chocolate and roast malts on a pale malt base, sort of straddling the line between a porter and a schwarzbier. There's also Hazelnut Brown, which uses the state nut. "It's the only beer we add anything to," Looney said, assuring me that the real deal—not extracts—are added to secondary fermentation. I guess they're entitled to at least one frill.

Chehalem Valley Brewing Co.

Opened: 2011.

Owners and brewers: John Price and Paul Looney.

System: 1-barrel.

Annual production: 100 barrels.

Distribution: On-site only.

Hours: Monday through Thursday, 5 p.m. to 9 p.m.; Friday, 5 p.m. to 10 p.m.; Saturday, noon to 10 p.m.; Sunday, noon to 9 p.m.

Tours: By request.

Takeout beer: Growlers mostly, and limited keg sales.

Gift shop: One T-shirt, one hat, and one pint glass.

Food: Order from Ye Olde Pizza shop across the way until they add a kitchen.

Claim 52 Brewing

1030 Tyinn Street, Suite 1, Eugene, OR 97402
(541) 554-6786 • Claim52Brewing.com
Twitter @Claim52Brewing

What with every other brewery making one (or more) IPA and making it their flagship, cofounder and brewer Trevor Ross figured he'd lighten things up. Hence, Claim 52 debuted with two core beers that are light in color, lighter in alcohol, and only light in hops by comparison: a Kolsch-style ale and an India Session Ale. (The India session ale is the IPA's sessionable kid brother, though Ross is mulling over calling it an "American hop ale" because unlike the British-style IPA, this one's pure Yankee.) Whatever you call the session-strength hoppy pale ale, it's my favorite emerging style because I get all the IBUs I crave and fewer ABVs so I can actually handle it. But I like Trevor's idea because, like its acronym, it leads to that aha! moment when you realize drinking too many full-strength IPAs takes its toll on your palate and mental acuity.

The brewery Ross and partner Mercy McDonald, a longtime friend, started in a warehouse out on the west side of town opened as a 3.5-barrel system with a 7-barrel fermenter. Did I say 3.5-barrel system? In actuality, Trevor brews "1-plus" barrel batches, thrice and simultaneously. His jury-rigged system literally consists of three identical kettles that yield over 30 gallons apiece. I asked Trevor if anyone else does that and it took him a split second to respond with "No!" Sounds crazy, yes, but such foxlike craziness also allows him to brew single-barrel pilot batches by only firing up one of the brew kettles if he so chooses. That's how I came to try Motueka ("mow-too-ay-ka") Extra Pale Ale, named for the new New Zealand hop akin to the noble-style Saaz.

Frugality necessitated the brewery's small size, which limits them to a little over two dozen accounts on rotating taps mostly around Eugene. Having said that, McDonald said they're in the

Beers brewed: Year-round: Claim 52 Kolsch, Southtown Session ISA, Lotus Eater IPA. Seasonals: Might be a strong ale or a wheat beer, including witbier, stout, DIPA, or my favorite if they have it, Bee Beard Braggot (5.5 percent ABV).

The Pick: Southtown Session is an India session ale, but in Ross's mind it's an American hop ale. Proffering 4.2 percent ABV and an impressive 60 IBUs, it's an impressive beer that tastes like an imperial pint's worth of hops in a half-pint's worth of booze.

"pre-planning stages" of scaling up to a "bigger, more reasonable" brewhouse, perhaps a 7- or 15-barrel. In the meantime, pop into the brewery during dock sales to start your weekends and try around seven different beers listed on a chalkboard next to a handful of Ross's homebrew competition ribbons. (His home, by the way, is situated in the old pioneer land Claim 52, which Ross knew since he's a land surveyor by trade.) Lounge on an old church pew or row of airport seats while listening to live music and noshing from local food trucks.

Claim 52 Brewing

Opened: 2013.
Owners: Mercy McDonald and Trevor Ross.
Brewers: Trevor Ross and Joe Buppert (assistant brewer).
System: 3.5-barrel.
Annual production: 500 barrels.
Distribution: Eugene mostly.
Hours and dock sales: Friday, 4 p.m. to 9 p.m.
Takeout beer: Growlers and kegs.
Gift shop: T-shirts and growlers.
Food: Local food trucks usually around.

Deluxe Brewing Co.

635 Northeast Water Avenue, Suite B, Albany, OR 97321
(541) 639-4257 • DeluxeBrewing.com
Twitter @SinisterDeluxe

The brewery's logo says "Est. 2011," but Eric "Howie" Howard and his wife, Jamie, opened the doors and unloaded the first keg of Deluxe beer in late September 2013. Then they had a "grand opening" in December because, as Jamie put it, "We just wanted to have a party and celebrate." Things take longer when you do them yourself.

And while we're clearing things up, the logo also calls it a "brewing co." but the Howards really founded a "brewstillery" since they built and launched Sinister Distilling simultaneously. They proudly refer to this synergistic paean to fermentation as "Albany's first brewstillery." (The brewery occupies Suite B and the distillery requires walking through a threshold into Suite D, mostly for legal reasons.) It's only Albany's second brewery after Calapooia a short walk down the street.

Howie started homebrewing in 2005 and joined the local club, Heart of the Valley Homebrewers, which helped him win several awards for his beer. He was even elected president of the club. He went to work part-time at a small brewery nearby to learn about the business end of things, and in 2011 began the journey of starting Deluxe, that rare brewery that focuses exclusively on German-style lagers. The distillery side is focused on creating a range of whiskeys—augmented by the fact that Howie gets to brew his own wash, aka distiller's beer—though he said he can see doing rum and gin, too. Their location near OSU makes the Wild Beaver Amber Lager a local smash.

Deluxe Brewing Co.

Opened: 2013.
Owners: Eric "Howie" and Jamie Howard.
Brewer: Eric "Howie" Howard.
System: 15-barrel.
Annual production: 250 barrels.
Distribution: Willamette Valley.
Hours/Tours: Tuesday through Friday, 4 p.m. to 9 p.m.; Saturday, noon to 9 p.m.
Takeout beer: Growlers and dock sales.
Gift shop: Shirts and growlers.

Beers brewed: Year-round: Resurrection Pre-Prohibition Pilsner, Perfect Sin Schwarzbier, Wild Beaver Amber Lager.

The Elk Horn Brewery

Elk Horn Brewery

686 East Broadway, Eugene, OR 97401
(541) 912-3846 • Facebook.com/elkhornbrewery

Expectations for Elk Horn run high because Colleen and Stephen Sheehan's Southern cookin' food truck, Delacata, was voted Best Food Cart by *Eugene Weekly* readers two years running. In their third year of operation, they started building toward a brewpub. Famous for their fried catfish honoring Stephen's native Mississippi (Colleen is from Eugene), Delacata parked outside neighboring Ninkasi and Oakshire until, as Colleen put it, "We got too busy to work breweries." With Elk Horn, they'll pair their own food with their own beer, plus cider since Colleen worked at nearby Sweet Cheeks Winery, a minority partner with the built-in license to produce cider and mead.

Whereas the cart runs out of food, a full kitchen enables Elk Horn to sling what Colleen calls "Southern meets Northwest fusion." Aware that Eugene's collective diet is heavy on healthy veggies, there will be nods to that clientele, but Delacata's shirts read simply "Fried" and the aroma of peanut oil envelops them. Colleen had me drooling talking about bacon mac and cheese, pimento cheeseburgers, and cheddar-jalapeño hush puppies on the menu that's college-friendly in terms of student bodies and budgets. Then again, in addition to elk burgers, she plans on offering elk steak specials. Since Mississippi isn't synonymous with skinny, I wonder what beers will pair with weekend brunch, à la rotating beignets and Bananas Foster French toast.

The Elk Horn Brewery

Opened: 2014.

Owners: Colleen and Stephen Sheehan.

Brewer: Sam Scoggin.

System: 7-barrel.

Annual production: TBD.

Distribution: On-premises.

Hours: Monday through Friday, 11 a.m. to 10 p.m.; Saturday to Sunday, 9 a.m. to 10 p.m.

Takeout beer: Growlers.

Food: Northwest ingredients, Southern flair: shrimp po'boys, elk burgers, hush puppies.

Beers brewed: Year-round: IDK Blonde, Ducks Blue Ribbon Pale Ale, Sasquatch's Shadow Stout, Dry-Hopped Amber, IPA, and a Wheat Ale series among twenty taps including ciders.

Eugene City Brewery
(Rogue Ales Public House)

844 Olive Street, Eugene, OR 97401
(541) 345-4155 • Rogue.com
Twitter @TrackTownAles

The Rogue Ales Public House, a.k.a. Eugene City Brewery, opened in 2004 with a storied past. On this spot nearly 140 years earlier existed the initial Eugene City Brewery. Before Prohibition it fell under the ownership of Portland beer baron Henry Weinhard, although Rogue's historians say the newly named Weinhard's Beer and Ice Depot only made the latter. (The beer came from Portland.) The block waited roughly a century to see a brewery again until 1996, when West Brothers BBQ transitioned into a brewpub (briefly). The interim business was called The Dive Bar, which explains the portholes around the pub floor, offering unique views of the brewery below bathed in sapphire-blue lights, making everyone look like Smurfs.

The brand name Track Town Ales is in deference to U of O's track program, made famous by coach Bill Bowerman (Nike's cofounder) and running legend Steve Prefontaine. Triple Jump Pale Ale pairs with playing Track & Field on the vintage arcade console. Former brewers Christina Canto and Sam Scoggin designed Chai Porter and Pole Vault Coffee Porter (aged in Rogue Dead Guy whiskey barrels), respectively. Native recipe Honey Orange Wheat was a holdover from West Brothers but wisely eliminates using real orange juice.

Beers brewed: Year-round: Triple Jump Pale Ale, 200 Meter Ale, Pole Vault Porter, Honey Orange Wheat. Seasonals: Many.

The Pick: Track Town Chai Porter. For fans of "dirty chai," a.k.a. "dirty hippie"— the combo of espresso latte and Masala spiced chai— this tasty beer marries porter's roast coffee notes with cardamom and ginger from spicy chai.

Eugene City Brewery (Rogue Ales Public House)

Opened: 2004.

Owner: Brett Joyce (See Rogue Ales, page 172).

Brewer: Steve Distasio.

System: 7-barrel.

Annual production: 413 barrels.

Distribution: Eugene.

Hours: Monday, noon to 10 p.m.; Tuesday through Thursday, noon to 11 p.m.;
Friday and Saturday, noon to midnight; Sunday, noon to 9 p.m.

Tours: Head downstairs.

Takeout beer: Bombers of Rogue and Rogue's Track Town beers and growler fills.

Gift shop: Apparel, glassware, and more. Vintage Nikes not for sale.

Food: Rogue staples like Kobe Bleu Balls. One menu distinction is barley and duck soup.
Go Ducks.

Extras: Back patio. Two dozen Rogue beers on tap. Bingo Wednesdays. Other live
entertainment.

Falling Sky Brewing

1334 Oak Alley, Eugene, OR 97401
(541) 505-7096 • FallingSkyBrewing.com
Twitter @FallingSkyBrew

With four people having so much input at the creation of a new brewpub, I'd worry about the risk of too many cooks in the kitchen or brewers in the brewhouse. But with Falling Sky, it feels like everyone gets what they want. Fortuitously, what they want and what patrons want seem to overlap quite congruously. The local alternative weekly fishwrap, *Eugene Weekly*, put Falling Sky as a finalist in the following Best Of categories: Bar Grub, Place to Drink in the Sun, Brewery, Burger, New Restaurant, and New Business. As they pointed out, "That's a Best of Eugene record."

Cofounder Jason Carriere had just gotten into homebrewing in 2002 when the local homebrew supply shop went under. So he bought it. He also moved it, enlarged it, and changed the name to Falling Sky (not in the Chicken Little sense but in that this is Oregon and it rains a whole lot). Employees came and went but one such hire, Scott Sieber, never left. A couple of years later, the same became true for Mike Zarkesh. For his part, Carriere said he has always seen himself as a "caretaker of future brewers," as evidenced by some of the local pros who started out as customers. When Sieber and Zarkesh presented him with their business plan for a local brewery, the pieces fell into place for Falling Sky Brewing.

The other cofounder, Rob Cohen, completed the puzzle. He and Carriere met playing pickup basketball. Cohen had restaurant experience and dreamed of opening a locavore deli market (think NYC meets Willamette Valley). During my initial visit, I was already greatly impressed with the food menu that makes no concessions to brewpub conventions. The post-Easter menu's daily lunch

Beers brewed: Rotating: Fifteen taps such as Brubeck Bitter, Dark Heart Munich Dunkel, The Dozens Extra Pale, Echoes English IPA, Eugener Weisse, Fallen Sky Juniper Rye, Pan Galactic Gargle Blaster, Gargle Blaster Dry Hop IPA, Don't Panic IPA, Pouring Porter, Reelin' In the Oats Stout, Sky Nectar Braggot, Spelt Rebel Dinkelbier, The Tourist English IPA, Who Loves The Sun Winter Spice, Wind-Up Bird Best Bitter, and Zig Zag Smoke Ale.

The Pick: Blue Balloon. As a Belgian-style ale this would've been tasty enough with pear esters and toasty malts, but cask conditioning and added coriander, pink peppercorns, and cardamom create an intriguing, intricate experience of nicely spiced (not spicy), smooth sipping. Hope this one comes back.

special included a rabbit pâté sandwich. Executive Chef Corey Wisun developed a cult following as cofounder of Field to Table Catering and dazzled folks at the farmers market, so the opportunity to use his local farm resources for a full-time kitchen panned out perfectly. Both the food menus and beer menus are in constant flux.

Carriere and Cohen wasted no time in adding a second location in town in the brewery-happy Whiteaker District, replete with its own Eastern European-style bakery and deli. Falling Sky Pour House and Delicatessen—Brewcatessen? Delicatessery?—features staples like tongue sandwiches and house-cured pastrami. Plus they make their own pickles, pretzels, bagels—everything is made, smoked, etc., on the spot—and treats like a chocolate-hazelnut babka, by no means the lesser babka. As a huge fan of both Jewish delis and brewpubs, I love that this one fills the knish niche.

Of course, when I'm at a deli, I wash down my pastrami with Dr. Brown's Black Cherry soda. But they've one-upped that. Besides brewing, Zarkesh makes inventive sodas. You might find a root beer or ginger ale (or carrot-ginger ale), but you're just as likely to find a Blackberry Coriander soda, and the spice addition makes it especially food-friendly. Because they're sweetened with honey and contain about half the sugar of regular sodas, kids might not crave them (though I met one of Carriere's kids—both partners have two young'uns—and his young son vowed he loved the root beer, made traditionally without extracts). Another thing the Pour House offers is a full bar with house soda cocktails. And to think the soda program started as a result of making syrups to add to their Berliner Weisse, as is the tradition with that tart wheat beer.

Having said that, it's still all about the beer. The focus is on sessionable beers in predominantly European styles, even if that means dusting off nearly extinct styles like a German dinkelbier, made with spelt and refreshing like a German wheat ale. What they generally don't make are hop bombs. Hops can overpower the palate (plus they don't have a hop back, which is almost a prerequisite for Northwest styles). Then again, batch number 100 was Chicken Little Imperial IPA, which returns on occasion, and sometimes you'll find Another IPA on. Sieber and Zarkesh heard and responded to the customers.

On the flipside, I'm happy to point out batch number 200 was a pre–Prohibition-style lager with light bitterness. Since they love adding New World twists to Continental styles, Wild Oregon Logger used Willamette hops and rice grown in Eastern Oregon.

The best way to experience several of the fifteen styles always on tap is with a tasting flight (six 4-ounce samples served on a cloud-shaped tray). Some of my favorites included Citragasm, Zig Zag Smoke, Juniper Rye, and a braggot made in collaboration with nearby Nectar Creek Honeywine (a braggot is half ale, half mead). If you like a particular beer, get a whole pint and then a second one because odds are good you may not see it again. Personally, it's this very notion I find endearing. It forces patrons to explore and be open to new ideas.

As for the two locations, both entail ordering at a front counter. The brewpub is behind the homebrew shop, but there's no bar. No bar! Upon entering, the brewhouse is behind a wall of windows to the right with communal tables made from salvaged fir trees to the left. No two-tops either. Seeing people come together around 6:30 p.m. is the "most satisfying part," according to Carriere. I found that being able to soak up some sun on the patio on a day when the sky wasn't falling felt rather satisfying. In the thriving Whiteaker, the deli is much longer and narrower and also has communal seating. Here, the back patio includes a sand space (it's not boxed in) for kiddoes so the whole family, including fur children, can hang out and enjoy the food, from a plate of corned beef hash for brunch to a NY cheesecake for dessert.

Falling Sky Brewing

Opened: 2012

Owners: Rob Cohen and Jason Carriere.

Brewers: Mike Zarkesh and Scott Sieber.

System: 8.5-barrel.

Annual production: 1,000 barrels.

Distribution: Mostly two Eugene pubs.

Hours: Sunday through Wednesday, 11 a.m. to midnight; Thursday through Saturday, 11 a.m. to 1 a.m.

Tours: Just ask.

Takeout beer: Growlers.

Gift shop: T-shirts hang in the pub and homebrew shop.

Food: Creative, seasonal menu items. The brewpub specializes in progressive plates that offer both healthy and/or comforting options such as a portobello Reuben, a field (veggie) burger, and a smoked beef dip with caramelized onions and horseradish aioli. The deli focuses on a mashup of Eastern European and Northwest modern that includes beef, duck, or lamb pastrami, not to mention sliders made with a ground beef and pastrami blend on house-baked buns, plus a classic Reuben.

Extras: "Let it Pour" special (25 cents off pints when it's raining). Brewers Harvest pairing dinners.

Other location: Falling Sky Pour House & Delicatessen (790 Blair Blvd., Eugene; 541-653-9167).

Fire Mountain Brewery / Outlaw Brew House

10800 Northwest Rex Brown Road, Carlton,
OR 97111
(503) 852-7378 • FireMountainBrewery.com
OutlawBrewhouse.com
Twitter @FireMtBrewery

Wineries generally beat breweries hands down with their settings: verdant valleys along pastoral country roads. Urban taprooms and beer gardens are fantastic, but if the point of enjoying beer is to relax, what's more relaxing than being surrounded by trees and fields? Fire Mountain Brew House is in Carlton in the Willamette Valley wine country, forty-five miles from Portland, and trades farms for food carts and horses for hipsters. In fact, it's not in quaint Carlton, but rather six miles up a rustic road. To get here, follow the signs owner Henry Gorgas staked in the ground that look like signs guiding visitors to nearby wineries.

Those wineries dot the valley's landscape because they need to be in proximity to the vineyards. Breweries proliferate in urban centers because their raw ingredients—malted barley and kiln-dried hops—don't need to be converted into their fermented beverage quite as fresh. Taking advantage of this fact, Gorgas specializes in European styles using many grains and hops rich in those countries' *terroir*, such as British Maris Otter malts and Saaz hops from the Czech Republic. That's just part of how he fulfills his motto: "brewed old school." No computers. Everything's touched by his hands, just like the large garden he tends on his thirty-acre property (where he composts spent hops and yeast). He rushes neither the mash times nor fermentation times.

The brewhouse occupies two structures—the brewery is basically a large workshop in a barn, and he added a second building for cold storage—and that's where I found the man with the graying goatee. When I visited and asked Gorgas for the story behind calling his brewery Fire Mountain, he responded, "Which of the three do you want?" I preferred this one: "Grandpa said he wanted to

Beers brewed: Year-round: Bad Henry IPA, Bogart Northwest IPA, Steam Fired Stout, Oregon Pale Ale. Seasonals: Tan Line Summer Ale, Carlton Lagered Ale (Kolsch), Hangman Winter Fest Ale. Outlaw: Uncle Teds Dark Ale, Cold Cold Billy DIPA, Single Malt German Blond Ale.

The Pick: Bogart NWIPA. If the regular IPA is Bad Henry, Bogart could've been called Worse Henry since the ABV remains almost the same at 6.9 percent. The hops bill with seven citrusy Northwest varietals packs in 99 IBUs and smacks of grapefruit pith.

retire on Fire Mountain . . . where the beer is cold." That's not how the Marshall Tucker Band song goes, as I recall. Alas, Gorgas mentioned that this is hardly retirement material since he's yet to turn a profit, but Fire Mountain is growing and he recently added the brand Outlaw Brewing so he can double shelf space at retailers who carry his beer. Although Outlaw beers just started showing up, he registered the name at the same time as Fire Mountain. (Don't even ask him about the wings joint up in Portland by a near-same name that added their own brewery, especially since he has a curmudgeon streak that fellow cranks find relatable or possibly endearing.)

Outlaw Brewing was also what he called his homebrewing operation in 1999. Like all homebrewers, Gorgas picked up a mash paddle because he wanted to drink the kind of beer he liked. And he likes clean beers. From his trio of IPAs—Bad Henry, Bogart, and Outlaw's Cold Cold Billy Double IPA—to his Kolsch-style Carlton Lagered Ale, which tastes closer to what you find in Cologne than many American interpretations, he credits his untreated well water for taking care of proper pH levels. And he takes the time to mash and sparge in steam-fired kettles (hence Fire Mountain's Steam Fired Stout that's rich yet finds the balance between dry Irish and malty Export stouts) and fer ment in time-consuming durations like a homebrewer without consideration for rushing beer from tanks to shelves.

Because visiting the brewhouse does require some commitment, you can often find Gorgas and his wife, Sherry, pouring at local beer festivals. Then again, it's more fun sampling from his farmland, even if none of his beers are farmhouse styles. And then there's the irony of visiting a brewery that's proudly, entirely analog yet requires a GPS just to find it.

Fire Mountain Brewery / Outlaw Brew House

Opened: 2009.
Owners: Henry and Sherry Gorgas.
Brewer: Henry Gorgas.
System: 15-barrel.
Annual production: 400 barrels.
Distribution: Oregon and Alabama. Yes, Bama.
Hours: Sunday, 11 a.m. to 6 p.m.
Tours: Sundays.
Takeout beer: Growlers and bottles.
Gift shop: Growlers, T-shirts, and an apron.

Flat Tail Brewery

202 Southwest 1st Street, Corvallis, OR 97333
(541) 758-2229 • FlatTailCorvallis.com
Twitter @FlatTailBrewing

Situated on the Willamette River waterfront, Flat Tail is frequented by local residents more than OSU students, but this Beaver-centric brewpub is festooned with school colors, black and orange. Brewmaster/co-owner Dave Marliave is happy his easy-drinking Rough Cut IPA and Tailgater Kolsch are in high demand, but he's developing quite a wild beer program for beer nerds and he digs that families flocking to the pub are parented by beer geeks. Persicus, a blend of Kolsch and Hibiscus Oatmeal Blonde, is aged in Pinot barrels with wild yeast strains and peaches for a delightfully tart, refreshing beer like a spritzer made with mango lemonade and those great Italian tannic "orange" wines. It's not exactly the stuff you'd expect at a brewpub that offers frickles (fried pickles).

"I've been brewing Kolsch since my days at Oregon Trail," Marliave said. Not only is Oregon Trail Corvallis's oldest brewery, it also opened in early 1987, meaning it's older than Marliave, who wasn't yet twenty-one when he landed the gig.

Tailgater is an ale that undergoes lager-like cold fermentation. "I love brewing lagers," Marliave said, but Flat Tail's good problem is that he only has time to brew them in the winter. Like lagers, the Kolsch takes several weeks to condition, and the extra tank time isn't a luxury he has in the summer. The grain bill is mostly German Pilsner malt and some malted wheat (and 100 percent noble German Tettnanger hops). It's a style that's still coming into its own in America, unlike its birthplace of Cologne; good luck finding anything but Kolsch there. (Corvallis also has considerably fewer gothic cathedrals.) GABF judges awarded it silver in 2013. While accolades are nice, Tailgater is Flat Tail's best-selling bottled beer (possibly going into cans), and it's better to win over customers than judges.

Beers brewed: Year-round: Tailgater Kolsch, George Cones Pale, Rough Cut IPA, 6 A.M. Coffee Stout, Little Green Dry-Hopped Session Saison, Mustache Rye'd Red, Session Wheat, Eight Man Amber, Seriously Low Budget. Seasonals: Wetsuit Black Kolsch, El Guapo Cucumber Lime Habanero Blonde Ale, and "a ton of one-offs."

The Pick: Lemon Diesel. Using Flat Tail's Corvaller Weisse as a base beer (because it wasn't brewed in Berlin it's not a Berliner), this light, tart wheat ale aged for two years, picking up citrus-like acidity thanks to its house-wild yeast. No lemons were harmed. It debuted at Belmont Station's Puckerfest and stole my heart among impressive sour ales.

He also loves witbier, a Belgian-style wheat beer marked by adding orange peel and coriander. The wheat he uses is grown thirty miles south; they generally trade grain for beer. What's more, by the time he's done, you'd be hard-pressed to call it a witbier. Sometimes grapefruit goes in. Other times he adds lemon and ginger. Most often he inoculates it with the strain of *Brettanomyces* he isolated from a plum.

"I got plums from a local at the bar," he recounted. "They had this blow-you-away aroma. From the guy's backyard. I just about dropped it there in the brewery. The juice of the fruit was incredibly flavorful but the thick, white powder—it was caked with yeast—was where the aroma came from. So I floated the plums in wort, and that batch was Local's Only Wit. That beer was fermented with plums in essence."

"You didn't pitch anything but plums?" I asked incredulously, figuring he'd tossed in a few plums after inoculating with brewer's yeast.

"Correct!" he assured me, before outlining how he sent a culture to Wyeast Labs, where they discovered three primary strains, now Flat Tail's proprietary cocktail of critters. Standard brett can be Brett B (*bruxellensis*), C (*claussenii*), or L (*lambicus*), but this is Brett F. He described it as, "If fruit leather were actually made of leather." I'd missed out on Locals Only, but the next batch, repurposing the *Portlandia* catch phrase "Put a bird on it" into Put a Bird on Wit, floored me with its uniqueness and sheer desirableness.

It doesn't hurt that the brewery's building was built in 1910 as the Corvallis Creamery, and Marliave's certain the microbes used over a century ago remain in the rafters. "It's why we do such authentic lambics," he said with a smile.

Flat Tail Brewery

Opened: 2010.

Owners: Dave and Emma Marliave; Iain and Tonya Duncan; and Jason and Carrie Duranceau.

Brewer: Dave Marliave.

System: 15-barrel.

Annual production: 1,500 barrels.

Distribution: Oregon and California.

Hours: Daily, 11 a.m. to 11 p.m.

Tours: By appointment.

Takeout beer: Growlers and bottles.

Gift shop: Shirts, hoodies, and hats, all black and orange (OSU colors).

Food: Finger foods, e.g. wings, rings, and frickles. The Beaver Dam burger has avocado, fried egg, peppered turkey, bacon, cheddar, and grilled onions—damn good.

Gilgamesh Brewing

2065 Madrona Avenue Southeast, Salem, OR 97302
(503) 584-1789 • GilgameshBrewing.com
Twitter @GilgameshBrew

The Epic of Gilgamesh, a five-thousand-year-old Mesopotamian poem that I only know because I double majored in Religious Studies, details how our hero's nemesis-turned-BFF, Enkidu, becomes civilized once he's introduced to wondrous beer. World leaders, take note.

As for my introduction to Gilgamesh Brewing, it transpired over a Filbert Lager. Nut brown ales are great, but contain nary a nut. So as long as brewer Matt Radtke—one of the four Radtke men at the brewery, including brothers Mike and Nick and their father, Lee—decided to buck the style, why not build a nut beer on an entirely different base? They source filberts (better known as hazelnuts, the official state nut) from Hunt's Hazelnuts just up the road. Matt said they're chopped and roasted before adding 8 pounds' worth per barrel to the mash. Nut oils are notoriously perilous to beer, but he explained that they give a bit of creaminess to the pilsner base, which finishes with great honey-baked bread flavors. It was developed as a homebrew for Nick's (the middle brother) wedding.

After much difficulty finding a place to anchor the brewery (it was initially in some woods near Turner on the other side of I-5, with a series of short-lived public houses around Salem), they set up as a proper brewpub called The Campus. An ornate copper sign hand-fabricated by Lee is indicative of how the Radtkes, whose family has lived in the Salem area for well over forty years, built everything by hand, from the top of the roofs to the bottom of the fireplace set in the wall in such a way that it crackles and warms patrons on the inside and outside on the patio. Woodwork, metalwork, electrical, and plumbing: From the front- and backbars to the tables themselves, as well as some great landscaping, "We all were there seven days a

Beers brewed: Year-round: Mamba (gruit), Hopscotch, Vader Coffee CDA, Oedipus IPA. Seasonals: Shiitake Bock, Stunt Double IPA, Ridgeway IPA, Cranberry Saison, O'Doyle Rules Irish Red, Filbert Lager, DJ Jazzy Hef, Pumphouse Copper, Coffee Cordial, Mean Eileen Black Lager, Millennium Falconer ISA, Mega Mamba.

The Pick: Mamba. That rare gruit—a beer devoid of hops—which is not just intriguing but also tastes great and is quite popular. Brewed with black tea and tangerine zest, this murky orange ale's herbal and deep citrus flavors nearly mimic some big American hops but offer an impressionist rendition.

week," Matt said, "putting in long hours trying to get the place open." Despite being surrounded by business and industrial parks, Gilgamesh is surprisingly situated in a tranquil, grassy spot with Pringle Creek running through the covered back patio. Kids love playing on the short bridge. For adults, a flight of eleven samples provides the fun.

I hate using this word, but Gilgamesh excels at weird beers. Yes, there are IPAs like Oedipus, some that pack 100 IBUs, and an old school, light-bodied copper ale. Spring and summer offer an American organic wheat beer, DJ Jazzy Hef that tellingly contains jasmine tea. Tea is one of the two primary ingredients in their flagship beer, Mamba, a gruit (hop-less beer) shaped by black tea and generous tangerine peel. Then again, Mega Mamba is so copious with the small orange fruit's peels that it's described as a "thick nectar dangerous delight," which is right on the money. It's so viscous it's the citrus smoothie of beers.

I also tried Shiitake Bock featuring local, organic mushrooms in a coppery, malt lager base. While I've had beer made with mapley-sweet candycap mushrooms, this beer is one umami tsunami, creating a unique pairing for certain dishes, including the house burger or lamb flatbread sandwich. Then there's Vader, a coffee CDA that delves deeper into its characteristic dark, roasty flavor by adding cold brewed coffee sourced from nearby Governor's Cup. It's a winner on its own, but try a blend that I made with my samples, something I call a Black Mamba (Vader and Mamba), wherein tangerine and coffee flavors with a touch of dry cacao nib flavor simulates a Borgia mocha.

It's no surprise Gilgamesh sponsors the Oregon State Fair's homebrew competition, and the Specialty and Experimental Beer category. As such, they succeed in their mission to brew "a beer for everyone."

Gilgamesh Brewing

Opened: 2010.

Owners: The Radtke family (brothers Mike, Nick, and Matt, and dad Lee).

Brewers: Mike Radtke (brewmaster) and Justin Bier (assistant brewer).

System: 17-barrel.

Annual production: 1,500 barrels.

Distribution: Oregon.

Hours: Monday through Thursday, 11 a.m. to 10 p.m.; Friday and Saturday, 11 a.m. to midnight; Sunday, 11 a.m. to 9 p.m.

Tours: By request.

Takeout beer: Growlers, 22-ounce bottles, and dock sales.

Gift shop: Shirts, hats, and hoodies.

Food: Creative burgers, sandwiches, and sides. The Cuban sandwich is amazing.

Golden Valley Brewery

980 Northeast Fourth Street, McMinnville, OR 97128
(503) 472-BREW (2739) • GoldenValleyBrewery.com
Twitter @GoldenValleyPub

Golden Valley Brewery feels like a brewpub that is a restaurant first and brewery second, but when you consider that their beef is sourced from the Kircher family's own Angus Springs Ranch, that's not a bad thing. It just means that I consider the burger first (the GVBBBQ comes topped with Tillamook white cheddar, amazing pepper bacon, and tangy barbecue sauce) and then choose the beer I want to go with it.

During my last visit, that meant I missed by a day my golden (pardon the pun) opportunity to try Black Panther Imperial Stout, a nearly 10 percent stout aged in Panther Creek Winery French oak barrels. It'd take a single minute to walk over to the winery and procure said barrels—or a glass of their pinot since McMinnville is famous for its pinot noirs. This is also likely the source of Golden Valley's great tasting flights served on arching staves so that samples appear as a rainbow of beer colors. Rejoice (if not forewarned) that this is no shrinking violet of a flight—staves hold ten samples. The beer near the middle will be Red Thistle Ale, their original flagship that yins with "imported malts" and yangs with noble hops. Seasonals are likely to dominate on either far end, according to where we are in our orbit around the sun. On the blond side, you'll find French Prairie Blanche (akin to a Belgian witbier) in the spring, but I lean toward some that arrive later in the year, like Atlas Elevator Bock (as the "ator" suffix suggests, it's a hearty doppelbock) and Tannen Bomb, which arrives in time for Christmas.

IPA-wise, the year-rounder is Chehalem Mountain, which is more on the redder, maltier side. Summer guests are treated to Bald Peak IPA, which in comparison is much brighter and citrusier. In

Beers brewed: Year-round: 3rd Street Wheat, Perrydale Pale, American Pale, Chehalem Mountain IPA, Red Thistle Ale, Dundee Porter, Muddy Valley Oatmeal Stout. Seasonals: Winter: Tannen Bomb, Black Panther Imperial Stout, Atlas Elevator Bock. Spring: French Prairie Blanche, Geist Bock. Summer: Bald Peak IPA, Carlton Kolsch, Red Hills Pils, 20 Mile Pale. Fall: Saint Paul Fresh Hop, Oktoberfest Lager.

The Pick: Tannen Bomb. A veritable malt bomb—125 pounds of malts per barrel—this winter warmer pours the color of (but isn't aged on) bourbon, and is spiced with enough hops to yield 40 IBUs. At 8 percent alcohol, it's made for enjoying by the fireplace, whether it's snowing outside or not.

both cases, brewmaster Jesse Shue uses whole cone hops. Golden Valley is his seventh brewing gig around the Northwest; he took over in 2013 when Mark Vickery left to launch Grain Station Brew Works located two blocks away. Shue said that fits in nicely with owner Peter Kircher's hopes to see McMinnville turn into a beer destination like it already is for wine, and the beer-wine combo is something only Hood River also has going for it.

But as mentioned earlier, the meat remains a big draw at Golden Valley, and not just juicy burgers. Steaks are hand cut and dry aged. Despite a recent threat from the FDA, luckily it remains almost standard practice for breweries to send local cattle ranchers their spent grains and oftentimes there's synergy with the farms: Brewpubs serve the beef from cows that their spent grains helped feed. Since the Kirchers own both the brewpub and Angus Springs Ranch, with seventy-six acres of pastures right outside McMinnville where they raise their organic beef, the result is a worthy filet mignon for thirty-five dollars and a 12-ounce rib eye for thirty dollars. For Shue's part, he likes his steaks with Dundee Porter or Muddy Valley Oatmeal Stout.

Golden Valley Brewery

Opened: 1993.

Owners: Peter and Celia Kircher.

Brewer: Jesse Shue.

System: 7-barrel.

Annual production: 1,500 barrels.

Distribution: Willamette Valley, Portland.

Hours: Monday through Thursday, 11 a.m. to 10 p.m.; Friday and Saturday, 11 a.m. to 11 p.m.; Sunday, 11 a.m. to 9 p.m.

Tours: By request.

Takeout beer: Bottles, growlers, and kegs.

Gift shop: Shirts and glassware.

Food: Owning Angus Springs Ranch means you get the freshest burgers and steaks. The menu offers something for everyone.

Other location: Second pub (1520 NW Bethany Blvd., Beaverton; 503-972-1599).

Grain Station Brew Works

755 Northeast Alpine Street, Suite 200, McMinnville, OR 97128

(503) 687-BREW (2739) • GrainStation.com

When Mark Vickery, former brewmaster for Golden Valley two blocks away, and Kelly McDonald, managing partner of the Granary District, conceived of Grain Station Brew Works, they envisioned it as a communal effort. Looking at the popularity of Community Supported Agriculture (CSA), they launched a CSB. Instead of subscribing to a CSA and receiving farm-fresh kale or rutabagas, folks can "pubscribe" to this Community Supported Brewery and receive brewery-fresh beers such as Bet the Farm IPA or Hank's Dark Ale (named after Mark's dog). It supports local agriculture inasmuch as the hops and even barley come from area farms. Think of it as a mug club, but with more perks.

The brewery is in McDonald's renovated barn, mere steps away from a nineteenth-century cereal elevator from back when this was a grain station. It shares space with Garden Shed produce and MEAT, a butchery owned by Grain Station chef Kyle Chriestenson. A café, food trucks, and a dog groomer also have roots in the district (yes, dogs are welcome in the beer garden). Rounding it out, there are six wineries. McMinnville is, after all, wine country. Mark said he makes sixty cases of Pinot a year, but sorry, that's just for (good) friends and family.

Grain Station Brew Works

Opened: 2013.

Owners: Mark Vickery and Kelly McDonald.

Brewer: Mark Vickery.

System: 7-barrel.

Annual production: 500 barrels.

Distribution: 100-mile radius of McMinnville.

Hours: Monday through Thursday, 11:30 a.m. to 10 p.m.; Friday and Saturday, 11:30 a.m. to 11 p.m.; Sunday, 11:30 a.m. to 9 p.m.

Takeout beer: Growlers and dock sales.

Gift shop: Shirts, glasses, and growlers.

Food: Pizzas, burgers, and salads.

Events: Oregon Brews & BBQs in September. Germanic Christmas Market in December.

Beers brewed: Year-round: Haystack Gold, Nut Red, Bet the Farm IPA, Sprout Hefe, Hank's Dark Ale (CDA), Grain Station Stout, White Ape (white/wheat IPA). Seasonals: Planning on several, including wine-barrel aged ones.

Heater Allen Brewing

HEATER ALLEN
HANDCRAFTED LAGER BEER

907 Northeast 10th Avenue, McMinnville,
OR 97128
(503) 472-4898 • HeaterAllen.com
Twitter @HeaterAllenBeer

John Fogerty belting out "Around the Bend" over the brewhouse speakers generally means one thing: the Bobtoberfest playlist is on. It's not all CCR all the time; Elton John keeps Bob happy during mashing, though the Rocket Man doesn't play nonstop during the eight-week conditioning period. That's how long it'll be until the popular festbier will be ready to celebrate Rick Allen's brother, Bob. Before he passed, they threw him a living wake and played his favorite classic rock tunes and freighted in a bunch of German lagers.

When Allen started his all-lager brewery in 2007 (its name comes from his wife Jan's maiden name and his surname), people thought he was crazy. He'd been homebrewing for twenty-five years already, but craft breweries just didn't make lagers—they take too long to condition and are therefore more expensive to make. And yet, not only is he still brewing and lagering (or storing), the brewery also has doubled in production size and opened a taproom for fans who love exploring the wide range of lagers from their flagship Pilsner to the malty Dunkel and chocolaty Schwarz, and even the spicy Baltic Porter, a classic style (unlike regular porters that are ales).

Lagers comprise about 90 percent of the world's industrial beer production. They aren't just less time efficient; they're less forgiving. The yeast requires bottom fermenting at colder temperatures compared to ales, their warmer, top-fermenting counterparts in the beer kingdom. Furthermore, small brewers focus on ales as a point of differentiation from the big boys with their adjunct lagers. That's precisely what made Allen and his all-malt, all-lager brewery prescient. (Okay, brewers hate being pigeonholed, so there's a Bavarian-style wheat ale.)

Hoppy ales will never disappear, but there is a growing interest in clean, crisp lagers. Coastal Lager is the closest Allen gets to Northwest style, but it's really a toasty Vienna lager hopped with

Beers brewed: Year-round: Pils, Coastal, Schwarz. Seasonals: Hugo Bock, Mediator Doppelbock, Rauch Dunkel, Lenz Bock, Isarweizen, Bobtoberfest, Dunkel, Kolsch, Sandy Paws Baltic Porter, Abzug.

The Pick: Pils. The users of RateBeer.com rank this as the single best pilsner. Not in Oregon or among American-brewed pilsners, but out of every one in the world. Straw colored with a grainy aroma and sweet grassy flavor, it's infinitely refreshing.

citrusy Cascades and Magnums with just a touch of English malts for added appeal to pale ale fans. But at Heater Allen, Czech Saaz hops are king and 80 percent of their production is Bohemian-style Pilsner.

"All of our beers are good food beers compared to IPAs," said Allen from atop his brewdeck. "IPA is a terrible food beer. Pilsner goes so well with seafood and appetizers. Our darker beers are very versatile. Restaurants gravitate toward our beer." That manifests itself in Heater Allen's having turned down restaurants calling for kegs since Allen couldn't keep up with demand. It also helps that in 2009, his daughter Lisa—truly a Heater-Allen—became the assistant brewer. She'd just graduated from college when her dad started the brewery and initially embarked on a career in wine, but has since seen the light. "I remember him brewing when I was little but I wasn't really that interested in it until around high school," she said. She is now a member of Pink Boots, the professional association for women in the brewing industry.

The taproom not only gives visitors a place to drink the freshest pilsner possible (compared to the Continental ones that often arrive in America stale and heat damaged after their cross-Atlantic journey) but also provides another opportunity for hands-on, lips-on education among those still learning about beer who sometimes don't realize that all pilsners are lagers but not all lagers are light pilsners. A glass of earthy Dunkel (which means "dark" in German) or ashy Smoky Bob sets their tastebuds straight. This is still very much wine country, but luckily people who go wine-tasting increasingly love mixing things up by throwing in a brewery visit. And I'm intrigued by the discussions Lisa has had with their neighbors at Remi Winery, so there may be a dark and malty wine barrel-aged Doppelbock coming soon.

Heater Allen Brewing

Opened: 2007.

Owner: Rick Allen.

Brewers: Rick Allen (head brewer) and Lisa Allen (assistant brewer).

System: 15-barrel.

Annual production: 600 barrels.

Distribution: Oregon.

Hours: Friday, 3 p.m. to 6 p.m.; Saturday, noon to 5 p.m.

Takeout beer: 22-ounce bottles.

Gift shop: T-shirts.

Food: Delivered from Third Street Pizza, blocks away. Snacks like pretzels, peanuts.

Extras: Sandy Paws, the holiday release, raises money for the McMinnville Education Foundation by raffling the opportunity to feature beloved pooches on the label.

Hop Valley Brewing Co.

Original brewpub: 980 Kruse Way, Springfield, OR 97477
(541) 744-3330 • HopValleyBrewing.com
Twitter @HopValley
Production brewery: 990 West First Street, Eugene,
  OR 97402
(541) 485-BEER (2337)

For a brewpub that opened on Friday the 13th (in February 2009), Hop Valley is experiencing a run of good luck. Credit what each of the five partners brings to the table. Trevor Howard, a 2004 graduate of Oregon State University's Fermentation Science Program, cut his teeth at Rogue Ales in Newport before transferring to their Eugene City Brewery, bringing him home to his native Eugene. His deft hop kung fu earned him a loyal following with patented Northwest styles of beer, hence Hop Valley's hop-laden formulae. Not enough alpha acids in your 90 IBUs citrus salad of Alphadelic IPA, hopped with Simcoe, Cascade, Cluster, and Palisade? Here, have an Alpha Centauri Binary IPA.

When he and his father, Ron Howard (not *that* Ron Howard) started talking about opening a brewery, that's when the elder Howard's associate, Jonas Kungys, came into the fold, along with his business partner Chuck Hare, who brought his bar and restaurant experience. All they needed was a restaurant with a brewery.

Lo and behold, the long defunct Spencer's Brewpub east of Eugene across I-5 in Springfield had become Sophia's Bavarian Restaurant (not Sophia's Bavarian Brewpub), so upstart Ninkasi Brewing took over the brewery portion. Soon, Sophia hung up her dirndl and Ninkasi opened their Eugene brewhouse. What's funny about the location—and hopefully telling about the trending direction of Americans dining out—is that amid sky-high signs for places like Denny's and Outback, there's some four-stories-tall real estate letting people know they've arrived at Hop Valley Brewing Co. Restaurant & Tap House.

Beers brewed: Year-round: 541 American Lager, Alpha Centauri IIPA, Alphadelic IPA, Czech Your Head Czech Pilsner, Double D Blonde Ale, VIP Vanilla Infused Porter, Imperial Red. Seasonals: Festeroo Winter Ale, Pollination Summer Ale, Proxima IPA, Stepchild Red, Natty Red, The Heff, Mr. Black Dry Stout, Hoptoberfest, and more, plus Dr. Ziggy's housemade root beer.

The Pick: Alpha Centauri Binary IPA: This imperial IPA prides itself on being hop-forward—not to mention hop-backward and hop-sideways—which it is, thanks to immensely high alpha hops including Simcoes and Amarillos, but it furtively boasts a near-creaminess, boosting up the prickly, piney flavor.

The name Hop Valley accurately connotes the Willamette Valley's 150-year-old cash crop. Photos of said crops and the Native American tribes that would come down from the hills to work the harvest hang in the restaurant section. Hop Valley Brewing works with local farmers, some of which are fourth-generation hop growers, to make fresh hop beers during the harvest.

Trevor likes to sit at the pub and listen to the beer-drinking crowd's feedback. In 2013, Hop Valley underwent a major expansion and built a separate 60-barrel brewery in Eugene's burgeoning "brewery district," the Whiteaker. Occupying a repurposed barn and maintaining some of its rustic past with reclaimed wood and corrugated sheet metal— although on the whole it feels quite modern in its aesthetic and use of digital draft lists to make it clear what's on each of the twenty-four taps—the Eugene brewhouse is for production brewing, enabling them to surge past the Springfield restaurant's 4,000-barrel capacity. But the beautiful part is that now the pub's original 15-barrel brewery is their pilot system. Trevor and cohorts get to play. And the two hundred folks who can bring the tasting room's awesome, 4,000-square-foot patio to capacity—the hops growing around it are cool and when it's chilly the firepits keep it hot—get to enjoy beers such as Figgie Smalls or Peace & Carrots. The former is a Belgian pale ale with Mission figs; the latter is a saison with carrot blossom honey, originally brewed for Trevor's wedding. Honeymooners aside, there's a lot to love among the solid list of IPAs, expanding list of lagers, little things like mozzarella-stuffed garlic knots, and impeccable things like the inviting patio.

Hop Valley Brewing Co.

Opened: 2009.

Owners: Trevor Howard, his father Ron Howard, Jonas Kungys, Chuck Hare, and Jim Henslee.

Brewer: Trevor Howard.

System: 60-barrel (production facility); 15-barrel pilot system (brewpub).

Annual production: 12,000 barrels.

Distribution: Northwest.

Hours: Restaurant: Sunday through Thursday, 11:30 a.m. to 11 p.m.; Friday and Saturday, 11:30 a.m. to 1 a.m. Tasting room: Sunday through Thursday, 11:30 a.m. to 10 p.m.; Friday and Saturday, 11:30 a.m. to 11 p.m.

Tours: By appointment.

Takeout beer: Kegs, growlers, bombers, and cans.

Gift shop: Apparel, glasses, dog collars with bottle openers, and disc golf discs.

Food: Starters, salads, and sandwiches. Try the Double D Blonde-braised ribs.

Long Brewing Co.

29380 Northeast Owls Lane, Newberg, OR 97132
(503) 349-8341 • LongBrewing.com
Twitter @LongBrewing

Paul Long was an electrical engineer, so that should tell you something about the way he approached homebrewing as his retirement activity. Engineers don't tinker and they don't dabble. He instantly started accruing homebrewing awards. Big ones. It started with the American Homebrewers Association's National Homebrewers Conference—the largest and most auspicious competition—where he earned the bronze for his American IPA in 2002. He placed third again in 2004, this time for his American Light Lager. In 2005, Long received the AHA Ninkasi Award, buoyed by his first-place finishes for his Vienna-style Lager and Kolsch. Think of the Ninkasi Award as the Heisman Trophy for amateur brewers.

Clearly, the idea of Long going pro wasn't a long shot. Thus began his second career in 2009. His four gold medal–winning beers at the NHC and his Blonde Ale, winner at the Masters Championship of Amateur Brewing, carry on as five of his seven commercial offerings.

Though Long was born in Independence, an hour's drive south deeper into the Willamette Valley, which once held the title of "Hop Capital of the World," he confessed, "I was more of a wine fan." Most visitors the high-tech "farm boy" gets at his brewery are actually on wine tours. But let's come back to that.

Long's 3.5-barrel all-steam system is his own design. Professional accolades and awards are beginning to replace the homebrewing ones such as North American Beer Awards. His Kolsch, Vienna, and IPA earned medals or ribbons. Add in his porter and Wee Heavy Scotch Ale (pointing out that his malt bill for each calls for eleven malts, he advised, "They're not that simple,") and you've got a lineup "from DC to daylight." It's a frequency spectrum reference he makes quite a bit. Old engineering jokes die hard, but it's fitting for such a relatively small range of beers in terms of flavors, colors, and strengths.

Beers brewed: Year-round: Linda's Lager, Kolsch Style Lager, IPA, Paul's Porter. Seasonals: Blonde Ale (summer), Vienna Style Lager and Wee Heavy Scotch Ale (winter).

The Pick: Paul's Porter. This goes beyond the style guidelines of a classic porter without venturing into a chocolate or imperial porter by amping up roast quality and alcohol kick for a robust flavor that walks the fine line between rich and decadent.

Long's bestseller is the IPA, and the high demand requires that every other batch brewed is the hop-heavy one. He even does a Fresh Hop IPA during harvest that sees as many as nine pungent varietals living up to their potential. His next best-selling beer, by his account, is either the Kolsch or the porter, my most favorite of his beers and the one that I think speaks best to what his brewery is all about. No surprise that it's called Paul's Porter. "I call it that not because I'm vain, but because it's not to style . . . it's exactly the way I like it," he said.

I have an affinity for breweries named after the founder, such as Eberhard Anheuser and his son-in-law Adolphus Busch, Frederick Miller, and Adolph Coors. True, breweries named after their place of origin show local commitment, but bearing the founder's name puts reputation on the line. Double that for Paul's Porter (the alliteration in that and the Linda's Lager named for his wife is not coincidental). "The chocolate and coffee flavors are prodigious, but nary a cocoa or coffee bean is used," Long commented as we sipped it in the brewhouse. "If you use the right malts, you don't have to."

The name Long could've been an ironic twist on the short walk from his home to the brewery in a shed in his yard. The nearby, highly regarded Allison Inn and its restaurant, Jory, carry some eight hundred wines but only eight beers. (How misguided.) The menu lists them as Paul Long IPA and Paul Long Porter. Long Brewing isn't just a company to them—it's Paul himself. His self-distributed beers are only found in high-end outlets, including another esteemed Newberg restaurant, The Painted Lady, and Portland boutique markets. "I take my beers very seriously," he said, adding, "especially at this price point." Bombers are in the ten-dollar range. "Half my market is winemakers," he said, standing next to a Pinot Noir barrel that he refilled with porter. Nearly the entire other half is comprised of wine drinkers who buy by the case. "I get limos that come by that've been out wine tasting . . . More often than not they'll say, 'This is the best stuff I've had all day.'"

Long Brewing Co.

Opened: 2009.
Owner and brewer: Paul Long.
System: 3.5-barrel.
Annual production: 50 barrels.
Distribution: Limited Portland and Willamette Valley.
Tours: By appointment only.
Takeout beer: Paul's happy to welcome guests who want to buy a case to go.
Gift shop: There's a shirt hung on the wall.

Mazama Brewing

33939 Southeast Eastgate Circle, Corvallis, OR 97333
(541) 230-1810 • MazamaBrewing.com
Twitter @MazamaBrewing

Creating a Belgian-style brewery might seem like a bizarre direction for a couple like Jeff and Kathy Tobin, whose love of brewing began with the pursuit of the perfect Bavarian-style hefeweizen, given that German brewing is all about purity and tradition. But ultimately, the Tobins are BJCP-certified (Beer Judge Certification Program) experts who seek out different flavors. And just like our friend the banana-and-clove hefeweizen, Belgian ales are redolent of winter spices and dried fruits. With a Belgian blond, dubbel, and saison, Mazama is one of the few purely Belgian-style breweries in Oregon. But like those others, it's still Oregon, so fear not, there's Hop Eruption IPA.

Hop Eruption—playing off the brewery's namesake volcano (down in Southern Oregon and dormant for nine thousand years) that created the state's only national park, Crater Lake—was actually the first release, as both a nod to hop-happy brewer Aaron Spotswood and also, Jeff admitted, "our acknowledgement that we're market driven. I have nothing against IPAs. We attempt to make the most delicious IPA that we can."

To Belgian-up the hoppy offerings, there's also White Wedding, which is a hybrid of American IPAs and Belgian witbiers, as well as a straightforward witbier (wheat ale with coriander and orange peel) called Wizard Island Wit, named after the small tuft of dry land in Crater Lake atop Mt. Mazama.

The Tobins have always been adventurous in their brewing aspirations, starting with ditching their ultra-basic homebrewing kit after just one batch back in 1984. At the time they lived in Vermont, where places like Catamount were among the first microbreweries anywhere on the East Coast. "We tasted them and thought, yeah, this is

Beers brewed: Year-round: Blonde, Pyroclastic Porter, Hop Eruption IPA, Saison D'Etro, Grand Cru, Dubbel. Seasonals: Petite Belgique, White Wedding (white IPA), Wizard Island Wit, Cherry Sour, Peach Sour Sunrise, Nightside Eclipse (bourbon imperial porter).

The Pick: Grand Cru. For a brewery that aims to brew to style, this is the beer they get to let their hair down with since there's no grand cru style. The fruity esters serve advance notice of the impending pear and spice notes that first hit your tongue accompanied by aggressive effervescence. Despite the 10 percent ABV, it's surprisingly dry and ultimately lives up to its many comparisons to Duvel, the touchstone of Belgian strong pale ales.

pretty good," said Jeff. A move to Colorado further accelerated their love of progressive beer, but when Hewlett-Packard relocated them to Corvallis, the wheels started turning for not just enjoying the local craft-brewing scene but also contributing to it. A 2011 trip to beer's holy land, Belgium, proved to be the straw-colored blond ale that broke the camel's back and inspired plans for a nanobrewery. Those plans were quickly ditched in favor of a full production brewery, and Jeff segued from a reliable career as an electrical engineer to a passionate one as a brewer in 2013.

"We manage multiple yeast strains," he said as he showed me the lab, a scarcely capitalized nanobreweries feature. It's those yeasts, he added, "that really define our beers . . . Kathy and I mostly drink Belgian ales—weird, wonderful beers."

A visit to the Mazama Taproom—located two miles outside downtown's cluster of breweries but on Route 34 on the way to town from I-5—offers an intimate place to try said wonderful beers. As time permits, they will release more barrel-aged beers. One of the first from this program, a bourbon-aged Baltic porter called Nightside Eclipse, won Best in Show at the inaugural Portland-version of Bend's Big Woody festival of barrel-aged beers, while a pair of Belgian Lambic-style sour beers (one made with cherries and another with peaches) has also earned high praise. Best of all, Mazama is sandwiched between Two Towns Ciders and Nectar Creek sparkling meadery for a trifecta of delicious fermentations.

Mazama Brewing

Opened: 2013.

Owners: Jeff and Kathy Tobin.

Brewers: Jeff Tobin, James Winther (assistant brewer), and Aaron Spotswood (brewer and "yeast wrangler").

System: 20-barrel.

Annual production: 400 barrels.

Distribution: Oregon.

Hours: Wednesday through Friday, 3 p.m. to 9 p.m.; Saturday, noon to 9 p.m.

Tours: By request.

Takeout beer: Growlers, bottles (and probably cans soon), and dock sales.

Gift shop: Hoodies and tees.

Food: Small bites including Liège-style waffles.

Events: Dark Days Winter Ale Fest (January) and Starkbierfest (March). Monthly beer dinners.

McMenamins High Street Brewery

1243 High Street, Eugene, OR 97401
(541) 345-4905 • Mcmenamins.com/HighStreet
Twitter @CaptainNeon

McMenamins brewpubs have made their homes in old ballrooms, boarding schools, farms, railway stations, and churches. High Street, built in 1905, once served as a flophouse. McMenaminized in 1988 as their sixth brewery—Eugene's first since Prohibition—High Street brewed their first gruit (unhopped beer) and spontaneously fermented ale (raspberry lambic from a wine barrel).

Jenny Gomez, High Street's manager since the day McMenamins converted it from the High Street Café, said one of the first customers to walk through the door "was an old hippie who used to hang out here." Considering Eugene's history with the Country Fair and many Grateful Dead shows, it's fair to say this pub has seen more than its share of hippies. (Imagine that at a pub called High Street.)

Brewer Hanns Anderson likes the Grateful Dead, but he's just as prone to crank Bad Religion while brewing down in the subterranean brewhouse where anyone of above average height needs to duck. Luckily, the awesome beer garden behind the house provides ample room to stretch out and relax.

McMenamins High Street Brewery

Opened: 1988.

Owners: Brian and Mike McMenamin (see page 92).

Brewer: Hanns Anderson.

System: 6-barrel.

Annual production: 700 barrels.

Distribution: On-premises and at some other McMenamins pubs nearby.

Hours: Monday through Saturday, 11 a.m. to 1 a.m.; Sunday, noon to midnight.

Tours: Walk-ins when brewer is available.

Takeout beer: Growlers.

Gift shop: Limited apparel and gift items.

Food: McMenamins pub grub. Try the shredded pork with mozzarella and fried onions.

Beers brewed: Year-round: Hammerhead Pale Ale, Terminator Stout, Ruby, IPA. Seasonals: Wunder Bär Munich Dunkel, Grandma Betty's (Mosaic-hopped pale ale), Boysenberry Cream Stout, various IPAs, and many more.

The Pick: IPA. Hanns brews a "traditional NW IPA" (redder and maltier) but he wanted to create a lighter IPA—in color, not flavor or bitterness. This 100-plus-IBU quaffer features 14 pounds of hops (Nuggets, Simcoe, and Citra) per 6-barrel batch and tastes like California sunshine.

McMenamins on Monroe

2001 Northwest Monroe Avenue, Corvallis, OR 97330
(541) 758-0080 • McMenamins.com/Monroe
Twitter @CaptainNeon

Community Supported Agriculture in the brewery world is a hot model or marketing angle, but the Oregon State University community has fervently supported the Monroe Brewery since it opened on one of the campus's main commercial drags. Just imagine this place, adorned with a wall full of sinks, packed from faucet to drain during OSU football games. During *and* before, I should say. If a big game starts at noon, doors might open at 9 a.m., meaning one lucky Beaver's drinking the first beer by 9:01. Harnessing that fandom, a popular house blend is a Black and Orange, but brewer Gary Nance the pub's first and only brewer, leans toward fundamental styles.

Oh, and those sinks? Rumor has it that the pub originally didn't have the regulation number of sinks. So now this quirky water feature ensures appliance compliance.

McMenamins on Monroe

Opened: 2006.

Owners: Brian and Mike McMenamin (see page 92).

Brewer: Gary Nance.

System: 6-barrel.

Annual production: 750 barrels.

Distribution: 3rd Street and a few nearby McMenamins pubs.

Hours: Sunday and Monday, 11 a.m. to 11 p.m.; Tuesday and Wednesday, 11 a.m. to midnight; Thursday through Saturday, 11 a.m. to 1 a.m.

Tours: Walk-in tours when the brewer is available.

Takeout beer: Growlers.

Gift shop: Some shirts and other limited items available on-premises.

Food: McMenamins menu of burgers, sandwiches, pizzas, salads, bowls, and snackies.

Extras: Opens early on game days. Two free pool tables.

Beers brewed: Year-round: Terminator Stout, Ruby, Hammerhead Pale Ale, IPA. Seasonals: Safeside Wheat, Lefty's Porter, Wade's Choice DIPA, Achin' Back IPA.

The Pick: Wade's Choice Double IPA. Named for manager and hop fiend Wade Williams, it's a crowd pleaser for those who dig big hops and, yes, big alcohol. Centennial, Nugget, Santiam, and Galena hops pack a piney punch, and it's a frugal option for students, who get to drink three beers' worth in just two pints.

McMenamins Thompson Brewery

3575 Liberty Road South, Salem, OR 97302
(503) 363-7286 • Mcmenamins.com/Thompson
Twitter @CaptainNeon

Before the Liberty Road structure became the Thompson Brewery and Public House, in 1984 it was a restaurant called Peter's Little Bavaria, serving cuisine and imported beers from the Old Country with a side of folk dancing. The restaurant is responsible for the Bavarian maps that still adorn the wall in the bar area. More importantly, the building dates back to a farm where the Thompson family from Minnesota settled in 1905. Fred Thompson, who fought in the Spanish American War, felt the Willamette Valley with its timberlands and orchards was their land of plenty. His father, Franklin, was a veteran of the Civil War and allegedly spent his last years here haunted by Confederate soldiers' ghosts.

The sudsy, twentieth-century bookend to this land's use is Salem's current, first post–Prohibition brewpub. Brewer Jen Kent said everyone who works here has seen or heard Thompson's ghost, and she noted that he's "a bit of a prankster." In other words, make sure your chair's still there when you go to sit down. When I asked if he drinks her beer, she instantly replied, "I hope so."

Her beer is made by herself and "her boys": Larry, Curly, Moe, and Shemp. They're not stooge brewers, but the grundy fermentation tanks are something of a McMenamins hallmark. The mash tun and actual brewing vessels are all female. Because the Thompson has twenty taps, four of which are devoted to the company's core beers and four more to wine and cider made at the Edgefield property, Kent gets to experiment with up to twelve taps. As part of company lore, this is the brewery that first whipped up Black Widow, an imperial porter with licorice root that's now a Halloween seasonal McMenamins mainstay. In addition to the now-classic rendition, Kent made one she calls Black Widower with the addition of sweet woodruff.

Beers brewed: Year-round: Hammerhead Pale Ale, Terminator Stout, Ruby, IPA, Pole Ax Lager. Seasonals: Black Widow Porter, Red Riser IRA, Jam Session ISA, and many more.

The Pick: Pole Ax Lager. Indelible at the Thompson Brewery, this opaque amber lager's mix of two-row, Munich, and black malts creates a honeyed brown bread base brightened with Chinook and Cascade hops.

She often adds culinary ingredients to her batches, frequently on the dark side of the spectrum. To Terminator Stout she has added coffee and vanilla. The Big Lebrewski is a stout that The Dude would be happy to bowl for. Sadly, I didn't get to try her Spanish Coffee Porter she mentioned, brewed with cinnamon and nutmeg. I'm sensing a trend, since she also makes a beer on the light-in-color side called Pot of Gold, a golden ale embellished not with pots of liquid coffee but their beans.

Of course, lagers are frequently on tap and in demand here, too. Pole Ax Lager, a dark amber, hoppy lager originally made by Chris Oslin who's now up at Cornelius Pass in Hillsboro, remains a house favorite. And Jen's Hoodie Love, a strong, Citra- and Cascade-hopped lager that's as dark and fragrant as a rainy day, has become one of her signature winter warmers.

Comfort might be the pub's biggest allure. Down on the farm, the space is warm and cozy inside, just as you'd imagine a settler's house would be, and in nicer weather, the fir and cedar trees towering overhead are so inviting. I like to think the Thompsons aren't haunting it so much as just hanging out, not ready to pay their tab.

McMenamins Thompson Brewery

Opened: 1990.

Owners: Brian and Mike McMenamin (see page 92).

Brewer: Jen Kent.

System: 7-barrel.

Annual production: 750 barrels.

Distribution: On-premises and to three nearby pubs.

Hours: Monday and Tuesday, 11 a.m. to 10 p.m.; Wednesday and Thursday, 11 a.m. to 11 p.m.; Friday and Saturday, 11 a.m. to 1 a.m.; Sunday, noon to 10 p.m.

Tours: Walk-in tours when brewer is available.

Takeout beer: Growlers.

Gift shop: Mc-merch (shirts and other limited items).

Food: McMenamins pub grub. Their tots are world class, but save your appetite for the Stella Blue Fries, a plate of fries topped with blue cheese and bacon.

Events: Annual Barley Cup, a beer fest among McMenamins brewers, judged by the local Capital City Homebrewers club, the last Saturday in June.

Ninkasi Brewing Co.

Perpetuate Better Living

272 Van Buren Street, Eugene, OR 97402
(541) 344-2739 • NinkasiBrewing.com
Twitter @NinkasiBrewing

When Ninkasi co-owner Nikos Ridge and his childhood friends coined "total domination" as their catchphrase, they must've been prescient. Years later, Total Domination is the best-selling IPA in Oregon where IPA is the best-selling style of craft beer. This beer alone has a 1 percent market share. Most of the largest craft breweries, across their portfolios, don't enjoy 1 percent of their home state's beer market. There are roughly two hundred breweries in Oregon—which might as well mean five hundred different IPAs are brewed here—so when one in every hundred beers (including the mega brands) consumed is Total Dom, it must make others teal with envy. (Glimpsing their packaging and ever-expanding brewery reveals that teal is Ninkasi's color.) The other co-owner, Jamie Floyd, intuited that would make a great name for the beer that first introduced Ninkasi to the world in 2006.

It's not that the Eugene-based brewery—named after the ancient Sumerian goddess of beer—schemed to control the massive IPA market, for in those days it didn't exist. "At the time," said Floyd, the public face of the company, who rocks a silver streak in his hair as well as tons of tattoos, "[IPAs] were not easily accessible on the shelves. We saw that opportunity. Even though what we're known for doesn't seem like it," he added, referencing the fact that Ninkasi has grown into the country's thirtieth largest craft brewery (and third largest in Oregon) on the strength and reputation of their IPA and even hoppier double IPA. So it's not just his opinion, although he is a man who holds—and shares—many. "We started out as a niche brewery

Beers brewed: Year-round: Total Domination IPA, Believer Double Red, Tricerahops Imperial IPA, Oatis Oatmeal Stout, Vanilla Oatis, Quantum Pale. Seasonals: Renewale (winter), Spring Reign (spring), Wunderbler Kolsch (summer), Maiden the Shade IPA (summer), Oktoberfest (fall), Sleigh'r (early fall). Rare & Delicious Series: Includes Hop Fraiche, Total Crystalation Fresh Hop Ale, Nuptiale, Redunkulous Dunkel Weiss, Critical Hit Barley Wine. Prismatic Lager Series: Pravda Bohemian-Style Pilsner, Lux Helles Bock, Venn Dortmund-Style Lager.

The Pick: Tricerahops. Indeed, this lumbering, fearsome double IPA tastes like it could be a triple, or tri-IPA, roaring with 8.8 percent ABV and 100 IBUs derived from citrusy Centennial, Chinook, and Cascade hops, as well as more floral aromatics derived from Palisade and Summit, making one beer that dominates even Total Domination.

not brewing other people's beers and not competing in the mainstream of recognition that was the Oregon lineup." Believe it or not, in 2006 only Oregon's biggest brewers and a select few upstarts packaged IPA; it didn't have a foothold outside the hophead nook. At best, you could find one on draft at brewpubs. In a sense, this particular brand played a role in that tectonic shift.

What I love is that now that Ninkasi has established itself as a formidable wielder of hops—Believer is a double red ale, similar to an IPA but with darker malts, and Tricerahops became the first double IPA bottled in the Pacific Northwest in 2007—they are formulating new beers in their Prismatic Series exclusively for lagers. Even though roughly 90 percent of the beer drunk throughout the world is an industrial lager, craft breweries rarely turn their focus toward them. (Floyd mentioned that batches eight and nine at the brewery were lagers.)

Quick aside about Believer: Floyd sports a tattoo of that logo, but it's not the only Ninkasi brand name inked into his flesh. His other arm is adorned with "Critical Hit" and a twenty-sided die that has landed on twenty, but it doesn't honor Ninkasi's Barley Wine. Rather, it depicts Floyd's uber-nerdy side that's enamored with role-playing games. Ninkasi even turned a Dungeons & Dragons event at a Southeast Portland beer hall (called Beer) into an annual party to commemorate the last of the year's kegs of Critical Hit Barley Wine. (Incidentally, I got to enjoy a glass of a beer called Little One, made from second runnings of Critical Hit, named for the pyramidal four-sided die.)

Homebrewing, like D&D, is pretty nerdy, so it's no surprise Floyd fermented his first batch at the age of seventeen. He developed professionally at Steelhead where he actually began in the kitchen (he continues to teach cooking classes for culinary students, folding in beer as an ingredient) but had long held ideas for starting his own brewery. Ninkasi enabled him to bring his recipes for Total Domination, Believer, and Tricerahops to life. But now there's a talented team of brewers, with Mark Henion at the helm, and a wide range of beers. Total Dom is 60 percent of their total production, which began greatly increasing once their new, 90-barrel brewhouse came online in early 2014. Lately, expansion is a major factor in the craft beer industry, but this one, and please pardon my attempt at a D&D reference, gains a level.

"Everyone else is upping their game. What I love is that we're creating a platform in which other people have to up their game," geeked Floyd. The new brewery resides in a LEED-certified building across the street from their 55-barrel brewhouse, bringing their eventual capacity to 350,000 barrels. The Ninkasi campus has expanded to encompass four city blocks with sustainability efforts at every turn, including something of a technological innovation: a hop strainer that puts more hops in their beers (always brewed without extracts) and keeps less brewing water from being squandered.

The campus also includes a LEED-certified administrative building with a recording studio, a climbing wall, indoor bike storage for employees, and three employee and hospitality bars. Those will come in handy because there's also a 7-barrel pilot system where brewers get to experiment with beers that'll nearly exclusively be tapped in the ten-handle tasting room and around town. Some of those creations may turn into packaged releases under the R&D Series—Research and Development, yes, but technically "Rare & Delicious."

All of these things contribute to why Ninkasi has made *Oregon Business* magazine's list of 100 Best Companies to Work For two years running. (The fact that it's the only brewing company to make the list says something about Ninkasi, as well as the publication's lack of a beer soul). That ninety-plus employees (and gaining twenty-five per year) get to rock climb at work is cool, but profit-sharing and 401(k) plans are better. "For me, that's the best award I've been given," Floyd said. "We want great jobs for people. It's soul-satisfying work. We're trying to create a level where there's happiness between your home life and work life." That's why their motto is "Perpetuate better living." Floyd concluded: "Beer is a part of what makes our whole society great. And it's our goal to make society great."

Ninkasi Brewing Co.

Opened: 2006.

Owners: Jamie Floyd and Nikos Ridge.

Brewers: Jamie Floyd (founding brewer), Mark Henion (head brewer), Chris Archer, Dana Robles, Richard Masella, Simon Sothras, and Tim Sanborn.

Systems: 90-barrel, a 55-barrel, and a 7-barrel pilot system.

Annual production: 115,000 barrels.

Distribution: Oregon, Washington, Alaska, California, Idaho, Nevada, Montana, and British Columbia.

Hours: Sunday through Wednesday, noon to 9 p.m.; Thursday through Saturday, noon to 10 p.m.

Tours: Monday through Friday at 2 p.m. and 5 p.m.; Sunday at 4:30 p.m. Tours last one hour.

Takeout beer: Growlers, bottles, and dock sales.

Gift shop: Huge variety of apparel, glassware, and swag including skateboard decks.

Food: Barroom snacks like nuts and popcorn. There's usually a food truck parked outside the tasting room's doors.

Oakshire Brewing

207 Madison Street, Eugene, OR 97402
(541) 688-4555 • OakBrew.com • Twitter @Oakshire

Talking to Oakshire's brewmaster, Matt Van Wyk, at the brewery—soon to be the old brewery—I learned that the brand-new Oakshire Brewing in 2008 was really the old Willamette Brewing from 2006. Brothers Jeff and Chris Althouse had built a 4-barrel brewery in industrial West Eugene that brewed 300 barrels its first full year. Not bad for a starter brewery. Thanks to a few hiccups (let's just say the name Willamette is pretty popular in the fertile Willamette Valley), they were gifted the necessity/opportunity to relaunch and rebrand. Once they rebranded in 2008 as Oakshire—a wholly made-up name synthesizing the strong and independent oaks found nearby and the concept of shire as a community—and worked out the kinks, people were immediately enthusiastic about this new brewery.

Wiser still, the Althouses then hired Van Wyck, who'd gained a bit of notoriety in the industry after earning Small Brewer of the Year in 2006 at the GABF for his work at the Chicagoland brewery Flossmoor Station. In beer geek lore, his single batch of bourbon-aged barleywine, Wooden Hell, lives on. (Among beer traders and collectors, it's considered a "white whale" because of the near impossibility in landing a bottle.) Still, he required no arm-twisting to move to Eugene; he already had family here, plus he and his wife pined for terrain more varied than the flats of their native Midwest.

It didn't hurt that immediately upon taking over the brewhouse, Oakshire earned a silver medal at GABF for Overcast Espresso Stout. I love this beer and am grateful it's part of their year-round lineup. In Oregon, we love our locally roasted coffee around the calendar every bit as much as our locally crafted beer, but most breweries only bring out coffee beers in the winter. As Van Wyck conducted a tour of the brewery where they used the

Beers brewed: Year-round: Watershed IPA, Oakshire Amber Ale, Overcast Espresso Stout. Seasonals: Hellshire, The Perfect Storm DIPA, Oregon Imperial Ale (for annual OBF), O'Dark:30 CDA (spring), Line Dry Pale Ale with rye (summer), Big Black Jack Imperial Chocolate Pumpkin Porter (fall), Ill-Tempered Gnome Ale (winter). Brewers' Reserve Series includes Framboise. Single Batch Series.

The Pick: O'Dark:30. In a region so heralded for its black and bitter beers that it derived the Cascadian Dark Ale appellation, O'Dark:30 goes extra dark and dank with resiny pine and oily coffee flavors, with the Northwest citrusy hops mimicking an Italian espresso when they drop in a lemon rind.

15-barrel system to make 20-barrel batches in heavy rotation, so as to fill 80-barrel fermenters, I stopped at the twin toddy makers. Honestly, given their smallish size, I thought maybe they were to keep the staff of around twenty-four employees buzzing, but Van Wyck explained that the cold water extract is expressly for Overcast. Ten pounds of whole beans from Eugene's Wandering Goat Coffee Co. are ground at the brewery and yield 5-gallon batches of toddy, meaning a total of 100 pounds of beans per tank of the medium-bodied oatmeal stout.

Incidentally, Wandering Goat is across the street from the public house that opened in 2013; brewing operations will move to the public house by mid-2015. Every Tuesday at 6 p.m., they tap a new beer in the Single Batch program that Van Wyck heads up. One such batch was called Goatshed IPA, a coffee-infused version of their most popular beer, Watershed IPA. Watershed is already quite bitter with 70 IBUs, so the coffee's natural bitterness became entangled in the hop bitterness, not unlike their great spring seasonal O'Dark:30 Cascadian Dark Ale.

"We're still a small production brewery, but we're growing all the time," Van Wyck said, before adding, "We still get to act like a small brewery." The Public House is in the Whitcaker, redubbed the "Brewery District," and some of the Single Batch beers are occasionally on cask, which is always fun. There's no kitchen in the wide, airy space, but there's always at least one food cart and often live music by happy hour. Speaking of single batches and happy, Hellshire has become Oakshire's own "whale," something of a spinoff of Wooden Hell. It changes every vintage but is typically a blend of strong ales—imperial stouts, barleywines, or the like—that have been aged in various barrels.

Oakshire Brewing

Opened: 2008.
Owners: Brothers Jeff and Chris Althouse.
Brewers: Matt Van Wyk (brewmaster) and Tyler West (lead brewer).
System: 15-barrel.
Annual production: 10,000 barrels.
Distribution: Oregon and Washington.
Hours: Daily, 11 a.m. to 10 p.m.
Tours: First Saturday of the month.
Takeout beer: Growlers, bottles and some cans, and dock sales.
Gift shop: Apparel and glassware.
Events: Hellshire Day. Zwickelmania is already the most incredible statewide open house for breweries that falls on President's Day. Oakshire treats the crowds and turns it into the release day to pick up bottles of Hellshire from the source.

Plank Town Brewing Co.

346 Main Steet, Springfield, OR 97477
(541) 746-1890 • PlankTownBrewing.com
Twitter @PlanktownBrew

As the college town of Eugene gets more bustling and boom-ier, some residential and business attention is shifting east of I-5 to Springfield, which is where Bart Caridio found the perfect location for his new brewery. The catch is that Plank Town Brewing—the name comes from Springfield's old nickname back when streets got so impracticably muddy that folks had to lay down wooden planks—wasn't the initial brewing company he had in mind. As one of the owners of Eugene's iconic Sam Bond's Garage since the early nineties, this amazing 7,000-square-foot corner space on Main Street landed on his radar as a possible place to locate Sam Bond's Brewing, which eventually found a home in the Foundry Building back over in Eugene (see page 280). His business acumen told him this was just the spot, but for what? Seeing as Sam Bond's Garage, Eugene's first rotating tap pub, arguably led the way for the rundown Whiteaker District's transformation into the Brewery District with four other breweries and public houses now, maybe Springfield's second brewery after Hop Valley will revitalize this city's downtown.

Besides happening upon the great location, the ball started rolling when Caridio and his partner headed up to Corvallis to visit Block 15 Brewing to see, as Caridio said, "why they were so popular." Part of the reason was the amazing beer made by their outstanding brewer, Steve van Rossem, a veteran of the Willamette Valley brewing scene. He was the inaugural brewer at McMenamins High Street in Eugene in 1992 before heading to the short-lived West Brothers, but really made his mark at Block 15. A chance meeting between van Rossem and Caridio at that brewpub led to a discussion about this new brew venture. Lo and behold, van Rossem signed up. "He was

Beers brewed: Year-round: Saaz-all, B3 (Bart's Best Bitter), Extra Pale Ale, ExSB Experimental Special Bitter, Black Knight Dark Lager, L'il Red Ryder, Riptooth IPA, Streetcar Stout. Seasonals: Optical Illusion (dark mild), Odd Fellow Wit, Reggie English IPA, Foggy Scotsman Porter, Blazing Caber (wee heavy), Contemplator Doppelbock, UnObtainium DIPA.

The Pick: B3 (Bart's Best Bitter). Rare is the British best bitter found during this era of hopmania, but this exceptionally light (4.1 percent ABV) and slightly grassy (18 IBUs) ale is ideal for those who seek out lagers or beers that foster conversations rather than dominate them.

interested in shaving an hour each way off his daily commute," Caridio semi-joked.

Caridio is the business guy, and van Rossem is the beer guy. The main reasons a beer called B3, or Bart's Best Bitter, is Plank Town's flagship is because van Rossem wanted to honor his boss, whose beer palate runs toward the milder side, and because, quite frankly, not everyone is a devout hophead. Having said that, before house beer arrived on tap the bestsellers were two of Oregon's most bitter IPAs. Riptooth, his new Northwest robust IPA, beat out all challengers in a blind tasting of IPAs from across the valley held at The Bier Stein, one of Eugene's (and all of Oregon's) best taphouses. Another intensely flavorful brew is Li'l Red Ryder, what van Rossem calls a "Cascadian red ale" (the CDA's redheaded stepchild?), with a full body from caramel and rye malts, European hops for bittering, and Northwest citrusy, spicy hops for flavor and aroma to complement the rye.

There are twenty taps behind the British-style, horseshoe bar. Not all are house beers since there are also guest beers, ciders, and sparkling mead from nearby. Van Rossem currently brews toward the local palate but hopes to expand it and appeal to more adventurous taste buds by creating a barrel-aging program for things like oaked stouts and sour beers, or "whatever Steve wants to brew," Caridio said. For now, a happy medium is easily spotted atop the bar where two cask pins (half-firkins) may contain Bart's Best Bitter, an IPA, or something more experimental. The bar ties the room together with wooden features and furniture, bringing a bit of the old plank vibe inside the new Plank Town.

Plank Town Brewing Co.

Opened: 2013

Owner: Bart Caridio.

Brewers: Steve van Rossem and John Crane (assistant brewer).

System: 10-barrel.

Annual production: 1,200 barrels.

Distribution: Eugene.

Hours: Monday through Thursday, 11 a.m. to 11 p.m. Friday, 11 a.m. to midnight; Saturday, 10 a.m. to midnight; Sunday, 10 a.m. to 11 p.m.

Tours: By request

Takeout beer: Growlers and dock sales.

Gift shop: Shirts and stuff along the side wall.

Food: Upscale pub-friendly burgers, salads, seafood, vegetarian, and seasonal specials.

RAM Restaurant & Brewery (Big Horn Brewing)

515 12th Street, Salem, OR 97301
(503) 363-1904 • TheRam.com/locations/or-salem
Twitter @TheRAM

Even among brewpub enthusiasts, there are those who, doggonit, just wanna know what they're getting on a consistent basis. Reliability, like a Swiss watch, is what chains like The RAM Restaurant & Brewery deliver. In terms of kitchen and décor, it could practically be Chili's, but where their beer list is a brief study in industrial lagers and behemoth imports (which also describes The RAM's bottle list), RAM's is a brewpub with a brewery on-site. What's more, beyond the six core beers, regional brewer Dave Leonard and head brewer Mike Paladino get to create any other kind of beers they'd like to suit the season or their whims.

"Regional brewer" seems to mean Leonard floats around Oregon and Washington. He told me that RAM operates nine breweries among its thirty (and growing) locations, beginning back in 1971 with the original RAM restaurant in the Tacoma, Washington, suburb of Lakewood. Co-founded by Jeff Iverson Jr.'s father, along with one of his fraternity brothers, the RAM Pub aspired to be more deluxe than just a pizza joint that served beer. It even included the concept of cook-your-own burgers. Then came an in-house brewery and the name Big Horn Brewing in 1995. Nowadays the burgers, steaks, and wings all come out of the kitchen. (Speaking of buffalo wings, I fell into the brewpub for some late-night beers and since in addition to the traditional daily happy hour from 3 to 6 p.m. there's also a second one from 10 to midnight, that explains my order of buffalo Gorgonzola mozzarella waffle fries.)

Beyond The RAM Restaurant & Brewery (which also operates in Idaho, Illinois, and Indiana), the company owns C.B. & Potts Restaurant & Brewery in Colorado, and C.I. Shenanigan's in Tacoma. As stated, not every store has a brewery on-premises. The reference to Chili's above is fitting since one that closed a little north in Wilsonville has been converted into Oregon's third RAM, with beers coming from Salem's brewery.

Beers brewed: Year-round: Blonde Ale, Hefeweizen, Big Red IPA, Buttface Amber Ale, Disorder Porter, 71 Pale Ale. Seasonals: Barry White Belgian, Brazen Nut Brown, Apollo IPA, Warrior IPA, Vanilla Cream Ale, Oatmeal Irish Stout (nitro), Oktoberfest, and more.

The Pick: Big Red IPA is liquefied big green hops with grass and citrus peel top notes on a pale malt base proving it's an India pale, not India red.

Leonard knows what he's doing. I can't fault him much on the flagship Buttface Amber Ale. It has some hops going, and I liked getting to say "Buttface" to the bartender's face. It also explains the shirt for sale that reads: "Came looking for a Blonde, got stuck with a Buttface." I admit I didn't even make a pass at the Blonde Ale.

Big Red, which isn't a red ale but the IPA, is serious West Coast liquid hops with grassy, citrusy tastes foisted on a truly pale malt platform the way some other brewers neglect to build their India pale ales. The brewer's choice beers included an Apollo- and Warrior-hopped IPA that was different from and almost just as good as Big Red, a vanilla cream ale that deftly blended a little vanilla sweetness to match the style instead of clobber it, and an Oatmeal Irish Stout on nitro with tempered bitterness and roast.

To round out the happy hour experience (or for the kids), there are arcade games and a pinball machine in the backroom, as well as billiard tables and—oy vey!—plastic darts. Plastic? Safer, yes, but not very sporting. Speaking of sporting (and not just all the TVs lined around the restaurant and horseshoe-shaped bar) RAM is a sponsor of USA Curling—you know, that sport where Canadians glide heavy teapots across the ice. If my misperception is the prevailing one, USA Curling and the RAM have a lot of work to do, so luckily 50 cents from each sampler tray (shaped like a big-horned ram's curls) goes toward the cause.

RAM Restaurant & Brewery (Big Horn Brewing)

Opened: 1995.

Owner: RAM International (privately owned by Jeff Iverson Jr. and family).

Brewers: Dave Leonard (regional brewer) and Mike Paladino (head brewer).

Annual production: 2,000 barrels.

Hours: Daily, 11 a.m. to "close" (at least midnight).

Distribution: On-premises only.

Takeout beer: Growlers.

Gift shop: T-shirts and more.

Food: Pub grub.

Other locations: Clackamas location (11860 SE 82nd Ave. #3050, Happy Valley; 503-659-1282). Wilsonville location (29800 SW Boones Ferry Rd., Wilsonville; 503-570-0200).

Salem Ale Works

2027 25th Street Southeast, Salem, OR 97302
(503) 990-8486 • AleInSalem.com
Twitter @SalemAleWorks

It helps that cofounder and brewer Justin Ego is often the guy behind the bar in the tasting room. I mean, it's always good and helpful when that's the case because then you can talk to the brewer about the beers' flavor profiles or ingredients and whatnot, but in this case, I could also ask him what the names mean. Some people are aware that a misery whip is the name for those two-person crosscut saws (as well as a big IPA dry hopped with spicy Columbus). But a pulaski? The house pale ale is named for the firefighting tool that's both an ax and a hoe. Ego was only too happy to point it out hanging on the wall among the other firefighting tools that he and co-owner Jake Bonham use in their line of duty, just as their respective wildfire-fighting parents did. (There's a picture of Ego and Bonham, college friends, helicopter rappelling near local wildfires.) As for the various saws on the walls and in the beer names? Hello, the name of the brewery is Salem Ale Works.

Ego, whose hair and beard are what you'd imagine Warren Zevon's werewolf in London to look like, related a funny story about their website. Even better, he told me over a sampler of Salem's beers served in a slice of tree with holes cut out to hold the glasses. As the duo was readying the brewery, they emailed some schmuck who'd registered SalemAleWorks.com, figuring the owners would then pay him a huge stack of cash for the domain. Hence, the brewery's URL is AleInSalem (which is appropriate for exactly the accounts they're seeking, such as Venti's and b2 Taphouse.) Besides, Ego pointed out, the other one looked like it read SaleMaleWorks, which is great if you're a gigolo, but not so great if you're selling liquid assets only.

As for the sampler, I should mention that Cast Iron CDA immediately became one of my favorite

Beers brewed: Year-round: Hootenanny Honey Basil, Cast Iron CDA, Drip Torch Amber Ale, Pulaski Pale Ale, Misery Whip IPA. Seasonals: Cloverfield Rye, Slow Roller Raspberry Mint, Mexican Oatmeal Stout, Spike Out Smoked Porter.

The Pick: Cast Iron CDA. If a beer can be both extreme and subtle, this is it. The darker malts make it smoky and ashy but not overly roasted and the 96 IBUs denote abundant alpha acids, yet it doesn't create that bitter-mouth face. It's packaged in an easy-drinking 5.5 percent.

examples of the regional style. The Cascade dry-hopping gives it that classic hop quality, and the malt-derived ash flavors work so well, perhaps because of the firefighting imagery. It's great to find a CDA that doesn't go over the top. All of the beers' flavors are kept nicely in check, even the Hootenanny Honey Basil, which avoids being a pesto beer but still would pair nicely with Italian or Thai since the honey actually dries it out a lot. Ego created the recipe on the spot in his kitchen, just from looking at the honey in the cupboard and the pot of basil growing. I didn't get to try Raspberry Mint, but it mirrors Hootenanny's origin story.

The tasting room toward the back of a strip mall near the airport only had five taps on when I visited a month after opening, but Ego plans on adding more to allow for additional seasonal or special releases. "But I don't wanna have three taps of 'weird beer,'" he said, making air quotes. "I don't want people to associate us with only crazy, experimental beers." His brewing focus will always be on well-built classic styles such as amber and pale ales. It's just that through years of homebrewing he has stumbled onto a few recipes that are "surprisingly good."

Salem Ale Works

Opened: 2013.

Owners and brewers: Justin Ego (head brewer) and Jake Bonham (assistant brewer).

System: 3-barrel.

Annual production: Almost 200 barrels.

Distribution: Mid-Willamette Valley.

Hours: Monday, 3 p.m. to 6 p.m.; Thursday and Friday, 4 p.m. to 9 p.m.; Saturday, 2 p.m. to 9 p.m.; Sunday, noon to 5 p.m.

Tours: The brewery is visible from the barstools.

Takeout beer: Growlers and limited bombers.

Gift shop: Branded growlers and stainless steel Hydro Flasks. And T-shirts.

Sam Bond's Brewing Co.

540 East Eighth Avenue, Eugene, OR 97402
(541) 246-8162 • SamBondsBrewing.com
Twitter @SamBondsBrewing

Nineteen years before launching Sam Bond's Brewing, Bart Caridio and some friends opened Sam Bond's Garage (407 Blair Blvd., one and a half miles east) as the first of four businesses. Then there was The Axe & Fiddle, a pub and music venue in Cottage Grove where Caridio lives, which he described as more of a listening room as compared to the Garage's pub-club feel. Earlier in 2013 he also co-founded Plank Town Brewing in Springfield (see page 274). And while I only saw the space where the fourth, Sam Bond's Brewing, wound up, I'm excited about the prospects, as are, no doubt, the future University of Oregon student residents of a high-rise apartment being constructed around the corner. What undergrad wouldn't want a brewery right outside their door?

Caridio, with old friends and fellow locals Mark Jaeger and Todd Davis, opened Sam Bond's Garage (so named for its earlier incarnation, a garage run by one Sam Bond) with the unusual premise of tapping eight different beers, a novel concept in 1995. Today, eight seems tame, but well-curated taps get the job done. The first house beer, Up Tempo, was tapped in December 2013. Sam Bond's Brewery only gets five taps at the Garage, the de facto tied house, including Instrumental IPA, naturally. Caridio also mentioned an exciting-sounding coffee-infused brown ale.

With no room at the Whiteaker District pub that dare not lose its patio, Sam Bond's Brewery set up in The Foundry, Eugene's oldest industrial building (1895). What a difference 118 years makes.

Sam Bond's Brewing Co.

Opened: 2013.

Owners: Bart Caridio, Mark Jaeger, and Todd Davis.

Brewer: Jim Montgomery III.

System: 10-barrel.

Distribution: Eugene.

Hours: Probably will be open daily, 3 p.m. to 10 p.m.-ish.

Tours: By request.

Takeout beer: Growlers and dock sales.

Beers brewed: Year-round: Dana's Alt, Instrumental IPA, Up Tempo Ale, Indie Red Ale, Oatmeal Stout, Renaissance Rye Ale, High Note Double IPA, Java Porter, Huakina New Zealand IPA, Sam I Am Beer.

Santiam Brewing

Santiam Brewing Company
Salem, Oregon

2544 19th Street Southeast, Salem, OR 97302
(503) 689-1260 • SantiamBrewing.com
Twitter @SantiamBrewing

Nine beer-loving friends who met weekly at "choir practice" to enjoy craft beer from Oregon and around the world launched this 3-barrel brewery in 2012. Four of them had homebrewing experience, including Ian Croxall, who'd been brewing since age fifteen (it's OK because he's British). Tucked into an industrial warehouse (conveniently near Raen Brew homebrew supply shop and taproom), in addition to the ten taps, you'll always find four "real ales" served on cask. In fact, the latter constitutes nearly half of the total pints (and half pints) pulled. Each week welcomes a new offering from the beer engine, where a solar-powered fridge cooled to 53 degrees keeps it truly cellar temperature and cask, not bright tank, conditioned. The "Santiam boys" may be a bunch of dudes, but they're not uncivilized.

Santiam, named for the nearby river that's Salem's water source (and not the emerging hop varietal of the same name), became the fifth of six breweries in the state capital with a population of only 154,000. They produce worldly styles with an emphasis on British beers, thus explaining why bitters and pales rule, but there's also a German pilsner, a hefeweizen, and sometimes a Maibock. One beer making a big splash is Pirate Stout Private Reserve, which Croxall first brewed at home in 2007. They refer to the base as a "sweet tropical export stout"—no bitter or acrid notes from overly roasted malts—aged for about six weeks in dark rum barrels procured from Rogue's distillery. And then they add toasted coconut. The non-reserve version replaces the barrel aging for maturation on rum-soaked oak chips, which I'm sure is nearly equally delicious, but the Private Reserve

Beers brewed: Year-round: Infiltrator Lager, Edel Weissbier, Bramble On, Double Top Bitter, Burton Strong Best Bitter, Spitfire ESB, Ecotopia NW IPA, St. Cutter's Double IPA, Coal Porter, Pirate Stout (rum barrel aged coconut stout). Seasonals: Cherry City Saison, Sangre De Christo Cabernet Stout, Fresh-hop Co-misseration Amber, Hoppy Frhoppy Fresh Hop Pale Ale, Unnamed CDA, Prince Charlie's Wee Heavy Scottish Strong, Cymru Welsh Olde Ale, 1859 Maibock, Summer Kolsch, four cask ales.

necessitates visits to the tasting room. During my last visit, "Naked Pirate" was one of the four real ales. In 2014, it became the back-to-back winner of the People's Choice Award at the Oregon Garden Brewfest in nearby Silverton.

The Pick: Pirate Stout is a rum barrel-aged "tropical export stout" (7.9 percent ABV) with a fudgy base of chocolate malts and de-bittered black malt that sails through the Bahamas in a dark rum barrel, picking up a crew of toasted coconut flakes. Fans of Malibu Rum and Mounds bars are the obvious targets, but the allure of this rich, sweet, voluptuous stout is very easily enjoyed as the meal, not just dessert.

There's no Jolly Roger or anything with a skull and crossbones, but there is a Union Jack. Flags hang from the ceiling and typically denote the styles of beers you're likely to find in the tasting room. There's Old Glory. I'm not sure if the German flag has a nickname, but there's one of those, too. There's a Welsh flag because, yes, they make a Welsh old ale called Cymru (that's the Welsh name for Wales). There are plans to hang a Scottish flag.

Croxall is the most senior of the brewers and the man behind Cymru. Here I must mention that his wife, Emily, painted the fun beer-themed art around the room. Jerome Goodrow is the youngest brewer, the only one who's full-time, and the creator of another intriguing, distinctly Santiam beer called Sangre De Christo. Legend has it he was sitting on the couch with his wife, who was drinking Cab Sauv, and he was drinking stout; he blended the two in his glass and dug the results. Santiam doesn't have a winery license, so they use Cabernet grapes in the vinous beer.

The 3-barrel system—the brewery was entirely self-financed by the partners—is adjacent to the bar. Kegs only find their way to over a dozen local accounts and, if Portlanders are lucky, a couple are delivered up north. One of the permanent off-premises spots to find Santiam beers is Venti's, which has two locations in town (Venti's Café and Venti's Taphouse in South Salem). It helps that one of Santiam's owners, Matt Killikelly, is regarded as Venti's Beer Czar. It's his czarist obligation to make sure Venti's taps only the best twenty-four beers he can coerce from breweries.

Directly across the street from Venti's Café in the historic Reed Opera House, Santiam recently opened the Downtown Annex with six taps ("and an occasional cask ale"). Like the original taproom with a bar and communal tables but no kitchen, this isn't a brewpub, but guests can order from a limited menu to have Venti's popular food shuttled across the street.

When boys get together over beer, they say a lot of things. In case it wasn't apparent, "choir practice" entailed no singing but plenty of drinking (mostly homebrews) and they talked politics, religion, and all the topics that are generally off the table during convivial conversation.

In the case of Santiam, it's a good thing the harebrained idea to actually brew professionally and create a non-homebased pub where others can carry on the conversations didn't simply vanish with the last drops of beer.

Santiam Brewing

Opened: 2012.

Owners: Jerome Goodrow, Ian Croxall, Jim Smiley, Brian Kelly, Matt Killikelly, Warren Bruhn, Loren Wuest, Bret Levinton, and Ed Litzer.

Brewers: Jerome Goodrow (full-time); Ian Croxall and Jim Smiley (part-time).

System: 3-barrel.

Annual production: 300 barrels.

Distribution: Salem and maybe Portland.

Hours: Monday through Wednesday, 4 p.m. to 8 p.m.; Thursday and Friday, 4 p.m. to 10 p.m; Saturday, 2 p.m. to 10 p.m.; Sunday, 2 p.m. to 7 p.m.

Tours: Ask an owner on-site.

Takeout beer: Growler fills.

Gift shop: Growlers, T-shirts, and gift certificates.

Food: Carts.

Events: Rock the Cask Bar anniversary party on second Saturday in July.

Other location: Downtown Annex (189 Liberty St. Northeast, Suite 107, Eugene, 97402).

Seven Brides Brewing

990 North First Street, Silverton, Oregon 97381
(503) 874-4677 • SevenBridesBrewing.com
Twitter @7BridesBrewing

The nutshell story of how Seven Brides (the brewery, not the musical) came about and earned its name is that all five partners grew up together in Silverton, a small agricultural town in the mid-Valley, home to fewer than ten thousand people. Among these five men— brothers Phill and Karl Knoll, brothers Ken and Jeff DeSantis, and Josiah Kelly—are seven daughters. That makes three of them fathers and two are uncles to the namesakes, who ranged from teenagers to babies in 2008 when these men, all beer lovers, figured it'd be pretty cool to turn their love of homebrewing into a way to afford seven future weddings.

Back then, they practically invented the nanobrewery by getting Jeff's 15-gallon homebrew system licensed in his garage. They couldn't afford even one wedding's worth of flowers on the 15 barrels they sold their first year. Now they're making over 1,500 barrels annually, and none of the daughters are still even close to marrying age, so the venture is working according to plan. What's more, when I met Jeff at the brewery, he mentioned that both of his daughters, the two oldest, are interested in studying brewing, so they may get more than some wedding beers out of the family business.

The pint-sized partners also explain the girl-centric names for some of the beers: Becky's Black Cat Porter, Lil's Pils, Lauren's Pale Ale, Emily's Ember (an amber), Oatmeal Ellie, and Paige's Purple Wheat. Fear not, none of the guys named their daughter Drunkle. Also no reason to fear—of course they make an IPA.

According to Jeff, when his daughter, Lauren (nicknamed Lou), found out she'd be commemorated by this hoppy brew, she said, "It's a monster and named after me!" So Frankenlou's IPA is now available, including in pint-size cans.

Beers brewed: Year-round: Frankenlou's IPA, Becky's Black Cat Porter, Lil's Pils, Lauren's Pale Ale, Emily's Ember, Oatmeal Ellie, Paige's Purple Wheat. Seasonals: Drunkle, Hazelbock, Abiqua Black IPA, Weezinator Doppelbock, Bridezilla IIPA, plus barrel-aged and other seasonal beers.

The Pick: Frankenlou's IPA. Although named after a little girl, this IPA is far from dainty or frilly, roaring with 105 IBUs, courtesy of Oregon hops. Big, sticky pine and citrus notes abound but the malt bill that boosts it to 7 percent ABV makes you want to hold her in your arms and never let go.

Attached to the brewery is a tasting room split with Vitis Winery, based simply on a friendship and an opportunity to provide a huge space for guests. It also helps that the brewery has access to freshly emptied wine barrels to age beers in on occasion.

One of the other cool opportunities this arrangement offers Seven Brides is the chance to turn wine drinkers on to craft beer. For Jeff's part, he might offer them Lil's Pils, the very approachable pilsner that's exceptionally clean, a testament to the brew crew. But he also delights in conniving those who have preconceptions about dark, "heavy" beers into trying Ellie's Oatmeal Stout, only to discover that chocolate and coffee notes are, unsurprisingly, really tasty.

Beyond their core beers, having a tasting room allows for a number of experimental beers. As for the visitors who come to taste wine, during my most recent visit there was a wild rice ale on. It was designed to appeal to consumers who, whether they realize it or not, are accustomed to beers made using rice as a cheap adjunct to lighten the body. For this recipe, the wild rice is really no cost-saving ingredient, and the fact that it was a top-fermenting ale instead of a bottom-fermenting lager provided interesting fruity aromas not intentionally found in lagers.

I, for one, can't wait to see what kinds of beers they'll eventually brew for future weddings. Perhaps they'll all be imperial IPAs, since daddies giving away their little girls must be both incredibly bitter and sweet.

Seven Brides Brewing

Opened: 2008.

Owners: Josiah Kelly; Phill and Karl Knoll; Ken and Jeff DeSantis.

Brewer: Phill Knoll.

System: 20-barrel.

Annual production: 1,600 barrels.

Distribution: Oregon, Washington, and Idaho.

Hours: Sunday to Thursday, 11:30 a.m. to 9 p.m.; Friday and Saturday, 11:30 a.m. to 11 p.m.

Tours: By appointment.

Takeout beer: Growlers and bottles.

Gift shop: Shirts, hats, and hoodies.

Food: Coleman Ranch steaks, sandwiches, salads, and healthy entrées (nothing fried).

Events: Oregon Garden Brewfest (late April), Anniversary party (late-May), Septoberfest, Men's Night Out (manly holiday shopping, early December).

Extras: Taproom allows minors until 8 p.m. Occasional live jazz. Seven Brides grows nearly four hundred acres of hops on a nearby farm, which provides nearly all of the hops they use.

Sky High Brewing

160 Northwest Jackson, Corvallis, OR 97330
(541) 207-3277 • SkyHighBrewing.com

The patio is four stories up (hence the name), making it the one place they don't deliver kegs by bike. The ground-level brewery is piloted by Laurence Livingston, who began brewing professionally in 1994 and was the acclaimed founder of Ring of Fire Meadery in Homer, Alaska. Getting to brew a wide and adept range of styles at the newest brewery in downtown Corvallis drew him to the Lower 48.

Sky High was founded by three pizza veterans—Scott McFarland, Mark O'Brien, and Brian Bovee—of American Dream Pizza, a family institution. The second level is all tasting room, but the third floor has a busy restaurant focusing on what the founders know best: pizza. The Sky High Burger with optional mozzarella and bacon simulates a pizza burger. But it's all about that rooftop garden overlooking the Willamette River and Riverfront Park, apropos of a pint of Panorama Porter.

Sky High Brewing

Opened: 2012.
Owners: Scott McFarland, Mark O'Brien, and Brian Bovee.
Brewer: Laurence Livingston.
System: 10-barrel.
Annual production: 500 barrels.
Distribution: Willamette Valley.
Hours: Sunday through Wednesday, 11 a.m. to 10 p.m.; Thursday, 11 a.m. to 11 p.m.; Friday and Saturday, 11 a.m. to midnight.
Tours: By request.
Takeout beer: Growlers/growlitas and dock sales.
Gift shop: Shirts, glasses, and posters.
Food: Pizzas, sandwiches, and more, including Turkey Pot Pie with Panorama Porter.

Beers brewed: Boundless Session Ale, Mountainous Stout, Monk's Mana, Freewheel IPA, Big Air XX IPA, June Bug Wheat Ale, Panorama Porter, Base Jump Amber Ale, Russian Imperial Stout, Dream-On Pale Ale, Bohemian Pils, Brew Kahuna NW Red Ale, Mighty Beavs Rye Bitter. Seasonals: Sky Bock Maibock. Old Dude Barleywine, Jingle Balz Winter Ale.

The Pick: Mighty Beavs Rye Bitter. Referred to as a "small beer," this is actually made from the second runnings of the Old Dude Barleywine mash and then augmented by 100 pounds of rye. The light body and flavorful malts with spicy rye, complemented by Kiwi hop varietals Pacific Jade and Gem, make it a distinct and ideal pizza pairing.

Steelhead Brewing Co. / McKenzie Brewing Co.

199 East Fifth Avenue,
Eugene, OR 97401
(541) 686-BREW (2739)
SteelheadBrewery.com
McKenzieBrewing.com

Two things that I recall from my first trip to Eugene—before it was home to all but two of the current ten breweries—are that the first living creature I saw when I pulled off I-5 wasn't a human but a duck, and that I had to hurry past another living creature, a hippie playing the banjo, to find safe haven inside the Steelhead brewpub. Founded in 1991, Steelhead Brewing quickly spawned more locations in California (though only the Burlingame one survives). I returned all these years later to find it nearly identical. Sure, the TVs that line the perimeter are modern hi-def flat screens—all the better for mighty Ducks fans to watch football and basketball action—but that's mostly it. Said fans still have the option to sit at the bar or in one of the comfy chairs with upholstery that, to my eye and touch, feels unchanged. The banjo player was gone, but I did have to brake for a brace of ducks waddling across the street as I pulled into downtown.

Oh, there has been one major change: the name. It seems a year before opening, Mad River Brewing down in Humboldt County debuted with an American pale ale it called Steelhead. It makes sense—rivers in both Humboldt County in California and here in the Willamette Valley teem with

Beers brewed: Year-round: Hazy Hef, James Blonde, Raging Rhino Red Ale, Bombay Bomber American Pale Ale, Hopasaurus Rex Imperial IPA. Seasonals: Orange Wheat, St. Bernard Brown, Anniversary Rye IPA, Unforgivable Darkness CDA, Pumpkin Ale, Twisted Meniscus IPA, Heat Miser winter warmer, Keller Kolsch, and a seasonal porter or stout.

The Pick: Raging Rhino Red, the very same beer that launched an impressive chain of GABF medals, remains an even-keeled elixir of toffee-like maltiness and fragrant, floral hops, yielding just 4.4 percent ABV. It's perfect for cheering on the Ducks.

the trout. Anglers flock to the McKenzie River, which runs a mere stone's throw from the brewpub. Hence, it makes perfect sense that Steelhead the brewpub would adopt the name McKenzie Brewing for their bottled offerings since Mad River owns the copyright to the name. All the minutia is best left to the lawyers.

What isn't up for debate or litigation is the fact that Steelhead/McKenzie is the winner of twenty-four GABF medals from 1991 to 2006 (half of which came from the Eugene brewing location). Four of the gold medals were awarded to various stouts (I wish I could've tried the Ghirardelli Square Chocolate Stout made at the Burlingame pub in collaboration with nearby Ghirardelli in San Francisco). And the imperial IPA, Hopasaurus Rex, has taken home both gold and bronze hardware.

It's not just Steelhead/McKenzie beers that win accolades. Steelhead/Bulldog root beers are big among the company's adult and kid fans alike. Co-created by former brewmaster Teri Fahrendorf—who is also the godmother of female brewers for creating the Pink Boots Society for women in the greater beer industry—there really are two separate recipes and two brands. Fahrendorf confirmed there are a sweeter, honey-vanilla version bottled both under the Steelhead and Bulldog labels, and a spicier, draft-only version that, to me, is part of the experience of visiting the brewpub. She said adults tend to prefer the "almost-dry version," sweetened with pure cane sugar, and that "it stands up to ice cream really well." And yes, the menu lists ice cream floats in both root beer and dark beer (stout or porter) formats.

Steelhead Brewing Co. / McKenzie Brewing Co.

Opened: 1991.

Owner: Cordy Jensen.

Brewers: Ted Fagan (head brewer) and Jake Foose (assistant brewer).

System: 10-barrel.

Annual production: 1,300 barrels.

Distribution: Oregon.

Hours: Daily, 11:30 a.m. to close.

Tours: The entire brewery is visible behind bar.

Takeout beer: Kegs, growlers, and McKenzie-brand bombers of core beers.

Gift shop: Shirts, hoodies, and pints on display by the entrance.

Food: Burgers, dogs, sandwiches, salads, and snacky foods.

Extras: Pizza & a Pint for $10.95, Sunday through Thursday after 5 p.m.

Vagabond Brewing

2195 Hyacinth Street Northeast, Salem, OR 97301
(503) 512-9007 • VagabondBrewing.com
Twitter @VagabondBrew

Among the new class of Oregon breweries is Vagabond, so new that when I visited in late 2013 they were still building out the brewery in a 5,500-square-foot warehouse in North Salem (conveniently located right off I-5). But I saw the corner of it with the chalk outline indicating where the bar was going to be. That bar now taps a dozen beers and coincidentally (or purposefully) fits twelve patrons. The core lineup consists of tried and true styles including an IPA, pale ale, red ale, and stout, but I was told to expect a rotating wheat beer with various fruit additions like raspberry or lemon. Even further down the line, they plan on implementing a barrel program for spirit-aged strong ales and wine-aged sour beers. Regulars and visitors can expect to find ever-rotating seasonals and one-off offerings, guest beers or other fermentations, and collaborations.

Those last two, guest beers and collaborations, are among the reasons to get excited about this brewery. The owners—Dean Howes, A.J. Klausen, and James Cardwell—are close friends and all served in the Marines. Cardwell was wounded in action, but luckily he can still wield his mash paddle. Even though they're all under thirty, they've collectively served nine tours and have been to over fifty countries, hence the name Vagabond. They're embracing being the new guys in the Oregon brewing community and helping out others is as much a part of their plan as being helped was. Cardwell got to help brew at other breweries to experience working on this scale. They all brew, but Cardwell wasn't shy about soliciting being an assistant on brew days elsewhere.

Their collaborative spirit doesn't end there. The warehouse that the brewery and taproom anchors is more like a retail mall, and while I don't see them brewing a beer that involves aquariums or crossfit gym equipment, there's already a stout collaboration in the works with Vul Coffee Roasters down the hallway. What's more, since the

Beers brewed: Year-round: Booted Brothers Pale Ale, Wild Ride IPA, Rail Rider Red, Northwest Passage Stout, Blond-ish Ale, All Rye All Rye All Rye, Hyperion Red IPA. Seasonals: Roamin' Chamomile Blonde, Gypsy Wagon Spice Ale, Black Triangle Ale, Jet Lagged Imperial Stout, Belgian Pale, Smoked CDA.

warehouse is so spacious, they built a large stage to host live music as well as comedy nights and author or speaker events. A panoply of televised Oregon games from the Blazers to the Beavers are projected on a large white wall above four awesome dartboards near the billiards table. And with Oktoberfest-style tables so guests aren't isolated from one another, Vagabond holds board game nights. Speaking of those dartboards, Vagabond plans on instituting a regulation tournament for a local league for the right kind of friendly fire.

Vagabond Brewing

Opened: 2014.
Owners: Dean Howes, A.J. Klausen, and James Cardwell.
Brewer: James Cardwell.
System: 4-barrrel.
Annual production: 700 barrels.
Distribution: Salem.
Hours: Monday through Thursday, 3 p.m. to 10 p.m.; Friday, 3 p.m. to midnight; Saturday, noon to midnight; Sunday, noon to 8 p.m.
Tours: By request.
Takeout beer: Growlers.
Gift shop: Hoodies, T-shirts, and growlers.

Viking Braggot Co.

520 Commercial Street, Unit F, Eugene, OR 97402
(541) 653-8371 • DrinkViking.com

This all-braggot brewery—beers made with a substantial amount of honey—dreamt up by University of Oregon Business School pals Daniel McTavish and Addison Stern makes anything but try-it-once novelty beer. Having said that, beyond the four core braggots always on at the taproom, the other two *are* quite likely try-it-now because they can never be duplicated. That aspect comes courtesy of hired guns Weston Zaludek and Perry Ames, childhood friends who, as U of O students, started the Brew of O homebrew club.

Zaludek had me sample many different honeys and showed me a honey unlike anything seen in a plastic teddy bear jar. It's completely raw, uncentrifuged, crystalized, and full of bee particulate. In other words, it's quite literally the bee's knees. And wings. And some stingers. He offered me a whiff. It's robust! I asked if we were to add the sum of these bee parts how many there'd be.

"Twenty or more, easy. I harvested it myself. Oh, oh, oh! I started keeping my own beehives. My brother and I. Six of them."

I asked if he has always been a beekeeper.

"No, but I've always been really into it," he said. "I always thought they were the coolest, but [then] I realized we could make money off them. This is our first harvest ever . . . cherry blossom, madrone, blackberry, wildflower. Stick your finger in that! This is what my childhood tasted like."

Weston's childhood clearly smacked of cherries and I'm curious to know what honey made from the madrone trees that grow along the coast tastes like. Next I wanted to know how they select the various honeys added to each recipe.

"Experience" for one, he said, but continued, "It's more just timing—whatever I can get my

Braggots brewed: Year-round: Reverence Red Ale with orange blossom honey, Battle Axe IPA with wildflower honey. Seasonals: Spring and Summer: Pineapple IPA, Honey Bush, Heather Flower Pale Ale, Gypsy Tears NW Ale. Fall and Winter: Valhalla Belgian Style Pale, Valkyrie Belgian Style Amber. And more.

The Pick: Pineapple IPA. The stars on this Viking ship are the exclusive one-offs, so most of Viking's offerings capture a moment in time. I hope they'll attempt to reproduce this IPA, made juicier than usual with entire raw pineapples plunked in, adding a vibrant pineapple aroma and aftertaste that still somehow emulates tropical fruit-tasting hops.

hands on." They like to use whatever is available in the moment. I call it the Great Cosmic Hive, which Zaludek seconds.

Zaludek told me that his friend, Barry the Bee Shepherd, often gets phone calls from people complaining that their kids are getting stung and asking him to please get rid of the hive. The very thought works Zaludek into a frenzy. "No, don't get rid of it! Let's go save it." This resulted in netting a hive that contained some 40 pounds of honey, all of which was added to a single 3-barrel batch that came to be known as Zombee (*sic*) Midnight Mash. And it wasn't just the amber liquid, but the honeycomb and all. "As we threw this hive from the side of a horse barn into our mash tun, bees stung Perry," Zaludek related. "They're all stuck in the honey—you can't get them out." To clarify, it's not so much that the bees stung Ames, but that unfortunately he grabbed part of the hive where some stingers jutted out. I mentioned how educational—and generally tasty—single-hop IPAs or single-varietal wines are, but that single-hive braggot is a new one for me. "Yep," Zaludek said with a wry smile. "It can never be replicated."

Next, Zaludek described a particular honey as "marshmallow." But what does that mean? "Meadowfoam. It tastes like marshmallows," he said excitedly, further explaining that they added it to a stout aging in a bourbon barrel, currently perched behind the wall of taps in the middle of the warehouse-based brewery. "It should taste like hot chocolate with marshmallows." Or perhaps bourbon s'mores. "We're not sure what to call this one yet."

Though that beer is modeled after a sweet treat, Viking's braggots aren't cloying; they usually contain about 30 percent honey that ferments out to dryness. Some would argue that makes their libations honey ales and not braggots. But Zaludek has a counter argument: "The BJCP [Beer Judge Certification Program] defines braggot as, 'A harmonious blend of mead and beer.' Well, what's harmonious? What do I want to drink a lot of? I don't want to drink something that sucks or is syrupy."

To the crowd gathered in Viking's beer garden—or rather, braggot garden—harmonious is closer to one-third honey content because they, too, are drinking a lot of this stuff. Weston offers me some Pineapple IPA. One whiff and it's clearly got fresh pineapple. It's fruity but not so juicy that you couldn't think it's perhaps just Simcoe hops.

"It's a pretty standard IPA recipe," Zaludek said. "All organic. We used over 50 pounds of sage honey [and] thirty raw, whole pineapples that we hand-chopped. The secret is where I pull the yeast off the bottom and crash it out, then put it into another fermenter over the pineapple, which acts as a fining agent."

That's what I like about Viking Braggot: there's wisdom behind the whimsy. Both Zaludek and Ames have prior professional experience; Weston still moonlights at Oregon Trail Brewery in Corvallis and Ames brewed at now-defunct Wakonda Brewing on the coast. Ames was then working at Falling Sky Brewing in town back when it was still only a homebrew shop."Brew of O had a flyer up and the Viking owners called up. They hired me on, then hired Weston a month later. So we home-brewed a bunch of batches of braggot, but will it work? We liked it, because of course you like your own stuff, but will people drink pints of this?"

Their homebrewer roots always shine through in their techniques and recipes that incorporate not just organic honeys but also organic herbs, teas, or anything else that floats their way.

That reminds me of Candy Mountain, the first thing they made at the braggotery. Zaludek said this beer, the first they made, was a Belgian strong ale featuring lemon peel, elderflower, green and white teas, and golden raspberries, then aged in a Pinot Noir barrel. "And a wild yeast strain that I caught." The members of Brew of O carried the equipment and the ingredients to make a braggot atop Spencer Butte, the highest point in Eugene. It might only be a short hike with a 700-foot elevation gain, but they carried 10 gallons of water and those kettles up there. The one thing they didn't bring was yeast to pitch. "It caught a wild yeast that tasted like hard lemonade," Zaludek said, which a microbiologist dubbed unique to the Willamette Valley.

Viking Braggot Co.

Opened: 2013.
Owners: Daniel McTavish and Addison Stern.
Brewers: Weston Zaludek and Perry Ames.
System: 3-barrel.
Annual production: 160 barrels.
Distribution: Eugene.
Hours and tours: Friday and Saturday, 4 p.m. to 10 p.m.
Takeout beer: Growlers and dock sales.
Food: Rotating food trucks.
Gift shop: T-shirts and barware.

Bend and Central

The picturesque and playful Deschutes River courses through this outdoor playground where the Cascade Mountains peer out over the high desert, providing a pristine water source for the twenty-six breweries that call this comparatively isolated paradise home. (There are more to come, and Bend resident Jon Abernathy maintains updates on his longest-running beer blog, TheBrewSite.com.) The town of Bend, which roughly eighty thousand people call home, receives much of the spotlight, but this is not a single-town destination. Even Visit Bend's highly successful *Bend Ale Trail*—a passport encouraging tourists to visit the breweries in the region—includes a brewery up in Sisters. It doesn't hurt that Sisters is the location of Central Oregon's annual *Fresh Hop Festival*.

Keeping watch of Sisters along its western ridge horizon are the *Three Sisters*, three volcanic peaks each topping 10,000 feet in elevation. Ogling them from not too far away is *Mt. Bachelor*, where winter and spring long *Mt. Bachelor Ski Resort* lavishes 3,300 feet of vertical across 3,600 acres on its visitors. Once that snow has melted, alpine enthusiasts who switch from two skis to two wheels see why many of the country's top mountain bikers live in the area.

Smith Rock State Park is another huge draw and the kind of setting people might describe as "pretty as a postcard," but you can't capture the wildness of this jagged, welded tuff (a.k.a. compressed volcanic ash) with its pinks and yellows. It soars straight up from the aptly named Crooked River and invites climbers at every level—elementary to insanity—up its five hundred climbing routes.

From hiking to fishing to kayaking, Central Oregon offers unparalleled outdoor opportunities. *Wanderlust Tours* is an adventure company that will take you spelunking down into the **Lava Caves** or paddling on the **Cascade Lakes**. The company also serves as a tasting guide through Cascade Lakes Brewing's beers (talk about synergy) on the Views and Brews Canoe trip; and return in the winter for Shoes, Brews & Views, even if snowshoeing sounds like more work.

Having this much fun is hard, thirsty work, but Bendites (including around 170,000 in the "metro" area) are up to the task. One local artist, known simply as the Beer Painter, uses porters instead of paints to create hoppy creations such as reimagining Rodin's *The Thinker* as *The Drinker*. Her work is displayed and available in the **Old Ironworks Arts District**, next to the ethereal **Sparrow Bakery**, purveyors of "ocean rolls." Neither croissants nor cinnamon rolls, these edible masterpieces are made of croissant dough rolled up like a sticky bun but with cardamom, vanilla, and an adult-level of sweetness.

As for visitors, there are accommodations for every budget, activities for every proclivity and skill set, and dining options for every taste. And then there's the grand poopah of family resorts, the 3,300-acre community of **Sunriver**, with golfing, rafting, kayaking, biking, and relaxing (a spa is like a brewpub for your nerves, right?). Naturally, the resort town welcomed one of the region's newest brewpubs, **Sunriver Brewing**, as well as the tiny but welcoming **Mountain Jug Beer Shop** for pints, growler fills, and bottles.

The Ale Apothecary

61517 River Road, Bend, OR 97701
(541) 318-9143 • TheAleApothecary.com
Twitter @DrugstoreBrewer

The Ale Apothecary will never be a spot on the well-trodden, sloshy Bend Ale Trail. It's ten miles out of downtown, way up in the mountains. There's no pub. No merchandise wall. Founder Paul Arney is a man who, after fifteen years at Deschutes working his way up to assistant brewmaster, set up his own brewery and has the finished Finnish *kuurna* to show for it.

Before I get to the family history of pharmacists that led to the Apothecary name, I should explain that the *kuurna* looks like a trough, or even a canoe, that Arney and some very helpful friends hand-carved over a few months out of an Engelmann spruce tree from his property above Bend, where a full dozen breweries also call the area home. The *kuurna* is used as a mash tun—it holds about 2 barrels by volume—for his Finnish-style Sahati ale and is indicative of how every little thing here is done by hand.

Arney's mom married a pharmacist. Druggists go back three generations in his family. And while he's not a pharmacist, the recipes he alchemizes tend to put his patients—er, patrons—in good spirits. "I do have this family lineage of people who go out in the land and gather stuff to make people feel better," he said.

Arney said his dad never pressured him to follow in his footsteps. "He saw the writing on the wall. There's no future in running a small drug store" the way his predecessors had. The sad irony, of course, is that there certainly was no future in operating your own brewing company in that same era when the industry was hell-bent on consolidation in exactly the same way Walmart, Walgreen's, Rite Aid, and Kroger have obliterated indie apothecaries.

On the flipside, young Arney was pressured into pursuing the sciences. "Being creative wasn't encouraged." Despite an undergraduate degree in

Beers brewed: Year-round: Sahalie, (TBFKA) La Tache, Sahati. Seasonals: Spencer, El Cuatro, Be Still, Sahalien.

The Pick: Sahalie. Once poured, this complex wild ale relinquishes a mélange of tropical, citrus, and pomaceous fruits, fermented on a bed of *Lactobacillus* and Joker's Wild yeasts, resulting in a refreshingly tart and acidic beer grounded by detectable Cascade dry-hopping.

geology, "At heart," he declared, "I'm driven to be an artist." As an under-grad, a chance encounter with a brewer up in Washington led him to become interested in and pursue his livelihood in brewing. While study-ing at UC Davis's elite brewing program, Arney shot off letters to some three hundred breweries around the Pacific Northwest. Deschutes, the fifth largest craft brewery and twelfth biggest overall in the country, was one of only two to respond (with a job offer, no less). That's part of the reason we can enjoy their Flemish brown-style The Dissident.

Arney stands simultaneously at the center and the precipice of the craft-brewing industry. While some would argue it is an industrial soci-ety, there are brewers like Arney who still view it as a partially unchar-tered frontier. "I saw this movement of people interested in esoteric beers," he told me. "Brewers are science driven. I want this to be art driven. It's liberating."

His initial blog posts laid out his vision for being the "American Orval" in that he was going to only brew one ale, called Sahalie, and do it well. To mention one casual yet salient matter: "This is not a farmhouse brewery. This is a mountain brewery." When Arney's fami-ly moved here, they didn't have running water. They fetched it from the stream below. His one-beer–style concept has since evolved into six brands. One of them, Spencer, is Sahalie ale with the addition of wild black currants picked from the river that runs alongside the mountain brewery.

By converting his garage into the brewery, Arney is saving money, rather than renting an industrial space downtown, but this also means he's not doing what the other eleven breweries in Bend are doing. He's happily a part of the community but proudly removed from it. He's a jovial recluse.

Ten miles and a world away from Deschutes, Arney works in his brewery, surrounded by about two dozen oak barrels for aging, each emblazoned with names of departed relatives, including Paul and Pauline, his grandparents. The barrel named Staci isn't used for gentle maturation—it's actually his mash tun named for his wife. ("It's sym-bolic. She gives me a lot.") I stuck my nose into a barrel marked La Gordita, which was brimming with foam that smelled like a cocktail made with peach and watermelon Jolly Ranchers. The liquid's on its way to becoming El Cuatro, which is aged in brandy barrels, complete-ly unhopped, and fermented with a blend microflora. That includes Oregon-cultivated Wyeast yeasts, a pair of *Brettanomyces* strains, and whatever floats in on the winds via the windows he leaves open during fermentation. "Every beer has brett," Arney said of the notoriously wild and wily critters. "Can't avoid [them] at this point."

At one point, I'm handed a beer called La Tache. It's 8 percent alcohol but tastes only half that potent. Arney credits a long, slow fermentation, which doesn't produce fusel alcohols like other stronger beers do, rendering them enjoyable only once the booziness burns off. He refers to La Tache (technically named The Beer Formerly Known As La Tache, or just TBFKA, with the backstory involving a small puppy, a large French winery, and the desire to not get litigious) as a table beer, a sort of Northwest Berliner Weisse. It's light, slightly tart, and awesome.

There's know-how and applied science in these beers, but there's plenty of Mother Nature's imagination as well. And they're only available in a handful of retail accounts around Oregon: Portland, Eugene, and of course Bend retailers such as Broken Top Bottle Shop and Ale Café, plus a few in Vermont as a quirk of craft beer distribution. There's also his Ale Club, the guaranteed and direct way to procure his latest prescriptions, but it's capped at one hundred and sold out in no time flat. Arney did promise that he plans to grow that number slightly.

Arney can't make a fortune off the amount of beer he's turning out. He could spend less time working on it, but his philosophy on labors of love is that they should entail as much work as possible. In lieu of corking and caging the 750-milliliter bottles, he and Staci hand-tie champagne knots around each bottle. He said it's about "connecting with each bottle," but also about branding, going so far as to call it "metaphysical marketing." It really is an outward expression of how, as I said, every little thing here is done by hand. "I want my kids to see me follow my dreams," Arney said, referring to his son, Spencer, and daughter, Sahalie (pronounced "sa-HAY-lee").

Like the river water and the spontaneous metabolizing critters, even when not seen they can still be heard or just sensed running wild. And since Arney "can't pay the bills writing a novel or poetry," he concluded that making ales that are entirely influenced by history (and biochemistry and botany) would be both "art-driven" and "liberating," so he might as well make a go of it brewing what he does best.

The Ale Apothecary

Opened: 2012.
Owner and brewer: Paul Arney.
System: 1.5-barrel.
Annual production: 50 barrels.
Distribution: Oregon and Vermont.
Tours: By appointment only.
Takeout beer: 750-milliliter bottles.

Below Grade Brewing

BELOW GRADE BREWING

SERIOUSLY UNDERGROUND ALES

Bend, OR 97701
(541) 408-1050 • BelowGradeBrewing.com
Twitter @BGBDean

Below Grade's motto, "Seriously Underground Ales," is an apt one since it's not only a super small batch nanobrewery (all of a whole barrel), but also literally in Dean and Bridget Wise's basement. Having been bit by the homebrew bug in 1992, when the Wises built their home, Dean laid out the basement with his home brewery in mind, right down to floor drainage.

"As a homebrewer, you can do what you want," said Dean. He has Richie Cunningham boyish looks yet a salt-and-pepper goatee (when he sports one). "I never paid attention to the cost of ingredients because it was for me." And as a commercial brewer? "Now I've continued that. I've changed nothing." In this way, he said his beers don't just compete with bigger commercial craft beers but also fit into the top tier. And yes, he still only brews what he likes. No crazy adjuncts or bizarre flavors here.

One arena Below Grade certainly doesn't compete in is distribution. The Wises self-distribute their beer to a handful of accounts around town, and the bottles fly off shelves nearly as quickly as they land. Dean said when he delivered to Cork, the wine and beer bottle shop, "all five cases of bottled IPA sold the first day." You can nearly always find a Below Grade beer or two on tap at Broken Top Bottle Shop and Ale Café (named after the extinct composite volcano twenty miles due west), except when they're sold out. When I met Dean and Bridget there, the IPA and Volksvitzen were on tap. The latter is a South German-style weissbock, also called a weizenbock, which is easier to wrap your head around if you think of it as

Beers brewed: Validation Imperial IPA, Old School English-style Ale, Volksvitzen South German Weissbock, Jackaboy Pale Ale, Dangerous Kate Imperial CDA, Nevermind White IPA, Identity Crisis Farmhouse-style Sour IPA, RB/X Red/Brown Experimental Ale.

The Pick: Call Dangerous Kate a Black IPA or an Imperial CDA, it doesn't matter to Dean. It's simply about the tango of prominent hops and roasted malts entangled in the nose and on the tongue. At 8.5 percent alcohol and over 100 IBUs, perhaps it's more of the Lambada.

an imperial Bavarian hefeweizen. And this strong wheat beer clocks in at 6.7 percent alcohol.

The one place you're sure to find their ultra-fresh beers, fittingly, is the NorthWest Crossing Farmers Market on Saturdays all summer long. It runs from 10 a.m. to 2 p.m., and as Dean recalled, "The first day at the farmers market, we sold 200 pints, even with those hours. You'd be surprised how many people bought a beer at ten o'clock. And we were the last to close." You can fill your reusable bag with bombers to go along with your broccoli and bok choy, or enjoy a glass or even a tasting flight right at the market. Dean and Bridget are always on hand with six taps, and they're happy to sell you a growler or refill your own. I recommend filling yours with Jackaboy Pale Ale or, for the undaunted, Dangerous Kate Imperial Cascadian Dark Ale. The names are not happenstance. They're named after their teenaged twins. (Dean's father gave Jack that nickname, while Kate is actually their daughter's middle name.)

Dean, who grew up here and sends his kids to his old middle school, says his goal is to turn Below Grade into a vehicle that can pay their mortgage and put their kids through school. Beyond that, Jack has apparently expressed interest in becoming a brewer, a notion that met with his dad's full support. To do that, Dean knows they'll need to ramp up production big time, probably to 1,500 barrels a year. Having said that, "I have no aspirations of running a 50-barrel brewhouse," he expressed. "I like having a connection with the people that consume your product."

Below Grade Brewing

Opened: 2011.

Owners: Dean and Bridget Wise.

Brewer: Dean Wise.

System: 1-barrel.

Annual production: 50 barrels.

Distribution: Central Oregon.

Gift shop: Find Below Grade gear on the website.

Extras: Dean and Bridget offer six beers at the NorthWest Crossing Farmers Market (corner of NW Crossing Drive and NW John Fremont Street by Compass Park, www.NorthWestCrossing.com).

Bend Brewing Co.

1019 Northwest Brooks Street, Bend, OR 97701
(541) 383-1599 • BendBrewingCo.com

Bend Brewing Co., strictly referred to as BBC by Bendites, is very much a local's hangout. Although former brewmaster Tonya Cornett built a legacy with her award-winning beers like Hop Head Imperial IPA and Outback X (their most decorated beer) that led to being named Best Small Brewpub at the 2008 World Beer Cup, this isn't the beer nerd hangout in town. It is, nevertheless, a strong pull with tourists given its prime location overlooking the section of Deschutes River known as Mirror Pond, both in frosty winters and gorgeous summers when a seat on the back patio is prime real estate.

Founded by Jerry Fox and Dave Hill, who had already been business partners at Bend Wood Products, these two had the foresight to realize Bend was destined to be more than just a one-brewery town. (It took seven years for Bend to receive its second brewery after Deschutes opened in 1988, compared to ushering in seven more over the last two years.) "We had no experience in brewing beer, only drinking beer," Fox used to say. Not only did they need help brewing the beer, they also needed help managing the house. In short order, he called his daughter, Wendi Day, who was working and living in Seattle, to ask if she'd consider the position and move back to Bend. Fortuitously, she and her husband did plan to move back, even if not initially on that accelerated schedule, but it worked out for the best. Her dad retired in 2000, though as Day explained, "He continues to consult and help around the brewery to this day, for which I am truly grateful. I could not have asked for a better teacher in business and customer service."

Beers brewed: Year-round: High Desert Hefeweizen, Metolius Golden Ale, Elk Lake IPA, Outback Old Ale, Pinnacle Porter. Seasonals: Big Eddy Bitter, Paulina Pale Ale, Hop Head Imperial IPA, Nitro Oatmeal Stout, Doppelbock, Outback X, Ching Ching Pomegranate-Hibiscus Berliner Weisse, Wicked Medicine, One Loudah, and Scottish Heart.

The Pick: Ching Ching. With a strong lineup including highly decorated Outback X Strong Ale, picking just one was tough. Ching Ching isn't just delicious and refreshing—it's one of Oregon's most coveted beers. As pink as it is tart, it derives the former from hibiscus flowers, but the tartness stems from *Lactobacillus*—and the puréed pomegranate of course—which gives this otherwise traditional German-style sour ale an amazing finish.

With a pub this small, attentive service is not a problem. It's typically packed with families or groups of friends, and barflies nab the stools in the sliver of the bar that excludes minors. It just so happens that's the spot that enables patrons to peer upward into the brewhouse, visible through three-paneled picture windows. More in the line of vision is the wall of medals and ribbons lining the wall. Many were earned by Cornett, and many of the newer ones are still for beers that she wrote the recipes for but current brewer Ian Larkin has taken over admirably.

"The transition from Tonya to Ian could not have gone more smoothly," said Day. "Ian confidently took on the challenge of head brewer after working with Tonya for three years, which is evident through all of the awards Ian has won during his tenure." Putting a fine point on that tip, she specified the amount at seventeen, but that's just so far. Among Larkin's well-received creations is Scottish-style Scottish Heart and Belgian-style Wicked Medicine, a dark, strong ale that earned a gold medal at the North American Beer Awards in 2014 and bursts with over-ripe fruit and mulling spice flavors.

With ten taps, there's something for everyone, but everyone seems to love Outback X, the aforementioned winningest beer in the house. It's an old ale, meaning it's not quite a barleywine, nor is it a double IPA. At 9.5 percent ABV, it rather tastes like dried fig and pear and some rum-soaked raisins and warms more with each swallow. For winters I'll take Outback X, and in the summertime I want Ching Ching to quench my thirst. As for in between and any other time, I'll happily take Hophead Imperial IPA.

Bend Brewing Co.

Opened: 1995.

Owner: Wendi Day.

Brewers: Ian Larkin (brewmaster) and Josh Harned (assistant brewer).

System: 10-barrel.

Annual production: 1,000 barrels.

Distribution: Oregon.

Hours: Monday through Saturday, 11:30 a.m. to 11 p.m.; Sunday, 11:30 a.m. to 9 p.m.

Tours: By appointment.

Takeout beer: Bombers and growler fills.

Gift shop: Shirts, hoodies, and hats line the walls as you enter. Pint glasses and hydroflasks, too.

Food: Burgers and sandwiches rule this beer-friendly menu, with half-priced apps from 4 p.m. to 6 p.m., but I dig the grilled veggie muffaletta.

Boneyard Beer

37 Northwest Lake Place, Suite B, Bend, OR 97701
(541) 323-2325 • BoneyardBeer.com
Twitter @BoneyardBeer

Heading to the Boneyard tasting room from the office or the brewhouse itself, it helps to suck in your beer gut when squeezing between the eighteen fermentation tanks crammed into a former garage, since the space was designed to hold, well, far fewer than that. Said tanks range from 20 to 40 and up to 60 barrels apiece. Still, sixteen of them are the black top hats out of which the magical rabbit that is Boneyard RPM IPA emerges.

The tasting room is one of the only places where you're guaranteed to find RPM available; its rampant popularity cannot be overstated. Cofounder and brewmaster Tony Lawrence said that practically 90 percent of their production—they produced 15,000 barrels in 2013 and will do 25,000 in 2014—is strictly RPM. And they still cannot make it fast enough to serve markets from Eugene up to Seattle.

"Brew 1" is the name for the original 20-barrel brewhouse that remains in effect for the foreseeable future. How the roof even stays on considering how many kegs are stacked up and seemingly bursting through the ceiling, I'm not sure. For the sake of Lawrence and his partners, the husband-and-wife team of Clay and Melodee Storey, I really hope "Brew 2" affords more breathing room, both in the literal sense and so they can stop pulling their hair out over the best problem a brewery can have: keeping their accounts in liquid hops.

Once Brew 2 is operational it'll help them reach their projected production of 40,000 barrels, thanks to fermenters with up to 200-barrel capacities. "Our goal is to make the most beer possible," said Lawrence. "I sure hope that we're staying focused on making exceptional quality beer for the region, first and foremost. We're a sold-out brewery, and the retailer and distributor is always

Beers brewed: RPM IPA, Hop Venom DIPA, Notorious Triple IPA, Armored Fist Imperial CDA, Black 13, Diablo Rojo, Fuego Rojo (with habaneros), The Backbone (espresso stout), Wit Shack Wit, Femme Fatale, Skunkape IRA, Bone-A-Fide Pale Ale, Bone Light ISA, Suge Knite Imperial Stout, Shotgun ISA (rotating single hop).

The Pick: RPM IPA. Bright, juicy, and explosive, this is an IPA that lives up to the hype. Equal parts West Coast IPA (pale and pineapply) and Northwest IPA (piney and aromatic but not overly bitter at "only" 50 IBUs), the four varietals of local hops make this a classic Oregon IPA.

clamoring for more." They're brewing so constantly they need to replenish their grains every other day. They bought a canning line but never had the time (or space!) to use it, so they'll remain draft only, also "for the foreseeable future." They're aware these are great problems to have, and it's all the irresistible RPM's fault.

Lawrence and Storey sort of shrug off the IPA's success as just science. But there's no denying there's something about this beer. "If you give everyone the same recipe, same raw materials in the same day and say, 'Go at it,' you'll get as many different outcomes as participants," Lawrence theorized. It's true. And they'd likely all come out redolent of grapefruit and pineapple, pine needles, and a touch of caramel. Asked to break down RPM's best attributes, he didn't hesitate: "It's clean, balanced, and interesting. Now of course I want interesting to be in that number one spot, but I'd never push cleanliness down to position two or three."

That leaves little tank space for Boneyard's other brands that, trust me, are equally worth ordering. Yes, there's the Double IPA Hop Venom and the Triple IPA Notorious for those for whom the amply hopped RPM doesn't quite do it. Newer to the résumé is Bone Light, dubbed an India Session Ale because of its hop bill—100 percent Mosaic—but at 4 percent ABV with a light gold color, it's modeled on pilsners. But Boneyard is not a one-trick pony, or a one-hop rabbit. Their dark beers include Black 13 (thirteen total ingredients, 13 IBUs), The Backbone (stout with some chocolate and cold-pressed coffee in conjunction with Bend's Backporch Roasters), and the corpulent Suge Knite Imperial Stout. These three are all richly delectable, even if their collective 66 IBUs register less than Hop Venom's 70 IBUs. Perhaps the middle ground is Armored Fist, an imperial Cascadian Dark Ale with a powerful punch of 80 IBUs, though it's hardly middle of the road.

Given the difficulty of finding the variety (or any Boneyard beers with regularity), it's always best to go straight to the source to sample their beers. Brew 1, the only location with a public tasting room, is in a funky industrial part of town. The first taste is free; after that you're hooked. In addition to finding a wide array of hoppy manifestations, if you're lucky you'll find Diablo Rojo (a solid, malty, Northwest red ale) alongside its habanero-infused hermano, Fuego Rojo. There's a surprising amount of chili beers around the state, and the heat varies with each batch, but this one's gotta lotta burn to it.

Speaking of variation, one thing Lawrence and the crew aren't worried about with Brew 2 is "flavor matching," keeping RPM and the family completely consistent with how they tasted off Brew 1. "I'm excited about making RPM better," said Lawrence. The 40-barrel system, like

Brew 1, is a hodge-podge or "boneyard" of parts, but the main skeleton was once nestled in Yakima at Bert Grant's, the very first brewpub in post–Prohibition America. I like knowing that, sort of like how in olden days brewers would take the mysterious sludge from the last batch (flocculated yeast) and inoculate the new batch with it, the future of Boneyard beer has a taste of history.

Boneyard Beer

Opened: 2010.

Owners: Tony Lawrence; Clay and Melodee Storey.

Brewmaster: Tony Lawrence.

System: 20-barrel at Brew 1 and 40-barrel at Brew 2.

Annual production: 25,000 barrels.

Distribution: Oregon and Washington.

Hours: Daily, 11 a.m. to 6 p.m.

Tours: By request at Brew 1 only.

Takeout beer: Growlers only.

Gift shop: Shirts, hoodies, hats, socks, baby onesies, aprons, sunglasses, and glassware.

Food: None.

Bridge 99 Brewery

63063 Layton Avenue, Bend, OR 97701
(541) 280-1690 • Facebook.com/pages/Bridge-99-Brewery/
330744700395411

It's fortuitous that the angler's paradise on the Metolius River near the town of Sisters is marked by Bridge 99 Brewery. And that number is, according to legend, how many bottles of beer are on the wall, but in the case of one of Bend's newest breweries, there are zero bottles of Bridge 99 on the wall.

Bridge 99 beers, such as their Wizard Falls IPA or Candle Creek, a pale ale that owner-brewer Trever Hawman simply refers to as an "American ale," are all named for features in the Willamette National Forest near the brewery's namesake. You can only find them on draft and only reliably at Wubba's BBQ Shack (63055 Layton Ave.) forty miles away in Bend. Sometimes there's a tap at the Platypus Pub where the taproom-turned-brewpub collaborates with Hawman on Platypus IPA. But the exclusivity makes Wubba's—a Klamath Falls institution that recently opened a second shack in Bend—something of a de facto Bridge 99 brewpub. This works for Hawman, who's already eyeing a spot directly across the street to expand his 1.5-barrel brewery into 4 or 7 barrels and create a smokin' beer garden.

After I enjoyed a flight of his beers and a plate of Wubba's nachos loaded with beef, pork, and chicken, Hawman excitedly showed me around the space he's envisioning. He has lots of ideas and infectious enthusiasm, so here's to hoping everything unfolds according to plan.

Bridge 99 Brewery

Opened: 2013.
Owner and brewer: Trever Hawman.
System: 1.5-barrel.
Annual production: 300 barrels.
Tours: By appointment.
Distribution: Bend.
Food: BBQ courtesy of Wubba's BBQ Shack, (WubbaBBQShack.com).

Beers brewed: Year-round: Camp Sherman ISA, Brown Trout Stout, Candle Creek American Ale, Wizard Falls IPA, Rock Crawler Red. Seasonals: Winter Trail (vanilla oatmeal brown sugar dark chocolate caffè stout).

The Pick: Camp Sherman ISA. Whether it's a session IPA or just a light-bodied pale ale, Camp Sherman is appreciably clean and aromatic.

Cascade Lakes Brewing Co.

2141 Southwest First Street, Redmond, OR 97756
(541) 923-3110 • CascadeLakes.com
Twitter @CascadeLakesAle

With the recent release of Cascade Lakes Brewing Co.'s twentieth anniversary IPA, I realized their beers are like your old college sweatpants that you still like to wear at breakfast twenty years later. So many pairs of pajamas or flannel pants have entered your pajama drawer since, but Old Reliable remains comfy and warm.

Cascade Lakes has been brewing in Redmond since 1994—before all but one of them (Deschutes), though the brothers who started Cascade sold the business in 2000. But with flagship styles such as a beer they just call Rooster Ale, really a vintage pale ale plus a blond ale, a brown, a porter, and an IPA, it still has that cozy mid-nineties vibe.

Having long outgrown the original 4-barrel brewing system, the brewery, still in its original location, now brews 25 barrels at a time. What they've gained in beer capacity they've lost in people capacity; in lieu of a tasting room there are now five public houses (7th Street Brew House and Red Dog Depot in Redmond, Cascade Lakes Lodge and Cascade West in Bend, and Tumalo Tavern in Tumalo.) But it's 7th Street Brew House and Cascade Lakes Lodge that are truly the flagship pubs, as opposed to taprooms that have a bunch of Cascade Lakes beers.

While Bend draws more après ski and après river or trails visitors, Redmond hosts a horseshoe tournament. Seventh Street is housed in an actual house that segued into a pub back in 1996. The manger, Kevin, has been with the company since 2002 and is a card-carrying member of the National Horseshoe Pitchers Association. What's more, he pitched himself to second place at the Northwest finals up in Yakima, Washington.

During my recent visit, I saw what epitomizes this pub. A gentleman was celebrating his ninetieth birthday here surrounded by his entire family, many spilling out past the fire pit and onto the

Beers brewed: Year-round: Blonde Bombshell, 20" Brown, Monkey Face Porter, Cyclops IPA, Rooster Tail Ale. Seasonals: Project X NW Pale Ale, Slippery Slope, Snow Park Pale, Waist Deep Weiss, Paulina Lake Pilsner, India Red Ale, Riverside Red, Into the Darkness CDA, Silverback Imperial Stout, as well as draft-only beers.

The Pick: 20" Brown is a well-built, malt-centered ale, a touch lighter in color than other browns but heavy where it counts: in the nuts, that is, the nutty, creamy flavor that pairs well with many menu items.

regulation 50-foot horseshoe court (40 feet from pin to pin, less for women and the elderly, just like golf). When you make it to ninety, you get to celebrate anywhere you want. Don, the birthday boy, chose the Brew House. As if the point needed hammering home, there's a sign above the bar that reads, "Friends and Family gather here."

Admittedly, it's not a beer geek crowd, although the mug club is quite popular among local hopheads. There are thirteen taps with house beer, plus one for Coors Light. But Rooster Ale is the same pale ale that it's been since day one. Blonde Bombshell is light bodied and lightly hopped with Liberty. They even call it "low carb" on the menu. My personal favorite is the throwback style of brown ale. It's an endangered species of the craft-brewing ecosystem but the malty-nutty 20" Brown shows why it's worth preserving.

Cascade Lakes Brewing Co.

Opened: 1994.

Owners: Rick Orazetti, Doug Kutella, Ron Kutella, and Chris Justema.

Brewers: John Van Duzer (brewmaster), Peter Bishop, and Phil Brey.

System: 25-barrel.

Annual production: 5,000 barrels.

Distribution: Oregon, Washington, and Idaho.

Hours: 7th Street Brew House: Monday through Thursday, 11:30 a.m. to 10 p.m.; Friday and Saturday, 11:30 a.m. to 11 p.m.; Sunday, noon to 10 p.m. Cascade Lakes Lodge: Sunday through Thursday, 11:30 a.m. to midnight; Friday and Saturday, 11:30 a.m. to 1 a.m.

Tours: By appointment only.

Takeout beer: Bottles, growlers, and dock sales.

Gift shop: Garb and glassware.

Food: Nothing at the brewery. Pub menus feature burgers, salads, starters (mostly of the fried finger food variety), and pizza.

Extras: Very family-friendly (kids eat free on Sundays at the Lodge). Patios are dog-friendly (Bow Wow Bingo every Thursday with half the fees benefiting the Humane Society). Horseshoe season begins the first Monday in May.

Other locations: 7th Street Brew House (855 SW Seventh St., Redmond; 541-923-1795). Cascade Lakes Lodge: 1441 SW Chandler Ave., Suite 100, Bend; 541-388-4998).

Crux Fermentation Project

50 Southwest Division Street, Bend,
OR 97702
(541) 385-3333 • CruxFermentation.com
Twitter @CruxBrew

The brewing company, er, fermentation project from industry vet Larry Sidor is at the heart of what makes Bend great. It's as close to Bend's nexus of Arizona Avenue and Highway 97 as a business can get. It's got a cozy patio to gather during Sundowner (their happy hour). And despite being in the Old Mill Zone in a former AAMCO station, you can enjoy a beer with unfettered views of Mt. Bachelor, which lords over this majestic high desert playground. Obviously in this burg, dubbed Best Dog Town in America by *Dog Fancy* magazine, the patio's Fido-friendly. But, being a brewer, the name and logo (four arrows directing outward and four aimed centrally) capture Sidor's crucial belief in what such facilities should be about: beer, specifically, and the beer experience in general.

"They're intentionally interpretive," cofounder Paul Evers said of those arrows indicating Crux's direction(s). They point to the four basics of brewing (malt, hops, yeast, and water), but also explore the possible directions beer can go in (which I interpret as gravity, color, bitterness, and flavor, or a more visceral, historical palate).

Brewmaster and cofounder Sidor previously brought us gorgeous beers like Deschutes's complex and mutable imperial stout The Abyss and the experimental IPA Hop Henge. Before that eight-year stint, the Oregon native (mostly Corvallis and La Grande) spent twenty-three years working at Olympia, including after it fell under Pabst's ownership. The beers he crafts today are a far, far cry from "Oly," PBR, and those American light lagers.

Among his range of native styles exists a handful of IPAs. Instead of focusing on hops grown nearby, his Outcast relies on the pungent flowers from Down Under. Full-bodied Half Hitch is an imperial IPA made with Mosaic hops, a personal favorite bursting with guava-voom. And though Off Leash

Beers brewed: Year-round: Outcast IPA, Off Leash NW Session Ale, Half Hitch Imperial IPA, Impasse Saison, Doublecross Strong Dark Belgian Ale, On the Fence Northwest Pale Ale, Porter, Nitro Stout, Pilsner. Seasonals: Scotch, Marzen, experimental IPAs. Brewdeck Series: Belgian Gale. Banished Series: Tough Love Russian Imperial Stout, Barrel-aged Doublecross, Freakcake Oud Bruin, Better Off Red Flanders Red Ale

The Pick: Half Hitch. Mosaic hops are the varietal fronting this well-rounded imperial IPA where pilsner malt allows the hefty body and 10 percent ABV to defer to aromas and flavors of a veritable fruit cocktail of guava and mango.

isn't an IPA, it's a playful puppy with Citra, Centennial, and Crystal for fans of the burgeoning Session IPA style. They also access experimental hop varietals that will showcase throughout, and not just American ones.

As Outcast indicates, Crux loves looking to points beyond for inspiration, from Flanders and Franconia to Bavaria and Bohemia. The Banished Series (banished to oak barrels), includes Freakcake Oud Bruin and a barrel-aged Better Off Red Flanders Red. Freakcake contains roasted Belgian aromatic malts and fruity esters augmented by lemon and orange zest, then refermented with *Brettanomyces* and flecked with sour cherries, raisins, cranberries, figs, dates, and currants for a mildly acidic finish. The slightly tart Better Off Red, styled after the "Burgundies of Belgium," is put in Pinot Noir barrels for nearly a year to pick up oak and yield cherry flavors. Between Olympia and Deschutes, Sidor also had delved into winemaking, which explains his vintner's touch.

Evers's professional credits include creating packaging and branding for other breweries (e.g. Deschutes), so I thank him for not only packaging Crux beers in 500-milliliter bottles, but also putting stronger Banished beers in 375-milliliter bottles. The metric measurements dovetail with their 10-hectoliter brewery rather than an 8-point-something-barrel one. It's both attractive and state of the art, with the copper kettles displayed nicely to the left of the bar, proffering twenty taps of mostly house beer, and a dining area upon entering. Fermenters are showcased behind the bar. Inside it's all wood (both reclaimed and casks used for aging). Another "rustic" feature is the gooey Grilled Cheesy that might make you lower your lids in tasty delight, but keep 'em open until the last rays disappear behind the mountains.

Crux Fermentation Project

Opened: 2012.

Owners: Larry Sidor and Paul Evers.

Brewer: Larry Sidor (brewmaster).

System: 10-hectoliter (8.5-barrel).

Annual production: 1,900 barrels.

Distribution: Bend, Portland, and Seattle.

Hours: Tuesday through Sunday, 11:30 a.m. to 10 p.m.

Tours: Ask any server—all of them have been trained.

Takeout beer: Growlers, bottles including the Tasting Room Series, and dock sales.

Gift shop: Apparel and glassware.

Food: Gastropub offerings. The Grilled Cheesy comes on Asiago-crusted, spent-grain bread with pepper jack, cheddar, and goat cheese with diced bacon and spicy pickles.

Events: Cruxapalooza anniversary (last Saturday in June) and Cruxtoberfest (September).

Deschutes Brewery

901 Southwest Simpson Avenue, Bend, OR 97702
(541) 385-8606 • DeschutesBrewery.com
Twitter @DeschutesBeer

Gary Fish founded Deschutes Brewpub in 1988 as the first brewery in Bend. Since the eighth annual GABF in 1990, Deschutes has brought home the festival's hardware all but three years (a whopping forty medals and counting). Black Butte Porter is the best-selling porter in America, and The Abyss Imperial Stout has been perennially ranked one of the best beers on the planet (because it is) since its debut in 2006. As a sort of marriage of the two, the brewers have concocted an annual Imperial Black Butte; they started with Black Butte XX to commemorate the porter's twentieth anniversary in 2008.

Deschutes—named after the glorious river that runs through Bend—maintains the original 12-barrel brewpub downtown and expanded into a veritable compound a mile away where the 220-barrel brewhouse (plus a 50-barrel system on the side) offers tours, a museum, and of course one of the largest gift shops you'll find at a brewery.

Deschutes is now the country's fifth largest craft brewery. Fish realized very early on that they could stake their claim in the frontier that was eighties' microbrewing with scary-looking opaque beers. "We initially had three beers: Cascade Ale, Bachelor Bitter, and Black Butte Porter. Light, medium, and dark [in color]," he told me. He noted that their early distributor had mused that they "could duke it out in lighter-color beers, or take dark beers and own that smaller pie. [Because] nobody's pushing on this end of the envelope, let's establish the dark beer market."

I'm not sure what's more impressive then—that Black Butte is the biggest porter in the country, or that it's their second bestseller after their

Beers brewed: Year-round: Mirror Pond Pale Ale, Black Butte Porter, Obsidian Stout, Inversion IPA, Chainbreaker White IPA, Fresh Squeezed IPA, Green Lakes Organic Ale, Armory XPA, Cinder Cone Red, Pine Mountain Pilsner, Bachelor Bitter (pub draft only). Seasonals: Red Chair NWPA and Jubelale. Bond Street Pub Series: Hop Trip and Hop in the Dark CDA. Reserve Series: The Abyss Imperial Stout and The Dissident Oud Bruin. Conflux Series: Collaboration beers.

The Pick: The Abyss is a seasonal imperial stout wherein each vintage gets a tweaked treatment involving adjuncts and barrel-aged components, with consistently divine results. It offers the sensation of drinking blackout fudge cake with espresso frosting, or perhaps fig compote, or vanilla bean gastrique, but always memorably delicious.

pale ale, Mirror Pond (most of the brands are named after local features and landmarks, in this case a section of the river near the pub). Speaking of hoppy ales, the Oregon beer market is so hop-forward that IPAs account for one in four beers sold in-state and of them, Deschutes Inversion IPA is the second bestseller.

Craft beer consumers are a savvy lot. Brewers at Deschutes—starting with Oregon legend John Harris who helmed the pub's system, through the rapidly expanding program that previous brewmaster Larry Sidor captained, to contemporary brewmaster Brian Faivre—continuously conjure up a range of brews from easy-drinking beers to complex ales. "The idea of establishing a flagship wasn't part of our vision," Fish explained. "Nobody could predict where this industry was gonna go in twenty-five years. We were just trying to make payroll on Fridays."

Now the brewers virtually have a blank check to experiment with whatever recipes tickle their whimsy, and they have tapped scores of beers to show for it. Plum Line, a wild ale that rested on tart Italian plums in Pinot Noir barrels, barely reared its sour face outside the barrelroom. Some of the fun beers that made it to the majors are Hop in the Dark, a Cascadian Dark Ale (a.k.a. Black IPA) that's the perfect marriage of dark roasted malts and bodacious hops. The playful inverse of that is Chainbreaker, the first White IPA, another mutt style that's half Belgian witbier, half IPA. Having experimented with Citra hops before it was even a patented hop varietal (something the big craft breweries have the advantage of doing), the brewers found hops with just the citrusy notes that would play nicely with witbier's telltale orange peel and coriander.

"There was a significant [number of] customer[s] that was drinking hefeweizen and Belgian-style witbiers that we weren't serving," Fish said, knowing that they could "create a flavor profile that made sense." He was rightly proud of the fact that Chainbreaker, partially the offshoot of a collaboration beer with Kansas City's wheat-heavy Boulevard Brewery, debuted as the "number one new craft introduction" in the United States, no matter how tongue in cheek the concept of a White IPA may have been. It has been emulated frequently ever since.

Six-packs are convenient, but the best way to experience their beer is fresh in town (Deschutes has brewpubs in Bend and, as of 2008, Portland). The production facility has expanded and matured in ways inconceivable at its inception. As one of the most environmentally conscious breweries in the world, their green initiatives include resource conservation, waste reduction, and renewable energy. That's no small matter considering they churn out a quarter million bottles a day, all in recycled glass of course). All that liquid ferments in five 1,300-barrel tanks with room and plans to add five more. (Side note: Each fermenter holds about as much as Oregon's twenty-five or thirty smallest breweries produce all year.) The production goal is to hit the million-barrel mark in 2020.

Having said that, the brewing system they started with is the same one still in use today at the pub where it all started. A restaurant expansion provided plenty more seating when long wait times became an issue (especially since it's very popular with families), which of course draws more people, so there's still often a wait. Once inside, the wood and brick décor is attractive, but in nice weather hopefully you can enjoy the outdoors via the upstairs balcony.

As a fan of British bitters, Bachelor Bitter (named after Mt. Bachelor, which lures skiers and boarders) was one of the beers Deschutes debuted with, but it didn't fare well as a bottled brand, even when they changed it to Bachelor ESB. However, it remains popular on draft (even when faced with twenty-four taps). Just ask Fish. "It's a staple for our locals here in Bend," he said. "We get bludgeoned every time it isn't available." Visitors really owe it to themselves to try a glass to get a sense of the brewery circa 1988.

Deschutes Brewery

Opened: 1988.

Owner: Gary Fish.

Brewers: Brian Faivre and Cam O'Connor (cobrewmasters); Sean Garvin, Tim Alexander, and Ryan Schmiege (co-assistant brewmasters); and Veronica Vega (pub assistant brewmaster).

System: 220-barrel, plus another 50-barrel brewhouse and a 12-barrel pilot system at the pub.

Annual production: 340,000 barrels (brewery); 1,000 barrels (pub).

Distribution: Twenty-seven states and provinces.

Hours: Brewery: Saturday and Sunday, noon to 5 p.m. Pub: Sunday through Tuesday, 11 a.m. to 10 p.m.; Wednesday and Thursday, 11 a.m. to 11 p.m.; Friday and Saturday, 11 a.m. to midnight.

Tours: Free guided tours daily at 1 p.m., 2 p.m., 3 p.m., and 4 p.m.

Takeout beer: Bombers, growlers, and even kegs.

Gift shop: Beyond apparel galore, they sell everything from bar mirrors to golf balls. Want a Deschutes snowboard? They've got those.

Food: Solid pub staples and some creative offerings, using as much locally sourced and housemade food as possible. Try the baby back ribs in Black Butte Porter barbecue sauce.

Events: The Abyss release party (second Thursday of November). Anniversary party (June 27).

Other location: Pub (1044 NW Bond St., Bend; 541-382-9242).

GoodLife Brewing Co.

70 Southwest Century Drive, Bend, OR 97702
(541) 728-0749 • GoodLifeBrewing.com
Twitter @GoodLifeBrewing

Straightforward. If forced to sum up GoodLife Brewing in one word, that'd be the one I'd choose. Step into the 22,000-square-foot building and one of the first things that strikes your eye is that the warehouse, an old racquet club, dwarfs the actual brewing system. This is by design. Rare is the brewery that's planned from day one to be able to grow into its space—only a few years in and they've already added more and bigger fermentation tanks—as evidenced by the other Bend breweries that have had to relocate to accommodate growth. Furthermore, the tasting room is pretty meat and potatoes since there are tables, chairs, a bar, and four walls. It's all that's needed and nothing more. But, weather permitting, you can sip a sampler flight of beers or pints of Descender IPA outside, where the massive beer garden around the corner awaits. It's also pretty straightforward, although it's dolled up with the inclusion of a large and inviting firepit, brewery games such as cornhole and horse balls, and some furry, four-legged friends since Bend is, as Bendites like pointing out, "DogTown USA" as declared by *Dog Fancy* magazine.

Man's second best friend is beer, and GoodLife breeds their beers loyal and true. They owe their pedigree to brewmaster Curt Plants and the technique he adopted called hop bursting. In short, it's the process of adding lots of hops post–boil in the whirlpool to increase aroma and flavor without packing in the excess bitterness that comes from hop additions early in a batch's boil. The result are fragrant, delicious beers that are remarkably balanced since there are fewer IBUs than expected.

Now, some folks align themselves with the Sweet As Pacific camp, GoodLife's second pale ale, bursting with New Zealand-grown Pacifica hops, which lend softer, sweeter fruit flavors on a grain bill that includes some wheat. But I'm in the

Beers brewed: Year-round: Descender IPA, Mountain Rescue Pale Ale, Sweet As Pacific Pale Ale, Scottish Heart. Seasonals: Pass Stout, 29er Brown, Redside IRA, Comatose IIPA, Evil Sister, 150 Hippies Fresh Hop.

The Pick: Mountain Rescue. The mélange of hop—classics such as Cascades and Centennials, plus Pacific Jade and Bravo—varietals and caramel malts result in perhaps the best Oregon-brewed pale ale, floral, citrusy and ideal for enjoying after (or during) Bend's myriad recreational options.

Mountain Rescue camp, their original pale ale that smacks of sharp herbal tea with orange zest and dried flowers. Admittedly, the majority may constitute the third camp, the one touting Descender IPA as GoodLife's best beer, but I find that the brewery is in the rare position where their pale ales shine brightest. With either the Mountain Rescue or Sweet As Pacific stance, the point is that GoodLife succeeds not by proffering unreasonably bitter beers that rely on brewing acrobatics, but by offering perhaps the best classic pale ale from Oregon, and beyond. Who knows—it may one day bump Firestone Walker Brewing's Pale 31, a beer that Mountain Rescue emulates, from the top of the podium at GABF.

Visit in September and get a whiff of 150 Hippies. It's so named for its use of 150 pounds of fresh hops grown and donated by local hop growers, not necessarily for the number of said hippies who contributed their yard's harvest. (I have never owned a tie-dye shirt but I do grow some hops and am generally a proponent of peace and love, so I'll confess I'm something like 9 percent hippy.) Furthermore, visit on a Thursday and you'll catch a stream of Bendites coming in for Locals Day to fill their growlers for only seven bucks. They sure do get to live this brewery's namesake.

GoodLife Brewing Co.

Opened: 2011.

Owners: Ty Barnett and Curt Plants.

Brewer: Curt Plants.

System: 30-barrel.

Annual production: 9,000 barrels.

Distribution: Oregon, Idaho, and Washington.

Hours: Daily, 11 a.m. to 10 p.m.

Tours: By appointment.

Takeout beer: Bombers, cans, and growlers.

Gift shop: Threads, caps, barware, and, yes, beer soap.

Food: Pub fare such as bourbon-baked brie and "Bacon Squared" (a jalapeño stuffed with thick-cut bacon and cream cheese topped with more bacon), plus sandwiches, salads, and more.

Juniper Brewing Co.

Redmond, Oregon

1950 Southwest Badger Avenue, Redmond, OR 97756
(541) 548-2739 • JuniperBrewing.com
Twitter @JuniperBrewing

Curtis Endicott and Scott Lesmeister had both lived in Redmond for over a decade when they met through mutual friends—"over a beer of course," Endicott amended—and subsequently grew into homebrewing buddies. Spurred by friends and family and even some early homebrew competition accolades, they culled fourteen favorite self-designed recipes to serve as core and occasional offerings at Juniper Brewing, which opened in March 2014.

Destined to be the flagship at this 2-barrel brewery with a 575-square-foot tasting room is Old Roy IPA, named after "an ancient and magnificent juniper tree that has been a fixture at our homebrewing location [and which] long ago we named Old Roy," Endicott said. Old Roy's silhouette is also the inspiration behind their logo. But naming rights don't end there. "Some unbelievably good friends have stood by us and pushed us into believing we could make our dream a reality," Endicott said. Jolly Black Ale is named not for a pirate buddy as I'd guessed but for their friends Scott and Donna Jolly, though he did allow that he envisions "a very happy skull and cross bones" as a potential label.

Jolly Black's spinoff is Espresso Black, but it's surprisingly coffee-less, belying the rich roast in each sip. Then again, the name Juniper Cream Ale might fool some into thinking it would have juniper berries in it, but Endicott said they're working toward incorporating juniper wood chunks. Not from Old Roy, I hope . . .

Juniper Brewing Co.

Opened: 2014.

Owners and brewers: Curtis Endicott and Scott Lesmeister.

System: 2-barrel.

Annual production: 200 barrels.

Distribution: Central Oregon.

Hours: Monday to Thursday, 4 p.m. to 8 p.m.; Friday, 4 p.m. to 9 p.m.; Saturday, 11 a.m. to 9 p.m.; Sunday, noon to 4 p.m.

Takeout beer: Growlers.

Gift shop: Shirts and caps.

Beers brewed: Year-round: Jolly Black Ale, Juniper Cream, The Milkman Wit, Old Roy IPA, Pat-Kat Porter, Taproot Red. Seasonals: Espresso Black Ale, German Alt, Kolsch, Saison, Blonde, Raspberry Cream, Black IPA, Scottish Wee Heavy, Summer Ale.

McMenamins Old St. Francis School Brewery

700 Northwest Bond Street, Bend, Oregon 97701
(541) 382-5174 • Mcmenamins.com/OldStFrancis
Twitter @CaptainNeon

There are swankier hotels in downtown Bend if you're only looking at the rooms themselves, sure, but no other accommodations provide as unique and holistic an experience as this former Catholic school, built in 1936. Walk down the hallways of McMenamins Old St. Francis and black-and-white photos transport you back to behold some of the collared faculty from the thirties, the city champ football teams of the forties, and an inexplicable snapshot of young girls holding stuffed buck heads (the explanation detracts from the bizarreness that is part and parcel of the McMenamins hotel package). Guests can also enjoy a rejuvenating soaking pool, open until midnight, included in the package.

Even non-guests in the nineteen parochial classrooms-turned-suites or the four bungalow cottages can delight in Old St. Francis's grounds. Each of the bars has its own taps. O'Kanes Bar opens to a terrific, secluded patio with multiple firepits at which people sit around getting toasty, cold weather or not. The scent of cigars hangs in the air—as with many McMenamins properties there's a cigar bar that was grandfathered in—and even as a non-smoker, when the aroma mixes with the fire and ash, to my nose it smells fairly nice. In terrible weather, catch a flick in the cozy movie theater set up like a large den, or ideally there will be a band (they book great local and traveling acts) performing in Father Luke's Room.

The downstairs brewery is in the former school's lunchroom. When Old St. Francis opened in 2004, the original brewer was Dave Fleming, whom I like to call Oregon's bumblebee brewer because he buzzes around from brewery to brewery as if pollinating beers. A year later, despite only

Beers brewed: Year-round: Hammerhead Pale Ale, Terminator Stout, Ruby, IPA. Seasonals: Sunshine Pilsner, Father D's Kölsch, Golden Sparrow, Immigrant Irish Red, Gunslinger IPA, Parson Brown, Imperial Parson Brown, and more.

The Pick: Immigrant Irish Red. This is a "pitcher beer," appealing to everyone in your party. First brewed in 2010 when Curly garnered first place at the intra-company Barley Cup at Thompson's Brewery in Salem, this Irish Red's creamy mélange of malts (including Maris Otter, Franco Belges, and CaraMunich) and mix of citrusy (Cascade) and earthy (US Golding) hops pack 5.1 percent ABV. It's also a "conversation beer," as if each pint is another kiss of the Blarney Stone.

having spent six months at the McMenamins' brewers stable, Mike "Curly" White threw his hat in and was selected to take over based on the reception of his beers at the Fulton Pub in Portland. The Southern California native (who's neither bald as one might expect nor curly haired . . . anymore) moved to Oregon for college, fell in love with it, and fatefully moved to Bend where he met his now-wife. Good thing, since he credits their young daughter as his muse. "I have five to six taps that I get to play with," he said. "I hate to say 'wow-factor,' but I enjoy opening people's eyes to different ways to enjoy good beer." He insisted that locals (regulars) are "all about" the core brands like Hammerhead or Ruby, but with so much inspiration from other breweries in town—this was the fourth among Bend's eighteen and counting—Curly's brewing philosophy is to be consistent but always have fun. Partly because of the location's relative isolation but mostly because his beers are so popular, 90 percent remain on premise rather than go to other pubs. He said all twelve kegs of Aristocrat Imperial IPA kicked at the rate of one a day.

Because Bend is a big winter destination for snow-sport lovers, Curly's popular holiday seasonal is Parson Brown (named after the snowman in the meadow of the Christmas chestnut "Winter Wonderland"). He even beefed up the hoppy brown ale with an Imperial Parson Brown. Lighter, summertime ales often get named Father this-or-that, playing off the Catholic school roots. No matter the season and whether the water is frozen and powdery or melted and flowing down the river, Bend is blessed with ideal water quality (religious school background notwithstanding) that enables Curly to brew light Kolsches and heavy imperial porters without having to treat it. "It's gonna be good nine hundred times out of nine hundred times," he said.

McMenamins Old St. Francis School Brewery

Opened: 2004.

Owners: Mike and Brian McMenamin (see page 92).

Brewer: Mike "Curly" White.

System: 6-barrel.

Annual production: 1,150 barrels.

Hours: Open daily. Bar and pub hours vary.

Tours: Walk-ins when the brewer is available

Takeout beer: Growlers.

Gift shop: Apparel, glassware, and gift items.

Food: Burgers, pizzas, salads, a gluten-free menu, and a bakery on-site.

Extras: Four separate bars. High Gravity Extravaganza (mid-January). O'Kanes Cask Series releases every last Wednesday of the month.

Oblivion Brewing Co.

Bend, OR 97701
(541) 306-8590 • Facebook.com/pages/Oblivion-Brewing-
Co/489874801094000

Darin Butschy's pedigree traces back to Firestone Walker Brewing (really, the brewhouse that Firestone purchased in 2001: San Luis Obispo Brewing, whose Blueberry Ale I confess to drinking back in college). Oblivion arrived on Bend's beer scene in September 2013 and made a splash more like an Olympic diver's than a tubby kid's cannonball.

Three of Butschy's beers went on tap at Broken Top Bottle Shop and Ale Café in town, the de facto springboard for area nanobreweries. The good thing about that timing is that it was during fresh hop season. Oblivion's Fresh Hop Pale Ale features Centennial and Cascade hops grown in Tumalo, not ten miles north. Whether or not it makes an appearance at the local fresh hops festival in the town of 3Isters is still to be decided, but it's yet another good reason to spend part of your beercation at Broken Top. And Oblivion plans to put some beers in pint cans, so you can take your beercation home with you.

Oblivion Brewing Co.

Opened: 2013.
Owners: Darin and Meghann Butschy.
Brewer: Darin Butschy.
System: .5-barrel but expanding to 10-barrel.
Distribution: Bend.

Beers brewed: Year-round: Oblivion Extra Pale, Polar Star Pale, Knockout Stout, Backside IPA, Golden Aurora. Seasonals: DSB (Darin's Special Bitter), Winter Red IPA, High Point Pilsner, Aurora Golden, assorted fresh hop beers.

The Pick: Fresh Hop Pale Ale. A clean, session-strength pale ale (5 percent ABV) of nice clarity, it leaves a pleasant taste of apricot and nectarine, though this ephemeral beauty is only available late summer or early fall.

Old Mill Brew Wërks

803 Southwest Industrial Way, Bend, Oregon 97702
(541) 633-7670 • OldMillBrewWerks.com
Twitter @OldMillBrewWerk

Breweries established in Bend typically outgrow their original locations. Hence Old Mill Brew Wërks moved a half mile away, still within the Old Mill District almost by necessity (otherwise it'd be Old Mill Adjacent Brew Wërks), for some sweet upgrades. They upsized to 10 Barrel Brewing's old 10-barrel brewery. There's also now a killer deck overlooking the Deschutes River, and the Les Schwab Amphitheater hosts concerts and two awesome beer festivals: Bend Brewfest and Old Woody (all barrel-aged beers). Old Mill runs a small barrel program. The bourbon-aged Schizophrenic Stout nails it, and oaked Rabble-Rouser Imperial Red, no shrinking ginger at 8.5 percent ABV to start, yields caramel maltiness embellished with vanilla and maple sweetness. Brewmaster Mike McMahon conjures up pleasers like Irreverence IPA and old-school amber plus new brew tricks.

Chef Rudy Garcia's pub bites include bleu cheese and roasted red pepper polenta on a bed of tomatoes drizzled with white wine sauce and tasty balsamic. No mere poppers, the chipotle-lime cream cheese stuffed jalapeños come wrapped in bacon. Finish with beer ice cream (the flavor and style changes), especially if it's Shrunken Pumpkin Ale season.

Old Mill Brew Wërks

Opened: 2011.

Owners: Courtney and Mark Stevens; Sean and Genie Kelley; and Tim Vezie.

Brewer: Michael McMahon.

System: 10-barrel.

Annual production: 250 barrels.

Distribution: Central Oregon.

Hours: Monday through Thursday, 11 a.m. to 9 p.m.; Friday and Saturday, 11 a.m. to 10 p.m.

Takeout beer: Growlers, dock sales, and bottles coming soon.

Gift shop: Garb and glasses.

Food: Salads, burgers, and a Scotch Egg as an entrée.

Beers brewed: Year-round: Irreverence IPA, Neurotic Blonde Ale, Rabble-Rouser Imperial Red Ale, Schizophrenic Stout, Brew Wërks Amber. Seasonals: Eccentric ESB, Shrunken Pumpkin, Winter Warrior Lager, Seasonal Brown, Imperial IPA.

The Pick: Party Girl Pale. Billed as a "Central Oregon Pale Ale," it's a "lightly hopped session IPA" but is more of a pale ale or Central Oregon pale ale, as stated.

Platypus Pub / The Brew Shop

1203 Northeast Third Street, Bend, Oregon 97701
(541) 323-3282 (Pub) • (541) 323-2318 (Brew Shop)
PlatypusPubBend.com
Twitter @PlatypusPubBend

If the idea of a convenient, all-in-one stop in Bend offering a huge selection of bottles, great taps, pizza and other tasty dishes, homebrewing supplies and, most recently, its own house beers makes you raise your hands in the air exclaiming hallelujah, you wouldn't be the first. This divine beer business occupies a former church.

Founded in 2011 as The Brew Shop—both a contract brewer and homebrew supply store where you'll now also find endless chillers (okay, it ends when it hits six hundred beers, ciders, and meads)—the downstairs was expanded to include The Platypus Pub. The family-friendly pub with its fifteen great taps offers more than just pizza; there are also dartboards and live music. Regulars need not worry: the frequent Meet the Brewers nights showcasing breweries around Central Oregon and beyond shall continue.

But the feather that capped the late 2013 remodel is Platypus Pub beer. The first release was Platypus IPA, contract-brewed by Bridge 99, and the second release was Flat Tail Pale Ale.

Platypus Pub / The Brew Shop

Opened: 2013 (The Brew Shop opened in 2011).

Owners: Tom Gilles and Jeff Hawes.

Brewer: Contract for now.

Annual production: TBD.

Distribution: On-premises.

Hours: Monday through Friday, 10 a.m. to 7 p.m.; Saturday and Sunday, 10 a.m. to 6 p.m. (Downstairs pub closed Mondays).

Takeout beer: Growlers and dock sales, plus around 500 bottles of craft beer.

Food: Pizzas.

Gift shop: T-shirts, growlers, and more.

Beers brewed: Platypus IPA and Platypus Flat Tail Pale Ale.

Rat Hole Brewing

384 Southwest Upper Terrace Drive, Suite 108, Bend,
    OR 97702
(541) 389-2739 • RatHoleBrewpub.com

Let's address the name issue first so we can move on to the beer. Unless I'm an exterminator, having the word Rat in the name of my business probably wouldn't be my first choice. But I assure you no rats were harmed in the making of Al Toepfer's beer. As his story goes, he moved to Bend in late 2010 upon retiring from his twenty-five year career in the navy. His brother-in-law had an outbuilding on his property, adjacent to the ten-acre lot the Toepfers now live on, and Al knew it was perfect to brew in. But, as he put it, "When I opened up the cistern and looked inside, I said, 'Wow, this is a rat hole.' Literally."

OK, so the rats weren't harmed, just dislocated. And there's something else. The décor is Southwestern themed. It's not remotely Bend-y, but Al's wife, Susan, in his words, "is real big on Indian heritage." So along with the painted cow skulls and Indian knives, drums, and blankets, there's a diorama, and it ain't no elementary school project in a shoe box. The diorama depicts skeletal rats bellying up at a bar, called the Rat Hole Saloon, which predates the brewery. Not that it makes it any less gross to me.

So now we can move on. Beer-wise, there's no questioning Toepfer's decisions. (While we're clearing up names, it's pronounced "TUP-fer.") Weeks into launching Rat Hole Brewing, he won two medals at the 2013 Denver International Beer Competition for his Rotation Red (Mild category) and Vanilla Porter (Robust Porter category). Even before that, his homebrew competition awards were numerous. With five year-round beers and usually seven or eight on tap, he plays around with his seasonal concoctions. My favorite seasonal during my visit was Haystack Hazelnut Brown, brewed with filberts added to the mash. Since the food menu matches the décor with New Mexican cuisine and small plates, I asked if he has already done or has plans to do a chili beer and,

Beers brewed: Year-round: Rotation Red Ale, Vanilla Porter, Sickle Bar Saison, Fencepost Porter, Rathole IPA. Seasonals: Pumpkin Spice Ale, Haystack Hazelnut Brown, Summer Lemon Wheat.

The Pick: Haystack Hazelnut Brown. This robust brown ale base, a tad shy of porter territory, sees hazelnuts added right into the mash. The oils create a distinct nutty coating that's still shy of syrupy yet almost like a cola.

since anyone from or with a passion for New Mexico has a stance on the matter, would it be with green or red chilies? Green are his favorite, though he envisions doing a Belgian tripel with both red and green chilies, known in the Land of Enchantment as "Christmas," which is perfect considering it'd be a winter or Christmas warmer.

The brewery remains off the grid, but the plan all along was to open some sort of tasting room in town. When the Old Mill Brew Wërks moved out of this location and into a new one just a few blocks away, the Toepfers leapt at the lease. "Some people come in expecting something divey" befitting the name, Toepfer said, but instead guests are treated to a cozy space that seats about thirty inside, plus more at the beautifully decorated bar featuring art made from barley malts of various hues. The patio fits about two dozen, and the firepit makes it usable in the winter. A pint of chocolaty Fencepost Porter made with chocolate malts and oatmeal is a perfect accoutrement to said firepit. Or for those who prefer vanilla over chocolate, there's a version made with vanilla beans.

Rat Hole Brewing

Opened: 2013.
Owners: Al and Susan Toepfer.
Brewers: Al Toepfer and Ken Deuser (assistant brewer).
System: 2.5-barrel.
Annual production: Pub only.
Distribution: Oregon.
Hours: Monday through Saturday, noon to 10 p.m.
Tours: None (brewery not on-premises).
Takeout beer: Growlers.
Gift shop: Shirts and glasses in the back.
Food: Tapas, salads, and pub grub. Try the red chili pork burrito.

Riverbend Brewing and Sports Pub

2650 Northeast Division Street, Bend, OR 97701
(541) 550-7550 • RiverbendBrewing.com

Everyone in brewery-happy Bend knew of Rivals Sports Grille, but owner Gary Sobala converted it into a brewpub with a 10-barrel brewing system, hired Daniel Olsen (formerly of Deschutes Brewery and 10 Barrel), and changed the name to Riverbend Brewing and Sports Pub. Fittingly, it's located on a river bend across from Riverview Park. Incidentally, Olsen has now been brewing for over half his life, getting his professional start at age seventeen. I guess they don't card brewers in Colorado.

There were already eighteen taps, which won't change, but instead of mostly local craft beers on draft now nearly half are hyper-local. Sobala said the Bud Light and Coors Light handles stay since this is, after all, half sports bar and not everyone who fills the 175 seats is into craft beer. As for those house beers brewed directly across the parking lot, in addition to Riverbend IPA, of course, Olsen said he's looking forward to doing more dark beers. The third house tap was a dry Irish Stout. His first winter seasonal in 2014 was a wintermint stout. As for future offerings? Imagine watching The Big Game while quaffing a Flemish Red, if Olsen's plans come to fruition.

Riverbend Brewing and Sports Pub

Opened: 2013 (née Rivals, 2008).

Owner: Gary Sobala.

Brewer: Daniel Olsen.

System: 10-barrel.

Annual production: 1,500 barrels.

Distribution: Central Oregon.

Hours: Sunday through Thursday, 11 a.m. to 11 p.m.; Friday and Saturday, 11 a.m. to midnight.

Tours: By appointment or possibly upon request.

Takeout beer: Growlers and dock sales.

Gift shop: Hoodies, tees, and glassware.

Food: Extensive menu of pub grub classics, a la the Super Nacho Platter, fish and chips, guacamole bacon burger, and pulled pork pizza. And for dessert: fried Twinkies.

Extras: Daily poker tournament. Fifteen big-screen TVs. Sunday brunch.

Beers brewed: Year-round: IPA, Blonde Session, Irish Stout, Pale Wheat Ale, Red, Nut Brown, Saison, XPA, Imperial IPA. Seasonals: Wintermint Stout.

Silver Moon Brewing

24 Northwest Greenwood Avenue, Bend, OR 97701
(541) 388-8331 • SilverMoonBrewing.com
Twitter @SilverMoonBeer

Silver Moon was sold to new owners in 2013, but Tyler Reichert built it over a dozen years earlier as Bend's third brewpub. Reichert, a ski bum, moved to Bend in 1998 and decided to fund his primary hobby via his secondary one, so he bought a homebrew supply shop. He added a 1.5-barrel nanobrewery to the store, and five years later production at Silver Moon increased more than fivefold when the brewery landed in its current Greenwood Avenue location, mere blocks from its only predecessors, the Deschutes Brewpub and Bend Brewing Co. By 2005 the McMenamins had come to town and opened the Old St. Francis School Brewery, making Bend a town of "just" four breweries, all within less than a mile walk of one another.

I got to sit and enjoy some Silver Moon beers with Reichert shortly before he sold the business, not realizing the rebranding that was in store for Silver Moon. Reichert had said he never saw the wellspring of breweries coming in Silver Moon's early days, though he added, "Bend hasn't seen a brewery fail yet."

Hopefully, that day will never come. New owners Matt Barrett and James Watts are both from the high-tech world, but Barrett also owns two SNAP Fitness locations in town and Watts started the uber-popular Cycle Pub here, so he's not new to the beer scene.

To ensure longevity, Silver Moon will keep brewing its award-winning beers, including four auspicious GABF medals in the past few years. Those began with Bridge Creek Pilsner in 2010. The next year they brought home two more for Legacy Lager and Dark Side Stout. The 2012 medal was actually for their 2010 Old Trainwreck Barleywine in the Aged Beer category. One of the most impressive aspects is that these cover a breadth of beer styles.

Beers brewed: Year-round: Hounds Tooth Amber, Lifeguard Blond Ale, Crazyhorse DIPA, Jingo Jango ISA, Snake Bite Porter, Hopnob IPA. Seasonals: Legacy Lager, Dark Side Stout, Twisted Gourd Pumpkin Ale, Hoppopotamus Fresh Hop Ale, Get Sum Pale Ale, Hoptagon DIPA, Voodoo Dog India Session Red.

The Pick: Hoppopotamus Fresh Hop. For those bullish about fresh hops, this whale of a fresh hop ale is truly all about Cascades. It's one of the hidden gems when Oregonians go mining for fresh hop beers.

Among the beer lineup IPAs take center stage, as expected, and Silver Moon brews four of them. Their best-selling creation and year-round version, Hopnob, clocks 6 percent ABV and 65 IBUs. Hop Fury resides in the "Northwest IPA" category (7.7 percent alcohol, 70 IBUs). Then there's Hoptagon Imperial IPA (8.6 percent ABV), replete with five Northwest hop varietals and evidently off the charts of the bitterness scale. My personal favorite, however, is the ephemeral Hoppopotamus, a fresh hop IPA made with entirely Oregon-grown Cascades. I'm grateful this one gets bottled and distributed to Portland.

Beyond solid core beers and ever-changing seasonal offerings—there are eight taps in total, though Watts told me that will be increasing—Silver Moon has woven its way into the fabric of downtown Bend. In 2007, Reichert augmented the brewery into a full-bore brewpub, with sandwiches and pizzas comprising most of the menu. Families with kids are welcome until 8 p.m. I love when brewpubs make their own root beer and Silver Moon's is one of the best. Later in the night, the taproom, known as the Moon Room, turns into a sweet little music venue where the cover charge typically runs five dollars.

Sitting in the pub hoisting a few pints or making your way through a flight, don't be tricked into thinking you're peering directly into the brewhouse. One of the floor-to-ceiling murals—and the new owners have already added another as part of their facelift that also included newfangled digital tap boards—there's one that's simply, incredibly lifelike. And if you suspect you've had one too many because you could swear you're seeing fairies alighting on kettles and tanks, relax: there really are Monet-inspired beer faeries. Perhaps they're the ones making the beers magically delectable.

Silver Moon Brewing

Opened: 2000.
Owners: Matt Barrett and James Watts.
Brewer: Stuart Long.
System: 12-barrel.
Annual production: 2,400 barrels.
Distribution: Oregon and Northern California.
Hours: Monday through Thursday, 11:30 a.m. to 10 p.m.; Friday and Saturday, 11:30 a.m. to 2 a.m.; Sunday, 11:30 a.m. to 8 p.m.
Tours: Email info@silvermoonbrewing.com to schedule.
Takeout beer: Growlers and bottles.
Gift shop: Clothing, posters, glassware, and, uh, yellow leather gloves.
Food: Burgers, sandwiches, and various handhelds and finger foods.

Smith Rock Brewing

546 Northwest Seventh Street, Redmond, OR 97756
(541) 279-7005 • SmithRockBrewing.com

Smith Rock is a popular climbing and hiking spot out in the high desert overlooking the Crooked River. It's also the eponym for the small brewpub in Redmond located eight miles away that has become a popular watering hole for outdoorsy types from near and far. What's great is that after (or before) spending a day basking in the monolithic glory of the state park, patrons can bask in the sun in the pub's surrounding beer garden or find warmth around the firepit when necessary. Arrive early to stake your claim since seating is limited.

The brewpub was originally conceived as a production brewery—but fortuitously for diners it didn't pan out that way—and is a full-on family affair. Among the four owners, Don Frederickson and Danielle Stewart are brother and sister, Natalie is Don's wife, and Kevin is Danielle's husband. But the staff is a veritable family tree. Kevin and Danielle's son, Scott, is the head chef; daughter Marlee does prep work, and even brother Trevor has helped in the kitchen. Danielle, the one with restaurant experience, is the pub manager. Natalie, the lone Oregon native, is the master brewer and recipe creator while Don (the first to homebrew) and Kevin handle much of the day-to-day brewing on the too-small half-barrel system. That explains why there's often just one house beer on tap, though a 3-barrel system is in the works.

Natalie said they'd eventually like to have six house taps—including two rotating or seasonal ones—and that they're always experimenting, in part thanks to obtaining unreleased, unnamed hops that usually only the big guys get. Their contract with Hop Union means there's always Citra hops in Morning Glory IPA. Of course, fresher's always better, and their Tumalo Fresh Hop Pale ale, made with hops plucked right in Deschutes County, earned Smith Rock Brewing the people's choice award at the 2013 Fresh Hops Fest in nearby Sisters. Natalie said she's particularly enamored

Beers brewed: Year-round: Morning Glory IPA, Porter, Crooked River Brown. Seasonals: Smith Rock Scottish Ale, 8 AM Pale, Tumalo Fresh Hop IPA, Misery Ridge IPA, Sweater Weather Barrel-aged Imperial Oatmeal Stout, and more.

The Pick: Crooked River Brown. Maybe it's because my dad is from New York, but this English Brown resembles a New York Egg Cream with its chocolaty creaminess and medium carbonation. Someone has to salvage the brown style.

with their Oatmeal Pale Ale, but I've yet to find it tapped during my visits. Their darker beers are another strong suit, offering a porter, both oaked or un-oaked, and the equally chocolaty Crooked River Brown.

Food-wise, freshly prepared specials mean the menu is frequently in flux, although Natalie noted the emphasis is on the burgers. You might find a Caprese burger or a jalapeño popper burger, but the standard Smith Rock Burger features gorgonzola, bacon, and caramelized onions. Speaking of onions, they fry up some of the best anywhere and hand prepping them is nearly a full-time job. The mini corndog on the kids menu is also hand battered and tasty enough for kids over twenty-one (I can verify).

Ultimately, while it may be the arduous climbing the sheer walls of Smith Rock or mountain biking that draws people through or to Redmond, this is a sweet spot whether your day was rigorous or relaxing. The indoor space, a former Italian restaurant, offers various smaller rooms instead of one large space, so it's always cozy, especially if there's room by the fireplace in the back. And the beautiful shot of Smith Rock right as you walk in means you can bask in its glory over a few pints without fear of all that climbing chalk or sweat from your brow getting in your beer.

Smith Rock Brewing

Opened: 2012.

Owners: Natalie Patterson and Don Frederickson; Danielle and Kevin Stewart.

Brewers: Natalie Patterson (master brewer); Kevin Stewart and Don Frederickson (co-brewers).

System: 25-gallon (less than 1 barrel).

Annual production: 50 barrels.

Distribution: On-premises only.

Hours: Tuesday through Thursday, 11:30 a.m. to 8 p.m.; Friday, 11:30 a.m. to 9 p.m.; Saturday, noon to 9 p.m.

Tours: None.

Takeout beer: Growler fills.

Gift shop: T-shirts.

Food: Creative pub food from scratch. The bratwurst corndog with epicurean onion rings is a winner.

Extras: Enjoy the beer garden in nice weather or the fireplace in inclement weather.

Solstice Brewing Co.

BREWING COMPANY
Prineville, Oregon

234 North Main Street, Prineville, OR 97754
(541) 233-0883 • SolsticeBrewing.com
Twitter @SolsticeBrewing

Long before it became a brewpub, this space had a history of serving as multiple local watering holes for the residents of Prineville, a city of fewer than ten thousand. One of my favorites that Solstice Brewing owner-brewer Joseph Barker mentioned was a "fake cowboy bar." But he then noted, "this is real cowboy country." Directly across Main Street there's Prineville Men's Wear with cowboy boots and Stetson hats aplenty. Barker figured at least 75 percent of the patrons are ranchers, though when the weather's nice weekenders and beer tourists stop by in droves.

The environment and pace suits Barker just fine. He grew up in La Grande in Eastern Oregon, where there was Blue Mountain, an early nanobrewery in the nineties, and more recently Mt. Emily Ale House. Barker moved to Portland for college in 2004 and pushed to start a brewery there, but not only is it more expensive, he also found that once he turned his focus to Crook County, he "got more done here in two weeks than in two years in Portland." That's how they do it out in the country. Besides, with Solstice located not too far from Bend and Redmond, it's adjacent to well-educated beer towns, and since there's a pub involved, they have great access to good ranch beef. I don't know who the competition is, but the brewpub was voted as the winner for slinging the best burgers in Prineville. And the sausages are simmered in the house brown or dark ale. While I'm at it, the onion rings and cod-based fish and chips are battered using Prinetucky Pale.

As for the beer, Barker and co-owner Timothy Czuk began brewing in 2012, once they'd procured the old five-barrel system from Terminal Gravity up in Eastern Oregon. The fermentation tanks came from Double Mountain after they upsized, too. The first beer out of the brewhouse (which is somewhat visible from the bar stools) was Prinetucky Pale. With an ABV of 5.2 percent

Beers brewed: Year-round: Prinetucky Pale, Show Me the Honey Wheat, Double Dam IPA, Last Day IPA. Seasonals: Walton Lake Lager, Needs a Name Brown, Boot Stomp'n Stout, Chocolate Porter, Warpaint Red Ale, Winter Solstice, Summer Solstice.

The Pick: Prinetucky Pale. Locals like their boots and trucks dirty but their beer clean, and this pale ale achieves that with German Magnum and Crystal hops for an emphasis on being crisp and refreshing over big impact.

and sufficient hop profile, packing 41 IBUs, it remains the bestseller even over Last Day IPA, which spurs the body and flavor up to 6.6 percent and 60 IBUs. Whereas Last Day goes blonder than Prinetucky, Double Dam is a double IPA with a huge malt body giving it a redder color, nearly 8 percent alcohol, and just under 100 IBUs.

On the grain side, Barker's fond of brewing and drinking dark beers and said he adds oatmeal to the stouts and porters. He may make a "stout porter" as a nod to the style's historical origin "just to mess with people who clamor for one over the other." I enjoyed Boot Stomp'n Stout, but from the flight Barker pulled for me at the bar, I really dug Needs A Name Brown. Two beers that certainly don't need better names are the hearty Winter Solstice and bright Summer Solstice. "The name 'Solstice' attaches us to the seasons . . . and the planet," Barker said. "It represents the rhythm of life."

I also couldn't help but notice the eclectic tap handles. Barker pointed out that a customer whose hobbies include making taps explains why one is a fishing pole, one is an actual grenade (not live, I should hope), and another is the butt of a rifle. The brown ale needs a name? How about Rifle Butt Brown?

As I said, Barker enjoys the pace of life in Prineville that draws people for its fishing, climbing, biking, and hiking opportunities, even if it's less of a destination than nearby Bend or his old stomping grounds of Portland. When business or personal stuff brings him to either of those, he calls that "going to town." And "town," he explained, "is anywhere bigger than here."

Solstice Brewing Co.

Opened: 2010.

Owners: Joseph Barker and Timothy Czuk.

Brewer: Joseph Barker.

System: 5-barrel.

Annual production: A few hundred (800 capacity).

Distribution: Central Oregon.

Hours: Monday through Thursday, 11:30 a.m. to 9 p.m.; Friday and Saturday, 11:30 a.m. to 10 p.m.; Sunday, 11:30 a.m. to 8 p.m.

Tours: By request.

Takeout beer: Growlers.

Gift shop: T-shirts.

Food: Apps, salads, sandwiches, entrées, and plenty of Breese Ranch beef burgers. Steins burger comes with center-cut bacon, ham, cheddar, and a fried egg.

Extras: Kids play area.

Sunriver Brewing Co.

57100 Beaver Drive, Building 4, The Village at Sunriver, OR 97707
(541) 593-3007 • SunriverBrewingCompany.com

Before owner Brian Cameron installed the actual Sunriver Brewery in late 2013, he had opened the Sunriver Brewhouse (a jog from the brewing facility) in The Village at Sunriver over Fourth of July, 2012. It's the top-rated restaurant on TripAdvisor.com and, for what it's worth, number two is a white tablecloth restaurant. You can keep your fancy linens—I'll take the Brewhouse's fried avocado, accurately described by Cameron as a deconstructed then reconstructed chips and guacamole, with the breading around each slice supplanting the need for tortilla chips.

Already I've fallen into the trap. Should you come here for the house smoked pork and steelhead or for the beer? The obvious answer is "both" (and not merely in the sense of the amazing pretzel that's boiled then baked with their black ale and served with stout mustard). It's also worth noting that Sunriver, located twenty miles south of Bend, is a major resort destination. The Brewhouse in the Village—which also includes art galleries, ski, bike, and board shops, and an eternal duel between a healthy produce stand and a donut shop—is just a four-minute bike ride from the resort, a mere fraction of the thirty-three miles of bike trails here. Soon you'll need all your fingers and toes to count the breweries in Bend, but considering the population and number of vacationers, Sunriver needed one of its own.

Cameron is one of the two thousandish folks who actually live here year-round. He grew up in the Portland suburb of Tigard but initially moved to Bend at the turn of the millennium. He hadn't moved back to Portland for long when, bam, he had what he called "an epiphany at 11:30 p.m." The timing was unfortunate for his wife, who had to listen to him hash it out until 3 in the morning.

Beers brewed: Year-round: Vicious Mosquito IPA, Trail Pale Ale, Chalk Rock Amber, Baselayer Black Ale, Lazy River Lager, Bog Frog India Wheat Ale, Grandma's Original Ale. Seasonals: Shred Head Winter Ale, Fuzztail Hefeweizen, Hop Shop Series.

The Pick: Base Layer Black Ale. By using midnight wheat instead of traditional roasted malts in the grist, this beer—neither stout, nor porter, nor schwarzbier—offers smooth chocolate notes without the telltale astringency or other bitter flavors traditional dark beers produce, all on top of a surprisingly light body.

Part of the inspiration, he disclosed, was that Portland is just too rainy. "I wanted to be dry. I wanted my son to wake up dry." Central Oregon loves to flaunt its three hundred days of sunshine. (My wife is dying for me to have the same epiphany.)

"I had an interest in the beer business before," Cameron elaborated. "I always wanted to do a Cheers type of bar, where everybody knows your name. I didn't want a 'bar' because bars are where you go to get drunk. I wanted a [social] hub. I didn't know how to pull it off until 11:30 at night."

So with help from his parents Marc and Karol—"My mom is probably the boss of the whole damn thing," he quipped —Sunriver Brewing started to roll. As for the beer, they initially contracted house beers to Phat Matt's up in Redmond (now closed), but right as Cameron was securing the brewing system, several trustworthy brewers in the local industry suggested the same person he should try to land as Sunriver's brewer: Brett Thomas, who had just departed from Silver Moon in Bend. Brett is an award-winning professional brewer but said that he still draws inspiration from his "three binders' worth" of homebrewing recipes and notes. Not only does he get a new 15-barrel brewery, he also gets a 3-barrel pilot brewery to "play mad scientist" without having to worry about selling 15 or 30 barrels' worth. So when visiting, definitely try whatever's on the rotating brewer's tap. Just hope there's room at the bar because the restaurant gets packed.

Sunriver Brewing Co.

Opened: 2013.

Owners: Brian Cameron; Marc and Karol Cameron.

Brewer: Brett Thomas.

System: 15-barrel.

Annual production: 1,500 barrels projected for 2014.

Distribution: Central Oregon.

Hours: Sunday through Thursday, 11 a.m. to 10 p.m.; Friday and Saturday, 11 a.m. to 11 p.m.

Tours: Yes.

Takeout beer: Growlers and dock sales at brewery, packaged.

Gift shop: Shirts, hoodies, and glassware.

Food: Creative salads, sandwiches, and apps like fried avocado.

Extras: Large kids play area, and not one but two patios.

10 Barrel Brewing Co.

1135 Northwest Galveston Avenue, Bend, OR 97701
(541) 678-5228 • 10Barrel.com
Twitter @10BarrelBrewing

As expected, 10 Barrel Brewing began with a 10-barrel brewing system that originated as a scheme to brew and sell some beer so as to afford the local lifestyle of skiing, fishing, and enjoying the overall quality of life—a phrase echoed repeatedly in Oregon, and Bend in particular. Within five years, the brewery became so popular (a classic NW IPA called Apocalypse with an orange glow that's resiny but juicy as a fruit salad helped) they added a 50-barrel system. Some might call them 60 Barrel since they retained the original system as a pilot brewery, but I say if they just wait, at their pace of growth they'll need to expand again and it'll be easier to rebrand by adding a zero: 100 Barrel Brewing.

I'm joking about the name, but 10 Barrel is already close and will get closer to those collective 100 barrels of production before long. It started by opening a public house in Bend's residential River West neighborhood, which immediately became a hub for locals who walk or ride up to it. It's common to see people enjoying a pint of Apocalypse—not surprisingly their best-selling beer by over 50 percent—or the benevolent black ale called S1nistør by the firepit with their dogs lounging at their tired feet after a rough day on Mt. Bachelor. That's exactly what Jeremy Cox—who founded the company with his twin brother, Chris, and runs it with father-and-son duo Brad and Garret Wales—said was their ambition all along. "Most of us at 10 Barrel have kids, so we definitely think about them as well as our adult patrons. We all have dogs. We wanted to make it the most comfortable place to get good food and good beer," Cox said. The pub's so receptive to minors, children's pizzas are served on Frisbees (sorry, only the kids' pies).

Beers brewed: Year-round: Apocalypse IPA, O.G. Wheat IPA, S1nistør Black Ale, Pub Beer. Seasonals: Swill grapefruit radler, Crush sour series, Pray For Snow, Rye'm or Treason, and more.

The Pick: Swill. Brewer Tonya Cornett developed a Berliner Weisse-style sour wheat beer (it won a gold medal at GABF) that was then used as the effervescent base for Swill, 10 Barrel's radler that's ideal on warm, sunny days, especially since it's only 4.5 percent alcohol. This stuff tastes like fresh juice, drinks like beer, and is prudently available as a six-pack in the summer.

Cox said they "designed it for Bend," but those attributes are hardly restricted to this town. Next came an additional pub, this time east of the state line in Boise. To captain its 10-barrel pilot brewery, 10 Barrel hired one of the most decorated brewmasters in the country, Shawn Kelso, formerly of Barley Brown's in Baker City, so he was already over halfway closer to Boise than Bend. Next up was a brewpub in Portland's central Pearl District near where other transplanted brewers like Deschutes and Rogue have set up pubs. With its 10-barrel system, that brings 10 Barrel up to a collective 80 barrels. But Cox hinted that they're considering other Northwest destinations as far as Montana for future outposts. Like I said, 100 Barrel Brewing.

At the heart of the brewery is brewmaster Jimmy Seifrit, previously brewer at Deschutes, who was instrumental in setting up the new brewhouse; and Tonya Cornett, formerly of Bend Brewing Co., who along with Kelso does R&D batches. "Our dream team came together," Cox said. In the early days, tank space was limited so variety came in the form of taking one beer, often S1nistør, and adding off-the-wall adjuncts during secondary fermentation. Cinnamon sticks. Warheads candy. Red Vines. The latter smacked of sitting in a movie theater eating red licorice.

A main focus and passion of Cornett's is the sour beer program. Call it her Berliner Period, if I can draw a comparison between Picasso's warmer and vibrant Rose Period and her tangier, vivacious Berliner Weisses. Given the moniker German Sparkle Party, her base Berliner medaled at GABF and has been known to put on various flavors of party pants soured with *Lactobacillus* for 10 Barrel's Crush series. Barrels are filled with it and fruits are added during aging and secondary fermentation, hence Apricot Crush, Cherry Crush, and more challenging iterations like Pumpkin Crush. Cox called Cucumber Crush probably the most unusual and popular. I don't particularly love cucumbers, but I got to try that beer at the annual Fruit Beer Fest (cukes are botanically a fruit, not a veggie) and it was so good I had to wait in line again for seconds—a second helping, that is; the line itself for this sumptuous beer lasted minutes.

Berliners traditionally added flavored syrups to their Weisse, so this is an artistic evolutionary step. Germans also commonly mix beer with juice or soda to make a radler. Swill is 10 Barrel's grapefruit-forward radler. "Our goal was to produce the ultimate lawnmower beer," Cornett said. "We also wanted to make it approachable to people who don't usually choose beer. The reaction has been phenomenal. It's geeky enough for beer enthusiasts and drinkable enough to win over the wine cooler crowd." Given Oregonians' propensity for riding bikes (often from a brewpub to a taphouse), it's worth noting that *radler* is German for "cyclist."

Many of their regular beers can be found in 22-ounce bombers, so when my wife and I hit the Bend pub (long before we knew there'd be a Portland one), we opted for pub-only offerings. The first one I had was Lavender-Infused S1nistør. It's a difficult beer to pair with food, but is a very intriguing flavor—not unlike drinking a roasty Schwarzbier while sitting in a tub filled with bath oil. My wife got the Triple Chocolate Stout, an insanely tasty, chocolaty beer further ameliorated by a nitro tap, meaning smaller nitrogenated bubbles lending a ceaselessly smooth mouthfeel, but nowhere near too sweet to enjoy.

The pizzas are 10 Barrel's most popular offering, but being sand-wichvores, we went piggy, me with the flatiron pork topped with beer-infused apple chutney and she with the BBQ pork with S1nistør Black BBQ sauce. It was winter so we ate inside, but that didn't stop plenty of folks from sitting around that great firepit. Being outdoorsy in Bend never goes out of season.

10 Barrel Brewing Co.

Opened: 2006.

Owners: Brad and Garrett Wales; Jeremy and Chris Cox.

Brewers: Jimmy Seifrit, Tonya Cornett, and Shawn Kelso.

System: 50-barrel + 10-barrel + 10-barrel.

Annual production: 25,000 barrels.

Distribution: Idaho, Washington, Oregon, and British Columbia.

Hours: Sunday through Thursday, 11 a.m. to 11 p.m.; Friday and Saturday, 11 a.m. to midnight.

Tours: Fridays, 3 p.m. to 4 p.m.; RSVP to seeshinytanks@10barrel.com.

Takeout beer: Growlers and bottles (and cans of Pub Beer) at pub. Dock sales at brewery.

Gift shop: Apparel and glassware.

Food: Plenty of meaty and no-meaty sandwiches and pizzas. The All American Cheeseburger Pie comes with special sauce (Thousand Island), lettuce, cheese, pickles, and onions . . . no sesame seeds.

Events: Pray for Snow party with the burning of a 30-foot snowman around Thanksgiving weekend.

Other locations: Production brewery (62970 Northeast 18th Street, Bend, OR 97701; 541-585-1007). Portland brewpub (1411 Northwest Flanders Street, Portland, OR 97209).

Three Creeks Brewing Co.

721 Desperado Court, Sisters, OR 97759
(541) 549-1963 • ThreeCreeksBrewing.com
Twitter @ThreeCreeksBrew

I first met Zach Beckwith, who honed his chops at Lompoc Brewing, when he was the inaugural brewer at Pints, a half-pint-sized brewery in Old Town Portland. But when the opportunity to brew at Three Creeks opened up he seized it, since it's not uncommon for families in Portland to long to move to pastoral Central Oregon. Considering his wife gave birth shortly after mine did, I absolutely see the allure of having our sons grow up together since Sisters—along with its chic neighbor Bend—provides as much of a natural playground for kids (and adults) as the burgeoning brewing scene does for area brewers.

In fact, that's exactly what Beckwith was brought in for. He inherited a core lineup of beers—the summer tsunami of Knotty Blonde Ale slakes the thirst of mountain bikers and kayakers—and loves that he's "free to create new beers and change everything else as I see fit." For the summer-ending, barrel-aged beerfest in Bend called Little Woody, Beckwith devised Double Hoodoo Voodoo aged in Pinot.

He did so behind the glass wall that separates the tavern side of the brewpub from the brewhouse. Three Creeks is housed in a large log cabin–looking building but is smartly divided into two areas. Turn left and you find yourself in the family-friendly restaurant. About face and pass through the swinging doors, like what you'd expect to find in a Western saloon, that lead to the twenty-one-and-over portion. So while little kids would probably get a bigger kick out of watching the three-man brew crew (Beckwith along with staff brewers Terry and Aaron) in rubber boots working among the gleaming tanks, since the contents are strictly for really big kids it makes sense, and Beckwith said he doesn't mind the audience. No matter your scene, there's a comfy setting for you.

As for the future of Three Creeks, Beckwith said they're considering a major expansion (welcome to the club) that would include a 30-barrel

Beers brewed: Year-round: Hoodoo Voodoo IPA, Old Prospector Pale Ale, Knotty Blonde, Anvil Amber, Firestorm Red, Stonefly Rye, Raptor Rye IPA, FivePine Chocolate Porter. Seasonals: Hodag CDA, Cone Lick'r Fresh Hop Pale, Rudolph's Imperial Red, and more.

The Pick: Stonefly Rye is an unfiltered rye ale that appeals to pale ale fans for its spiciness and wheat beer fans for its fruity esters and haze that denote refreshment. At only 4.6 percent ABV, it's great for outdoor folks seeking to remain active.

production facility built in Sisters because the current 10-barrel pub system is "maxed out." They'd like to distribute more bottled beer, which is tough when a solid half of what they produce is sold through the pub. Just don't look for any zany beers to be packaged. "Everyone tries to do something different," Beckwith said. "My goal—and [I'm] trying to get the crew to get on board—is to make the beer truly better. It's almost more of a risk, and why you see us with plans for [a] production brewery. We're in it for the long haul here." Around here, the native CDA (Cascadian Dark Ale) is now his idea of a popularly accepted style, and he gave props to Dave Fleming, one of his predecessors here (and who is mentioned in several other chapters), for creating the winter seasonal 8 Seconds India Black Ale, "one of the first of what would become CDAs in the Northwest." That beer has been replaced by Beckwith's recipe for Hodag, first brewed to commemorate Hoodoo Ski Area in Sisters on the occasion of their seventy-fifth anniversary.

Ask Beckwith what his favorite indigenous style is, though, and he answers, "I love making fresh hop beers," which is perfect since one of three fresh hop beer festivals thrown in Oregon is here in Sisters. "They're one of the last styles that we can call our own around here," he said.

Three Creeks Brewing Co.

Opened: 2008.

Owner: Wade Underwood.

Brewer: Zach Beckwith.

System: 10-barrel

Annual production: 2,100 barrels.

Distribution: Oregon.

Hours: Sunday through Thursday, 11:30 a.m. to 9 p.m.; Friday and Saturday, 11:30 a.m. to 10 p.m.

Tours: By request.

Takeout beer: Bombers and growler fills.

Gift shop: Plenty of T-shirts and garb including cycling jerseys, along with glassware, disc-golf discs, and more.

Food: Wide-ranging menu to please all tastes, from mature palates to young whippersnappers. I love Hawaiian pizza and this one made with smoky pulled pork and Old Prospector Pale Ale barbeque sauce rocks.

Events: March Maltness featuring eight malty beers and IPApril featuring ten hoppy ones. In nearby Village Green Park, Sisters hosts a Fresh Hop festival (late September).

Wild Ride Brewing Co.

332 Southwest 5th Street, Redmond, OR 97756
(541) 516-8544 • WildRideBrew.com
Twitter @WildRideBrewing

Some of the five owners of Wild Ride Brewing grew up in Redmond; all have hometown pride and all are thrilled to join Central Oregon's brewing community. As they built toward launching the enterprise, co-owner Brian Mitchell said they landed on the name innocuously, yet fittingly. "One day one of us described the planning process as a 'wild ride,'" he said. It not only had a nice ring to it but also is "How we'll run our brewery. 'What's your wild ride?' has become our theme . . . In a place such as Central Oregon there are so many outdoor activities." Truly, locals have a wild thirst for beer and lap up anything new they can find.

Brewer Paul Bergeman moved to Redmond with a decade of experience including Laurelwood in Portland and Kona Brewing (because while Oregon trumps Hawaii in local craft beer, the Aloha State wastes Oregon in terms of warm ocean water). From the day Wild Ride opened they had a dozen taps with, as Mitchell put it, "a style we feel provides a choice for any beer drinker." And not just local drinkers. "We hope to reach the 10,000-barrel mark within five years," he added.

Wild Ride Brewing Co.

Opened: 2014.

Owners: Scott Satterlee, Brian Mitchell, Paul Bergeman, Chad Hinton, Erik Steers, and Steve Downey.

Brewer: Paul Bergeman.

System: 20-barrel.

Annual production: 1,500 barrels (projected).

Distribution: Oregon and Washington.

Hours: Sunday through Wednesday, 11 a.m. to 9 p.m.; Thursday through Saturday, 11 a.m. to 10 p.m.

Tours: Check for event listings.

Takeout beer: Growlers, dock sales, and 22-ounce bottles.

Gift shop: Shirts, snapback hats, pro-style hats, trucker hats, growlers, pints, and beer soap.

Food: Visiting food trucks.

Beers brewed: Year-round: 3 Sisters American Red Ale, Big Booty Golden Ale, Bitch Stout, Brain Bucket IIPA, Fly.P.A., Hopperhead IPA, Stand Up and Shout (coffee and vanilla stout), Whoopty Whoop Wheat, Mount Up Maple Brown, Cole's Trickle, Ride the Rail Pale Ale. Seasonals: A-Bomb SMaSH IPA, Medusa's Pleasure, Barrel Aged Bitch Stout (to be released late in 2014), Barrel Aged Brown.

Worthy Brewing Co.

495 Northeast Bellevue Drive, Bend, Oregon 97701
(541) 639-4776 • WorthyBrewing.com
Twitter @WorthyBrewingCo

Between its natural beauty and rotating outdoor recreational pursuits, Bend continually lures expats from Portland's brewing community. Another plus is the high desert's sunny weather. I'd add the pace to that list, but Bend's brewing industry is growing so quickly the pace is perhaps becoming even more breakneck. The rapid growth was just the point for brewmaster Chad Kennedy, who left Laurelwood (and soon brought his lead brewer, Dustin Kellner, with him) to pursue Worthy Brewing. I wondered how much the name was a nod to Roger Worthington, beer-loving attorney and primary investor. Around their first anniversary, Kennedy mentioned they had outpaced their own production goal for the first year by topping 3,000 barrels; in short order, they've grown into one of Oregon's twenty largest breweries. He also corrected me about my supposition of the name.

"Actually, the Worthy and Worthington thing was just a coincidence," he said. "It's actually more about a goal to strive for, and telling folks that they're worthy of good beer, food, etcetera. It's the antithesis of this brewer-as-rock-star BS that we're seeing. Crafting great beer is about the person drinking it—not the person making it."

Worthy's solid lineup of beers is distributed to Washington, Idaho, and soon California. "Our beer is distributed [throughout the] West Coast, and then within five to ten years working out towards the Mississippi," Kellner added. "But Bend is really our market." Surprisingly, given Bend's double-digit brewery population, Worthy was the first brewery and pub on the east side, where there's a growing portion of the (people) population. If you're coming from Old Town or somewhere on the west side, the drive down Greenwood Avenue

Beers brewed: Year-round: Worthy IPA, Easy Day Kolsch, Worthy Pale, Lights Out Stout (vanilla cream stout), Worthy Imperial IPA, Eruption Imperial Red, The Contender Triple IPA. Seasonals: Dark Muse Imperial Stout (winter), Porter (spring), Farm Out Saison (summer), Powder Keg (fall). Series: Heart and Soul (draft only).

The Pick: Eruption. Worthy calls this an IRA—Imperial Red Ale—which also qualifies it as an India Red Ale to me. The sunset-red hue accurately suggests toffeelike caramel maltiness, but the star is the 6 pounds of hops per barrel, including plenty of "C" hops (Cascade, Centennial, and Crystal) and two cool "M" hops—the lemongrassy Meridian and a personal new favorite, Mandarina Bavaria from Hallertau, for a touch of tangerine.

past the extinct volcano that is Pilot Butte, popular with urban hikers and dog walkers, leads directly to this most welcoming brewpub.

Let's start with the beer. Kennedy's focus is on production brewing, which the 30-barrel system (for starters) amply handles, but he was itching to get the 5-barrel pilot system in gear so there's always unique stuff on among the dozen taps as part of the Heart and Soul Series. There's a wide spectrum of beer styles, but the central focus is on hoppy beers. The flagship is Worthy IPA, which achieves the required malt balance to the fragrant hop bill composed of Nugget, Centennial, Meridian, Crystal, and Horizon and accounts for 70 percent of their volume. There's an Imperial IPA, and in the middle of the Standard Reference Method (SRM)—the spectrum used to measure beer color—is an imperial red called Eruption that's rapidly gaining followers. On the dark end, Badlands Black IPA, a Heart and Soul batch, tastes like holding cocoa nibs and grapefruit peel in your mouth. Biggest of all, The Contender is a true hop volcano that blasts past both the 10 percent ABV and 100 IBUs markers. It burns with smoldering "C" hops like Chinook, Cascade, CTZ, Centennial and Amarillo, Citra, and Simcoe—stuff some smaller breweries would be happy to get their hands on.

In many facets, Worthy assembled a dream team of brewers, reps, and other veterans. Worthy CEO Chris Hodge spent eighteen years with Columbia Distributing, which, not surprisingly, is Worthy's distributor. Another noteworthy top veteran is Dr. Al Haunold. For background, Worthington, who cofounded Indie Hops—a hop distributor for independent breweries—sponsors Oregon State University's hop breeding program. In the United States, there are breeding programs in the public and private sectors, and OSU's falls under the USDA's umbrella. With Indie Hops sponsoring their hop breeding, Worthy was able to recruit the legendary Dr. Haunold to its team after he retired from the USDA in 1999.

Sure, hoppiness seems to be almost everyone's focus, but how many breweries have sixteen hop varietals growing in their quarter-acre hop yard? Amble through the garden boxes and it's like walking around the world—and through time—in terms of hop agriculture. There's a bine of Keyworth's early United Kingdom hops from the late 1800s (the U.S. Goldings have roots in eighteenth-century Canterbury) and Perle hops with German ancestry. You'll also find Dr. Haunold's veritable, verdant, and aromatic curriculum vitae, spanning from his work with the USDA at OSU in 1972; to his development of the most formidable of American hops, Cascades; and up through his Newport hops that hit the market in 2002. All of this results in a greenhouse dubbed the "Worthy Hop House," where they develop new varietals. Hence, the back row of trellises, behind the Santiams and Sterlings, are labeled simply "2010 #1" and may show up in Worthy's (or other breweries') beers in the future. "It's safe to say there will never be another public servant like Dr. Alfred Haunold," lauded Kennedy. "Al will go down in history as 'the People's Hopmeister' who helped put the aroma in craft beer."

Not for nothing, the garden also grows herbs and veggies that make their way onto the pub's menu. The restaurant expanded practically the minute after Worthy opened. Initially, everything hot came out of the 800-degree pizza oven. That's right—a brewpub with no fryer. Sounds good to me, but Bendites demanded French fries. I do concede: What's a brewpub burger without fries? So, going back to what Kennedy said about the beer but substituting fries or poppers, "telling folks that they are worthy of good [fries]" and that it's "about the person [eating] it," they folded that into the kitchen expansion.

The artistically designed interior, including mosaics along the walls and floor as well as the spacious and inviting beer garden that's more like a park (total capacity is around 250) means that everyone's welcome, and it often feels as if everyone *is* there.

The entirely modern brewhouse and pub do have one rather unique connection to Oregon's past. From the bar to the bathrooms, several thousand feet of boards made of Old Growth Douglas Fir were repurposed from the demolition of the Oregon Mental Hospital, the very same nineteenth-century Oregon State Insane Asylum that served as the setting of novelist Ken Kesey's seminal *One Flew Over the Cuckoo's Nest*. The film was shot on location. Maybe that's where the rich, mocha flavors of Cuckoo Kawfee Porter get that hint of nuttiness from.

Worthy Brewing Co.

Opened: 2013.

Owners: Chad Kennedy and Roger Worthington.

Brewers: Chad Kennedy (brewmaster) and Dustin Kellner (head brewer).

System: 30-barrel (to start).

Annual production: 10,000 barrels.

Distribution: Oregon, Washington, Idaho, and Vermont.

Hours: Sunday through Thursday, 11:30 a.m. to 10 p.m.; Friday and Saturday, 11:30 a.m. to 11 p.m.

Tours: Available by appointment; email tours@worthybrewing.com.

Takeout beer: Growlers, bottles, cans, and dock sales.

Gift shop: Shirts, hats, bike riding gear, glassware, and more.

Food: Pizzas plus sandwiches and snacks. For Oregon *terroir*, try the Oregon Pear pizza that's also topped with Rogue Creamery gorgonzola and local hazelnuts.

Southern

The State of Jefferson was nearly America's fifty-first state. The Jefferson Movement swept this region of Southern Oregon and Northern California where residents planned to form a breakaway state, incensed that the capitals of Salem and Sacramento were guilty of taxation without representation. They made plans for an elaborate State of Jefferson rebellion to occur on December 8, 1941. The bombing of Pearl Harbor is to thank/blame for this nonexistent secession state. Sixty years later, locals are revisiting the idea in earnest. The main reason I hope they don't secede is because Oregon would lose up to twenty-five breweries.

Equally vital is Southern Oregon's rich farmland, including plenty of vineyards. This wine country receives many visitors, and wine-tasters' new openness to trying beer has led to a recent boom in breweries along the more populous Interstate 5 corridor throughout Roseburg, Medford, and Ashland. The latter has been home to the **Oregon Shakespeare Festival** since 1935. Arrive any time between February and November, as over 400,000 fans do each year, and you can catch one of the Bard's masterpieces.

Others are drawn by the region's startling beauty off the freeway; the Rogue and Umpqua valleys and their respective rivers offer fantastic rafting and salmon fishing. **Highway 138**, dubbed the "Highway of Waterfalls," makes for a gorgeous drive that leads to even more breathtaking hikes whether you're angling for steelhead or not. If spelunking is your thing, the half-mile underground tour of **Oregon Caves National Monument** includes fanciful stalagmites and stalactites galore.

But the most can't-miss feature is probably **Crater Lake National Park** in Klamath County, so those simply shooting up I-5 miss out. Inside the caldera is the second deepest lake in America, nearly 2,000 feet deep, and you simply have to see the resulting blue hues to believe they're real. From I-5, if you're driving up Crater Lake Highway (62) that shadows the Rogue River, the fresh berry pies at **Becky's Café** in its own little town of Prospect are practically worth the haul. If you're traveling through or to Klamath Falls via the Green Springs Highway (66) from Ashland, the scurrying chipmunks and errant wild turkeys reveal that you're entering a pastoral, wooded area. Heed the circling hawks overhead as you bank hard curves over this road that's fun yet requires serious eyes on the road with hands at ten and two.

BricktownE Brewing Co.

44 South Central Avenue, Medford, OR 97501
(541) 973-2377 • BricktowneBeer.com
Twitter @Bricktowne

BricktownE's location was built in the 1890s, according to owner and craft beer crusader Craig McPheeters, and a brothel used to operate upstairs. You could call their Workin' Gal BrownE Ale, which busts a nutty flavor and mouthfeel, an homage. For today's working folks, there's Blue Collar Cream Ale, a session beer that goes down nice and easy.

As a dosimetrist—the radiation oncologist who decides on chemotherapy treatments—McPheeters's day job paid better than brewing, hence he contained his hobby to a 1-barrel system in his garage, the same one on which he made his first commercial batches. BricktownE's capital "E" denotes Craig's affinity for English-style ales, but while there's the brown, an ESB, and Rogue Trail English IPA (67 IBUs), most popular are HopJaw American IPA (98 IBUs) and Ore-Gunslinger Double IPA (100-plus IBUs). The latter, boasting 4 pounds of hops per barrel and featuring a cap gun as the tap handle, made by Dennis McPheeter (Craig's father—this is a family operation), "keeps the pub going."

BricktownE Brewing Co.

Opened: 2013.

Owners: Craig McPheeters and Scott Parker.

Brewers: Craig McPheeters and Neil Smith.

System: 5-barrel.

Annual production: 300 barrels.

Distribution: Around town.

Hours: Monday and Tuesday, 2 p.m. to 10 p.m.; Wednesday through Saturday, 11:30 a.m. to 10 p.m.; Sunday, noon to 6 p.m.

Tours: "Have a peek." It's in the back.

Takeout beer: Growlers, limited bottles, and kegs.

Gift shop: Apparel and growlers.

Food: Starters, salads, sandwiches, sausages, and more. Pulled pork nachos!

Beers brewed: Year-round: Workin' Gal BrownE, Ore-Gunslinger DIPA, Applegate Pale Ale, HopJaw American IPA, Rogue Trail English IPA, Siskiyou Pass ESB, Blue Collar Cream, Table Rock Red, Barrique Black Ale (vanilla porter), Calypso Cowboy Tropical IPA, Rock Steady Wheat Stout. Seasonals: Summer Swelter Lemon Wheat, India Red, Bricktoberfest.

The Pick: Ore-Gunslinger. Employing the newly popular hop-bursting technique (only late-addition hops) using Centennial, Citra, Cascade, and Columbus and dry-hopping with them as well creates this super citrusy DIPA roaring from the aroma.

Caldera Brewing Co.

590 Clover Lane, Ashland, OR 97520
(541) 482-HOPS • CalderaBrewing.com
Twitter @CalderaBeer
Taphouse: 31 Water Street, #2, Ashland,
OR 97520l; (541) 482-PINT (7468)

When I popped into Jim Mills's office at the back of Caldera's production area behind the public house, he was wearing shorts and flip-flops, looking every bit the quintessential surfer boy that he is so he doesn't look his age, which is only his mid-forties. He wears his love of Hawaii on his short sleeves, which explains Caldera's Toasted Coconut Chocolate Porter and another called Red Sea, a collaboration brew with Big Island Brewhaus in Kona that's a delectable imperial red ale with chocolate, molasses, pink peppercorns, and Himalayan pink salt added for richness and spice, not unlike a sweet and savory molé. It'd go great with fish tacos, but this isn't the middle of the Pacific and the surfing in Ashland is terrible.

These days, Mills likes the expanding Southern Oregon scene, and beer-wise a lot of that has to do with the recently expanded Caldera. If he seems a bit young to run one of the largest breweries in Oregon and the largest by far down south, keep in mind that he started it in 1997. The Portlander brewed for Rogue Ales from 1990 to 1992 when they still had their original Ashland-based brewery.

After awhile of quiet yet steady growth, Caldera started winning a few beer competitions and in 2005 became the first brewery in the state to put its product in cans. The package is increasingly prevalent now, but at the time it was still perceived as something only industrial, inferior brands were sold in. At the same time, it led to a few years of growing pains. Caldera is now at the point where it distributes to well over a dozen states scattered around the country and a few overseas destinations, too.

Beers brewed: Year-round: Canned: Pale Ale, IPA, Ashland Amber, Lawnmower Lager, Pilot Rock Porter. Draft: Pilsener Bier, Dry Hop Pale, Dry Hop Orange. Caldera Kettle Series bottled releases: Hopportunity Knocks, Ginger Beer, Rose Petal Imperial Golden, Vas Deferens (with orange bitters and blood orange zest), Rauch Ür Bock (smoked lager), Old Growth (imperial stout), Mogli (oaked imperial porter with chocolate), Hop Hash IPA. Seasonals: Draft: Helles Lager, Hibiscus Ginger Beer, Vanilla Wheat, Cauldron Brew, Toasted Coconut Chocolate Porter, South Side Strong, Oatmeal Stout, Kihei Snow, Roasted Hatch Chili, Kolsch, Belgian-Style Dubbel, Good Bean Coffee Brown, Double Hemp Brown, No Grain No Pain (gluten free), Mother Pucker Raspberry Sour.

Also in 2005, Caldera opened its taphouse, in the spot where Rogue had flooded, as an outlet for people to enjoy the array of Caldera beers on draft in a cozy atmosphere. Ashland Creek, the headwaters of the Rogue River, snuggles up against this below-street-level hideaway with a fireplace for chilly nights. The friendlier-than-usual beertenders know regulars not only by name but also by order, even with twenty house beers on tap. The food side leans toward fries, rings, wings, and burgers, but the veggie Miles Burrito is delicious, a bit spicy, and pairs nicely with a beer like Dry Hop Orange (which doesn't contain any citrus fruit but could've been named India Orange Ale). If there's a game on, expect it to be on the big screen but it's behind the stage until a band kicks in.

The newer and more polished Public House at the front of the larger production facility—there's a 30-barrel system, with the original 10-barrel system now used for pilot batches that make their way onto the twenty-eight taps behind the bar—includes a restaurant with less emphasis on the fried and features pizzas and housemade pastas as well as its own bakery that repurposes spent grains. Even non-vegetarians would love to sink their teeth into the black bean burger with Dry Hop Orange avocado crème fraiche. Illustrating how much larger the environment is, the walls surrounding it are lined with 4,567 bottles of varying origins and vintages yet don't make the space seem at all crowded. The view of Grizzly Peak is a nice touch.

Part of the 28,000-square-foot facility is a larger canning line. The original packed up to 60 cans a minute. The new one can do 1,400. To move that much product, one of the first new offerings is Lawnmower Lager, named for those light beers that make tending to one's lawn more manageable, and it retails for around six bucks a six-pack. It's not one for the beer geeks and it's the only one that doesn't use whole flower hops (oh, and Hop Hash IPA uses bricked hops), which is a testament to their multitude of hoppy offerings such as Hopportunity Knocks, a Centennial hop bomb topping 100 IBUs. The canning line, additionally, will start to see beverages other than beer, i.e. root beer. The line of craft sodas—an area I believe is far underrepresented—includes a ginger ale with 30 pounds of organic ginger. Mills designed the recipes, and they don't entail extracts. Just don't confuse the Ginger Ale with the Ginger Beer, which is actually beer with alcohol.

Speaking of alcohol, the second phase of the expansion is to add a distillery to make spirits such as bourbon, vodka, and gin.

I can only hope that one day, once they get some good house bourbon barrels going, they'll use them to upgrade what is already one of their finest offerings, Mogli, named in honor of a gorgeous black lab who, in the words of Shakespeare, shuffled off this mortal coil. (Ashland is also the home of the virtually year-long Oregon Shakespeare Festival.) No doubt the chocolate imperial porter would've been awesome enough on its own, but it's then aged on bourbon-soaked oak. It's certainly sweet and best served with or as the dessert course. Let this chocoholic's liquid dream warm up and the bourbon's vanilla notes reveal themselves, along with rum-soaked tobacco. Best of all, this once seasonal beer is now available year-round. Another amazing treat from my last visit was intended to be a replica of Red Sea, just like Mills brewed in Kona, but they accidentally left Mogli's bourbon, chocolaty oak spirals in the fermentation tank. The resulting warming vanilla notes (or maybe it's the near 9 percent ABV that made me glow) round out this beer that's only available in Ashland, but it's a lot easier to drive to than Kona.

Caldera Brewing Co.

Opened: 1997.

Owner: Jim Mills.

Brewers: Jimmy Mills (brewmaster), Adam Benson (lead brewer), Jon Bieckel (brewer), and Fred Martinez (assistant brewer).

System: 30-barrel production and 10-barrel pilot.

Annual production: 5,800 barrels.

Distribution: Oregon and fifteen states coast to coast, plus Puerto Rico and a few foreign countries including Japan, China, Brazil, and Sweden.

Hours: Daily, 11 a.m. to 11 p.m. Taphouse: Sunday through Thursday, 2 p.m. to 10 p.m.; Friday and Saturday, 2 p.m. to midnight.

Tours: By appointment.

Takeout beer: Growlers, bombers, cans, and keg dock sales.

Gift shop: Shirts, caps, and glassware.

Food: The menu at the brewery's on-site public house offers pizzas, sandwiches, specials, children's items, and beery desserts. The centrally located taphouse menu contains burgers and fried pub grub.

Conner Fields Brewing

The Haul: 121 Southwest H Street, Grants Pass, OR 97526
(541) 226-8490 • ConnerFields.com

CONNER FIELDS BREWING

Outside Grants Pass in the rural Applegate Valley is a veritable beer geek destination that sadly can't be visited. In a rehabbed barn surrounded by the Conner Family Vinery, or what you and I might call a vineyard, Jon Conner makes delicious and distinctive farmhouse ales. He'd love to add a hop yard, too. Fortunately, he and Fulcrum Dining's Chad Hahn are creating a tasting room/marketplace/restaurant called The Haul—more of what Conner calls a pour house—that will be the public face, but more on that later.

Conner, who usually sports a gray beard or mustache and curly hair, moved to Southern Oregon after seventeen years in Brooklyn, along with his buddy, Josh Fields. In Brooklyn, the roommates were sculptors—which is to say starving artists—so home-brewing became a natural way to keep themselves in cheap beer. Conner's welding skills came in handy creating the Conner Fields 1.5-barrel brewery (with plans to upsize to 8.5 barrels). Fields later split, but the name stuck and sensibly so, since the brewery is literally in grape fields.

Initially, Conner's stable of quality saisons and various ales were sold primarily at the Grants Pass Growers Market in pre-filled growlers. He also alternates appearances at Growers Markets in Medford and Ashland. He tries to always have a lighter beer, a darker beer, and a hoppier one. All manners of non-traditional grains, ginger, or grapes find their way into his recipes. A favorite among the local winemakers, and one of my personal preferences too, is the Zin Saison made with Zinfandel grapes hand-plucked right outside the barn-based brewery.

He loves giving out samples to get non-dark beer fans to buy his porter. For both hopheads

Beers brewed: Seasonals: Frank Lloyd Rye IPA, Cream Lager, Bankrupt State (California Common), Shark Attack! (IPA), Robot Small, Afterglow (dry-hopped pale ale), Zin Saison, Gold Coast (ginger saison), Eric (smoked porter), Landlover (American brown), Dry Stout.

The Pick: Robot Small. Although the grain bill contains predominantly two-row malted barley, it's the 30 percent rice that gives this beer its characteristic dryness. Even though super lemony Sorachi Ace hops from Japan lend it both big citron notes and some guava flavors, it is still more a Northwest ale than a Japanese lager, and delectably so.

and those who claim they don't dig hops, Conner offers a taste of Robot Small. It's a creative, hoppy beer with a light body from a grain bill that's 30 percent rice and made more bright and refreshing with Japanese Sorachi Ace hops. It's not bitter, just flavorful. He pitches an ale yeast frequently used to ferment Kolsches, Helleses, and "steam" beers, then lagers it at a cooler temperature. "I do wanna do a Big Robot as an imperial," he told me, though he's not sure how much higher alcohol or full bodied he'd build it.

Overall, Conner Fields offers around fifteen different beers, though none as a year-round flagship. It's not as if the family vinery grows zin grapes throughout the year, or that such a refreshing, slightly sour beer wouldn't hit the spot no matter the season. What he does always have available are wine barrels: Zinfandel, Tempranillo, and even port and sherry ones. "I will be barrel aging," he said, "but no brett [*Brettanomyces*] or I'll be kicked out by all the winemakers," he added, since it's no secret that while some brewers like employing funky microorganisms, they're a winemaker's nightmare.

In the end, Grants Pass doesn't have the same vibrancy as New York or number of beer drinkers, but Conner enjoys converting winemakers. Once The Haul opens in late 2014, Conner anticipates having twenty taps of primarily Conner Fields beer but also wineries including sparkling wine, cold brewed coffee, and cocktails on draft. "We are having a small, curated market with organic vegetables, charcuterie, cheese, and [other fermentations]," he explained. He called the cuisine of the farm-to-table eatery "New American," but it sounds like this pour house in the heart of Josephine County will be distinctly New Grants Pass.

"I fell in love with it here . . . I prefer to work in the country. I like opening the door and seeing that," he mused, pointing to the vineyard, "especially after living in Brooklyn."

Conner Fields Brewing

Opened: 2012.
Owner and brewer: Jon Conner.
System: 1.5-barrel.
Annual production: 35 barrels.
Distribution: Southern Oregon.
Extras: The brewery is not open to the public yet, although there are plans to add a tasting room. Prefilled growlers are available at local farmers markets.

Draper Brewing

7752 Highway 42, Tenmile, OR 97481
Draper Drafthouse: 640 Southeast Jackson
Street, Roseburg, OR 97470
(541) 672-5417 • DraperBrewing.com

The city of Roseburg is, just now, finally etching its place on the Oregon beer map. It was a smart move, then, for Sam Draper Eslinger, who decided to open a tasting room in the downtown area, since it's safe to say his hometown of Tenmile will never, ever be a beer mecca. That's where his actual brewery is located, in the barn next to his house along Highway 42, seventeen miles southwest of Roseburg proper. It's where his folks settled on thirty acres in the agricultural community rife with vineyards and orchards. As such, people interested in visiting Draper Brewing and sampling the beers can please stop popping in on him at home, thank you.

Unlike beer barons from Anheuser and his son-in-law Busch to the modern era's Widmers, Eslinger elected not to go the usual route for his brewing company. There are a lot of things he does differently from larger brewing companies. He has experience at some small-by-most-standards breweries including Lost Coast and Mad River, both in Humboldt County, which makes sense since he's originally from Northern California. Mad River happens to be one of my favorite breweries from that area, so it stands to reason that he has folded some of the tricks he picked up there into his own operation. Really, they're not tricks at all, since that almost implies shortcuts. His techniques entail using high-quality Maris Otter malts, using only real fruit (he handpicks the pears in his Pear Tripel and plums in his sour plum ale from his backyard), and brewing in the Old World tradition with an open fermenter for primary fermentation. Plus all his packaged beers undergo secondary fermentation because bottle conditioning adds more character.

As for the Tenmile brewery, Eslinger told me about a perk of his wine country surroundings. When it came time to graduate to a 5-barrel sys-

Beers brewed: Year-round: IPA, DIPA, Cream Ale, Chocolate Porter, Brown, Red. Seasonals: Wine barrel-aged ales, Blueberry Wheat, Blueberry Saison, Pear Tripel and one-offs.

The Pick: Chocolate Porter. It's desserty, but not goopy or too sweet to actually enjoy through the end of the pint since it's medium bodied (5.6 percent) and tastes like your pint is rimmed with cocoa powder thanks to the addition of cacao nibs. If only it came with a scoop of vanilla on the lip.

tem, since no one actually makes any money doing 1-barrel batches like he did at first, Sam went around to the wineries and Frankensteined his own system. (Yes, you can scrub and wash away hornet nests and other debris off stainless steel dairy tanks.) As for a winery effect on the Roseburg drafthouse (besides selling draft wine), he usually has a wine barrel-aged number available in a cask-conditioned firkin, like the red wine-aged Stock Ale I really dug. It was vinous and dominated by a sour cherry aroma but tasted almost like a cross blend of porter and Flemish Red ale without any sort of lactic character.

Because Eslinger likes Belgian styles and dark ales, that's generally what he brews. Despite not being a huge hophead himself, he makes a Centennial hop-driven DIPA because he observed that when he had one on a guest tap—of the dozen handles usually eight are Draper beers—it always kicked quickly. I'll add that he also likes traditional English styles and even has a beer engine to serve cask-conditioned ale, usually a British bitter, but it breeds some confusion.

The Draper Drafthouse is almost more of a clubhouse than a bar, as tipped off by the Princess Leia cutout among the cans of Duff Beer and a mirror ball in the entrance window. There are also pinball machines, dartboards and shuffleboard, and classic arcade consoles. Eslinger told me that the long space formerly served as a martini bar, a bakery, and local republican headquarters, but I gotta say: a brewpub works best. Not that beer is brewed on-premises, or that hot dogs and chips and salsa constitute a pub menu, but he has established a very cool hangout.

Draper Brewing

Opened: 2010.
Owner and brewer: Samuel Draper Eslinger.
System: 5-barrel.
Annual production: 150 barrels.
Distribution: Mostly around Umpqua Valley, but as far as Portland.
Hours: Tuesday through Saturday, 3 p.m. to 11 p.m.
Tours: Not available.
Takeout beer: Growlers and 22-ounce bottles.
Food: Basic snacks like chips and salsa. BYO is OK.
Extras: Thursday nights are Beers for Beards, so don a follicle face mask and get a buck off your pint (including women with real or fake ones).

Fire Cirkl

16110 Jones Road, White City, OR 97503
(541) 646-8871 • FireCirkl.com

Apropos of my destination, the vocalist soothing me from my car radio sang, "Meet me at the edge of the world." Southern Oregon University's station—with a format heavy on Dobros and musical saws—comes in weakly after passing Table Rock well off I-5, heading deeper into ranch country. The song guided me to Fire Cirkl, founded by retired fighter pilot James Romano in 2012. Romano flew F-14s through four deployments over thirteen years in the navy. He then transitioned back into civilian life as a pilot for American Airlines. If that sounds boring by comparison, it was. Over a dozen years later, he pursued his entrepreneurial dream of earning an MBA. His goal? Build a company that'd allow him to live where he wanted, do what he wanted, and follow his passion. That apparently means living on a ranch way above Medford, surrounded by more horses than people, and going from homebrewer to commercial brewer. He doesn't make regular ol' beer, but ancient braggots. "I'm interested in bringing back new flavors," he said.

At his 6-barrel brewery with a new tasting room, he makes braggots with 50 percent mead and 50 percent ale, though he's not allowed to label it as such. To understand why, ask the feds. But his products are certified 100 percent organic despite there being "no real money in making things organically." If regular honey is expensive, the organic stuff constitutes 75 percent of his expenses. He toyed with the idea of going the half-million-dollar, 20-barrel route, but Fire Cirkl is smaller and self-financed, hence the remote locale.

Braggots brewed: Naughty Heather, Dragon's Blood, Deer Catcher, One-Eyed Ginger.

Romano pulls his recipes from antiquity. "Hops only go back five hundred years in the ten thousand-year history of beer. Why are we going in the direction of hops? There's a market here that isn't being served," Romano explained. "I love reading about the Druids, the Greeks, Romans, Sumerians, and Native Americans."

Some consumers want beer over braggot, so he's bowing to modernity, somewhat, and expanding. Even then, he's developing mostly gruits, calling them pre-hopped beers rather than un-hopped.

The Pick: Naughty Heather. Built on a red ale in terms of malt bill, this hop-less beverage features organic heather tips and other flowers, is fermented with Belgian yeast to reach 11.4 percent ABV, and finishes sweet like strawberry-hibiscus juice.

"I've got a dark ale that uses all the same herbs that go into French absinthe . . . Wormwood provides bitterness in lieu of hops," he said.

I got to sample a few of his braggots, including one of his flagships, Dragon's Blood, which starts as a porter fermented with wine yeast. There are plenty of New Zealand hops—Pacific Gem and Hallertau—in it. It might appeal to barleywine fans or just wine fans, as the aroma is quite fruity like a Zinfandel. The first sip offers coffee-like bitterness but it finishes like squirting a honey bear bottle into your mouth, albeit one filled with blackberry or currant honey. But that's Romano's catch. Braggot needs to be fifty-fifty, otherwise he considers it honey beer.

Romano conceived of Fire Cirkl in 2007 and hoped he wouldn't be too late by the time he got it going. When bottles showed up in 2012, he was surprised he was actually the first. I have no clue where he gleaned this stat, but he said that even today, "seven out of ten people have not heard of mead." He followed that with a statistic from his own research, informing me that nine out of ten people who try his braggots really like them, even if they like one over another. And to think, a year later with the opening of Viking up in Eugene, Oregon now has two dedicated braggot-making meaderies/breweries—braggoteries—along with a new retail space in Portland called Bee Thinking that doubles as Mead Market. Insert mead is buzzing pun here.

As such, Romano is hopeful that the audience for meads and braggots picks up in the future to resemble the ancient past. Naughty Heather's label copy conjures Druids, Celts, and Picts from thousands of years ago who deemed heather sacred. Deer Catcher alludes to the Rarámuri of the Barrancas in Northwest Mexico, famous for hunting deer not with rifles but by running them down to exhaustion, hence the inclusion of organic white sage for good respiration. All this begins to paint a clearer picture of Fire Cirkl and Romano himself, and why he had the company logo resemble the Zia sun symbol, in which the four points or directions symbolize body, mind, spirit, and planet. "We're doing our part to improve the human experience," said Romano.

Fire Cirkl

Opened: 2012.
Owner and brewer: James Romano.
System: 6-barrel.
Annual production: 50 barrels.
Distribution: Oregon.
Hours: Possibly Fridays and Sundays; check before you visit.
Takeout braggot: 750-milliliter bottles.

Griess Family Brews

220 Southwest H Street, Unit B, Grants Pass, OR 97526
(541) 450-9090 • GFBrews.com

The name Griess Family Brews doesn't mislead. More than a mom (Susie Griess) and pop (Dave Griess) operation, their son, Travis, in his mid-twenties, is the brewer. The other son, Patrick "PJ" Griess, handles the IT side of things, and his wife, Leah, set up the company's Facebook page. The brewhouse occupies the 200-square-foot outbuilding in Travis's backyard.

A homebrewing operation with really supportive parents, Griess Family Brews filed in April 2013. They soon sold a growler of their first beer, Little Orphan Amber, to a family friend (talk about being supportive), though the Growler Guys two hundred miles away in Bend staked its claim as the first retail account. Not that the Griess family plans on selling the beer far from home—they opened a tasting room in Grants Pass.

Travis plans on brewing beyond their British styles. "We want to do some German styles, too, because of our heritage," he said, ("Griess" rhymes with "rice"), though he hasn't done any lagers yet. Not that Germans only make lagers. There's a cute note on the Facebook page showing a glass of Rogue's Mom Hefeweizen with a comment from Susie: "Hey Travis are you listening? A Hefeweizen for your mom. Hint, hint."

Beers brewed: Year-round: Grandpa Hall and Oats Oatmeal Stout, Little Orphan Amber, Cousin Jimmy Hoffa IPA. Seasonals: Grandpa Stagger's Stubborn Stout, Winter Warmer.

Griess Family Brews

Opened: 2013.

Owners: The Griess family (mom Susie, dad Dave, sons Travis and PJ, and daughter-in-law Leah).

Brewer: Travis Griess.

System: 1.5-barrel.

Annual production: TBD.

Distribution: Southern and Central Oregon.

Hours: Tuesday through Thursday, 4 p.m. to 9 p.m.; Friday and Saturday, 4 p.m. to 10 p.m.; Sunday, noon to 10 p.m.

Tours: Taproom coming soon to downtown.

Food: BYO.

The Pick: Grandpa Hall and Oats. Named after Grandpa Griess (actually Grandpa Hall). Some oatmeal stouts pick up a lot of body from velvety oats but this one retains a lighter body like an Irish stout, but with the sweetness from those added grains. If Little Orphan Amber's poor, this one's a rich girl.

JD's Sports Bar and Brewery

690 Redwood Highway, Grants Pass, OR 97527
(541) 471-0383 • JDsSportsBarAndBrewery.com

JD's slogan is: "Cold beer. Hot wings." Upon entering, you're struck not by the visage of a modern brewpub but by a throwback sports bar, lots of TVs (twenty total), six pool tables (free on weekdays), and a jukebox stocked with classic rock. Food-wise, the Pure Insanity wings claim they'll have you begging for your mommy. The menu itself isn't fried, but half of its offerings are.

JD's has been around for over twenty years, but it wasn't until recently that off-track horse betting was replaced with a brewery (though plenty of video poker machines greet you directly upon entering past the "biker parking only" sign). Brewer Jerry Elder is a veteran of the Southern Oregon brewing scene, having brewed at still-operating and now-defunct breweries alike.

There are eighteen different beers on tap, including macro Lights, but house beers wisely sell for the cheapest, at $4.25 per pint, and those quarter savings add up after a few rounds. Having said that, I often have good luck with lottery machines when doing max lines at max bet, and I even managed to win a couple pints' worth on the penny machine and genuinely enjoyed them.

Although all of the promo items on the walls—including in the bathroom—are for domestic macros and a few of the larger brewing companies like Deschutes, there's a cardboard cutout of John Wayne, wearing a Panama hat and keeping watch over the spacious, open-walled brewery.

JD's Sports Bar and Brewery

Opened: 2013.
Owner: Jack DiMatteo.
Brewer: Jerry Elder.
System: 6-barrel.
Annual production: 150 barrels.
Distribution: Grants Pass.
Hours: Office: 7 a.m. to 2:30 a.m.
Tours: It's right there in the back.
Takeout beer: Growlers.
Food: Wings, burgers, and barbecue.

Beers brewed: Year-round: Patriot Pale Ale, LSD IPA, Farmer's Organic Wheat Ale, Knockout Stout, Paisan Porter, Monk's Obsession Red, Festivus Ale (holiday).

The Pick: Patriot's Pale Ale. It's a pretty good pale, true to the Northwest style with hop bite over a sessionable base boosted by sturdy pale malts.

Klamath Basin Brewing Co. / The Creamery Brewpub & Grill

1320 Main Street, Klamath Falls, OR 97601
(541) 273-5222 • KBbrewing.com

Klamath Basin Brewing is the fitting name for this brewpub, but as soon as you spot the cartoonish cow lording over the entrance it's clear why the equally suitable name is The Creamery Brewpub & Grill. The blue cow sign dates back to the Klamath Falls Creamery, which enjoyed a good fifty-year run before its current incarnation. The brewery actually first started selling beer made in cofounder Lonnie Clement's garage. Thanks to local support, Clement and partner Del Azevedo were able to open the brewpub in 2005, but locals continued to call it The Creamery. One of its original Crater Lake Ice Cream neons still adorns the pub.

Rather than dwell on the building's icy past, this is the only brewery that gets to flaunt such a hot present. Thanks to a distinct, geothermal combo of hot rocks and water akin to Yellowstone's famous geysers—don't worry, Klamath Falls doesn't smell like sulfuric rotten eggs—the city figured out how to tap into this natural resource to do things like keep sidewalks snow free (from December until as late as June in Southern Oregon's High Country) and provide the brewery's heat source. (The fireplace by the easy chairs helps, too.) As brewer Corey Zschoche explained it, "City geothermal water comes into our building between 180 and 190 degrees." That means they always have a jumpstart at getting the strike water up to temperature before mashing in.

When Zschoche started in 2009, he inherited Clement's and Azevedo's recipes. "Crater Lake Amber was the first beer they brewed in the garage commercially," he said. "It still harkens back to that garage-based recipe." He confessed—more like assured me—that he upped the hopping on their IPA, which features Summit, Chinook,

Beers brewed: Year-round: Headstrong Blonde, Notch Eight IPA, Rebellion Red Ale, Backroad Vanilla Porter, Defiance DIPA, Crater Lake Amber Ale, Hard Hat Hefeweizen, 51st State Pale Ale. Seasonals: Bare Knuckle Brown, Linkville Lager, Oktoberfest, Fresh Hopican Pale Ale.

The Pick: Backroad Vanilla Porter. While the pub is known for its blue cow, this beer reminds me of a brown cow—a milkshake made by adding chocolate sauce to vanilla ice cream. Alternating between the sweetness of vanilla beans and the bitterness of roasted chocolate malts, this porter works accompanying a meal or dessert.

Cascade, Falconer's Flight, and Simcoe for a winning mélange of Northwest aromatics. He also introduced a fresh hop version of the pale ale. There's now the year-round 51st State (formerly Pelican Butte) and autumnal Fresh Hopican, playing off the pelican name, that employs tropical Mosaic hops.

On Zschoche's clock, the IPA has become the best-selling draft beer in the huge pub, while the vanilla porter remains the top seller among bottled offerings. He painstakingly slices enough vanilla beans (with help from an assistant) for a 30-barrel double batch, which makes his hands quite sore but leaves them smelling great. He then adds a mesh bag full of the beans, once the porter has undergone primary and open fermentation, into secondary fermentation. Rogue Creamery down in the valley uses the brew to make their Vanilla Porter Cheddar.

Finally, given the family-oriented atmosphere of the pub, I had to ask him about the Butt Crack Brown Ale. "Well . . ." Zschoche said with a sigh, "the story that I heard was Lonnie was trying to think of a name for the brown ale when he saw Del working away in the brewery. Del may have been flaunting a bit of ass cleavage." Alas, most of the beers were rebranded in 2014 so it's now called Bare Knuckle Brown. (I wouldn't flinch at seeing Del's bare knuckles.) Mercifully, even though the brewery today is situated right behind the bar with a glass wall, I didn't have to see Zschoche squatting over any brewing equipment. He said it definitely makes him feel like a zoo animal but acknowledges it "adds to the pub." That's true, although you can't see it from the massive patio that's packed to the gills all summer long with locals and folks making their way up to or down from Crater Lake National Park. And while Clement and Azevedo aren't very active in the brewpub's day-to-day operations, it's not uncommon to see them hanging out with regulars whom they know by name.

Klamath Basin Brewing Co. / The Creamery Brewpub & Grill

Opened: 2001.

Owners: Lonnie Clement and Del Azevedo.

Brewer: Corey Zschoche.

System: 15-barrel.

Annual production: 1,450 barrels.

Distribution: Oregon, Washington, and Northern California.

Hours: Daily, 11 a.m. to 9:30 p.m.

Takeout beer: Growlers and bottles.

Gift shop: Threads, hats, and soaps made using Crystal Springs IPA and Vanilla Porter.

Food: Burgers, sandwiches, pelican potato skins with pulled pork and bacon.

McMenamins Roseburg Station Pub & Brewery

700 Southeast Sheridan Street, Roseburg, OR 97470
(541) 672-1934 • Mcmenamins.com/Roseburg
Twitter @CaptainNeon

With the exception of the many chandeliers, painting of dogs playing poker, and brewery itself, much of what you see at McMenamins Roseburg Station is actually from Roseburg's Southern Pacific Railroad depot, built here in 1912.

Historical photos line the walls, including one of President Taft being welcomed here. Ironically, Taft opposed Prohibition, but before his administration Douglas County voted to go dry, thus padlocking the Roseburg Brewing Co.

McMenamins isn't the first post–Prohibition brewery here, but it's now the oldest. Tom Johnson keeps locals in Roseburg-themed beers such as Wissler's Wheat, named after Ezra Wissler who settled here in 1852. While plenty of Johnson's beers are decidedly modern, including Diamond IPA and Purple Rain (a malted rye- and wheat-based ale with blackberries), patrons are ushered back in time via features such as vaulted ceilings with tongue-and-groove wainscoting and the original urinals in the men's restroom.

McMenamins Roseburg Station Pub & Brewery

Opened: 1999.

Owners: Brian and Mike McMenamin (see page 92).

Brewer: Tom Johnson.

System: 7-barrel.

Annual production: 800 barrels.

Distribution: On-premises and nearby pubs.

Hours: Monday through Thursday, 11 a.m. to 11 p.m.; Friday and Saturday, 11 a.m. to midnight; Sunday, noon to 10 p.m.

Tours: Walk-in tours when brewer is available.

Takeout beer: Growlers.

Gift shop: Mc-merch (shirts and other limited items).

Food: McMenamins pub grub.

Extras: In September, Hopqua is a fresh hop beer with backyard hops picked by regulars from the Umpqua Valley. On St. Patrick's Day, Pub Crawl turns this into standing room only.

Beers brewed: Year-round: Hammerhead Pale Ale, Terminator Stout, Ruby, IPA. Seasonals: Thielson Porter, Wissler's Wheat, Hopqua Fresh Hop Ale, Purple Rain, Diamond IPA, Jam Session ISA, and more.

The Pick: Diamond IPA. As if it contained a freight train's worth of Simcoe, Perle, and Santiam hops, this classic West Coast IPA strikes its balance between 6.5 percent ABV and 62 IBUs, which explains the heavy aroma of bitter citrus peel.

Mia & Pia's Pizzeria & Brewhouse

3545 Summers Lane, Klamath Falls, OR 97603
(541) 884-4880 • MiaAndPias.com

Seventeen miles north of the California border is this ma-and-pa pizzeria named Mia & Pia's, run not by anyone actually named Mia or Pia, but by Rod Kucera and his wife, Jodi. As family lore has it, Rod's nephew John was the first grandchild for Rod's parents, but he couldn't quite say "Gramma and Grampa" when he was learning to speak; instead, it came out "Mia and Pia." When they opened the restaurant in 1987, they knew they had their name for the next family business. The first was running a dairy farm. "We had the largest raw milk dairy in Oregon . . . We were organic before organic was cool," Kucera said. But his folks got out of the dairy biz during the government's Whole Herd Buyout Program in 1986. Today, Kucera is the restaurant owner and brewer, but he didn't add the brewery until 1996. Before that, he was busy "sowing my wild oats in Oklahoma rodeoing."

I sat down in the welcoming back patio of the brewpub—a flight of a dozen beer samples set before me—with Kucera. He was dressed in a khaki brewery-branded shirt and shorts, safari hat and boots, with his brown and gray goatee and round-frame glasses. He looked like a Klamath bushman, not a bona fide professional bull rider. He did suffer "bruises and a couple trips to the hospital," but his worst injury occurred at the hooves of his own heifer on the farm and required seven screws and a plate. "I keep those X-rays up at the bar so I can prove I don't have any screws loose," he told me.

As for the patio, the first stop on our brewery tour, in the summer it's a veritable rainbow of flowers and verdant with trees and plants. Indoors there's a bank of arcade game consoles. The bar, somewhat hidden behind a wall and the mug club mugs that hang like crystal stalactites, is a respite from minors. In this remote town of twenty

Beers brewed: Year-round: Screamin' Eagle American Lager, Emmett & Anna's Pivo, Henley Hayfeweizen, RA Ale, Applegate Trail Pale Ale, Rod's Rodeo Red, Spencer Creek Amber Ale, Improvisor I.P.A., White Pelican Porter, Irish Stout. Seasonals: Peach, Marzen, Blast Off Barleywine, IPAs, fresh-hop beers, Country Bumpkin Pumpkin Ale, Irrigator Doppelbock.

The Pick: Rod's Rodeo Red. Brewed in honor of all the cowboys Rod rode with as a professional bull rider, at first glance the beer looks like a brown ale. It's even a bit nutty like a brown, but citrusy hops peek through and the mahogany red hue hints at its caramel malt base provide a mere 4.7 percent ABV for an easy ride.

thousand people, the pizzeria-brewery, unlike contemporary, sleek brewpubs, looks like an old neighborhood grocery store, and that's because it was. "We used to deliver milk to this store," Kucera said. It's not downtown like Klamath Basin Brewing, but it works for them. Then again, instead of boasting about using reclaimed wood, what's more environmental than reclaiming an entire building? The Kuceras installed solar panels, too, and RA Ale, a rather light IPA, takes its name from the sun god.

As for the brewery, I can't call the equipment "reclaimed" since it belonged to the family farm the whole time. One day in 1995, Kucera was driving in a rig alone, which meant he had the rare treat of getting to tune into the rock-and-roll station that his dad would've vetoed. He kept hearing ads for the Northwest Microbrew Expo, a beer festival that today is known as the KLCC Microbrew Festival over in Lane County. Having attended and sampled his way through the microbrews, "It was time to slow down drinking," said Kucera, setting up the story. As he sat down to kill some time, he heard a speaker discussing how fun it is to brew from scratch using stainless steel, and how a good source is old dairy equipment. When Kucera alerted the speaker that he was sitting on plenty of such equipment, having been banned from returning to the dairy business nearly a decade earlier as a result of the buyout, he was told, "You can sell that to a microbrewery! They make beer in those tanks." Kucera said that's when the lightbulb went off.

Cut to one year later: Kucera read homebrewing books, learned to use the internet to find supplies, and attended a seminar called "How to Build a Brewery with Milk Tanks." If that sounds conveniently like fate, he swears it's so. "To this day I've never brewed an extract [batch of beer]," he added. Which isn't to say he's loved every drop of beer he has brewed: "I was such a rookie, I'd never had a German hefeweizen." Yet he decided to brew a wheat beer as his first batch. "It was perfect, but I didn't know about the banana and clove aroma. I thought it was off; I was looking for an American hefe. I thought I got it wrong so I fed it to the pigs. They put on their party hats and lederhosen and had a great time."

Nowadays, Mia & Pia's uses two yeast strains, an American ale yeast and a lager one for the three cold-fermenting beers Kucera makes. Henley Hayfeweizen comes with a lemon wedge like most American wheats, Kucera having abandoned the traditional Bavarian profile back during his homebrew year. Speaking of American styles, there's also Screamin' Eagle American Lager, a ridiculously light-bodied beer, and in contrast, Improvisor IPA, a full-bodied number boasting 4 pounds of hops per barrel. But the topseller is Applegate Trail Pale Ale, named for the southern route of the Oregon Trail that passes through the basin and containing Cascade, Golding, and Perle hops.

Speaking of hops, there's a hop garden on the Kucera farm, out in the even more rural part of town where the brewery resides. It provides barely enough hop cones for the annual fresh-hop batch of beer, and the yield determines the style. A bumper crop means an IPA. A pittance might lead to a pumpkin beer, which sounds like an odd use to me, but the 206 members of the mug club get invited out to the farm to pick the hops and they love his pumpkin beer. One year a gate was left open and cows chewed the hops off the bines, leaving me to wonder how those eventual burgers tasted. Clearly, Gilbert—their border collie whom I call the hop herder—failed to protect them.

Another element found on the farm linking the original dairy to the current brewery is the old milk delivery truck parked on the driveway. It has been converted to a sweet beer truck, replete with tap handles on the side. It's the truck that Jodi's dad drove for the Kuceras when her family moved out to Klamath Falls from Nebraska. Jodi was just five at the time; Rod was ten. He laughed as he stated earnestly, "I used to babysit my wife."

Mia & Pia's Pizzeria & Brewhouse

Opened: 1996.

Owners: Rod and Jodi Kucera.

Brewer: Rod Kucera

System: 5-barrel.

Annual production: 230 barrels.

Distribution: On-premises.

Hours: Sunday through Thursday, 11 a.m. to 10 p.m.; Friday and Saturday, 10 a.m. to 11 p.m.

Tours: By appointment only.

Takeout beer: Growlers.

Gift shop: Apparel and glasses.

Food: Pizza. I liked the Funky Chicken with roasted chicken, olives, mushrooms, garlic, and bbq sauce. Special Combination includes six different meats, while Italian Garden targets herbivores.

Old 99 Brewing Co.

3750 Hooker Road, Suite A, Roseburg, OR 97470
(541) 670-9260 • Old99Brewing.com
Twitter @Old99Brewing

Three best friends with full-time jobs—hence why they take turns brewing—opened Old 99 Brewing Co. in August 2013 on their dinky brewing system. Within a month they expanded to their 3.5-barrel brewery and, thanks to 7-barrel fermenters, brew fifty-some kegs a month. It sounds like the startup does brisk business, but "We're sincerely not in this for the money," said cofounder Matt Hill. "If it works out to support three families," he continued, noting that he and fellow owners AJ Tuter and Bryan Ireland are each married with a couple of kids, "then awesome. But we brew beer because we like beer . . . beer that we like to drink."

Route 99 runs through Roseburg and beyond, but Hill and Ireland began as garage-based homebrewers and they both live on Main Street, which Hill said used to be old Route 99. I doubt they would've been allowed to name it after the street the commercial brewery is on, since Hooker Brewing Co. is just wrong. "We've thought about doing things like having a Red Light special," joked Hill.

Hooker Road runs parallel to and is sandwiched between new Route 99 and heavily trafficked I-5. Along with the other new and forthcoming breweries, they "want to make Roseburg a [beer] destination," Hill said.

Old 99 Brewing Co.

Opened: 2013.
Owners and brewers: Matt Hill, AJ Tuter, and Bryan Ireland.
System: 3.5-barrel.
Annual production: 250 barrels.
Distribution: Roseburg.
Hours: Friday, 4 p.m. to 8 p.m.; Saturday, noon to 8 p.m.
Tours: By request.
Takeout beer: Growlers and dock sales.
Gift shop: Shirts and hats line the side room; growlers are available.

Beers brewed: Year-round: Infidel CDA, Billy Bad Ass DIPA, Fogline Espresso Stout, Infrared Red, 99-01 IPA, Yard Sale Pale Ale.

The Pick: Fogline Stout. Although Old 99's IPA, black IPA, and double IPA are clean, top-notch Fogline is spiked with cold-brewed espresso for a great complementary— not show-stealing—flavor to a well-built stout.

Opposition Brewing Co.

545 Rossanley Drive, Suite 106, Medford, OR 97501
(541) 210-8550 • OppositionBrewing.com
Twitter @OppositionBrew

I entered Opposition Brewing just as a caravan of Arizona rafters heading for the Rogue River arrived and took over the small industrial space, a.k.a. The Bunker. The second of many signs—some humorous, some dead serious—I read on the walls alerted folks that "guns are welcome on premises." That made the first sign, "no minors allowed," all the more reasonable.

Opposition changed its name in 2013 after originating in 2012 as Apocalypse. A Bend-situated brewery that makes an IPA by the same name litigated this Medford nanobrewery into . . . wait, I just got the new namesake. Anyway, the couple behind Opposition, Nick Ellis and his wife, Erin, don't necessarily think the world is going to end, but if it does they're prepared to keep themselves inebriated until their number's up. Until that day, they'd like to sell you some beer (and some of the best brewery art shirts) while you enjoy some pints and a game of Ring the Bull. This new-to-me pub game requires a skosh of skill and panoply of patience as you swing a ring on a string and try to land it on a wall-mounted bull's nose ring.

Despite—or in defiance of—the name change, Opposition's brands remain the same. The Sixth Seal is not an IPA but a Northwestern Pale Ale, yet at 6.88 percent ABV and 88 IBUs I defy them to explain the difference, not that it matters. For this beer, Nick wanted to shoot for that balanced pale ale that doesn't tip the scales into "extra" or "imperial" boundaries, which is where he figures this Northwest pale ale lands (especially since most of the ingredients are Pacific Northwest grown), meaning well shy of "like eating a hop cone." The hop cones imbibed in their best-selling beer include Warrior for bittering and Zythos, as well as Centennial for the tangy citrus and aroma.

As for other aromatic beers, Nick said he'd love to do a collaboration beer with their landlord

Beers brewed: Year-round: The Tunguska Event (cream ale), Fallow Fields (brown ale), Devastated Sky (stout), The Sixth Seal (Northwest pale ale), Blast Radius (oatmeal pale ale). Seasonals: Purgatory Pomegranate Berliner Weisse, Dirty Hippy, Kalki, brewers' choice.

The Pick: The Sixth Seal. They call it a Northwest Pale Ale. Packed with 88 IBUs, it's hopped like an IPA but maltier than even an English IPA and pours more toasted orange.

and his former employer, The Human Bean, a drive-through coffee hut that started in Southern Oregon and has evolved into a bicoastal chain. Initially Nick told me about his vision of a White Chocolate Espresso "Stout" that would be pale just like that stuff called white chocolate that calls itself chocolate. In the end, the Human Bean collaboration brew turned into Krumpus, a double peppermint mocha stout. At over 8 percent ABV, it sounds like it certainly lends itself to some merry holidays.

The Ellises outlined several ideas for down the road—such as a sour beer made with the little-known salal berries that look like raspberries but taste like blueberries and grow wild in the Kalmiopsis Wilderness just off the Rogue River—but they're still focused on getting their budding brewery going. The frequently-packed tasting room shows they're getting by with help from their friends. The convivial space has brought fellow patrons together, and the Ellises said they've gone on camping trips with folks who started out simply as customers. I'm sure they'd be fun to camp with, and it was all I could do to not take Charlie home with me. He's the boxer-pit mix that guards the brewhouse against, or rather for, opposition.

Oh, and as for Ring the Bull? Nick pointed out that Dennis Poncia, the brewer, is really good at the game he called "the cat toy for humans." I'm ringing .1000, at least among my very last at-bull. Just don't ask me about my first fifty tries.

Opposition Brewing Co.

Opened: 2012.
Owners: Nick and Erin Ellis; Dennis and Penny Poncia.
Brewers: Nick Ellis (head brewer) and Dennis Poncia (brewer).
System: 1.5-barrel.
Annual production: 200 barrels.
Distribution: On-premises only.
Hours: Thursday and Friday, 4 p.m. to 9 p.m.; Saturday, noon to 9 p.m.; Sunday, noon to 7 p.m.
Tours: Impromptu upon request.
Food: None, but food trucks occasionally parked outside.
Takeout beer: Growlers and kegs.
Gift shop: Cool shirts designed in town by Legionnaire Apparel, hoodies, and glasses.

Oregon Trail Brewery

341 Southwest 2nd Street, Corvallis, OR 97333
(541) 758-3527 • OregonTrailBrewery.com

Oregon Trail Brewing is an anachronism of the pioneering class of microbrewing that endearingly retains a toehold even though annual production has diminished by a few dozen barrels each year. A home-brewer named Jeremy opened it in 1987 despite lacking a professional application. He leased the space inside the Old World Deli rent-free somehow for five years when the only others were BridgePort, Widmer Brothers, and Full Sail. Five years later it closed. The following year, it reopened, salvaged by Dave Wills (owner of Freshops mail-order organic hops) and Jerry Bockmore (who got his start brewing at Pyramid—née Hart Brewing—in 1989 before consulting for Star Brewing from an earlier era in Portland). If you meet Wills at the brewery, be prepared for him to ask you if you'd like to buy it.

Fred Eckhardt, Oregon's celebrated dean of beer writers, dubbed Oregon Trail Brown the "Beer of the Year" in 1989. Neither it nor the brewery has changed one iota. "No robots, no computers," said brewer Weston Zaludek, who also brews at Viking in Eugene. Oregon Trail did, however, welcome microbiologist Don Pfeifer to the fold in 2003 when he began running a lab not for pay but for beer. For real.

Oregon Trail Brewery

Opened: 1987 (reopened in 1993).
Owners: Dave Wills and Jerry Bockmore.
Brewers: Dave Wills and Weston Zaludek.
System: 7-barrel.
Annual production: 317 barrels.
Distribution: Corvallis mostly.
Hours: Monday through Friday, 11 a.m. to 5:30 p.m.
Tours: By request.
Takeout beer: Growlers, 2.25-gallon "party pigs," limited bottles of Bourbon Barrel Porter.
Gift shop: A T-shirt and a pint glass.
Food: From the adjacent Old World Deli includes quick-service sandwiches, chili, and "World's Best Brownies."

Beers brewed: Year-round: Wit, Brown Ale, IPA, Ginseng Porter, Bourbon Barrel Porter, Smoke Signal, Beaver Tail, Mosaic Red Ale.

The Pick: Ginseng Porter. This malty robust porter picks up an earthy, dirty kick from four types of ginseng root for an experience like drinking up the air in a Chinese tea or herb shop.

Portal Brewing Co.

100 East Sixth Street, Medford, OR 97501
(541) 499-0804 • PortalBrewingCo.com

This cozy corner spot founded by Mike Dimon and Theresa Delany offers a few tables, a comfy chair alongside a couch, and stools at the bar facing the dozenish taps (depending on what's available) jutting out from a copper backsplash. Delany may spring on you when you enter Portal Brewing and inform you of her daily specials—one of which was onion dip made using The Dark One, the house "Siberian" Imperial Stout—and that people have told her the bacon quesadilla is what they'd request as their last meal. For a buck more you can request IPA pickles. Yes, pickled in Riptide IPA.

Dimon mans the bar, proffering libations with a seafaring theme—Riptide, Hoptopus, Ahab's Hopoon, and of course Portal's Porthouse Porter. He has a penchant for the dark stuff, and while you can get a beer float in virtually any size you can think of, for another mere dollar you can end the evening with a sampler-size glass of the coconut brown ale afloat with Kona coffee ice cream for one of the best uses of a Washington that still exists.

Beers brewed: Year-round: Downtown Jackie Brown Ale (Coconut Brown), Tub Springs Northwest Pale Ale, Riptide IPA, Portal Porthole Porter, Donegal's Break Oat Stout, Buckwheat Blonde Ale, Reagan Red India Red Ale, Grace O'Malley's Irish Red Ale, The Dark One Siberian Imperial Stout, Ahab's Hopoon ESB, Sunset Cream Ale. Seasonals: Hoola Hop, Hoptopus Imperial CDA, Koko Blanco Coconut Cream Ale, and more.

Portal Brewing Co.

Opened: 2013.
Owners: Mike Dimon and Theresa Delany.
Brewer: Mike Dimon.
System: 1-barrel.
Annual production: 70 barrels.
Distribution: On-premises only.
Hours: Monday through Saturday, 4 p.m. to 10 p.m.
Takeout beer: Growlers.
Gift shop: Shirts, sweatshirts, and beer soap.
Food: Small menu of modest-sized nosh, including quesadillas and the classic Ploughman's platter.

The Pick: Donegal's Break Oat Stout. Stouts can be of the Irish variety or the oatmeal sort and this one's both by layering flavors of cocoa nibs and vanilla ice cream into a smooth nightcap.

Southern Oregon Brewing Co.

1922 United Way, Medford, OR 97504
(541) 776-9898 • SOBrewing.com
Twitter @SOBMedford

Dr. Tom Hammond, an anesthesiologist, founded Southern Oregon Brewing—the acronym S.O.B. is not an unfortunate oversight—as a way to segue from practicing medicine to perfecting brewing and drinking beer. "I wasn't sure if medicine was going to be the rest of my working life. I wanted to find something I was passionate about and was fun," he said. "Beer seemed obvious."

Naming his brewery Southern Oregon shows his dedication to his home of Medford since 1997. Born in Alaska, Hammond went to Seattle for med school, did his residency in Boston, and then first practiced in Tucson. But Southern Oregon's beers are entirely Northwestern, even if, or especially because, as Hammond put it, "I didn't have delusions that my homebrews would turn into commercial success," which led him to bring on Anders Johansen as his first brewmaster and Scott Saulsbury as the current one. Each was a twenty-year veteran and came to Southern Oregon from Deschutes Brewing.

Since 2007, Southern Oregon has brewed on the same 20-barrel brewing system in the same industrial space, but production has increased from some 800 barrels its first year to more than 2,000 today. That makes it the second largest brewery in the region where over half of the current breweries set up shop since 2010. The surge has come from within Medford or, catching many by surprise, up I-5 in Roseburg. "We want to be a regional brewery," Hammond expressed. "That being said, I don't think we've grown as [far] as I thought we would have after these years." Thus far, growth has come in the form of adding pint cans to the 22-ounce bottles already in distribution.

An interesting sign of regionalism is the fact that Nice Rack IPA and its DIPA big sister, Big Rack, aren't the biggest movers. Those would be what Hammond calls the dual flagships, Na Zdravi Czech Pils and Pin-up Porter. Na Zdravi—it means "To

Beers brewed: Year round: Na Zdravi Czech Pils, Nice Rack IPA, Pin-up Porter, Woodshed Red, Killer Rabbit ISA. Seasonals: Big Rack Double IPA, Old Humbug, Holy Water Maibock, Black Heart Imperial Stout.

The Pick: Na Zdravi. This ain't no over-hopped Northwest pilsner. Everything (save the water, naturally) is imported from the Old Country, and it's the lemony, grassy Saaz hops that make this sunny yellow lager immensely and refreshingly drinkable in the Czech style.

your health" in Czech—is an homage to a Czech doctor colleague. Eschewing citrusy aroma hops from Willamette Valley since that'd hardly fit the Czech pilsner style, this beer relies on Saaz, the benchmark of Bohemian hops. These earthy, low-alpha hops are just another way Southern Oregon cleans up among the crowd that drinks for refreshment, not bowling for bitterness. Better selling still is the year-round Pin-up Porter, brimming with espresso and smoke. Also from the dark side, Black Heart is a seasonal imperial stout that's malty and creamy, on the low end of alcoholic strength for the style guidelines (under 9 percent ABV) and, in my opinion, a fine beer to reach for twelve months a year.

A beer exclusive to the working-class taproom is Woodshed Red. Hammond calls it the locals' favorite, "It can't go off tap!" Like Nice Rack IPA, it also boasts 65 IBUs, but the malt bill containing Munich Dark, Vienna, and some flaked oats, among others, creates a richer beer with caramel notes and a woody flavor, though it's in no way oaked.

One aspect of the brewery's growth and expansion plans left out above is that Hammond finally added a patio to the front of the taproom that's now open on a daily basis. As the brewery grows, the good doctor keeps reinvesting the profits back into the company and community. Kids, parks, student athletes, animals, and more are all on the receiving end of Southern Oregon's philanthropic mission, as the brewery's profits go to a great many worthy causes more than into Hammond's pockets. Luckily, he still practices medicine but may spend more time in the brewhouse when he retires at age sixty or seventy. (He recently turned fifty.) Of equal importance are his three kids, who he knows are curious about the brewery. "I'd be lying if one of my motivations wasn't to create a legacy," he said. "*And* I sleep a lot," he added, as if emphasizing that his life, like his beers, is about staying in balance.

Southern Oregon Brewing Co.

Opened: 2007.

Owner: Tom Hammond.

Brewer: Scott Saulsbury.

System: 20-barrel.

Annual production: 2,500 barrels.

Distribution: Oregon and Washington.

Hours: Monday through Saturday, 3 p.m. to 9 p.m.; Sunday, noon to 6 p.m.

Tours: Saturdays at 4 p.m.

Takeout beer: Bombers, pint cans, and growlers.

Gift shop: Sweatshirts, shirts, caps, and pints.

Food: Rotating food trucks.

Standing Stone Brewing Co.

ASHLAND, OREGON
www.StandingStoneBrewing.com

101 Oak Street, Ashland, OR 97520
(541) 482-2448 • StandingStoneBrewing.com
Twitter @ssbc

Standing Stone Brewing gives the occasional nod to Ashland's reputation as the home of the Shakespeare Festival, like with Midsummer Dream, a pilsner-mimicking session ale that debuted during brewmaster Larry Chase's first July here. But really, the brewpub pays homage to something even more monolithic in the area: Pilot Rock, which towers over Oregon's Rogue Valley and California's Shasta Valley (Ashland is sixteen miles from the state line). The Takelma tribe of Native Americans referred to it, via translation, as Stone Standing Up.

Standing Stone Brewing occupies the historic Whittle Garage, built in 1925, and was established by Alex Amarotico in 1997. Naturally, a great aspect of brewpubs is drinking the freshest beer possible, but I believe that Standing Stone is the only one that processes their eggs and chickens on-site, too. Serving sustainably raised food at the pub came about organically.

"We'd been open for five years before we started thinking about serving wild Alaskan salmon, which is almost standard now," Alex's wife, Danielle Amarotico, said at the bar, just a few feet in from the entrance on the wall opposite the brewing system. After salmon came locally-raised buffalo. From there, the meat ball started rolling. "When you start doing things with a whole animal, you have to start rewriting the menu and doing things with all the parts," she said. "Everybody's had to learn the best ways to butcher a cow."

The next step wasn't logical, but it's quite impressive. Alex came up with the idea of doing a farm, initially specified for poultry. "We worked with the city and leased over 250 acres a mile up the road," she said. Thus, in 2011, they launched One Mile Farm. They have about twenty-five head of Black Angus and forty sheep, and each of the six thousand chickens consumed at the pub (from the chicken noodle soup to the grilled chicken

Beers brewed: Year-round: I ♥ Oregon Ale, Amber Ale, Twin Plunge Double IPA, Steel-Cut Stout, Noble Stout. Seasonals: Dear Abbey, Break Time (spring), 76 Hands Blackberry Ale, Midsummer Dream, Madrone Red, Oktoberfest, Barleywine, and more.

The Pick: Noble Stout: Whereas Steel-Cut oatmeal stout has good roast presence even though it's devoid of actual coffee, the good folks at Noble Coffee Roasters a couple of blocks away provide cold-pressed java to make a delicious, smooth, robust stout with an extra kick of joe. For hedonists, there's a Noble Stout Float on the menu.

breast atop the Cobb salad) was raised a mile away. With eggs like they get, it's no wonder people order egg dishes including a breakfast burrito from morning to midnight. "We even make our own mayonnaise," Danielle added. To sweeten the pot, they keep their own bees. No, the cattle aren't enough to satisfy Standing Stone's demand for beef (they sold twenty-four thousand burgers last year), but they're grass fed and sustainably raised in Southern Oregon. The brewery's spent grains and other by-products go to their farm for feed and composting. On a list of Oregon's 100 Best Green Businesses, Standing Stone routinely occupies second or third place.

It's not just food that's predominantly local and organic. A good example is the Noble Stout with cold-pressed coffee from nearby Noble Coffee Roasters. A great example is when Larry Chase took over the brewhouse and suggested, "Let's brew a beer with all Oregon ingredients." That means Ashland-grown hops and malt from Klamath Basin via Great Western Malting. A server came up with the name, I ♥ Oregon Ale. It's proven so popular at the pub that Chase said "even though it's not to style," it replaced the pale ale from before his arrival. An original Double IPA remains and is the pub's bestseller, but naturally Chase put his own spin on it, including boosting the juicy hop quotient and "dry-hopping the heck out of it."

Standing Stone is cozy year-round but especially when the back patio is open and hosting live music summer long. It's popular with Shakespeare buffs and hikers along the Pacific Crest Trail (easily spotted by their backpacks), but mostly it's a local hangout, which explains the expanding bike parking in front, especially since most of the seventy-five employees receive brewery-issued commuting bikes.

Standing Stone Brewing Co.

Opened: 1997.

Owners: Alex and Danielle Amarotico.

Brewer: Larry Chase.

System: 10-barrel.

Annual production: 500 barrels.

Distribution: On-premises and at Crater Lake National Park Lodge.

Hours: Open daily, 11 a.m. to midnight.

Takeout beer: Growler fills.

Gift shop: Apparel ("Powered by Beer" T-shirt depicts a keg recharging a bicycle) and glassware.

Food: Sustainably grown items from Standing Stone's One Mile Farms. Try the BBQ Burger, roasted beet salad, and the deep-fried Brussels sprouts with house basil aioli.

Swing Tree Brewing Co.

300 East Hersey Street, #7, Ashland, OR 97520
(541) 591-8584 • SwingTreeBrewing.com
Twitter @SwingTreeBeer

I liked Swing Tree Brewery—or the couple behind it, Brandon and Tanya Overstreet—before it opened. It's based on their lofty aspirations to make innovative and challenging beers (they want to build a coolship to make spontaneously fermented ales). They also know the company has to be grounded, so they debuted with crowd-pleasing beers like an India Pale Ale, wryly named Obligatory IPA.

Although I visited the business-park suite during construction, I found Brandon expanding on his professional brewing experience gleaned in Colorado and readying Swing Tree's half-barrel brewery and taproom that's now officially open. Because they opened quite modestly, I envision plans for a 7-barrel system to materialize sooner rather than later. However, the Overstreets want to keep things focused on serving Ashland and its surroundings and not grow much bigger.

Porch Swing Pale is an easy-drinking, still hoppy brew that was poured at their grand opening. By all accounts, another affable beer is Two Shilling, an English-style brown ale that's in such high demand it's often tapped out. The Overstreets believe that the Rogue Valley's microfauna resemble Belgium's Senne Valley, from where wild lambic ales hail. Beers like that take time and are very risky. IPA, on the other hand, is a sure thing. It's like shooting fish in a barrel, but they'd rather put that barrel to more interesting use.

Swing Tree Brewing Co.

Opened: 2013.
Owners: Brandon and Tanya Overstreet.
Brewer: Brandon Overstreet.
System: .5-barrel.
Annual production: 50 barrels.
Distribution: Southern Oregon.
Hours: Thursday through Sunday, 3 p.m. to 8 p.m.
Tours: By request.
Takeout beer: Growlers.
Gift shop: Shirts and glasses.

Beers brewed: Year-round: Obligatory IPA, Porch Swing Pale, Two Shilling English Brown Ale, Lonely Trike Red Ale. Seasonals: Dark beer, a wheat, a rotating IPA tap, and more, including cask ales.

Two-Shy Brewing

1308 Northwest Park Street, Roseburg, OR 97470
(541) 236-2055 • TwoShyBrewing.com
Twitter @TwoShyBrewing

The name? Three buddies from Umpqua Valley Brewers Guild (a home-brew club) always brewed two bottles shy of a case. Even as budding professionals, they started on a single-barrel system but bumped up to 3 barrels so they could keep beers on at their cinderblock-walled tasting room, which opened in late 2013.

Their focus, said cofounder Erik Nielson, is keeping Two-Shy Brewing beer on area taps. Mission accomplished at some of the forward-thinking spots such as O'Toole's Pub (328 SE Jackson St.) in the old Umpqua Brewery. That brewery is a 1990s relic, but Roseburg has worked out the kinks as far as brewing—and supporting—local beer.

Two-Shy brews mostly straightforward styles. "We got on an acronym kick," explained Nielson, who asked co-owner Lyle Hruda to design a cross between Fat Tire and an amber bock. "We called it DOA because the very first rendition was dead-on." The beer is a lifeblood of Two-Shy, so Dead-on Amber is the opposite of the popular acronym for dead on arrival. Phat Odd Stout, made with oatmeal, retained their homebrewed version's name and acronym, yet is the furthest thing from the vernacular meaning of POS (see UrbanDictionary.com).

The flowery Influence American Pale Ale resembles an English IPA. Ignition Double IPA is a gearhead-turned-hophead's liquid dream come true. As for seasonals, on the less straightforward side they made a "subtle" chocolate mint stout ("not mint-forward," declared Nielsen); how I wish I could've tried the truffles a local chocolatier made with it.

Two-Shy Brewing

Opened: 2013.
Owners: Lyle Hruda, Paul Singleton, and Erik Nielsen.
Brewer: Lyle Hruda.
System: 3-barrel.
Annual production: 125 barrels.
Distribution: Southern Oregon.
Hours: Friday, 4 p.m. to 6 p.m.; Saturday, 2 p.m. to 6 p.m.
Takeout beer: Growlers.
Gift shop: Threadware and glassware.

Beers brewed: Year-round: Influence APA, Dead-on Amber, Phat Odd Stout, Reformation Red, Everlasting ESB, Picnic Pale, Uberdunkelweizen, TSB Session Ale, Ignition Double IPA, Toby's Best.

Walkabout Brewing Co.

921 Mason Way, Medford, OR 97501
(541) 734-4677

Forget the notion of a walkabout as something Australians do during adolescence or just after university. Perth native Ross Litton embarked on his Walkabout in 1997 at the tender age of thirty-four, several years after he moved to Southern Oregon. A craftsman who fabricated his own brewing equipment, Litton initially set up the brewery at his house in neighboring Central Point, but after fifteen years he expanded to the current brewpub. Well, it's a tasting room that also offers a small food menu. The industrial location not only requires a bit of meandering across the tracks, but also is directly across the street from a Budweiser distributor. "We'll take them over someday," proclaimed Litton optimistically.

The sparse space doesn't offer an exceeding amount of decoration—a wooden boomerang constitutes much of it, and flight trays are "brewmerangs"—but the most important aspect is nicely showcased. The shiny brewery sits in the room directly behind the bar and is visible through a picture window. The more awkward tanks, like a funky square mash tun from the early days, along with spray-on insulation fermenters, are still in operation but situated behind the shinier vessels, which is no accident, Litton joked. I haven't been here during a Super Bowl party, but I imagine the custom, bar-height wooden table with mini field goals at either end, part of the year-round décor, is extra popular among armchair placekickers flicking handmade paper triangles.

The twenty-one-and-up pub hosts mostly an after-work crowd, though Litton showed me a large rectangular lawn around back that he hopes to turn into a spot where friends and families (but no pets, so leave your dingo at home) can gather for picnics. He's working on a firepit and would even like to install some grills so patrons can GYO steaks.

Among Walkabout's "Aussie-themed but Northwest-style" ales, the most popular is Worker's Pale Ale. The story behind the name, explained Litton,

Beers brewed: Year-round: Jabberwocky, Redback IPA, Wallaby Wit, Worker's Pale Ale, Walkabout GFA (gluten free). Seasonals: Point the Bone IPA, Summerhays' Honey Ginger.

The Pick: Jabberwocky Strong Ale. This is a strong ale in the United Kingdom sense, not Northwest. It's a 7 percent that reveals a bit of pepper and spice behind its wall of malt, which throws bits of chocolate and tobacco flavors.

is that, "My mate and I were drinking [Anchor] Liberty Ale one day and he suggested 'Working Man's.' I said, 'Women like to drink, too, so it's gonna be Worker's.'"

Nearly as popular is Jabberwocky, perhaps with the implication that each 22-ounce bottle implores you, in its best Lewis Carroll voice, to "drink me." The name of this 7 percent English-style strong ale is, in Litton's words, "a meaningless word." Drink too many of them, he chuckled, and you'll be speaking nonsense, too.

"I like my beers to go along with foods, not overly hopped where the hops are so present that it destroys the food," Litton stated at one point. He used the pairing of pepperoni pizza and IPA as an example, adding, "If you can't taste pepperoni in your burp, then it's too hoppy." Fair point. But that doesn't stop him from making three IPAs, starting with the most recent Session IPA, then the flagship Redback IPA at 6.5 percent ABV and nearly 60 IBUs, and finally Point the Bone, the bolder, Northwest-style IPA. The name, he explained, resulted from its initial Halloween release and he wanted the label to be scary—"When a witch doctor points a bone at you that means death"—but the beer is only scary delicious, tricked out with Cascade and Centennial hops for a tasty, grapefruity treat that became so popular it's now available year-round.

One of the best aspects of the new pub is that Walkabout can now brew rarer offerings like the lemon-ginger ale or intermittent beers incorporating strawberries (the stark red hue actually comes from hibiscus tea), not that restaurants in the area don't typically have Worker's on draft and perhaps an extra handle for seasonal releases. Personally, I'm hoping Litton brings back Croctoberfest the party, along with its Oktoberfest-style lager. Then again, if those barbecue grills get installed, I'd be afraid to hear everyone asking him to say, in his still thick Aussie accent, "Throw another shrimp on the barbie."

Walkabout Brewing Co.

Opened: 1997.
Owner and brewer: Ross Litton.
System: 7-barrel.
Annual production: 1,300 barrels.
Distribution: Oregon and Seattle area.
Hours: Monday through Friday, 3 p.m. to 8 p.m.; Saturday and Sunday, noon to 5 p.m.
Tours: Saturdays, or call for an appointment.
Takeout beer: Bottles, growlers, and dock sales by appointment.
Gift shop: Swag behind bar.
Food: "Munchies" like nachos and potato wedges and straightforward pizzas.

Wild River Brewing & Pizza Co.

595 Northeast E Street, Grants Pass, OR 97526
(541) 471-RIVR (7487) • WildRiverBrewing.com
Twitter @WRBrewing

I'm compelled to begin by editorializing that longtime residents of Southern Oregon, especially those who are into craft beer, perceive Wild River as just a pizzeria or a stand-by family restaurant that added their own beer a while back. No, it doesn't feature cutting-edge brew-pub design with reclaimed wood and lighting that is a twist on repurposed growlers or carboys. And there's very little in the way of Belgo-Northwest influence that's found in some pilot brewery programs, but the beer is clean and solid, the atmosphere is welcoming and not remotely intimidating to craft beer newbies, and the sustainable menu should be an inspiration to many other "locavore" restaurants. Plus, there's a speedboat hanging in the dining area (in the Grants Pass location).

Admittedly, yes, the Miller family of owners added the initial brewery to their nearby Cave Junction location in 1990, fifteen years after opening their first pizzeria, because they wanted their own German-style beers (increasing their margins) to serve with said pizza. Even at the time, basic tenets of "local, fresh, and distinctive" weren't as widespread among diners or beer drinkers. Jerry Miller and his wife, Bertha, founded Shady Oaks Pizza Deli in Cave Junction in 1975 and five years later added a store in Brookings Harbor, leaving its management to their son, Darrel, and his wife, Becky. A decade later, in 1990, they added what was originally called the Steelhead Brewery (no relation to the current brewery in Eugene of the same name). The Grants Pass spot came four years later with the introduction of wood-fired ovens for the pizza. Also in 1994, the restaurant and brewery was rebranded as Wild River.

Although the Grants Pass pub is huge, the Millers still found themselves short on seating so,

Beers brewed: Year-round: IPA, Harbor Lights Kolsch-style Ale, Nut Brown Ale, Bohemian Pilsener, FSR, Double Eagle Imperial Stout, Honey Wheat. Seasonals: Weizen Bock (spring), Blackberry Porter (summer), Oktoberfest (fall), Snug Harbor Old Ale (late fall), Cave Bear Barley Wine (winter).

The Pick: ESB. Previously the flagship before the IPA took over, this exceptional British-style pale ale defines balance in a beer with lightly-toasted nutty malts and present yet not abundant earthy hop spice. At 5.5 percent ABV and a potent-for-the-style 50 IBUs, get a pitcher for the table.

directly across the street they run a sister pub that's less kid-oriented. Minors are still allowed, but between the pool table right at the entrance and the fact that the banquet hall serves as a Rotary Club meeting space, kids tend to find the main restaurant more appealing (plus it's larger and warmer). Then again, across the street at the sister pub there are professional local artists on the eastern wall and decidedly less professional local and visiting artists on the other in the form of coasters featuring drawings, sketches, and doodles—many barfly Rembrandts working within the crayon medium—surrounding a large map of the United States where visitors mark where they're from.

A final word on the Wild River locations with two brewhouses to serve them all: they added a fifth (or as I think of it, a fourth and a half since the two in Grants Pass almost operate as one) store in Medford in 2006 and Grants Pass GM Shaun Hoback told me there are well over one hundred employees company-wide, about half of whom work in Grants Pass. As if that's not enough community support, the Millers don't put all the profits in their pockets. "They only collect rent," said Hoback. The pizzas and beers end up sponsoring parks, events, and all manner of local interests. "They're running [the company] for the community," he added.

I was even more interested in what brewer Scott Butts had to tell and show me. He is only the second brewmaster, beginning here in 1995, and has been upping the ante of both the beer and food programs ever since. It's one thing that he encouraged banishing GMOs from the menu—everything is made from scratch, down to sourcing locally milled flour for the pizza dough and bread rolls. But as an avid home gardener from a family of makers (his mom made wine but Scott developed his interest in beer from his homebrewing father, going so far as to make his own root beer as a kid), he talked the Millers into converting any available patch of soil into their own garden.

When he discovered that what he thought was a pumpkin growing along the parking lot turned out to actually be a kabocha—a Japanese winter squash—Scott seemed torn on whether to send it to the kitchen for one of their garden-fresh daily specials or use it in a beer. I voted beer. Tomatoes, basil, jalapeños and more all grow right outside the back door. That eggplant parmesan on the specials board? Before it was parm'ed, it was picked out back. Perhaps the best part is that Scott has hops growing, having started with one hundred rhizomes. (The ones encompassing the patio are merely decorative.)

As for his beers, Scott said the Honey Wheat is their bestseller, which speaks to their customers' desire for refreshing beers over progressive beers. Not that Scott's stuck in 1995. He makes forward-thinking beers, even if they're not geekily avant-garde. His unfiltered Blackberry Porter with ample berry and chocolate flavors has a loyal following. His English-style Cave Bear Barley Wine, which I had after it hibernated for a year, had amazing apricot preserve esters from citric acid and candi sugar. And Nut Brown Ale is a true British mild ale for newfound fans of session beers. It is 3.4 percent ABV, and I think it's only the color that scares regulars off of making this their usual.

It's not unusual to see schooners, their 23-ounce glasses, of Harbor Lights Kolsch-style Ale at nearly every table. Properly named so as not to trample on Cologne's Kolsch appellation, it is light in color and body and indefinitely quaffable. It's big among retirees who like that they're getting a hand-crafted beer still in line with beers they're used to. On that note, while chatting with Hoback he took a look around the house at the packed, silver-haired lunch crowd and said he knew everyone by name save for one young lady impressively sitting alone at a two-top working her way through a sample tray of eight beers, and whom I also spied leaving with a mixed six-pack.

Wild River Brewing & Pizza Co.

Opened. 1990 (brewery), 1970 (restaurant).

Owners: Jerry and Bertha Miller.

Brewer: Scott Butts.

System: 15-barrel in Grants Pass; 7-barrel in Cave Junction.

Annual production: 1,700 barrels.

Distribution: Five pubs only.

Hours: Each pub open daily; check for individual hours.

Tours: Upon request.

Takeout beer: 12-ounce bottles and growlers.

Gift shop: Shirts, glasses, etc.

Food: Predominantly pizza, but sandwiches and chicken, too, including gizzards as a side or app. Plenty of meaty pies, but try the Avocado Supreme (also in sandwich form).

Other locations: Across the street (533 NE F St., Grants Pass; 541-474-4456). Original 7-barrel brewery (249 N. Redwood Highway, Cave Junction; 541-592-3556). Brookings Harbor (16279 Highway 101 South; 541-469-7454). Medford: 2684 N. Pacific Highway; 541-773-RIVR [7487]).

Beer Festivals

With more than fifty-two brewfests a year, there is on average more than one organized beer event per week. The granddaddy is Oregon Brewers Fest (OBF), which has been running since 1988 and attracts over eighty thousand attendees at the height of summer. But there are festivals year-round dedicated to every imaginable aspect of beer: barleywines, organic beers, fruit beers, barrel-aged beers, and holiday beers that are frequently spiced and/or higher in alcohol to help warm the bones.

One of my favorites is also the silliest: BenFest. Established in 2011, it keeps on going. The sole point is to celebrate brewers named Ben, of whom there are surprisingly many (Widmer Brothers' Ben Dobler, Breakside's Ben Edmunds, Occidental's Engler, Lucky Lab's Flerchinger, Gigantic's Ben Love, and Deschutes-PDX's Kehs). It has even spun off into SeanFest (well, Sean/Shawn/ShaunFest), MikeFest, and ChuckFest to celebrate every Tom, Dick, and Harry (or rather Chuck, Charles, and Charlie) in the fun beer community. That reminds me how grateful I am that there aren't many brewers or publicans named Richard around here.

In terms of Beer Weeks, there are now seven to ten day-long celebrations in Portland, Medford, Central Oregon, Eugene, Corvallis, the North Coast, and Eastern Oregon, not to mention the bona fide Oregon Beer Month every June (and pretty much the other eleven months). Furthermore, there are events celebrating music and beer, carnivals for dogs, bikes, UFOs, and more than one for our favorite cash crop: fresh hops.

January

The Big Woody Barrel Aged Beer and Whiskey Festival, WoodyBeer.com/big
Leftbank Annex in Portland; established 2014
> The big counterpart to its older sister Little Woody in Bend, this is a showcase for wood-aged beers (and whiskeys) from across the region.

CellarFest, BaileysTaproom.com/Cellarfest.
Bailey's Taproom in Portland; established 2010
> All vintage, all the time. Get your barleywine and imperial stout on.

High Gravity Extravaganza, Mcmenamins.com/events/120483-High-Gravity-Extravaganza
McMenamins Old St. Francis in Bend; established 2014
"Go big or go home" is the motto at this festival of Central Oregon's high-gravity winter warmers.

February

Festival of Dark Arts, FestivalOfDarkArts.com
Fort George Brewery in Astoria; established 2012
In the middle of February-long Stout Month brewers send their darkest beers, demonstrating that there's none more black or tasty.

KLCC Microbrew Festival, KLCC.org
Lane Events Center in Eugene
A beer tasting event benefitting KLCC 89.7 FM and featuring over sixty breweries mostly from the Willamette Valley.

Hillsdale Brewfest, McMenamins.com
McMenamins Hillsdale Brewery & Public House; established 1993
The godfather of internal McMenamins breweries brewfests at the brewpub that started it all.

Malt Ball, Twitter.com/MaltBallPDX
Wonder Ballroom in Portland; established 2011
The *Portland Mercury* organizes the ultimate beer pairing: artisan brewers creating a unique beer for, and often with, musical artists to enjoy the beers during their sets.

Zwicklemania, OregonBeer.org/Zwickelmania
Breweries throughout Oregon; established 2008
Presidents Day Weekend, breweries host open houses with free tours and samples fresh from the zwickel.

March

Barleywine and Big Beer Tastival, BarleywineFest.weebly.com
Lucky Lab in Portland
At the NW Quimby pub, big boozy barleywines and other high-gravity beers warm from the soul outward.

Double EE, Beer & Cheese Festival, OregonBeerAndCheese.com
Rogue Creamery in Central Point; established 2013
A friendly bEEr and chEEse competition that challenges cheesemakers and brewmasters to create great tastes together.

Firkin Fest, Rogue.com/RogueEvents
The Green Dragon in Portland; established 2008
Thirty-plus Oregon firkins (unpasteurized, unfiltered, naturally carbonated in the cask and served at cellar temperature) for "real ale" fans.

Pouring at the Coast, PouringAtTheCoast.com
The Seaside Chamber of Commerce; established 2010
> It's a beer festival and homebrew competition right on the beach.

Spring Beer and Wine Fest, SpringBeerFest.com
Oregon Convention Center in Portland; established 1994
> Shake off the cabin fever with this celebration of grapes and hops every Easter weekend (March or April).

Triple IPA Fest, NWIPApdx.com
N.W.I.P.A. in Portland; established 2014
> You're once, twice, three times a hophead.

April

Cheers to Belgian Beers, OregonCraftBeer.org/events/CTBB
Metalcraft Fabrication in Portland; established 2007
> Participating brewers throw a dart to determine the color and strength of the beer they must brew, all inoculated with the same Belgian yeast strain selected by the previous year's winner.

May

Brewer's Memorial Ale Fest, BrewersAleFest.com
Rogue Ales in Newport; established 2007
> Benefitting Lincoln County animal shelters, over three thousand people attend, many with their pooches. Activities include a dog wash and a Brewer look-alike competition memorializing Brewer, brewmaster John Maier's black Lab.

Central Oregon Beer Week, CentralOregonBeerWeek.com
Throughout Central Oregon; established 2012
> Ample events all "week" long.

FredFest, FredFestPDX.com
Hair of the Dog Brewing in Portland; established 2006
> A mini but mighty beer festival held at the brewery in honor of beer writer and historian Fred Eckhardt. The fest began on his eightieth birthday. Eckhardt, renowned for his charitableness, selects a different nonprofit each year for the bash's proceeds.

Sasquatch Brewfest & Homebrew Contest, NorthwestLegendFoundation.org
Ninkasi Brewing in Eugene; established 2002
> This brewfest benefits the brewer-centric Glen Hay Falconer Foundation and showcases many local breweries, whose brewers often create unique beers for the fest.

Sasquatch BrewAm Golf Tournament
McMenamins Edgefield in Troutdale; established 2004
> Benefitting the Glen Hay Falconer Foundation, this golf tourney pairs amateur participants with pro brewers.

UFO Fest, UFOFest.com
McMenamins Oregon Hotel in McMinnville; established 1999
> A celebration of the infamous UFO sighting in 1950, the fest is replete with earnest lectures, a sci-fi parade, and more, plus special space-themed beers at the McMenamins hotel with its rooftop bar perfect for spaceship gazing.

Wild Ale Fest, SixteenTons.biz
16 Tons Taphouse in Eugene; established 2010
> Commemorating the taphouse's anniversary on the first Saturday of May, over seventy wild, funky, sour ales are available to sample.

June

Berries, Brews, & BBQs
French Prairie Gardens in St. Paul; established 2009
> All the namesake delicacies (including strawberry donuts and deep-fried strawberries) served in the middle of a strawberry patch.

Cider Summit PDX, CiderSummitNW.com
The Fields Neighborhood Park in Portland; established 2011
> When you need a respite from beer there's always cider, and this event showcases the many innovative cidermakers of the Northwest.

Eugene Beer Week, EugeneBeerWeek.org
Throughout Eugene
> Ample events all "week" long.

Fruit Beer Fest
Burnside Brewing in Portland; established 2011
> The first and largest annual fruit beer festival offers dozens of styles of base beer styles embellished with inventive fruit infusions (including some you don't think of as fruit).

Medford Beer Week, MedfordBeerWeek.com
Throughout Medford
> Ample events all "week" long.

North American Organic Brewers Festival, NAOBF.org
Overlook Park in Portland; established 2004
> Organic beer? Yes. But this is also about sustainable living, plus live music and fun for the whole family.

Oregon Brews & BBQs, OregonBrewsAndBBQ.com
The Granary District in McMinnville; established 2008
> Host Grain Station Brew Works is just one of around thirty-five breweries pouring to complement platefuls of smoky meats.

Oregon Garden Brewfest, OregonGarden.org
Oregon Garden in Silverton; established 2004
> This event moved to Father's Day Weekend, so bring Dad to sample some 130 beers while exploring the eighty-acre botanical garden, beers in hand.

PDX Beer Week, PDXBeerWeek.com
Venues all over Portland; established 2011
> "A 10-day celebration of craft beer in the greatest beer city on earth."

Rye Beer Fest, RyeBeerFest.com
EastBurn in Portland
> Sponsored by TapLister. Rye beers, rye foods, rye not?

Southern Oregon Craft Brew Festival, SOCBrewfest.com
Bartlett Street in Old Town, Medford; established 2011
> Southern Oregon's premier craft beer event features samples from local breweries and beyond.

Eastern Oregon Beer Festival, EOBeerfest.org
Main Street in La Grande; established 2014
> Celebrate the summer solstice while celebrating the breweries in the eastern corner of Beervana.

Barley Cup, Mcmenamins.com/1483-mcmenamins-brewfests-barley-cup
Thompson Brewery in Salem; established 1998
> Sample beers from several McMenamins breweries and a few from Salem and vote to see who'll hoist the Barley Cup.

July

Oregon Craft Beer Month, OregonCraftBeer.org/events/OCBM
Throughout Oregon
> Beer week, schmear week. The Guild celebrates all of Oregon beer all month long with over 450 events at breweries, beer bars, and more.

BenFest
Rotating host locations around Portland; established 2011
> The sole point is to make merry with the many brewers named Ben, with beers such as BENevolet Dictator and HaBENero and Juice.

Portland International Beerfest, Portland-Beerfest.com
Halladay Park (Lloyd Center) in Portland; established 2003
> This dog-but-not-kid-friendly fest features over 150 beers from around the state and the world.

Puckerfest, Puckerfest.com
Belmont Station in Portland; established 2007
> Believed to be the first American celebration of sour, wild, and funky beers, this week-long display is the next best thing to being in Brussels.

Oregon Brewers Fest, OregonBrewFest.com
Tom McCall Waterfront Park in Portland; established 1988
> Nearly thirty years strong and getting bigger and better every year. Enjoy IPAs, fruit beers, and more with thousands of fellow beer lovers who flock here from around the world to enjoy beers from some ninety breweries.

Roadhouse Brewfest, Mcmenamins.com/1484-mcmenamins-brewfests-roadhouse.com
Cornelius Pass Roadhouse in Hillsboro; established 2001
> This noncompetitive fest features brews from McMenamins breweries and nearby guest breweries.

Bite & Brew, TheBiteAndBrew.com
Riverfront Park in Salem; established 1994
> Beer, wine, and great food (and a Kid Zone) enjoyed in a great park.

August

Bend Brewfest, BendBrewFest.com
Les Schwab Amphitheater in Bend; established 2002
> Bend itself is a year-long brewfest, but this puts them all in one grassy area with many others.

Bronze Blues & Brews, BronzeBluesBrews.com
City Park in Joseph; established 1996
> Hot, live blues and cold, wet brews.

Lighthouse Brew Festival, Mcmenamins.com/events/122492-19th-Annual-Lighthouse-Brewfest.com
McMenamins Lighthouse Brewpub in Lincoln City; established 1995
> Company brewers pick a number, representing a beer style, out of a hat and then create it for this coastal event.

Little Woody Barrel-aged Whiskey Fest, TheLittleWoody.com
Des Chutes Historical Museum in Bend; established 2008
> Indulge in whiskey-aged beers alongside straight whiskey. Go big or go gnome.

Nano Beer Fest, NanoBeerFest.com
Max's Fanno Creek in Tigard; established 2008
> Over twenty small breweries at this small beer fest with live music.

September

Bend Oktoberfest, BendOktoberfest.com
Downtown Bend
> Bend brewed beers, Bavarian food, and wiener dog races.

Biketobeerfest, HopworksBeer.com/Biketobeerfest.com
Hopworks Urban Brewery in Portland; established 2009
> Celebrate two of Portland's favorites: beers and bikes.

Corvallis Beer Week, CorvallisCraftBeer.com/Corvallis-beer-week
Throughout Corvallis
> Ample events all "week" long.

Dogtoberfest, DoveLewis.org/Dogtoberfest
Lucky Lab (Hawthorne) in Portland; established 1994
> Suds in mugs and suds for pugs with a dogwash fund-raiser.

Hood River Hops Fest, HoodRiver.org/events-festivals
Downtown Hood River; established 2004

A beer festival that can only happen in this place at this time; enjoy several dozen beers made with the freshest hops possible.

Mid-Valley Brew Fest, Mcmenamins.com/1486-mcmenamins-brewfests-mid-valley
McMenamins High Street Brewery in Eugene; established 1997

McMenamins and guest breweries converge in this location central to brewers up and down I-5.

Mt. Angel Oktoberfest, Oktoberfest.org
In Mt. Angel; established 1965

Attracting some 350,000 people, this family-friendly festival is one of the largest Oktoberfests in America.

OMSI After Dark Brewfest, OMSI.edu/afterdark
OMSI in Portland; established 2011

Don't just drink beer, learn how it's made, why yeast is important, and how to grow hops. Age twenty-one and up.

Portland Fresh Hops Fest, Oregoncraftbeer.org/events/freshhopsfest
Oaks Amusement Park in Portland

The Guild brings a fresh hops fest to PDX.

Septembeerfest, Septembeerfest.org
Benton County Fairgrounds in Corvallis; established 2008

Regional brewfest from the Heart of the Valley Homebrewers.

Sisters Fresh Hop Festival, SistersCountry.com/Fresh-Hop
Sisters Village Green Park in Sisters; established 2009

A beer festival that can only happen in this place at this time; enjoy several dozen beers made with the freshest hops possible.

St. Paul Fresh Hops Fest
Jaycees Bullpen in St. Paul

The Guild brings a fresh hops fest to hop country.

October

Killer Beer Week, Brewpublic.com
Various locations including Portland, Corvallis, Eugene, and Bend

Beer blogger extraordinaire Angelo De Ieso fashioned Killer Beer Week to celebrate many facets of the Cascadian beer scene, from beer styles to brewers. Events include the Killer Pumpkin in Portland and a recovery brunch to cap the week.

Mid-Valley Brewfest, MidValleyBrewfest.com
Linn County Fair & Expo Center in Albany; established 2009

The Wedge, TheWedgePortland.com
Green Dragon in Portland; established 2007

The Oregon Cheese Guild's event is more of a farmers market-style cheese tasting event but you can find their perfect pairings from the Green Dragon's many beer taps.

Umpqua Brew Fest, www.UmpquaBrewfest.com
Douglas County Fairgrounds in Roseburg; established 2010
 Southern Oregon breweries pour beer to help conserve local watersheds and rivers.

November

Beer Pro/Am
FH Steinbarts in Portland; established 2013
 Local alt-weekly *Willamette Week* champions homebrewers and pro/am beers at America's oldest homebrew shop.

Boone's Ferry Autumn Ale Festival, Mcmenamins.com/events/109494-Boones-Ferry-Autumn-Ale-Fest
McMenamins Old Church in Wilsonville; established 2013
 Summer sippers are gone. Winter warmers haven't arrived. Drink seasonally (festbiers and pumpkin ales, etc.) with local McMenamins brewers.

Coffee Ale Fest, SixteenTons.biz
16 Tons Taphouse in Eugene; established 2010
 Not just stouts, but over twenty IPAs, bocks, and all manner of beers get the coffee infusion treatment for this perky beer fest.

December

Holiday Ale Fest, HolidayAle.com
Pioneer Square in Portland; established 2000
 Talk about saving the best for last. Over fifty winter warmers help fend off the holiday chill all under one warm, dry, massive tent.

Bottle Shops and Taprooms

Visiting breweries is great, but sometimes you want to try beer from more than just one brewery. Oregon is blessed with so many great retailers that do their darndest to offer the widest selection of draft or packaged beer possible, from the most popular IPAs to the hardest to find limited releases. The laws in Oregon are quite friendly for retailers and consumers, which means that many taprooms can sell bottled or canned beer to go as well as fill your growler (or sell you a new one) in 64-ounce, 32-ounce, or any ol' size you like, down to a sealable mason jar. In fact, growler filling stations have become all the rage and are too numerous to list; don't be surprised if the supermarket or gas station you find yourself in has a laudable selection.

Portland

Apex, ApexBar.com; 1216 SE Division St.; (503) 273-9227

Bailey's Taproom, BaileysTaproom.com; 213 SW Broadway; (503) 295-1004

Barrique Barrel, BarrelPDX.wordpress.com; 7401 N. Burlington Ave.; (503) 208-3164

Bazi Bierbrasserie, BaziPdx.com; 1522 SE 32nd Ave; (503) 234-8888

Beaumont Market, Facebook.com/pages/Beaumont-Market-Beer/315419459576; 4130 NE Fremont Ave.; (503) 284-3032

The BeerMongers, TheBeerMongers.com; 1125 SE Division St.; (503) 234-6012

Belmont Station/Bier Café, Belmont-Station.com; 4500 SE Stark St.; (503) 232-8538 (1,000+ bottles)

Bottles, BottlesNW.com; 5015 NE Fremont St.; (503) 287-7022

Bridgetown Beerhouse, BridgetownBeer.com; 915 N. Shaver; (503) 477-8763

Cheese Bar, Cheese-Bar.com; 6031 SE Belmont St; (503) 222-6014 (ltd. bottles with cheese and charcuterie)

Concordia Ale House, Concordia-Ale.com; 3276 NE Killingsworth St.; (503) 287-3929

Fred Meyer, FredMeyer.com; 3805 SE Hawthorne Blvd.; (503) 872-3300

Grain & Gristle, GrainAndGristle.com; 1473 NE Prescott St.; (503) 298-5007

The Hop & Vine, TheHopAndVine.com; 1914 N. Killingsworth St.; (503) 954-3322

Imperial Bottle Shop, ImperialBottleShop.com; 3090 SE Division St.; (971) 302-6899

John's Market, JohnsMarketplace.com; 3535 SW Multnomah Blvd.; (503) 244-2617

Hawthorne Hophouse, HawthorneHopHouse.com; 4111 SE Hawthorne Blvd.; (503) 477-9619

Horse Brass Pub, HorseBrass.com; 4534 SE Belmont St.; (503) 232-2202 (since 1976)

New Seasons Market, NewSeasonsMarket.com; a dozen Portland locations, and you can buy singles from six-packs

Roscoe's, Facebook.com/RoscoesPdx; 8105 SE Stark St.; (503) 255-0049

Saraveza, Saraveza.com; 1004 N. Killingsworth St.; (503) 206-4252

Tin Bucket, Growler-Station.com/tinbucket; 3520 N. Williams Ave.; (503) 477-7689

Uptown Market, UptownMarketPDX.com; 6620 SW Scholls Ferry Rd.; (503) 336-4783

Velo Cult, VeloCult.com; 1969 NE 42nd Ave; (503) 922-2012 (bike shop/taproom)

Yard House, YardHouse.com; 888 SW 5th Ave.; (503) 222-0147

Zupan's Market, Zupans.com; four Portland locations, each with nicely curated bottles and growler taps

The Coast

Cannon Beach Hardware Store & Public House ("Screw & Brew"), CannonBeach Hardware.com; 1235 S. Hemlock St. Cannon Beach; (503) 436-4086

Holy Toledo, 155 N. Main St., Toledo; (541) 336-4000

Vista Pub, 1009 Chetco Ave., Brookings; (541) 813-1638

Walt's Pourhouse, 1880 N. 7th St., Coos Bay; (541) 267-5588

The Wine & Beer Haus, 1111 N. Roosevelt Dr., Cannon Beach; (503) 738-0201

Hood/Eastern

Embers Brewhouse, EmbersBrewhouse.com, 204 N. Main St., Joseph; (541) 432-2739

Great Pacific, GreatPacific.biz, 403 S. Main St., Pendleton, (541) 276-1350

Pint Shack, PintShack.com; 105 4th St., Hood River; (541) 387-7600

Volcanic Bottle Shoppe, VolcanicBottleShoppe.com; 1410 12th St., Hood River; (541) 436-1226

Willamette Valley

Beerworks, 323 East Main St., Medford; (541) 770-9100

Bier Stein, TheBierStein.com; 1591 Willamette St., Eugene; (541) 485-2437 (1,000+ bottles, 30 taps)

B2 Taphouse, b2Taphouse.com; 4336 Commercial St. SE, Salem; (503) 991-5369

Corvallis Brewing Supply, LickSpigot.com; 119 SW 4th St., Corvallis; (541) 758-1674

Franklin's Bottle Shop, Facebook.com/FranklinsBottleShop/info; 241 Liberty St. NE, Salem

The Growl Movement, GrowlMovement.com; 5137 River Rd. N., Keizer; (503) 385-1064;
& 2990 Commercial St. SE, Salem; (971) 273-6533

Loggers Tap House, LoggersTapHouse.com; 2060 NW Stewart Pkwy., Roseburg;
(541) 671-2206

Market of Choice, MarketOfChoice.com; 1475 Siskiyou Blvd., Ashland; (541) 488-2773

O'Toole's Pub, OToolesPubRoseburg.com; 328 SE Jackson St., Roseburg; (541) 673-5152

16 Tons Café: SixteenTons.biz/blog; 2864 Willamette St.; (541) 485-2700. 16 Tons
Taphouse: 265 E. 13th Ave.; (541) 345-2003

Venti's Café & Taphouse VentisCafe.com; Two in Salem: (Basement Bar) 325 Court St NE;
(503) 399-8733; & (Taphouse) 2840 Commercial St. SE; (503) 391-5100

Central

The Brew Shop/Platypus Pub, PlatyPuspubBend.com; 1203 NE 3rd St., Bend;
(541) 323-2318

Broken Top Bottleshop, BTBSBend.com; 1740 NW Pence Ln. #1, Bend; (541) 728-0703

Brother Jon's Public House, BrotherJonsPublicHouse.com; 1227 NW Galveston Ave.,
Bend; (541) 306-3321

Gorilla Growlers (at Empire Carwash), Gorilla Growlers.com; 20425 Empire Ave., Bend;
(541) 318-8039

The Growler Guys, TheGrowlerGuys.com; 2699 U.S. 20, Bend; (541) 385-3074

The Mountain Jug, MountainJug.com; 56805 Venture Ln., Sunriver; (541) 390-0214

Newport Market, 1121 NW Newport Ave., Bend

Pig and Pound Public House, 423 SW 8th St., Redmond; (541) 526-1697

Breweries to Come

The first day I started working on this guidebook, there were about 150 breweries in Oregon. As of late 2014 there are practically 200, including a few on this list that opened after my deadline. There may soon be over 250.

Arbella Brewing (ArbellaBrewing.com; @ArbellaBrewing), SE Portland. Brewers: Henry Schmidt and Devin Owen.

Backside Brewing (BacksideBrewingCo.com), 1640 NE Odell Ave, Roseburg; (541) 580-1906. Owner: KC McKillip.

Benedictine Brewery (BenedictineBrewery.com), 1 Abbey Dr., St. Benedict in Salem/Mount Angel Abbey. Brewer: Father Martin Grassel.

Bethany Public House & Brewery (BethanyPub.com), 4840 NW Bethany Blvd., Portland; (971) 371-2954. Manager: Andre Jehan.

Bifrost (Facebook.com/BifrostBrewing), Corvallis. Owners: Jacob Oliver, Michael Galusha.

Brannon's Pub & Brewery (BrannonsBrewery.com), 3800 SW Cedar Hills Blvd., Beaverton. Owner: Kevin Brannon.

Celtic Raven (Facebook.com/claddagh.brewing), Dundee. Owners/brewers: Terrisa and Gregg Watson.

Climate City Brewing, Grants Pass. Owners: Christine Marie Meis, Mark Simchuk, Jodi Paquin, and Steve Baksay.

Culmination (CulminationBrewing.com), 2117 NE Oregon St., Portland. Owner/brewer: Tomas Sluiter.

Deception (DeceptionBrewingCo.com; @deceptionbrew), 1174 SW Highway 99W, Dundee; (971) 832-8054. Owners/brewers: Brian Wheatley and Ben Hoffman.

Defeat River (DefeatRiverBrewery.com, @DefeatRiverBrew), 473 Fir St., Reedsport. Owners/brewers: Levi Allen and Trevor Frazier.

Dog Barrel, 1092 NE Stephens St., Roseburg; (541) 643-5627. Owners/brewers: Tom and Russ Anderson.

Flyboy, (FlyboyBrewing.com), 15630 SE Boones Ferry Rd. #1A, Lake Oswego, (503) 908-1281. Owner: Mark Becker.

Gold Rush, 3278 Madrona Ln., Medford. Owners: Sid and Holly Dyer.

Grateful Deaf (GratefulDeafBeer.com). Owner/brewer: Ken Fisher.

Hard Knocks (HardKnocksBrewing.com), 1024 E. Main St., Cottage Grove; (541) 740-5625. Owners: Kate and Ben Price.

Late Addition (LateAdditionBrewing.com; @L8addition), Portland. Owners/brewers: Joel Pomeroy and Lance Means.

Leikam Brewing (LeikamBrewing.com), 1718 SE 23rd Pl., Portland. Brewer: Theo Leikam.

Mancäve Brewing (MancaveBrewingCompany.com; @mancavebeer), 540 Fillmore St., Eugene; (541) 632-3967. Owner: Brandon Woodruff.

Meteorite Brewery, 6930 Southwest 68th Avenue, Portland.

Montavilla Brew Works (MontavillaBrew.com), 7805 SE Stark St., Portland; (503) 241-2300. Owner/brewer: Michael Kora.

Moonshrimp Brewing (gluten free) (MoonshrimpBrewing.com), 8428 SW 22nd Ave., Portland; (503) 970-2234. Owner/brewer: Daniel McIntosh-Tolle.

Mt. Tabor (MtTaborBrewing.com), 124 SE 11th Ave., Portland. Owner/brewer: Eric Surface (Portland location of existing Washington brewery originally founded in Portland).

Northcraft Brewing (Facebook.com/pages/Northcraft-brewing/321740827894348), Roseburg or Winston. Owner: Chad Northcraft.

North Rim (NorthRimBrewing.com), 20650 High Desert Lane, Ste. #7, Bend; (541) 280-1330. Owner: Shane Nielsen.

Old Castle steampunk brewery (Facebook.com/OldCastleBrewingCompany), Hillsboro. Owner/brewer: Allen Marc Levy.

Ordnance Brewing/Neighbor Dudes, 405 N 1st St., Ste 104, Hermiston. Owner: Cherie Baker McLeod.

Oregon Public House, non-profit brewery and public house (OregonPublicHouse.com), 700 NE Dekum St., Portland; (503) 828-0884. Director: Ryan Saari. Brewer: Alan Taylor.

Plough Monday (PloughMonday.com), 25327 Jeans Rd., Veneta (541) 935-4004. Owners: Norm Vidoni II and Charlie Whedbee.

Roscoe's Brewing, 8105 SE Stark St., Portland; (503) 255-0049. Owners: Jeremy Lewis and Quyen Le.

Royale (RoyaleBeer.com), 55 NE Farragut St. #6, Portland; (971)-279-5587. Owner/brewer: Paul Bastian and partners.

Rusty Bucket (RustyBucketBrewing.com), Medford.

Salud Restaurant & Brewery (@SaludRoseburg), 537 SE Jackson, Roseburg; (541) 673-1351. Owner: Manny Anaya.

Shade Tree (Facebook.com/shadetreebrewery), Bend. Owner: Larry Johnson.

Steens Mountain Brewing, 150 W. Washington St., Burns; (541) 589-1159. Owner/brewer: Rick Roy.

Waltz (Facebook.com/WaltzBrewing), 1900 A St., Forest Grove; (503) 896-6057. Owner: Adam Zumwalt. Brewers: Karl Glatz and Michael Duron.

Wolves & People Farmhouse Brewery (WolvesAndPeople.com), Newberg. Owner/brewer: Christian DeBenedetti.

Zig Zag (ZigZagRiverBrewery.com), 23560 E. Lolo Pass Rd., Zigzag; (503) 622-1200. Owner: Rod Meyer.

Cheesemakers

Oregon beer is doubly delicious when paired with Oregon cheese. In 2013, I brought the Oregon Brewers Guild and the Oregon Cheese Guild together—of course there were guilds for each—to create the Double EE Festival celebrating both local classics: bEEr and chEEse. Participants collaborate to ferment ultimate pairings between partner creameries and breweries. These are the cheesemakers around the state. Call for tours and tasting room, if available.

Ancient Heritage Dairy (AncientHeritageDairy.com), 2595 Elm Ln., Madras; (541) 460-5032

Briar Rose (BriarRoseCreamery.com), 19231 NE Fairview Dr., Dundee; (503) 538-4848

Face Rock Creamery (FaceRockCreamery.com), Highway 101, Bandon; (541) 347-3223

Fairview Farm Goat Dairy (FairviewFarmDairy.com), 2340 SW Fairview Ave., Dallas; (503) 623-4744

Ferns' Edge Goat Dairy, (FernsEdgeGoatDairy.com), 39456 Hwy 58, Lowell; (541) 937-2093

Fraga Farmstead Goat Cheese (FragaFarm.com), 54655 NW Old Wilson River Rd., Gales Creek; (503) 367-7100

Goldin Artisan Goat Cheese (GoldinArtisanGoatCheese.com), 32880 S. Sawtell Rd., Molalla; (503) 810-1954

Juniper Grove Farm (Facebook), 2024 SW 58th St., Redmond; (541) 923-8353

La Mariposa Cheese (Facebook), 815 1st Ave. E, Ste. B, Albany; (541) 740-6835

Mama Terra Micro Creamery, Williams; (541) 846-9029

Oak Leaf Creamery, 795 Stewart Rd., Grants Pass; (541) 476-1290

Ochoa's Queseria (OchoasQueseria.com), shares with La Mariposa; (541) 228-7327

Pholia Farm Creamery (PholiaFarm.com), 9115 W. Evans Creek Rd., Rogue River; (541) 582-8883

Portland Creamery (PortlandCreamery.com); (503) 616-4443

Quail Run (QuailRunHollow.com), 29645 NW Quail Run Dr., Gaston; (503) 985-3573

Rivers Edge Chêvre (ThreeRingFarm.com), 6315 Logsden Farm, Logsden; (541) 444-1362

Rogue Creamery (RogueCreamery.com), 311 N. Front St., Central Point; (541) 665-1155

Tillamook (Tillamook.com), 4185 Highway 101, Tillamook; (800) 542-7290 (ext. 7)

Tumalo Farms (TumaloFarms.com); (541) 350-3718

Willamette Valley Cheese Co. (WVCheeseCo.com), 8105 Wallace Rd. NW, Salem; (503) 399-9806

Cideries

I've heard it said that the best gluten-free beer is a cider. But celiacs are not the only ones driving the current cider boom. Artisan cider, just a few years into the twenty-first century, has become a $600 million industry—the fastest growing beverage segment. One of the brightest stars on the American cider map is the Pacific Northwest, and several Oregon cideries own or have planted their own orchards. Furthermore, more breweries are getting winery licenses so they can make cider, too. Naturally, dry-hopped ciders are quite popular for those who can't choose between beer or cider. For the record, don't call it "hard cider" to folks in the industry. It's cider. That "soft" stuff is juice. You don't call grape juice "wine."

Also, just for fun, I listed the few mead makers, too.

Portland Metro

Alter Ego (AlterEgoCider.com), 404 SE 6th Ave., Portland; (503) 719-7000.

Bull Run Cider (BullRunCider.com), 7940 NW Kansas City Rd., Forest Grove; (503) 535-9796. By appointment only.

Bushwhacker Cider (BushwhackerCider.com), 1212-D SE Powell Blvd., Portland; (503) 445-0577. Opened in 2010 as the country's first cider pub, Bushwhacker makes its own ciders and attempts to offer every packaged cider available in Oregon on eight taps and in nearly three hundred bottles.

Cider Riot (CiderRiot.com), Portland. No public visits.

Finnegan Cider (FinneganCider.com), Lake Oswego; (503) 703-6786.

HUB Cider (HopworksBeer.com), 2944 SE Powell Blvd, Portland; (503) 232-HOPS.

McMenamins Edgefield Hard Apple Cider (EdgefieldWinery.com), 2126 SW Halsey Street, Troutdale; (503) 667-4352.

Portland Cider Co. (PortlandCider.com), 275 S Beavercreek Rd. #149, Oregon City; (503) 908-7654.

Rain Barrel Ciderworks (RainBarrelCider.com), Portland.

Reverend Nat's Hard Cider/Cascadia Ciderworks United (ReverendNatsHardCider.com; CascadiaCiderWorkersUnited.com), 1813 NE 2nd Ave., Portland; (503) 567-2221.

Rogue Cider (Rogue.com).

Sasquatch (SasquatchBrewery.com), 6440 SW Capitol Hwy., Portland; (503) 402-1999.

Square Mile Cider (Facebook.com/SquareMileCider), 929 N Russell St., Portland (Widmer Bros. Pub); (503) 281-2437.

Swift Cider (SwiftCider.com), Portland. No public visits.

Northeast and Hood River

Barlow Road Hard Cider (BarlowRoadHardCider.com), Mosier; (541) 645-0753.

Blue Mountain Cider (DrinkCider.com), 235 E. Broadway Ave., Milton-Freewater; (541) 938-5575.

Fox Tail Cider (FoxTailCider.com), 2965 Ehrck Hill Dr., Hood River; (541) 716-0093.

Gorge Cyder Works (OvinoMarket.com), 1209 13th St., Hood River; (541) 436-0505.

Hood Valley Cider Hard Cider Co. (HoodValleyHardCider.com), 4950 Baseline Rd., Parkdale.

HR Ciderworks (Facebook.com/HRCiderworks), 1930 Highway 35, Hood River.

Logsdon Farmbrew (FarmhouseBeer.com), 4785 Booth Hill Rd., Hood River County; (541) 399-4659.

Rack & Cloth (RackAndCloth.com), 1104 1st Ave., Mosier; (541) 965-1457.

Willamette Valley

Carlton Cyderworks (CarltonCyderworks.com), 320 SE Booth Bend Rd., Ste. B, McMinnville; (503) 857-2314.

Elk Horn/Sweet Cheeks (ElkHornBrewery.com), 686 E Broadway, Eugene; (541) 912-3846.

E.Z. Orchards (EZOrchards.com), 5504 Hazel Green Rd. NE, Salem; (503) 393-1506.

Farmhouse Cider (Facebook.com/farmhardcider), Dayton; (503) 395-8429.

Kookoolan Farms (KookoolanFarms.com), 15713 Highway 47, Yamhill; (503) 730-7535.

Nectar Creek Honeywine (NectarCreekHoneywine.com), 33848 SE Eastgate Cir., Corvallis; (541) 760-1343 (behind 2 Towns & Mazama Brewing).

2 Towns Ciderhouse/Traditions (2TownsCiderhouse.com), 33930 SE Eastgate Cir., Corvallis; (541) 207-3915.

Wandering Aengus Ciderworks/Anthem (WanderingAengus.com), 6130 Bethel Heights Rd. NW, Salem; (503) 361-2400.

Wildcraft Cider Works (WildcraftCiderWorks.com), 390 Lincoln St., Eugene; (541) 501-7031.

Central Oregon

Atlas Cider (AtlasCider.com), 900 SE Wilson Ave., Ste. H, Bend.

Far Afield Cider (FarAfieldCider.com), 1201 NE 2nd St. 180, Bend; (541) 639-8959.

Red Tank Cider (RedTankCider.com), 840 SE Woodland St., Unit 185, Bend.

Southern Oregon

Thompson Creek Organics/Apple Bandit (AppleBandit.com), Applegate; (541) 846-1718.

Portland Coffee Roasters

There are roughly fifty coffee roasters in Portland despite, or possibly because of, the fact that there are also fifty Starbucks stores in Stumptown, which just so happens to also be the name of the largest of the city's local roasters. We know this statistic thanks to Ruth Brown, my former colleague at Portland's alt-weekly *Willamette Week*. Perhaps that's a weird detail to include in a book about Oregon's beer, but in a city so rich with breweries that one of its many nicknames is "Beervana"—which really applies to the whole state—it speaks to the way Oregonians feel about and support all things handmade, small batch, and local, to the point of being from one's neighborhood and not just region. I'm not picking on Starbucks, as they have served a vital function in educating a wide audience about specialty coffee and better technique in making it, especially when you consider that every supermarket still has tubs of instant coffee on their shelves. Nevertheless, here are the Portland area's independent coffee roasters available to caffeinate you at the sole or flagship stores listed below. Roasters without a store are listed with only their website.

Altura Coffee Roasters, AlturaCoffeeRoasters.com

Badbeard's Microroastery, BadBeardsCoffee.com

Blac Coffee Roasters, BlacCoffee.com

Blue Kangaroo, BlueKangarooCoffee.com; 7901 SE 13th Ave.; (503) 756-0224

Boyds Coffee, Boyds.com

Bridgetown Coffee, BridgetownCoffeeExpress.com

Case Study Coffee, CaseStudyCoffee.com; 5347 SE Sandy Blvd.; (503) 477-8221

Cellar Door Coffee, CellarDoorCoffee.com; 921 SW 16th Ave; (503) 221-7435

Clive Coffee, CliveCoffee.com; 79 SE Taylor St.; (800) 520-2890

Coava Coffee Roasters, CoavaCoffee.com; 524 SE Main St.; (503) 894-8134

Coffee Bean International, CoffeeBeanIntl.com; 603 SW Broadway; (503) 243-6374

Courier Coffee, CourierCoffeeRoasters.com; 923 SW Oak St.; (503) 545-6444

Extracto Coffee, ExtractoCoffeeHouse.com; 2921 NE Killingsworth St.; (503) 281-1764

Greyhound Coffee Roasters, GreyhoundCoffeeRoasters.com

Happy Cup Coffee Co., HappyCup.com

Hawthorne Coffee Merchant, HawthorneCoffee.com

Heart Coffee Roasters, HeartRoasters.com; 2211 E. Burnside St.; (503) 206-6602

K&F Coffee, KandFCoffee.com; 2706 SE 26th Ave.; (503) 238-2547

Kobos Coffee, Kobos.com; 200 SW Market St. and 2355 NW Vaughn St.; (800) 557-5226

Marigold Coffee, MarigoldCoffee.com

McMenamins, Mcmenamins.com/406-mcmenamins-coffee-roasters-home

Mudd Works, MuddWorks.com; 537 SE Ash St., No. 108; (503) 236-2326

Night Owl Roasters, NightOwlRoasters.com

Oblique Coffee Roasters, ObliqueCoffeeRoasters.com; 3039 SE Stark St.; (503) 228-7883

Nossa Familia, FamilyRoast.com

Portland Roasting, PortlandRoasting.com

Red E Coffee, Facebook.com/TheRedECafe; 1006 N. Killingsworth St.; (503) 998-1387

Rose City Coffee Co., RoseCityCoffeeCo.com

Roseline Coffee, RoselineCoffee.com

Ristretto Coffee Roasters, RistrettoRoasters.com; 555 NE Couch St.; (503) 284-6767
    2181 NW Nicolai St.; (503) 227-2866
    3808 N. Williams Ave.; (503) 288-8667

Schondecken Roasters, RoseCityCoffeeCo.com; 6720 SE 16th Ave.; (503) 236-8234

Seven Virtues Coffee, SevenVirtuesPDX.com; 5936 NE Glisan St.; (503) 236-7763

Spella Caffe, SpellaCaffe.com; 520 SW 5th Ave.; (503) 752-0264

Spielman Coffee Roasters and Bagels, SpielmanBagels.com; 2128 SE Division St.;
    (503) 467-0600

Spunky Monkey, Monkeyroasters.com

St. Johns Coffee Roasters, StJohnsCoffee.com

Sterling Coffee Roasters, SterlingCoffeeRoasters.com; 417 NW 21st Ave.

Stumptown, StumptownCoffee.com; Five Portland locations. The original and only one
    that roasts on-premises: 4525 SE Division St.; (503) 230-7702

Trailhead Coffee Roasters, TrailheadCoffeeRoasters.com; 1847 E. Burnside St., No. 105

Urban Grind Coffee, Facebook.com/UrbanGrindCoffee

Water Avenue Coffee Co., WaterAvenueCoffee.com; 1028 SE Water Ave.; (503) 808-7083

World Cup Roasting, WorldCupCoffee.com; 1740 NW Glisan St.; (503) 228-5503

ZBeanz, ZBeanz.com

Ava Roasteria, AvaRoasteria.com; 4655 SW Hall Blvd., Beaverton; (503) 641-7270

Dovetail Coffee Roasters, coffeebeancoffeeroasters.com

Happyrock Coffee Roasting Co., HappyRockCoffee.com; 465 Portland Ave., Gladstone;
    (503) 650-4876

Longbottom Coffee and Tea, LongBottomCoffee.com; 4893 NW 235th Ave., Hillsboro;
    (800) 288-1271

BJ's Coffee Co., 2834 Pacific Ave., Suite C, Forest Grove; (503) 357-0969